PRAISE

An incredible time capsule.

-Stuart Bernstein

2

The Holy Paragon

Bob Karnes

Editor J. Thomas Hetrick

Pocol Press
Clifton, VA

4

POCOL PRESS

Published in the United States of America
by Pocol Press.
6023 Pocol Drive
Clifton, VA 20124
http://www.pocolpress.com

Publisher's Cataloguing-in-Publication

Karnes, Bob.
   The holy paragon / by Bob Karnes ; J. Thomas
Hetrick. – 1st ed.
   p. cm.
   Includes bibliographic references.
   ISBN 978-1-929763-12-2

   1.   Karnes, Bob—Childhood and youth. 2. High school
students—Virginia—Oakton—Biography. 3. Oakton (Va.)
I. Hetrick, J. Thomas, 1957- II. Title.

F234.O28K37 2002   975.5'291
                            QBI33-277

I wish to dedicate this book to Tim Kulik, AKA Emmette Ophasse. May a portion of his spirit live on in its pages.

MUSIC AND LITERARY REFERENCES

Adverts. from McDonald's Restaurant's, Schaeffer Beer, Utz Potato Chips.
Areteus the Cappadocian, "Insanity is but an extension of normal
    thought processes."
Bonneville Follies, *Fading Out With Glitter*, "Florida," 1973.
Bonneville Follies, *For Some People in Indiana*, "Go-Go Library," 1973.
Bonneville Follies, *Bonneville Follies in the Dark* , "If Tonny Could Say It,"
1987.
Bonneville Follies, "Life in PA," 1974.
Bonneville Follies, "Pepe La Pue," 1970.
Bonneville Follies, *From Under a Log*, "Killer Keating," 1973.
Bonneville Follies, *For Some People in Indiana*, "Wilber Tucker Woodson,"
1973.
David Bowie, *Diamond Dogs*, "Future Legend," RCA, 1974.
Robyn E. Burchfield, *Oakton Occasional*, 1975.
Death by Hanging, *Elmo Zudinski Romanoff*, "Peterson 2," 1973.
Death by Hanging, "Black in the Boy of Silver," 1974.
Death by Hanging, Elmo Zudinski Romanoff, "Words," 1973.
Elmo Zudinski Romanoff, *Crane and Crack*, "S.H.", 1973.
Ezrin Amphitron Talis (EAT), "The Art of Slaying Dragons,"1974.
Ezrin Amphitron Talis (EAT), *Worlds You Never See*, "Hunks," 1974.
Ezrin Amphitron Talis (EAT), "Lepreconic Mystic," 1975.
Ezrin Amphitron Talis (EAT), *Peachbottom and a Pickle*,
    "Life/Death in the Circle," 1974.
Harry Golden, The Unconquearble, *Washington Star*, 1971.
Grass Roots, "Sooner or Later," 1970 Dunhill.
Steve Harley, *The Best Years of Our Lives*, EMI, 1975.
Steve Harley, *The Human Menagerie*, EMI, 1973.
Steve Harley, *Love's A Prima Donna*, EMI, 1976.
Steve Harley, *Psychomodo*, EMI, 1974.
Steve Harley, *Timeless Flight*, EMI, 1976.
Insane Illustrated, 1973.
Jobriath, *Creatures of the Street*, "Liten Up," Elektra, 1974.
Robert Karnes, *9, Black, and Creepers*, "Come! Come! Elizabeth,"1975.
Robert Karnes, *Time is the Murderer*, "Death by Slow Girl,"1974.
Robert Karnes, *Valentine Trashcan Rain*, "Doves Have Two Wings," 1976.
Robert Karnes, *Valentine Trashcan Rain*, "Fairfax Fog," 1975.
Robert Karnes, "Neat-o Guts," 1972.
Robert Karnes, *It Was the Only Thing to Do Since the Mule Died*,

"Great at Last," 1972.
Howard Koretz, "Death in the Essence," 1973.
Howard Koretz, "Declared Change of Worship," 1974.
Howard Koretz, "Miss Loonies of Our Minds," 1973.
Howard Koretz, "Radioactive Faces," 1974.

PHOTOGRAPH CAPTIONS

Bob Jarvie (p. 28) My grandfather.

Intercepted Female Code (p. 30) A letter written in code by a female in my sophomore year biology class to another female in that class. It was intercepted by my lab partner Boni, and the two of us proceeded to have some jolly fun deciphering it, which as I recall, took all of 5 minutes.

Cheri Allen (p. 61, 244, 245)

The Colonel at the Final Folly (p. 66) A picture of Colonel Hash standing in the doorway to the radio room, just prior to joining us for our mock press assault on Peggy in the cafeteria.

EAT, Tonny, and I (p. 74) Taken by Elmo during the "In Name of Panic Karen" sessions, with Tonny playing my guitar and me peeking from behind the bar.

Tonny Live at Margate (p. 75) Tonny shaking it loose during the "Live at Margate" session.

Session Set-up (p. 77) The set up for the December 1973 "We were promised a female, but got stuck with a pillow" session.

A Behatted Trio (p. 78) Another photo from the "In Name of Panic Karen" sessions, with EAT giving the camera the finger and I reclining suggestively on the bed.

Another Trio Shot (p. 80) Tonny looks back in amazement at EAT and Bobney playing guitar.

Weirdly Lab Assistant (p. 98) EAT doing his "Weirdly Lab Assistant" impersonation.

Eat Attacking Me with a Knife (p. 99) As I was having dinner with the Lay's, I suggested it might be fun to have a picture of EAT attacking me with a knife.

EAT in White Wig and Matching Facial Powder (p. 100)

Knife Attack on EAT's Mom (p. 115) Knifing EAT's mother in the back as she read the daily mail.

Knife Attack on EAT's Sister (p. 117) A picture of me taking a knife to EAT's younger sister, who was obviously amused by our shenanigans.

American Gothic (p. 118) A picture of me standing in the front yard of EAT's house on Sandberg Street, giving my most convincing American Gothic pose (sans the wife). EAT's house was located in a small two street subdivision located across Gallows Road from what is now the Dunn Loring Metro Station. This subdivision (which included the Zarin and the Herrill households) was sadly demolished some years later (late 80's?).

Elmo the Man (p. 123) Elmo in mid-macho stance, taken in my room during one of the early DBH sessions. Just how early can be gleaned from the fact that I still had a black light poster on my wall.

Elmo with a Foot Bow-tie (p. 124)

Elmo on his Bed (p. 125) An early picture of Elmo sitting on that suspension bed of his, probably taken during my first visit to his house. I can tell it was an early photo because of the paltry size of his record collection, the entirety of which was sitting on the shelf just above his pillow. I can make out the spine of Led Zeppelin II, but nothing else. It was no less than a year after this photo was taken that Elmo's collection would outgrow that shelf.

Elmo posing with UHF antenna ears (p. 126).

Ganzer and Bobney (p. 144) Ganzer and myself standing in the middle of Beyer Avenue in Punxsutawney, about 3 doors down the street from Tonny's house.

Gary Garland and Bobney at Graduation (p. 145) A picture of Gary Garland and myself just prior to the graduation ceremony, with Gary attempting to make the point that the message on his button was more important than any pose he could effect for the camera, and me attempting to hold my hat on against the intense gusts of wind that were kicking up that day.

EAT and Bobney as Ascending Angels (p. 149) EAT and I dressed in the white clothes that signified our ascension to another plane of existence.

Sue Sudor Letter (p. 305) The letter to Sue Sudor, written in the fall of 1971. It should have been a letter of introduction, similar to the one I dropped in CA's locker two years later, but Tonny was so paranoid that Sue would recognize his handwriting that he left the job to me. In my defense, I contend that Tonny should have known me well enough to have imagined the complete farce I would make of this whole process. The two of us did not become the best of friends or find ourselves as freshmen insanists through the process of writing love letters together. We did so through the process of goofing off, of which I was often the primary catalyst, as this letter bears out.

In addition to the sort of misspellings one would expect to encounter in the work of someone of my relative youth, Tonny and I still get a chuckle out of the word "Canaverous." I imagine that the intended word was either "Cavernous" or "Carnivorous," with some confusion between the two resulting in a total brain fart. Oh well! We laughed ourselves silly all through the composition of the letter and for minutes afterward, a fact that overshadows any practical use this letter might have had in breaking the ice with Sue Sudor. I don't think Tonny was THAT interested anyway.

Gone Fishin' (p. 311) A classic picture of Tonny fishing in his own aquarium.

Ichabod Tooter (p. 337) Having lost his head, Tonny bends down to pick it up.

ACKNOWLEDGEMENTS

I wish to thank the following people:

Michael Rodriquez for the use of his computer.

Doug Lay (AKA Ezrin Amphitron Talus), Howard Koretz and Melody Rouzer for the use of their memories.

Jeff Bolton for providing the extra reverie needed to help keep me focused back in the 70's.

Thomas Hetrick (AKA Tonny Necessity Tooter) for his assistance in the design, layout, and editing of this book.

Bob Jarvie (AKA Poppy) for a level of inspiration that I will carry with me to my grave.

And last but not least – I wish to thank Oakton High School for being the backdrop of so many of my treasured memories. May this grand old building stand for generations to come.

13

IT WAS THE BEST OF TIMES

The inspiration to write this book came during a major clean up of my room in July of 1997. In digging through a file cabinet and a chest of drawers full of photographs, letters, journals, song lyrics, and other assorted memorabilia (much of which was from or related to my high school experience in some way), I realized the need for a more condensed chronicle of this period. The fact that most of the keepsakes I came across had a separate story attached to them made writing such a chronicle in encyclopedic form appear as the logical way to tell a story which was actually a multitude of smaller stories that would not easily lend themselves to the sequential order of a conventional book. I wanted the written equivalent of a photo album (or a yearbook if you will), something I could pull off the shelf 30 or 40 years from now and reminisce over. Although most of these memories were still relatively fresh after 20 to 30 years, I did not want to get any closer to their expiration date before deciding to go ahead with this project.

Having begun to write about these things, I began to ask the 20 somethings I worked with about their high school experiences. Their responses revealed not only how much of an unpleasant experience high school must have been for them, but that it was something they were embarrassed to even admit having taken part in, and why in God's name would I even want to write about such a topic, thus revealing that I too had once bore the burden of this disgrace? Having received this same disdainful reaction to the subject of high school before, I began to ask myself if I was unusually lucky to have the amount of fond memories of this period that I had. This was a strange thing for me to be pondering, after pouring through so many of my writings of the time, where the main message that comes through is what a social outcast I thought I was, but the gift of hindsight prevailed.

A good friend of mine, Howard Koretz, wrote in my junior yearbook, "I shall write on your gruesome grave – He hated school to the barbariously bitter core." Though this could be truthfully said about some of the claptrap I had to study there, any outward signs of discontent I displayed in front of Howard were likely the result of some very normal growing pains, despite how unusual my particular situation might have seemed at the time. I could not give the public school system greater praise than to express how much more painful these growing pains would have been without those classmates of mine who made life so interesting that I either forgot about my troubles completely or was inspired to make a game out of them. Yes! High school grew to be so interesting my senior year that I actually began to dread weekends.

But the question remains, was I having a disproportionate amount of fun? After hearing the enthusiastic recollections of other Oakton alumni such as Jeff Bolton, Scott Goodrick, and my old buddy EAT, I began to wonder if it wasn't simply that particular time and place that lent itself to a happier high school experience. And of course, when I use the word "happier," I mean to say happier in relation to the unfulfilling experience that high school seems to have become in the 80's and 90's.

Having gotten deep into the writing of this book over the winter of 1997/98, amazement and wonder began to overtake me regarding a number of things. Though occasionally an important piece to a particular puzzle would hang frustratingly out of reach of my searching memory, for the most part, I was astounded at how much clearer my overall picture of certain things became through the process of simply writing about them. I did receive a few chills down the back revisiting old mysteries, though enough mysteries were solved (or at least fitted with likely explanations) that I began to recommend this form of autobiographical writing to several of my friends for its therapeutic value alone.

Secondly, despite the man at odds with society that I may have fancied myself to be at the time, and despite the fact that I may have dowsed the fondest wishes of a few by refusing their invitation to become enemies, the fact that I made it through four years of high school without making a single personal enemy was no more astonishing to me than when I first realized it sometime in 1998. It did not jibe at all with my memories of having a talent to annoy-by-simply-existing to rival that of my friend EAT, and it's something I should explain, lest you read on about the various villains in this book, and it begins to appear as though I'm contradicting myself. With most of the bullying I had to endure in high school over with by my junior year, most of the people I thereafter had a problem with were people who actually refused to communicate with me directly or honestly, a strange reversal of circumstances. For the most part, I had left the era where my big lesson in life was "Boys will be boys," and had graduated to the age of discovering that "Girls will be girls." Whatever acts were being perpetrated against me or someone close to me were now being done so at such a distance that it was hard to sustain any anger for these people, much less consider them my enemies. Despite how easy it was to recapture the anger I felt over the transgressions of Brenda Paris and Robyn Burchfield, I have to include them in whatever blessings I give to the Oakton student body of the early to mid 70's for making my stay there such an interesting and eventful one.

The third and most rewarding shock of discovery that occurred as I began to get into the meat of this book was how easy it was for me to journey back and relive those times, to once again feel the love I felt for and camaraderie I shared with certain people, as well as the whole spectrum of emotions that welled up as each circumstance and impression retrieved from this microcosm of my life was examined individually. The more I wrote, the clearer were my memories of that time, to the point where I saw not only memories I had long forgotten, but things I did not see (or closely examine) at the time. Thus the last two and a half years of the 1990's were a time full of the childlike excitement of a treasure hunt for me; a fact that has further befuddled my fun-in-high school deprived acquaintances.

So what was life at Oakton High like back in that part of the decade of the 70's that Hollywood, bereft of any disco culture references, is at a total loss to explain? Well, to insure yourself of at least a partial answer to that question, I entreat you to read through this book two or three times before allowing any finished pictures to develop in your mind, and to keep in mind that the answer you receive will be more in the form of what life was like for Bob Karnes at Oakton High during the uncircumscripted early to mid 70's. You will not have to read very far before you get the idea that it was fairly out of the ordinary, and that I did my best to keep it that way. Having said that, I'm equally confident that whatever era you attended high school, you will eventually come across a passage that, for better or worse, takes you back to that time in your life. I hope that doing so brings many smiles.

ACTION BRAXTON

AKA Braxton Loughran, member of the WOHS C lunch triumvirate that included Wolfman Jeff and Jeff Kaiser. What made Braxton's on-air nickname appear to be an attempt at self-parody was the relative inactivity of the man himself. It was not that Braxton was a dullard or a pot-mellowed stoner, he simply seemed to be a determinably slow moving individual. Passively content is how I would describe Braxton. He seemed to have gotten his own joke as well, smiling knowingly whenever I would address him as "Man of Action."

The only question that remains for those of us who never heard Braxton's radio show is how different was his on-air persona? The joke would have been on the rest of us then, if he had adopted Doctor Sal's AM high volume razzmatazz and come across to his C lunch listeners as a real "Man of Action."

AL EARLY

Another enigmatic figure to emerge from the Margate Manor apartment complex. Al was one of the more legendary characters to come out of Tonny's 1972-73 sophomore year at Woodson High. Al was in Tonny's German class, where his habit of showing up late earned him the nickname of "The Late Al Early." At some point during the year, Al found religion, making his complete title –"The Late Reverend Al Early," which is also the title of a song I wrote in his honor for my April 1973 "Another Job for the Freudians" sessions.

Like Tonny, Al lived in Margate Manor, and over the course of the 72-73 school year, the two of them became friends. Tonny's accounts of Al's bizarre behavior brought to light two aspects of the late reverend that led me to consider converting him to insanity, although I would ultimately have to meet him in person to make a true assessment. The first of the two aspects was, oddly enough, Al's propensity for ranting about the lord. This was smack dab in the middle of a period where I was planning a major loon push into Christ United Methodist Church. From what little I knew about Christianity, I simply assumed that Christian youth would be friendlier and more accepting of loon behavior. This belief alone would, for a time, paint Christian youth groups as a new frontier for positive relationships. I hadn't yet associated Christians with lunacy in any other way, though in time Gary Garland, Scott Merrill, and Al Early himself would change all that.

This brings us to the second aspect, that being the strange behavior Al would exhibit in Tonny's presence. Unfortunately, as the transcripts of the Al Early interview that appeared in issue No. 2 of Insane Illustrated would indicate, Al's bizarre behavior seemed to be for Tonny's eyes only. And yet! All through our first meeting, I had the sense that he was, perhaps in the presence of a relative stranger, holding back his true self. As further proof of this, I offer Tonny's first question put to the late reverend from the transcript of the interview.

Tonny: First of all, I'd like to ask him why doesn't he act really weird in front of Bob, because Al, you know you can do it, you've done it many times in front of me.
L.R.A.E.: Because I'm tired, tired as a fly being chased by a toadfrog, cause I work all day and I'm dirty. Is that good enough? Hmmmmm.

Here is more tempered nonsense from late in the interview (or rather near the point where Tonny and I just gave up). It's as much proof as I can give, without the aid of seeing his accompanying mannerisms, how much Al was demonstrating his own insanity as he was stifling it.

L.R.A.E.: (gesturing to Tonny) Who is that kid?
Me: That's TNT, my co-reporter.
L.R.A.E.: Crapped on a log? He looks like more of what you said, TNT. I'm gonna blow his head up. It'd be a big improvement. Yours too.

Yes! Al was undoubtedly insane, but like Joe Gorsuch, he was vibrating on a different wavelength than we were, and so a certain distance was maintained. Recently, Tonny related that while Al was having a succession of relationships with various ladies (something Tonny and I could only hold in envious wonder back in the summer of 73), these relationships seemed to cause Al nothing but heartache and complaint. In fact, Tonny added that at times during the playing of a tabletop hockey league the two of them had going with Peter Brichant, Al would break down in tears over some girl. Tonny's feelings of envy soon became relief over being spared this particular pain of growing up.

ALAN BARKSDALE
A creation of Howard Koretz. Alan was an invisible third person who, like EAT's "Arvin Moobunga," would occasionally take enough conceptual form as to appear to be listening in on our conversations about him. In a recent phone conversation with Howard, I discovered that there really was an Alan Barksdale. He appears to have been someone who was instrumental during the formative days of the Washington Star newspaper. Tying this in with Howard's job as a phone solicitor for the Star dates Alan's arrival as sometime in the fall of 1974. As a senior year manifestation, Alan Barksdale took on a darker veneer than his relatively

benign predecessor - Arthur O'Harrison. Alan's name was only invoked as a presage to some form of hypothetical maleficium, a surefire way of putting that ghost-story tingle of morbid fascination into the air. By the spring of 1975, I had jokingly begun to treat Alan Barksdale as Howard's dark alter ego. In my senior will, I left to "Howard Korpse (not a typo) - Three barrels of my finest goats milk and the wish for a Good Mourning in memory of Alan Barksdale." Entry no. 3 in Howard's senior will, which was bequeathed at my request reads – "To the late Alan Barksdale, a smile on our radioactive faces to reassure us that Jesus still loves us."

It's interesting to note that while Alan was referred to in both entries as being one of the dearly departed, Howard and I would always speak of him in the present tense amongst ourselves. He was dead, but still with us, hence the continual wishes for a "Good Mourning." Actually! There is a bit of truth to this analogy, at least from Howard's viewpoint. In addition to his hazy memory of Alan as being a founding father of the Washington Star, Howard also confessed that he considered his job at the Star to be his way of actively assisting Alan by continuing the work he started, carrying on the legacy, if you will. This would mean that for a time during our senior year, both of us were agents in the cause of furthering the Barksdale legacy. It also really brings home the idea that Alan was more than a figment of Howard's macabre imagination.

That Alan Barksdale was a senior year phenomenon is underscored by a lyric from "Fairfax Fog," a piece I composed and recorded during the turbulent February/March 1975 period. The lyrics of the final section of the piece contain this not so subtle play on words.

Cheri, this is Alan Barksdale speaking
Calling you to wish you a Good Mourning

The *Washington Star* newspaper (and Alan's dream) died on August 9 1981. Howard recited the exact date from memory.

AMERICAN STANDARD

Most of my various musical endeavors from 1971-1976 were sectioned off into album length parcels. Sometimes they were actually conceived and recorded as concept albums with finite beginnings and ends. Soon after Tonny and I began recording as the Bonneville Follies, we were faced with the idea of coming up with a fictitious label to record on. One of us, I can't remember whom, had an American Standard toilet. From this discovery, the humorous practice of recording on labels named after brands of commodes was born. The Bonneville Follies recorded on the American Standard label. My solo recordings were produced for the

"Universal Rundle" label, and all of the Death by Hanging recordings were on the "Tuffy" label. Now there's 3 good trivia questions for you.

THE ARCH OF ARPOCHNEY

This was my formal title in the Insanist movement. If the trumpets had just announced my arrival, your court crier would announce me as "Bobney Arpochney Buskatootie, the Arch of Arpochney." My 1973 album "To Preserve the Archdom" was a work of self-preservation, you could say.

ARETEUS THE CAPPADOCCIAN

The most important historical figure in the Insanist movement. When I read his immortal words "Insanity is but an extension of normal thought processes," I knew instantly what a quotable quote it would become. It actually became an axiom that legitimized the movement's philosophy (just in case that ever became something we felt it needed).

ARVIN MOOBUNGA

A fictitious character born out of the uncanny fusion of EAT's imagination and his ability to originate on the spot. Arvin was similar to Howard Koretz's Alan Barksdale in that at times he appeared to be an exteriorized portion of EAT's own personality. You will read about Arvin in greater detail under EAT's entry, suffice to say here that even with no bodily presence to speak of, it was good to have Arvin's spirit around. This pygmy representative from the fabled South African People's Republic did seem to eventually develop his own persona, bolstering the illusion that our group had an extra member. He was one happy whooping spear waving pygmy, and he could have only come out of the 9th grade mind of his mirror image - EAT.

AS GOOD AS WOOD

In the Tonno-Bobney post British Insipids parlance of the 70's, the term "As good as wood" was used to describe something or someone who was proving to be unfit for the endeavor they were currently undertaking.

BARNACLE CLAVICLE

A barnacle encrusted crabbing pot fished from the waters off of Lido Beach by Tonny and I
during the first of our three visits to Florida. It was immediately felt to possess some special power or significance and upon being dubbed the "Barnacle Clavicle," was accorded recognition as the second loon oracle - behind the venerated "Kaisey Module." That both the Clavicle and the

Module were out of loon hands by the end of 1974 did not bode well for the Insanist movement. 'Tis wise to hold on to ones' oracles.

BEAUXKYA

A word used by Tonny and I to describe an attractive female. Though the word itself dates back to the summer of 1974, the height of its popularity was during the 1975-78 post-Oakton period. Tonny's 1980 composition "Sproutin' Titty Beauxkya" shows that it was in common usage even at this point.

It was derived from the root word "Whatabuttakeauxkya," which in turn came from the "Tonbooch? Whatahooch!" call and response used to distraction during the summer of 1974. Whatabuttakeauxkya became a loon way of saying "What do you want?" or "What can I do for you?" Somehow the word "Beauxkya," though unrelated in meaning, was derived from this. By the fall of 1974, it had completely replaced more archaic female adjectives such as "Beeba" (baby) and "Byate" (beauty). More personal usages of the word soon developed, like "Bubblin' Betty beauxkya" and "Peggy peauxkya" (to which Tonny would make the observation of Peggy that "She's the only peauxkya").

Like most slang, its development and its usage were governed by how easily or
unconsciously it could slip into the communication flow. For instance, Romina, Tonny's first girlfriend, would never have been referred to as a "Reauxkya." It just would not have sounded right. Such a word would not have flowed with the roll of the Bobney-Tonny meter, nor would it have complimented the hard A Hey and Pay sound of the Bobney-Elmo dialect. All loon dialects conformed to slang's organic growth law.

In itself, the word beauxkya had many variants. If a young lady was noticeably well formed, she was referred to as a "Body-beauxkya". If the lady was cute or pretty, but not necessarily a raving beauty, she was called a "Lil' beauxkya." Sometimes the last syllable was left off for emphasis, and the lady was emphatically referred to as a "Beauxk!" The degree of attack on the B and the length of extension of the center vowel told the listener just how much of a Boooooookya the speaker thought the lady was.

BETSY MINETREE

While hers was little more than a cameo appearance in the epic length film of my Oakton experience, her flash across the screen was at least noted in the lyrics of one of my songs.

Waiting outside the door of ICT
Watching the parade of Garrett and Minetree

The coup de grace, the smile from Peggy's lovely face
The following 15 seconds of Bobney in outer space

The latter two lines explain why I was given to waiting OUTSIDE the door of ICT for the bell to sound the end of third period, as my ICT teacher Mr. Poston so graciously allowed. While most of my attention was focused down the hall to my right in anticipation of the passage of Peggy Wallace (whose third period teacher routinely dismissed a few minutes early), distractions from the opposite direction would occasionally divert my attention. Among those distractions were my memorable last encounter with Walt Robbins, and of course – "The parade of Garrett and Minetree."

Gail Garrett was a pretty lady in her own right, but her friend Betsy was striking to the degree that the totality of her aura and appearance actually overshadowed her underlying natural beauty, which I only took full note of years later when I came across her yearbook picture. She had this amazing mane of dark curly hair and dressed as though she were some sort of star. The "Wow! She's so glitter!" reaction I had to my first spotting of Betsy led to a brief exchange with EAT on the subject of this exotic sparkling doe-eyed statuesque gypsy of a girl. EAT had apparently already taken note of Miss Minetree, whose fashion sense went a bit against the grain of the back-to-nature earth-tones of the early to mid 70's. Betsy stood out, and going against the grain to the end of standing out in the crowd was the quickest way to gain the respect of EAT and I in those days.

I remember overhearing some fellow talking about this girl who was driven to school in a limousine every morning. I also remember him going on to say something that led me to believe he might have been talking about Betsy Minetree. This made sense, as Betsy certainly dressed like someone who could afford the clothes she wore. Despite the reverence in which I hold the ladies of my old high school, Oakton could have used a couple more like Betsy Minetree.

The yearbook picture of my third period ICT class (taken in the fall of 1974 for the 1975 Paragon). I am seated on the far right – front row, garbed in black from head to toe. There are only two people in this photo who were not actually in that class. One of which is none other than Walt Robbins, who is seated directly behind the VICA sign, with his head turned to one side, caught in the middle of an impromptu whisper. Strangely, Walt would deliver his impassioned Doves Have 5 Wings speech to me directly outside the door to that ICT class (Room 129), as I was awaiting the bell to sound the end of third period.

BILL DYE

A music loving colleague of mine from the Flip Anderson, Carlton Thompson, Ray Denk alliance who was happy to find in me another person who had at least heard of the band Budgie. What Bill wrote in my senior yearbook illustrates how bonds can grow out of the simplest exchanges of arcane pop culture knowledge.

> Bob, click bang, what a hang. Well, it was far out to know someone who finally knew what was going on in the vinyl world. I hope you'll think of me while listening to Budgie
>
> -Bill Dye

Now that's a mid-70's testimonial if ever there was one. Aside from our communion of shared musical tastes, Bill's place in the annals of loon lore was sealed by his unwitting participation in the final folly of June 3 1975. Near the end of the school day, as the follies' participants had shrunk to just EAT, Tonny and myself, we found ourselves upstairs in the English hallway. We were joined briefly by Mitchell Robinson, and then Flip Anderson, who asked us what we were doing. After Mitch explained by demonstration that we were roaming the school sticking microphones and cameras in people's faces, I asked Flip if he knew what class Bill Dye had this period. When Flip gestured up one door to the right (room 237) and said –"Yeah, he's right in there," I turned to the others and in a stage directors tone directed them to follow me into Bill Dye's class, where we would interview Bill in the middle of his class. I asked Flip who Bill's teacher was in an attempt to get a feel for how this little interruption I was planning would be received. He told me a "Mr. Smith," and then showered me with reassurances that this Mr. Smith was cool enough to laugh at such an occurrence. That he did exactly that demonstrated how prepared our school had become to except the insanity it had always been in our nature to dispense. All along the trail of disruption we had left in our wake, there had been the sense that all one of us had to do was to calmly state that we were engaged in a senior prank, and our looniest behavior would have been accepted outright. We were now merely observing tradition, while at the same time, learning a lesson on how timing was everything.

It's clear from the audio tape how pumped up I was at this juncture, absorbing about 10 seconds worth of assurances from Flip before turning to EAT and Tonny with a formulated plan of action. Addressing Tonny in particular, I explained that we were going to interview a guy named Bill Dye. Mitch interjects with the announcement that his girl is meeting him outside at 1:30. The "I gotta be leaving soon" tone in his voice indicates that the approximate time was 1:20-1:25, just after the start of the 6th period. This jibes with the increase in extraneous clatter heard on the tape only a couple minutes earlier. The patter on the tape at this point goes like this.

Me: (attempting to get everyone's attention while at the same time keeping my voice down) Hey! Hey! Hey! Hey! Listen! Listen! We're going to take an interview of Bill Dye. OK?
Tonny: Well, who is he?
Mitch: I gotta be outside at 1:30 cause my girl's gonna be out there.
Me: OK! Well, what we're gonna do is just kinda walk in. We're just going to walk into the room, and we're going to interview the guy.
Tonny: Well, where is he?
Flip: Right here (gesturing towards the open doorway of the classroom), just go in.
Tonny: (to me) Well, Do you want me to be in the hall?
Me: Just go in the room. Just walk in.
Tonny: (skeptical) Well, I can't walk in there.
Me: (moving towards the door in the hope that the group would just follow me in) Let's just walk in here.

At this point I walk into the classroom by myself.
Me: (addressing the teacher in a tentative tone that really recalls how much I was making this up as I went along) Excuse me! We're taking this here for, uh, film documentary here -

At this point I've reached Bill's desk. He realizes that he is the focus of the microphone I'm
extending towards him and he recoils in a panic.
Bill Dye: (gesturing with his hands in a feeble attempt to shoo me away) I don't want this. Get out of here!
Me: - on Bill Dye, and we'd like to interview -
Bill Dye: What do you want, man? Get out of here!

Me: We'd like him to say a few words.
Bill Dye: (calming down slightly) Like what?
Me: Like, uh, What do you think of Oakton high school? Do you think it should be allowed to continue as an institution? Do you think it's worth the taxpayer's money? What do you think of the teachers? Do you think the teachers are adequate? -

At this point, laughter erupts in the room, and Bill is much more relaxed in the realization that the object of the folly was not so much him as it was the execution of the folly itself.

Me: - Do you think they get the job done?
Bill Dye: (humorously sidestepping the question in the presence of his own teacher) No comment on that one.
Me: (signaling back to Tonny) Cut!

A few more seconds of classroom laughter and the tape goes off as well. In the mid-80's, I would have dinner with Bill at a Thai restaurant in Clarendon, over which this incident was humorously recounted. I haven't seen Bill in 13 years, but I'd love to get back in touch with him. I've got a cassette recording that he needs to hear.

BIPPERTY-BOPPERTY HAT
Mentioned in the David Bowie song "Queen Bitch." What makes it worth mentioning here is my memory of the day the picture of the WOHS DJs was taken for the 75 Paragon. I donned my black vampire cape, and gave my face a death pallor with the use of my mother's white lipstick. EAT was insistent on being photographed wearing a "Bipperty-Bopperty Hat." Now you will not find the term "Bipperty-Bopperty" defined in any dictionary, and the rest of you will just have to take my word for it, but those of you who own a copy of the 75 Paragon can turn to page 250 and see for yourself just how successful EAT was at finding a Bipperty-Bopperty Hat.

BITEREW
In the Tonno-Bobnian vernacular, if something "Biterew" (like an album one of us had just purchased), it meant that it stunk real bad. If the San Diego Padres only won 52 games during the 1969 season, one could safely say they "Biterew."

BOBBY CROKE

Second only to Don Frank under the category of failed conversion attempts. It is only due to the fact that no evidence existed that Bob Croke attended Oakton other than during my sophomore year that the effort expended to convert him to insanity did not exceed that of Don Frank. Bob was in the same sophomore gym class that Joe Gorsuch and I had such fun goofing off in, and had the same serious but affable future-family man air as another acquaintance of mine - Bob Herbert. But while I never considered Bob Herbert ripe for conversion, I will go to my grave insisting that Bobby Croke had the metal. In addition to being loose enough to be called "Bobby" Croke, there was something in his nature that begged me to persist in my efforts to convert him to insanity. Apparently Gorsuch picked up on this too, because I recall Joe starting in on him at one point. But Bobby Croke, like Don Frank, steadfastly refused to even confess to insanity, and so would become one of the many transitory friends that would flow in and out of my life during my four years at Oakton, with only the song "Bobby Croke's Little Tune" to commemorate his passing.

Without the presence of Emmette, Elmo, Boni, or Kaiser to assist me in setting the standard, I can only imagine what kind of odd collective Bobby must have thought we had going, for with me in that gym class (besides Gorsuch) was Howard Koretz, both of whom represented the outer fringes of lunacy. The outer fringe of the lunatic fringe, if you will.

BOB HOCKMUTH

To call Bob Hockmuth one of the freaks of Oakton high would be to describe him succinctly but accurately in the vernacular of the period. But while Bob did have long hair, wore denim and smoked pot, he was also probably the greatest proof I could offer that at Oakton High in 1974, even the freaks had character. And a nicer less pretentious fellow I've yet to meet. The placid no-bones smile that can be seen in his senior yearbook picture was pretty much what you got with Bob. He was not a part of any clique or group that would cause him to scrutinize who he befriended, so his opinion of you was apt to be purely his own. We met in my senior year English class, with Bob breaking the ice by saying something to the effect of "You are someone who pretty much does his own thing." He then went on to profess his respect for this type of individual, an introduction that all but assured that we would become friends. This instantaneously placed Bob in the Mitchell Robinson, Marcia Carter, Melody Rouzer, Flash Franny, Stuart Argabright group of people who were attracted to me BECAUSE I was different.

Stepping out of my world and into Bob's was like taking a vacation out in the country. I'll never forget the time I followed Bob home after school (which was quite a hike through the woodsy burbs of Fairfax) with a bag full of albums to play for his edification, one of which was Eno's "Taking Tiger Mountain by Strategy." Upon reaching Bob's very colorful apartment, we settled down and started crankin' some tunes. Bob led in with Manfred Mann's Earth Band's "Get Your Rocks Off," which was an album that Brian Helms had recommended and was one that I always wanted to hear. Afterwards, I treated Bob to his first Eno experience, where-in he made a couple of observations that I felt were humorous enough to relate to EAT.

As we were listening to the music, Bob was puffing away on a joint while he was in all seriousness explaining to me how pot focused the senses and made one more aware of things. No sooner had he finished explaining this to me, as the record had just cycled through a couple choruses of "Put a straw under baby," he turned to me with a quizzical look and asked – "Put a WHAT under baby?" After commenting during the very next track on an interesting use of voice that was so obviously either a synthesizer or a treated horn, I began to wonder which of the five senses pot expanded one's awareness of. It certainly wasn't the sense of hearing. Be that as it may, we foraged into the first Hawkwind album in search of the sonic buzz that no movie about the 70's has ever gotten right.

On another occasion, I remember cruising around the back streets of Fairfax with Bob and his brother Rick in the Hockmuth station wagon. At some point I was offered a joint, which out of courtesy I took a drag on. While both Hockmuth's were slightly bemused when I reported feeling nothing, I must now shamefully confess that like our esteemed president, I did not inhale. Pot would continue to be the demarcation line between their world and mine.

Another amusing story from the stoner files was the early January 1975 modeling of the "Hockmuth Originals." Bob had converted a pair of jeans and a denim jacket into a torn, embroidered, patched and painted ensemble that would make one the talk of any Steppenwolf concert, or fit one perfectly for that long awaited sequel to "Easy Rider." Bob showed them to me when I was at his apartment and, with light bulbs going on, I asked Bob if I could try the ensemble on. Well, being as Bob was my exact height and build, the jacket and pants were a perfect fit. Taking this about as far as I could, I then asked Bob if I could borrow these "Hockmuth Originals," wear them to school, and return them to him in a week or so. This was more of a daring idea on my part than it might seem in light of what some kids wear to school today, because as I intimated earlier, this was something Bob would wear to a concert, not to school. In those days, school wear for even the freakiest of freaks was simple working class utilitarian denim, flannel and cotton. It was still quite conservative by today's standards.

This was as much an attempt on my part to bond with the Hockmuths as it was an impulse to commit an insane act. Though drugs would always separate the freaks from the insanists, I was willing to at least look the part for a day or two. Bob was very amenable to the idea as well, and so for one day my senior year, I dressed like an uninhibited head, which if the reactions of Tanya Herrell and Bonnie Tuggle were to be taken as indicators, was a step towards the norm from my usual achromatic apparel.

Bob Hockmuth has the distinction of having his name in the composer credits of my 1975 "9, Black and Creepers." I decided to make a song out of a poem Bob gave me entitled "The Ridgede Toad." The joke here is that after asking Bob about the title and being told that it was supposed to read "The Ridged Toad," I went ahead anyway and recorded the song as written, adding a hard "e" on the end and in effect, creating a new word. Why Bob didn't just erase or cross out the "e" I have no idea. Apparently eyesight can be added to hearing as one of the senses impervious to pot's enhancing capabilities. This became a good-natured but ongoing rib that would surface again in my senior will: To Bob and Rick Hockmuth (the dig-it kids) I left "My map of Great Britain, showing designated areas of possible Ridgede Toad infestations and my survival kit containing an amber bible, a bucket of black paint and a reservation for two at the Last Supper Club."

Though these things were bequeathed to both, any messages beyond the acknowledgement of their favorite expression ("Dig it!") were mainly directed to Bob. I was quietly wishing him the best of luck in finding the amber-hairded girl he writes of in The Ridgede Toad (with of course one final jab at his misspelling thrown in for good measure).

While I might use the word freak or head here to describe Bob, the truth was that Bob had his head screwed on straighter than I or just about anybody else I knew at OHS. Bob joins Mitchell Robinson near the top of my list of people that I wish I had kept in touch with after graduation. With the help of his brother Rick, I hope a 21st century reunion will go a little ways towards making up for lost time.

BOB JARVIE

Having become a British Insipid and then an Insanist, I would have to say that in an off hand way, my spiritual mentor was my Scottish grandfather, Bob Jarvie – AKA "Poppy" (who was the principal male role model in my formative years). Here was a man who kept a straight face handy just in case his wife needed reassuring that he hadn't lost it completely, but was clearly more himself with a smile and a joke on his lips. He had lost the small finger of one of his hands when he was young, and was given to sticking the stub of his pinky underneath his nostril, giving the illusion that he had stuck his whole finger up his nose. He would then wiggle his fingers and make this goofy expression, the memory of which recalls what I will always love and respect about him the most. Up until the day he died, the boy in him was still alive. He adapted well to adulthood, but he never allowed the world to kill the child within him, and I know that subconsciously I took great inspiration from this, despite the fact that I never found his jokes very funny. Something must have clicked inside me when at a fairly young age, I realized that 99% of the kids I went to school with weren't as fun to be around as my own grandfather. If my mom had given me the choice of going out to play with the kids in the neighborhood or going to visit my grandparents, I'd have taken my grandparents every time.

Bob Jarvie was my grandfather on my mother's side. His wife, Catherine Jarvie (AKA "Meemaw"), though somewhat of a portly straight-faced Oliver Hardy to my grandfather's Stanley Laurel, was nonetheless your typical doting cookie-baking grandmother who was very much a second mother to me. From December 1st 1960 until December 31 1977, they lived in a house on Buffalo Ridge in Falls Church, directly overlooking Seven Corners shopping center. Though I never actually lived in that house, I spent a great deal of time there growing up. From kindergarten through the 6th grade, I would be taken to my grandparents house after school, being picked up around 6PM (or as soon as I could be called in if I happened to be playing out in the neighborhood) by my single working mother. I would also spend many weekends and holidays there, accumulating many fond memories. Any disillusioning that would begin to take place during my high school years was the result of my discovering that the rest of the world was not like Buffalo Ridge.

At the beginning of 1978, my grandparents moved to Sarasota Florida for good, but the fact that they were here through my high school years pretty much cinched the fact that my grandfather's influence on me would be lifelong, and guaranteed his inclusion in this book. Aside from his influence on the mixture of old world and new world type of person I would grow up to be, my grandfather would, in one fell swoop, steer the course of my direction in high school by his involvement in the original Bonneville Follies. It may have been my idea originally, and I may have named the group, but 90 percent of the material on the December 1970 Follies recordings was picked by my grandfather. I was spending a lot of my weekends at Buffalo Ridge in late 1970, and perhaps I had just thought of a new use for my cassette recorder (which was fast becoming my constant companion), but I began following my grandfather around the house and coaxing songs out of him. I would harmonize and/or playoff what he was doing, but for the most part, I counted on him to get things going. Nonetheless, my passion for recording music was now lying in wait for Tonny to come along and put in the time, energy, and creativity to the Bonneville Follies that I could not have expected from my grandfather.

As it's doubtful that Tonny and I's friendship would have survived without the sustaining interest of the Bonneville Follies to carry us to that point of ingrained solidarity, my grandfather's influence here is superficial, but historically important. What qualifies him for a bronze statue on the grounds of Oakton High was his leading by example in the lesson that a sense of humor is a good thing to always have around. Though our respective sense of humors were markedly different from one another, it was the impression he left upon me that became the philosophical cornerstone of the Insanist movement, though I certainly added every illogical twist I could throw in. His humor was as goofy and corny as humor tended to be in the era he grew up in, revealing itself more through straight joke telling. My humor (for some reason) veered more in the direction of the British absurdist humor that led Tonny and I to label ourselves "The British Insipids," and tended to delight in bending the rules of logic and reason.

I would pay tribute to my grandfather's influence in a song on my January 1973 "And All My Animal Friends" sessions, and he would actually make an appearance on my early 1975 recording of "Come! Come! Elizabeth." He just happened to be visiting us when I was downstairs working on the recording of 9, Black And Creepers, so I coaxed him into chanting the following at the end of Come! Come! Elizabeth:

Dead Hunk and dead-end CA
DB, PM sometime doomsday

As I recall, he was a little pressed for time, but he did it anyway. He was that kind of guy. And of course, it turned out to be the perfect way to end that song. I should list some of the many treasured memories I have of my grandfather, such as him playing catch with me on the street on Buffalo Ridge, the two of us burying a shoebox full of dead cicadas in an adjacent field during the May 1970 installment of their 17-year invasion, him driving me down to Music Time at Seven Corners to buy me my first album –"Jimi Hendrix Smash Hits", playing countless dice rolling baseball games with me in a Manhattan hotel in August of 1968, and his yearly task of setting up the little train that ran around the Christmas tree downstairs. I could go on and on, and perhaps I will someday collect those cherished memories the way I am collecting these memories of my high school experiences. It brings a tear to my eyes contemplating the fact that I will never get a chance to thank him for all those memories. My greatest tribute to his memory, as the hard realities of adulthood come flying at me like bothersome mosquitoes, is to hold true to every tenet of the Insanist movement that mirrored his example of not allowing the world to take his sense of humor away. I shall do my best to live up to his example, though I still miss him greatly.

BONIFACE IGNACIOUS

Bill Berry was the second member of Oakton's student body (behind Steve Larsen) to be excepted into our high order. Bill immediately christened himself Boniface Ignacious. It was sometime near the end of my freshman year. Tonny was attending Fairfax High, Emmette was still in 8th grade limbo back at Luther Jackson Intermediate, and Kaiser was with us in body, but would waiver in his allegiance to the loon cause until things really got rolling about a month into

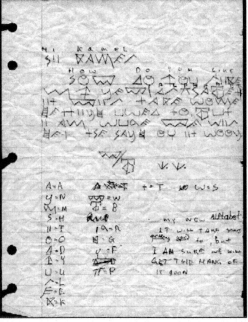

my sophomore year. Boni's spirit added much to the cause during the 72-73 school year. He assisted in conversion attempts, and was a major factor in the outcome of the Fleming-Judd election. His decoding of an antagonistic females written code led him to the formation of a loon alphabet. Extremely sophisticated - it was never decoded by the aforementioned female or anybody else.

Boni was a trumpet player, and was heavily involved in Oakton's music department. We recorded an album's worth of material in the spring of 1973. It was a classic session that amazed us both. However, our sense of accomplishment was dampened when the tape broke upon rewinding (this was before I learned my lesson NOT to buy 120 minute tapes).

During my sophomore year, loon activity was enhanced by having everyone onboard in at least one of my classes. If a folly was hatched by Kaiser, Howard and myself during my homeroom, it could be thrown by Emmette and Elmo in Mrs. Bryan's 2nd period Russian class, handed to Boni - my lab assistant in Mr. Komar's 4th period Biology class, and be in the planning stage by the end of the school day. If any of these links were by-passed, there was always, of course, the loon lunch table. Boni wore the ceremonial underwear, recited the lunacratic oath, and though we lost touch almost completely after my sophomore year, he is remembered fondly for his part in what was arguably the funnest year of my life.

BONNEVILLE FOLLIES

A book that gave a detailed account of our recording sessions, a complete discography and critique of each recording would be about twice the size of the one you're reading now. It's a goal of mine that someday such a book shall be written, but for my purposes here, a brief overview of the major events in the life of the band shall suffice. Like so many of the names and colloquialisms we've come up with over the years, "The Bonneville Follies" just sort of came out of nowhere. I think the original appeal of the name was in the old vaudeville/circus-like aura it projected. It's a good bet that I lifted the name from an actual group that I had on file in the back of my memory. It's an even better bet that all of the recordings I did with my grandfather in December of 1970 had a hand in pushing this memory to the forefront. The name was originally thought up to go with the music my grandfather and I were recording. Being the star of that duo, my grandfather chose most of the material we did from old songs that he knew, like "The Old Grey Mare" and "I Want a Girl just like the Girl (that Married Dear Old Dad)." As old as some of those songs we were doing were, they were undoubtedly the inspiration for the name.

In light of what I've given you so far, the "I Don't Know the Tune to This Song" sessions with my grandfather and I are the earliest Bonneville Follies recordings. The date of this duo's first session, December 5 1970, should be logged as the birth date of the group. These sessions were a series of four cassette recordings made throughout the month of December 1970. The first recording that Tonny and I recorded as a duo that gave us enough of a charge to want to continue was a number entitled "Pepe La Pue." While an explosion of recordings occurred in January of 1971, I believe that Pepe La Pue may have been recorded as early as November of 1970, shortly after our very first recording together "Oobla Ink Oink" was put to tape. Tonny and I were quite pleased with ourselves after creating Pepe La Pue. Using Tonny's father's Wollensack reel to reel tape recorder, we had successfully recorded our first pre-composed song. With its oft quoted opening line -

An Odious Odor, Oao! Oao! Oao! That is Pepe La Pue
He may say 'But, of course! But my butt is the source
That is Pepe La Pue

- it was apparent that whole new entertainment vistas had opened up. Add to that the laugh mileage we got out of listening to ourselves at a higher tape speed (as if anticipating the chipmunk's revival of the 80's), and the amount of recordings made in January makes sense. We were so amused by how we sounded sped up that this became THE way to hear the music of the Bonneville Follies into the fall of 1971. June's "Vomit Now" sessions began to break the mold, but by that time, oodles of recordings had been made, and the early Follies sound defined. Few regular speed versions of any of our pre-Vomit Now songs or jam sessions even exist anymore.

If Oobla Ink Oink and Pepe La Pue stand as the first Follies recordings of the more recorded duo of Tonny and I, then our mordantly insipid country/bluegrass send-up "Pickin' Your Nose" heralded the start of the "Interphase" sessions. These recordings were Tonny and I's first body of work, and a testimony of how busy we were that January. Interphase contained early jam sessions, such as "Slightly Organic" and the lengthy "Conglomeration," the song "Dedication to a White Ball," and the first "Guts Theatre" performances. In the beginning, our arsenal of instruments consisted mainly of various percussion devices, with only my acoustic guitar and Magnus chord organ to provide added coloring. Gradually throughout 1972, other instruments such as the mouth organ, toy piano, slide whistle and a little toy sax affectionately known as the "Dig That Sax Sax" began to appear in our recordings. While Tonny and I would come to view our kazoos as an important part of the Bonneville Follies, it was not until October of 1972, during the "Smackin' Crackin' on a Sunday" sessions that the kazoo even appeared in a Follies recording (and even then it was used sparingly).

The gradual addition of more musical instruments followed our direction towards becoming a totally music oriented group. In the first 6 months of our existence, parodies and skits such as Guts Theatre and "The Undersea World of Rodney Pumpernickel" were an equal part of the Follies output. During this period, the success of any recording we did was measured by how much laughter we derived from listening to it. Any successful musical moments that occurred were mostly accidental. Nevertheless, the impetus of those early jam sessions is especially inspirational to me at this point in my life. More than a means for Tonny and I to burn off some excess energy, they were products of the desire to allow our muse to take us where it will. As unfocused as Tonny and I were in our youth, moments of clarity would suddenly appear during these jam sessions, and I would be struck by the feeling that we were really connecting.

It's amusing to note how the titles of these jam sessions recall the implementation and/or the circumstances surrounding them. Conglomeration, for instance, was the
result of Tonny and I pulling every little shaker, whistle, percussive surface and noise making device into what was as much of a "Conglomeration" of sound as we could muster. Slightly Organic featured a recurring organ theme, hence the title. Moving into February of 71, Hodgepodge and a Bit of Pewter was perhaps most descriptive of the predominately percussive element in our music and how Tonny and I would satisfy our primordial urges to bang on a drum by quickly pulling together a hodgepodge of old junk, pots and pans and whatnot. The title of this particular jam is also a reminder that pewter kitchenware was utilized at some point during the recording.

Perhaps my favorite title of a Follies jam (and no less descriptive) was "Elephant Nose and Cat Gut" from Vomit Now. The "Elephant Nose" was a reference to the ivory keys of the organ (which were in fact plastic, but appearance counted for a lot in this instance). The "Cat Gut" was a reference to the strings of a tennis racquet that was strummed like a guitar to achieve a muted percussive effect.

As I mentioned earlier, skits like Guts Theatre and Ode to the Commode were an integral part of the Bonneville Follies early period, which concluded in June of 1971 with Vomit Now. Vomit Now was one of our most unusual and pivotal recording sessions. Pivotal because it marked the end of an era, unusual because of the circumstances it was recorded under. My folks and I moved out of Merrifield Village in May of 1971, but our lease would not expire until the end of June. The lag time with access to an empty apartment gave me an idea as well as a window of opportunity. The reverberant acoustics of our large (and now empty) apartment were calling out to be utilized in a Follies recording. So I gathered up all my instruments and had my mother drop me off at the apartment for the afternoon. A rendezvous with Tonny was easy enough, as he lived just across the street.

Once set up inside my now empty apartment, the session was underway. We began in my old room with a rather raw stripped down version of Alice Cooper's "Black Juju," which I suppose was intended to compliment the eerie ambiance. That was certainly accomplished with the landmark recording that followed, Tonny's pseudo-composed masterpiece "Wicked People of the World." Though Tonny was on the verge of cracking up at one point during the song, he held his composure long enough for "Wicked People" to become the Follies first serious original song. Of course, serious music was not what the Follies were all about, but this song did set the standard for future adherence to a more structured compositional approach, even if no precedent for seriousness was set.

This song is really a story in itself. While Tonny was in my former bedroom strumming the guitar and singing, I was banging on the wooden living room/dining room partition in an attempt to make full use of the acoustics. As I struck the partition with both hands on either side, I shouted out as if I was being flogged. As the sound reverberated down the hall, it dissipated until the effect was similar to that of someone inhaling and exhaling underneath and throughout Tonny's song. As Tonny's last vocal phrase and the last note of his guitar line had died down, one could better hear what I was doing. The song ends with a second or two of silence before I let out with a scream that would make me appreciate how much carpeting and furniture deaden sound.

Despite the dark tone of our two opening numbers, Vomit Now quickly turned into a parody and skit laden farce more typical of early British Insipids era Bonneville Follies, with musical content taking a back seat to self-entertainment. Moving from my former bedroom into the master bedroom, Tonny and I took to spoofing radio commercials such as – "Schaeffer is the one beer to have when you're having more than one," and the overplayed "McDonalds is your kind of place, a hap-hap-hap-happy place," and the classic Satchmo send-up – "Utz potato chips, for the fun of it, there's only one of it," and my less than reverent rendition of the musical portion of an add for an up and coming performance of Gershwin's Porgy and Bess.

But it was our rather straightforward rendering of the insidiously catchy Herbie's Ford radio add that really leads me back down memory lane, to the extent that I can still hear the original add in my head after 28 years.

Do-Dooo, Herbie's Ford, Do-Dooo
Meet Goldie, Herbie and Reg, The three Ford Knights who serve thee
The Robertson boys are the ones to meet
You'll find these other ones down the street
Do-Do, Do-Do, Do-Do-Do, Herbie's Ford, Do-Dooo

The genius responsible for composing this little ditty was acknowledged in our unembellished as-is cover version of it.

As alluded to earlier, while Tonny and I would occasionally thereafter record a skit (such as "Benchley Stenchly: The Butler Who Done Did It" and "A Web of Intrigue"), Vomit Now concluded the era of the skit. After Vomit Now (and perhaps partly because of Vomit Now), Tonny and I viewed each subsequent recording session as the making of a new album, each with a finite title and distinguishing characteristics all its own. All recordings made prior to Vomit Now which were sectioned chronologically into album length parcels for the sake of categorization were done so after the fact. Vomit Now was the first recording session that was distinct enough for Tonny and I to concurrently conclude that we had just recorded an album. As the realization that we were (at least in our own minds) recording groups of songs in album blocks began to solidify throughout 1972, so too did the conscious impulse to adjust somewhat to this conceptual format. We became more song oriented as a result of this minimal amount of self-awareness, and consigned our handful of post Vomit Now skits to the separate entities file.

Having said all this, Vomit Now was still very much a part of the British Insipids era that it concluded. Skits such as the Rodney Pumpernickel-inspired "Beta Particle," "Supernatural Theatre,", the "Mic Kicking Contest," and our wartime documentary hosted by "Gut Washterwong" and "His pile of army sergeants" (as Tonny called them) underscored this point.

The fact that Tonny and I no longer lived right across from each other made recording sessions occur much less frequently, a fact that in and of itself made the sessions more special. The early Fall of 1971's follow-up to Vomit Now was, in fact, the only recording made at Tonny's house on Country Hill Drive, where he lived during our Freshman year, although it was recorded over the course of two separate visits. "U235 Albump" was the only link between the British Insipids era Bonneville Follies and the "But Baby" sessions of early 1972. It's a crying shame that the tapes of these sessions were lost (although I'm praying that some miracle discoveries will be made as I'm pouring through my old tapes).

Although only my dim memory of U235 Albump can today serve as an assessment of how this missing link fits into the big picture, I do recall how much of a conduit it was between the old and the new, even in the way it was recorded. It began with a traditional percussion dominated jam, recorded onto reel to reel tape to be played back at a higher speed. Tonny's living room was strewn with metal cans, notebooks, toy hand drums, and other sundry devices. It was basically business as usual, except for the fact that the reel to reel that the jam was recorded on was borrowed. Although Tonny's father's Wollensack deck would remain useful as a playback machine until 1976; it was evidently unfit for recording purposes by this point. I remember being impressed with both the sound quality and our performance in the U235 Albump jam, though I would never hear the jam again after the day we recorded it. From this point on until I acquired my reel to reel recorder in August of 1972, all of the Bonneville Follies recordings (including the rest of U235 Albump) were recorded on cassette, necessitating the end of the era of the sped up jam. In fact, what little I recall of the rest of U235 Albump, it veered more in the direction of our early 1972 material, with even a couple attempts at serious songs (relatively speaking).

The first Follies sessions to be recorded in my new house on Maple Drive (February 1972) were a major step towards more coherent song structures. None of the music is sped up, and the original masters exist and are in good enough shape that one can finally hear what we actually sound like. Be that as it may, the specter of seriousness and a greater reliance on pre-composition were evident to the degree that very little of the British Insipids frivolity remained. Most of the songs were worked out beforehand, and some were even (God Forbid!) rehearsed beforehand. Although it is the songs that are remembered by Tonny and I for their identity and entertainment value, the instrumental jams that comprise at least 60% of the two albums worth of material that make up the But Baby sessions are of greater interest to me today. They reveal a growing (but as yet only partially developed) ability of Tonny and I to feel each other out as the music was unfolding. And while no astounding moments occurred during these jams that would cause Tonny and I to marvel amongst ourselves on how well we were clicking, it's clear that the impulse to pay greater attention to what the other person was doing was even then creeping into our jam sessions.

Beyond the But Baby sessions lay the longest period of relative inactivity (aside from the periods in-between our post high school reunion projects) in the group's existence. The period from February to October of 1972 was marked by an assortment of non-musical recordings such as our play by play announcement of a Fairfax High freshman basketball game, and my solo Guts Theatre performance "Neat-O Guts." One minor recording session at Tonny's new apartment at Margate Manor happened near the end of this period, but not much became of it. This period coincides exactly with the period in which Kevin Hans was living with us. I cannot say whether this was a factor or not, as would have been the case if, for instance, I felt uncomfortable having a recording session with Kevin in the house. It's likely that I did feel a bit self-conscious with Kevin downstairs. But on the other hand, it's difficult to imagine me having reservations about someone who donned the ceremonial underwear and recited the oath of adherence, as Kevin did. I may have felt that Kevin would want to join in on the session (as he probably would have) and this would have disrupted the chemistry that Tonny and I shared. As Kevin was asked to leave our home in August of 1972, my perspective now is that it was unfortunate (at least for the sake of musical diversity) that I squandered my chance to find out what the Bonneville Follies would have sounded like with Kevin Hans sitting in.

A more historically verifiable reason for this gap in Follies recordings is that around this time, my mother's disciplinary action for my poor grades in school was suspension of all access to radio, TV, stereo, and (unfortunately) tape recorder. As I was too young to drive and was not much of a party-goer, grounding me (which was the customary penalty for poor grades) made no sense in my case. Although I remember serving these sentences well, my mother gave up on this practice after a while, as evidenced by the veritable flood of Bonneville Follies, Death by Hanging, and solo recordings that were produced after the summer of 1972.

A major event occurred in August of 1972, which signaled the beginning of a new era in recording. My mother bought me a $125.00 Realistic reel to reel tape recorder, bringing all of us into the world of multi-track recording, and ushering in an era where at least an album's worth of music from one of the three aforementioned entities was being produced every month. The 1972/73 school year was not only the Insanist movement's glory days, it was a period of unparalleled creativity for the Bonneville Follies, a period in which 90% of all the songs Tonny and I would consider hits (if only in our own minds) were recorded.

Although a minor session in October of 1972 yielded our classic tribute to a fellow loon "Emmette-O," an excellent jam which featured my toy piano, and Tonny's utterance of the soon-to-be loon cliché "And a honky-tonk," it was a few weeks later that the real fireworks began. On the first weekend in November, Tonny and I assembled in my room and recorded Smackin' Crackin' on a Sunday, a session that upped the ante on the standards Tonny and I would set for future sessions. The intensity level of the opening track "What am I Doin' (I don't know)" set the pace for the entire session. Songs like "Polly Peanut Brittle," "Incident in St. Louis," and "She Left Me (For Another Man)" made this session an exclamation point in the theretofore haphazard history of the group. We had finally recorded an album's worth of good songs, and had done so while actually recapturing some of the old British Insipids spirit reborn in this thing we called "Insanity." Only weeks after this landmark session, Tonny and I reconvened for the recording "Fate will Come," which featured among other things, a reworking of "Pickin' Your Nose" entitled ""Pick Her Up." Also featured in this session were the Follies classics "Loadie, Get on Boardie" and "I Had a Little Girl," the latter of which contained the impromptu utterance from which the loon catch-phrase "Crane A Pode" (later Crane A Po) was derived from. Fate will Come started by picking up where Smackin' Crackin' on a Sunday left off, only to end up where the But Baby sessions left off, as a continuance of the development of a flow in our instrumental jams. From this point onward, many of the highlights in our music would actually be instrumental ones.

While I spent half of December and much of January painstakingly piecing together the most ambitious of my early solo projects - And All My Animal Friends, the next Follies recording session of note was February 1973's "From Under a Log." Second only to (or perhaps equal to) Smackin' Crackin' on a Sunday, this extremely successful session gave us "Beauties," "Arr Me Bucko! (Got Rum in Me Belly)," "Insipid Soul," "Cherry Smash," and Tonny's immortal "Out Like a Gator." The instrumental portion of Cherry Smash and Insipid Soul, as well as the "From Under a Log Jam" (pun intended) were proof that Tonny and I had honed our interaction to the point where our instrumental parts were beginning to sound almost composed.

Further proof of this symbiosis is found in the instrumental sections of the May and June recordings that made up "For Some People in Indiana." Culled from at least three separate recording sessions, this was arguably as close to an album of compositions as the Follies would get. "Bubblegum-Mania," "Wilber Tucker Woodson," "Go-Go Library," and instrumentals such as "All Things Must Piss" and the enormously successful "Electric" made For Some People in Indiana a fascinating (if fractured) mixture of ideas and approaches, two of which would be further explored in our next and final offering of the 70's —"Fading Out with Glitter." Go-Go Library was an experiment in pulling the lyrical content of a song out of a brochure on the spot as the song was being recorded, in this case a brochure on the Go-Go Library, "A library on wheels for some people in Indiana." The experiment was so successful, we decided to try it again on Fading Out with Glitter's "Tweetsie Railroad." "Gimme Some Lovin'" (a hilarious song that Tonny and I performed over the instrumental backing track of one of his father's old records) and "Wanna Play Some Hockey?" both utilized a two cassette delay method that would be used again on Fading

Out with Glitter. I stumbled upon this dual cassette delay method while experimenting with different effects during the recording of And All My Animal Friends. It was a labor intensive method of achieving a reverb and delay effect whereby a song was recorded on two synchronized cassettes and played back simultaneously while being recorded by a third recorder (usually my reel to reel machine). I say reverb AND delay because if both cassettes were synchronized correctly on the recording and the playback, one got a mild reverb effect for the first two minutes of the song. If the song went on much beyond that point, the two cassette machines would begin to slowly go out of phase with each other and a crude (but effective) analogue delay effect was achieved.

The song Wilber Tucker Woodson was (like the song "Beauties" from three months earlier) a tribute to Woodson High School's reputation as having an elevated babe factor. Despite the paeans to Oakton's fairest that you will read throughout this book, I must sadly admit that the reputation of being a babe school was not a reputation that Oakton High had or even deserved (though after reading this book, you may be able to argue the point that what our girls lacked in pulchritude, they made up for in heart). As I sang – "I heard you got some babes over there in Wilber Tucker Woodson," I was asking Tonny for confirmation of what other Luther Jackson alumni buddies of mine had previously imparted. And when Tonny responded with – "You bet we got some babes over here in Wilber Tucker Woodson," he was (in a good-natured way) rubbing it in a bit. I was still somewhat envious that Woodson had gotten the Ard sisters, the Cook sisters AND Susan Smith. But while these acquisitions alone had me agreeing with my Woodson buddies out of hand, I had by the time this song was recorded, attended at least one Woodson sporting event and was flabbergasted by what I saw. Though the song itself is just under a minute and a half in length, it brings back my conclusion (as well as the February 2 1973 basketball game that prompted it) that Woodson's reputation was well deserved. This song will by association always recall for me - a bit of local high school history.

Now before I get into the story of the Follies August swan song, there's an intermediate chapter that needs to be told. In July of 1973, Elmo and I went over to Tonny's apartment to record an album's worth of music on Tonny's balcony. Throughout 1973 and much of 74, I had this idea that I wanted to record a live album. As nobody I was recording with seemed to have an ounce of enthusiasm for this idea, it never materialized. However! Tonny and Elmo agreed to perform a set of tunes on the balcony of Tonny's third floor apartment, effectively giving a live show for anyone who happened to be passing through below. This recording was unique in that it contained elements of Death by Hanging as well as the more established Bonneville Follies, leaving the quandary of what name to put it under. Despite the fact that the sign Tonny and I propped up in the window of my stepfather's Ford Torino for our trip to Florida read "The Bonneville Follies on Tour" with the three of our names listed below, I shortly thereafter decided to christen "Live at Margate" as an official Death by Hanging album. My reasoning was to give a little extra push and support to a newly solidified entity. At this point, Death by Hanging represented the future, whereas Tonny's imminent move to Punxsutawney at the end of August meant that the Bonneville Follies as a band was not long for this world. The fact that Tonny and I named the album we began working on in late July Fading Out with Glitter was an acknowledgement that this was going to be the final Follies recording (at least for a while).

Like Vomit Now two years before, Fading Out with Glitter is a story in itself. It was recorded in three different stages, in three separate locales. The first 6 tracks were recorded in Tonny's bedroom at Margate. The next 6 tracks were actually recorded in the car en route to Florida (much to the dismay of my mother), and the remainder of the album was recorded in my grandparent's apartment in Florida. The opening track was simply entitled "Florida," and aside from being one of Tonny's best compositions, was the Follies most successful use of the dual-cassette delay effect. The song was written, of course, in anticipation of the trip that lay ahead of us. It was followed by our tribute to Gebhardt's Chili Con Carne (or as pronounced in the song with a loon inflection – "Chili Con Carnya"). This song was inspired by a can of Gebhardt's I found in the Hetrick's storage closet. I recall making some comment about the discovery, which no doubt led Tonny and I to look at each other knowingly until one or both of us let out with the by then familiar cry – "A NEW SONG!" Just about every Follies session had at least one song that was thematically derived from something observed just prior to the time of the recording, and Fading Out with Glitter was to be no exception. From Under a Log's "Cherry Smash" was inspired by the large bottle of cherry smash that was in my refrigerator, of which Tonny and I would drink from periodically throughout that particular session.

The compositions and relative orderliness of For Some People in Indiana made it the exception rather than the rule. After finishing up the song Florida, we didn't have squat planned for the rest of the album, and so continued the tradition of drawing our material from the next thought that entered our head, or as in the case of Chili Con Carne, whatever came into our realm of observation that was deemed song worthy. This is not to say that no work went into the album. Aside from the time consuming process that the dual-cassette delay effect we used on the first three songs was, I will never forget the work we put into the crude (and somewhat sonically compromised) multi-tracked chorus effect used on our adaptation of the Sonny James song "Young Love" entitled "Young Loon."

Finishing up the last of the material that was recorded at Margate was "Super Bobney," the theme song to Tonny's super 8 movie of the same name, which featured yours truly as a crime fighting super-hero. Beyond this point in the album, the recording resumes in the backseat of my stepfather's car en route to Florida, road ambiance and all. As if the din we were making wasn't enough of a strain on my mother's nerves, my stepfather took the microphone for an improvised little number of his own, giving a new definition to the word "shrill." The second half of the album was recorded in Florida at an apartment owned by my grandparents. It featured a number of Tonny classics that were less than a minute in length, such as "Anyway I'll Eat" and "Sarasota." During this phase of the Fading Out sessions, I took all the instruments into the shower stall with me and recorded a 7-minute piece entitled "The Bonneville Follies on Tour." Ever the one to experiment with different effects and acoustics, I was interested in the reverb that the shower stall would produce. Though I was delighted with the result on the tape, the volume was so enhanced by the reverb that my mother later told me there had been complaints from others in the building.

Being particularly creative during this final phase of our existence, Tonny wrote three songs that I would later polish up and record my own versions of – "Futile Preaches," "Laura," and "Little Guys of the World." While Tonny's late August move to Punxsutawney effectively halted the flow of Follies recordings, I continued writing and recording my own music at an insane pace, while working with Elmo and EAT in Death by Hanging. I also continued the rather laborious task of cataloguing all of the previous Bonneville Follies recordings (including ones that I did not have in my possession).

Lest you think this was the end of the Bonneville Follies, Tonny and I did record together again. While the only recording we did during my two week visit to Punxsutawney in the summer of 1974 was the "Woman in My Death" session in Ganzer's basement (which was dominated by Ganzer's guitar and my Death by Hanging influenced vocals, hardly qualifying it as a Follies recording), Tonny was spurred to write another song at my house on our two day stopover before embarking on our second trip to Florida. It was an autobiographical ballad covering the last year of his life, and expresses his dislike for Punxsutawney High School in no uncertain terms. "Life in PA's" first two verses spelled his feelings out pretty clearly.

1973 was a very bad year for me
It started pretty fair
I grew a little bit more hair
Now take that as you like
I even started riding my bike
But then the bad news came
Pennsylvania was to be my home
In 11th grade I went to PHS
Pretty bad school like all the rest
I couldn't stand it, I hated the place
But I hung on with a little bit of grace

This song quickly took its place with other Tonny classics such as "I Left You (You Deserved It)" and "Life in Virginia" as songs that were not recorded for or connected with any session that was collated into album form. When Tonny returned to the area for good in June of 1975, his interest in baseball had rubbed off on me a bit, inspiring us to record "A Web of Intrigue," a baseball-oriented mystery/soap opera. As the tape of this particular skit was quick to disappear, I can only recall that the story centered around a small-town baseball team called "The Intriguesport Webs," an announcer named "Joe Catchiola," and ended with an illicit love affair involving Cleveland Indians shortstop Jack Hiedemann.

The Bonneville Follies recorded three albums in the 80's – 1980's "Live at 45," 1984's "At Least Momster" and 1987's "Bonneville Follies in the Dark." Live at 45 was recorded in September of 1980 while Tonny was in town pending his ordeal in airforce boot camp and before leaving for his assignment in Japan. Live at 45 (harkening back to the in-transit recordings on Fading Out with Glitter) was recorded in my car on a trip to and from the Smithsonian Institute. What differentiated Live at 45 from those interstate recordings made 7 years earlier was that this time Tonny and I were sitting in the front seat instead of the back seat. I was actually singing, playing kazoo, and even some one handed drumming while driving the beltway and then 395 into the district. A more accurate title for the album would have been "Live at 65." I have a vivid memory of the two of us kicking into "Sproutin' Titty Beauxkya" on the overpass exit onto 395. In fact, I can remember at what point I was during the entire trip into DC and back by what song we were performing at the time. But lest you marvel at the foolhardiness of such an endeavor, I should remind you that driving (even on those roads) was a lot less stressful in those days.

Tonny and I might have been in greater danger of collapsing from the heat, because my car didn't have air conditioning, and on the afternoon ride back from the city, the temperature was well into the 90's, despite the fact that the beginning of fall was only days away. As one of the songs from our return ride rightly proclaimed, it was a "DC Scorcher." In fact, Live at 45 will always be a reminder of the hottest summer I can recall - 1980, with 90+ (or 100+) temperatures stretching from early July to late September without relief.

In 1984, I was keen on starting a band. With Awareness of Awareness, I got as far as a drummer who doubled on bass in the studio, a guitar player, and 6 songs written (three of which would resurface in later solo projects). In November or 1984, I began working on "In a Quiet Place." It's hard to believe that in the same year I bled such an effusion of dark romanticism, I was also involved in the recording of something as patently ridiculous as "At Least Momster." Yet this unforeseen return of the Bonneville Follies was the very thing Tonny and I needed to counteract the apparent seriousness of the world. To that degree, the last two Follies albums of the 80's were means of escaping the times they were recorded in, rather than exemplifications of them. Tonny's family troubles and my relationship travails had all but convinced us that we better stop being who we were and start being someone else, or at least begin adapting to a world that had little use for our brand of insanity. But while a full-fledged insanist revival was out of the question, it was good to discover (if only for an afternoon) that a Bonneville Follies recording session could have the same therapeutic value.

At Least Momster featured some vocals sung in an invented language that to my ears sounded like an abstract derivation of our insanist inflection, as if the accent that occasionally crept into our speech in the early to mid 70's was the result of having grown up speaking this language. Inventing a language to sing in was not a new idea, but inventing a language (which in this case amounted to random meaningless words) to fit a pre-existing accent WAS a new idea, as well as being one of my riskier attempts at experimentation. It's frightening how successful an attempt it turned out to be, given how out of character it was with the time in which it was recorded. Though songs like "Bean Story," "Abstractions of Historic Proportions," and "Rumpus in the Rumpus Room" demonstrated how simply getting together for the purpose of recording a Follies album was enough to summon the muse.

While Live at 45 still had the charm, naivete, and exuberance-run-amok feel of our early 70's recordings, At Least Momster and In the Dark were more or less adult approximations of those qualities. But while a certain out-of-our-element aura pervaded all but the silliest moments of these last two sessions, there was a certain "We could do this with our eyes closed" assuredness that made these recordings musically superior to Live at 45. During 1987's In the Dark (which begins rather tentatively with our Chill

Wills tribute – "Ya Darn Near Killed the Kid"), we were nonchalantly rattling off riffs and hooks that would have made us quite proud of ourselves back in 1973. And despite the loss of spirit and spontaneity, the sound was 100% Follies. In the Dark's closer, which was effectively the last song we've recorded to date, was an unapologetically insipid little number entitled "Downwind of a Thundergust." It was inspired by Tonny's reaction to the profusion of flatulence I was experiencing that day. The topical "If Tonny Could Say It" allowed Tonny to vent some rage (albeit humorously in the context of the song) about the maddening idiosyncrasies of a woman named Lois that he was sharing a townhouse with. Herein we discover that Tonny's brand of speech coloration had not dulled with the years.

She had that weaselly yelping dog, that fleebag jump up on the kitchen table, And then she expected me to eat off of that expectorated table

This humorous and typically Tonnian choice of words calls to mind an aborted project that Tonny and I had in the winter of 1989/90, that being to compile a double album retrospective of our work entitled "The Bonneville Follies: A Retroexpectorant." As the new millennium approaches, it appears as though shelved ideas such as this, as well as yesterdays pipe dreams like putting all of the existing Bonneville Follies recordings onto CD, and new digitally recorded Follies albums, just might be within our grasp. The future looks bright, but then as a member of the Bonneville Follies, it always did.

BONNIE TUGGLE

If I had to pick my top ten of who I would say were the strangest people I had come across in my four years at Oakton - Steve Larsen would hold the number 1 position, Leslie Chessman would be a close 2nd, and a strong third place would go to Bonnie Tuggle. People who knew what solid citizens Nora and Lauren Tuggle were, but who didn't know Bonnie, would invariably give me an incredulous look when I explained that for all the efforts of the Insanist movement to attract a female into the circle of loons, I had at last discovered in the person of Bonnie Tuggle, a female who was two steps shy of crossing the eccentricity line. In fact, well into my senior year and long after that crusade had been abandoned, Bonnie presented me with an unsolicited confession that she was insane.

Russian class seemed to attract the lunatic fringe. In my sophomore year Russian class, I sat next to Emmette and Elmo. In my junior year, I sat next to EAT. And in my senior year (as if fate were atoning for the absence of any of the former 3), Bonnie Tuggle. Bonnie sat directly in front of me in a back corner of the classroom, making in-class communication with her virtually interruption free. Bonnie was also given to wearing low back blouses, providing me with a scenic view that made abandoning my Russian class for the sake of my radio show a harder choice to make than it normally would have been.

Bonnie's face was a pictograph of caricatures, an ever moving show of expression, a well tuned and well timed accompaniment to her witty rejoinders, making her a fascinating and entertaining person to have a dialogue with. I'll never forget the mad glint in her eyes, so beautifully captured in her sophomore yearbook picture that graces the 75 Paragon. Its sudden appearance on her face hailed the expectancy embodied by both the watchful child and the bedeviled seductress that Bonnie seemed well on her way to becoming. It was a glimmer of moonlight in the daytime, signaling the suspension of all decorum, and looking at it now reminds me of Bonnie's uniqueness among the women of Oakton. She was, in fact, the only female I can recall at Oakton who I could feed a constant stream of non-sequitor silliness to and be matched tit-for-tat in a running dialogue.

By this time, I was not the loon I was in my sophomore year. A degree of war-weariness had taken some of the sparkle out of the mad glint in my eyes, and I could never quite get over being intimidated by what a fox Bonnie was. Here was this nutty angel of a girl, iced with yards of personality and sex appeal. Yet seeing her in action begged the question that haunts me to this day – "What was such a person doing in the Tuggle family?" In fact, I began to refer to Bonnie (as did EAT through osmosis) as a Tuggloid, which inferred something different from the ordinariness of her sisters, if not something removed from every other girl on the planet.

Kissing my Russian class goodbye for the sake of my radio show was not the end of the Bonnie Tuggle story. During the summer of 1977, I was employed as a deliverer for the Fairfax Mirror. I was delivering in a neighborhood on the northern edge of Vienna, when I happened to come across a mailbox with the name "Tuggle" on the side of it. It of course reminded me of Bonnie, but at the time I simply filed the discovery away. Flash forward about a year to June of 1978. After more than 3 years, it must have dawned on me what a cowardly fool I was for not asking Bonnie out, because the desire to act on my previous discovery became overwhelming. I looked up the name Tuggle in the phonebook, found a number that correlated with the address I had found the previous year, called the number and sure enough! Bonnie was home. She was surprised to hear from me, and cautiously asked how I had acquired her phone number, but in the next breath accepted my invitation to meet for lunch at a restaurant on 123 near the Nutley intersection. Though over lunch I noted that three years of maturing had added tints of seriousness and tentativeness to Bonnie's display of oddly interjected facial expressions, these subtle changes only slightly dulled the optimism I felt over Bonnie's acceptance to have lunch with me.

Her body language conveyed her unease at not knowing the reason for my sudden reappearance in her life, but she did not press the issue, nor did she seem anxious to leave. About 30 minutes into our lunch, I asked Bonnie out, making it understood that this time I was asking for a proper date. Her calm refusal made her aloofness seem suddenly more pronounced, yet Bonnie's uncanny ability to fidget openly and maintain an air of composure prevailed, giving the impression that she was ready to hear me plead my case. And plead I did. I spent 20 minutes or more emphatically trying to convince Bonnie to go out with me, but she wouldn't budge. With the opposite sex, I had always been one to take "No" for an answer way too easily, but Bonnie's confounded patience fueled my determination to not let her go without a confirmed date.

Still locked in a stand off, our conversation followed us to our cars, were I spent another five minutes in the hot June sun trying to bend Bonnie's iron will. Down to my last pitch, I asked Bonnie flat out why – "Why won't you go out with me?" Her answer was the thing that finally broke my resolve. She gave me a few sentences that boiled down to me being too much of a rebel. As one who had never been drunk or high, didn't smoke, had never been in trouble with the law, rarely misbehaved or got into trouble as a kid, never stole anything, was always respectful of my elders and authority figures bla-bla-bla, I couldn't fathom what Bonnie thought I was rebelling against - convention?

No sooner had this throw from leftfield completely crossed my circuits than Bonnie clarified herself by gesturing toward my mid-section, saying, "Well! Look at that shirt you're wearing," as if it was proof enough of what a rebel I was. As I had just thrown something on before coming, I honest to God had to look down to discover what she was talking about. My ill-timed choice of dress was a promotional Sex Pistols T-shirt with the cover of the "God Save the Queen" single on the front of it. The irony of how much of a catch phrase God Save the Queen was amongst EAT and myself during my WOHS days as Queen Viper was inescapable. On a date with any of the young ladies I work with today, this would be the nostalgic equivalent of wearing a Foghat T-shirt, but in 1978, it spoke to Bonnie Tuggle the way playing David Bowie records on my radio show spoke to Jeff Kaiser in 1974. By 1978, being musically ahead of my time had conditioned me to accept a tag of radicalism that in no way mirrored my actual personality, actions or beliefs. On this occasion, it would hand me the most wafer-thin excuse for a brush off from a female I would ever receive. The fact that any one of a hundred other off the cuff answers from her would have sounded so much more believable leads me to believe that Bonnie was being totally honest about her misgivings. I will tell you this much. It ended our conversation rather quickly. Not only would it have been beyond my ability to argue against such illogic, but my anger had overtaken my capacity for discussing this calmly, and on went the warning lights indicating I should leave immediately. Back home, my first thought was to call EAT and bemoan the fact that 3 years on, Oakton ladies were still giving me the slip.

BOUNCIN' BEAUTY

A term of Tonny's and mine throughout the 70's. I forget which one of us coined the phrase, though it does have Tonny's stamp all over it. Phrases or words were usually put into the loon slang pool through mutual usage, but as "Bouncin' Beauty" was always spoken with Tonny's sports-announcer accent, I think it's safe to say that he originally coined the phrase. A bouncin' beauty meant that when the lady walked, something was bouncin'. And believe me, in the days before vegetarianism, veganism, bulemia, and heroin chic, there were (or seemed to be) a lot more of them around our fair city.

BRENDA PARIS

I can unequivocally state that there was no one at Oakton High that I disliked (or had more reason to dislike) more than Brenda Paris. I was first introduced to Brenda by Tonny sometime in early 1973, and actually conversed with her on the phone a number of times before meeting her in one of the alcoves of Margate Manor. While not an unattractive girl per se, I felt such a suffocating feeling upon first meeting her that I decided then and there to slowly ease my way out of any further contact with Brenda.

This look of longing would cross Brenda's face at odd moments during that anticipated first meeting, but along with it would come the sensation that if I took advantage of the situation by leaning over and kissing her, I would be doing myself more harm than good. We did have a few more typically adolescent phone conversations about everything under the sun before I passed the torch along to Elmo. At some point during one of our later conversations, I mentioned Elmo to her. Not surprisingly, Brenda (who was clearly on the hunt for a boyfriend) developed an interest in hearing more about my friend. With obvious intent, I began feeding Elmo information about this girl who was interested in him. Also not surprisingly, I never heard from Brenda after her and Elmo had been given each other's phone numbers. Elmo then began the process I had undergone of having several lengthy phone conversations with Brenda leading up to an eventual face to face meeting.

I'm unsure of the exact time here, but I'm sure EAT would agree that early in the spring of 1974 was about the period where Brenda got her possessive hooks firmly implanted in Elmo. This was (not coincidentally) the period where EAT and I began to notice a change in Elmo. He was becoming less and less our friend, and more and more the property of Brenda Paris. This was a perfectly natural development up to the point where it became obvious that Brenda would have nothing to do with EAT and I. Brenda, who did not attend Oakton during the fall of 1974, would nonetheless meet Elmo periodically out in the faculty parking lot. She steadfastly refused to enter the radio station, an accommodation that would occasionally become an eye-rolling inconvenience to Elmo.

EAT (bless his little not-taking-shit-from-anybody heart) saw what Brenda was doing, called her on it, and they exchanged words on more than one occasion. EAT, who lived a stone's throw away from Elmo in the same subdivision, was more apt to run into Brenda than I was. EAT and Elmo's sister Donna therefore became my principal sources of information on the increasingly adversarial presence of Brenda Paris. At first, I construed Brenda's reluctance to enter the radio station as a reluctance to confront me. As petty as it sounds, Brenda may have harbored some kind of grudge against me for resisting her advances a year and a half earlier, though reports from EAT and Donna both revealed that Brenda's low profile was not being kept out of shyness or the wish to avoid embarrassment. Towards the end of 1974, Brenda's sociopathic behavior was appearing less like a personal grudge against me, and more like the byproduct of someone with designs on driving a wedge between Elmo and anybody else he theretofore had emotional ties with. Although Elmo, being the easy going guy he was, never allowed his dwindling fellowship with EAT and I to ever become a full fledged falling out, he may have been persuaded into believing that Donna, EAT and I were over-reacting unfairly to Brenda.

If the consistency of EAT and Donna's reports on Brenda hadn't convinced me, the first time I actually saw Brenda in the radio room certainly did. Despite the fact that Brenda had transferred to Oakton as a student sometime in mid-February of 1975, she still took great pains to avoid the radio station, and EAT and I in general. But one day, while hanging out with EAT while he was doing his show, Elmo came into the station for a few minutes with Brenda in tow. I had not seen Brenda in almost two years, and as such, was best suited for observing the physical changes she had undergone. Far from blossoming, Brenda had done a Tanya Herrell in reverse. She had put on a few pounds in her hips and backside, making her appear shorter. She was now wearing glasses (the same type of frumpy hornrims Tanya had ditched months earlier in favor of her Jazz-Dancer-of-the-Month look). But what really struck me were the changes in her face. Her once soft features now seemed hardened and fixed. Her big almost Bambi-like eyes were now narrow slits whose straightforward focus was so obviously a refusal to meet the gaze of anyone else in the room. She remained close to Elmo's side for the few minutes she was there, but more as a trained attack dog than as a loving companion. On top of all this, it was the unnervingly dense atmosphere she brought into the room that made me realize that I was viewing the living proof of what EAT and Donna had been describing for months. Really! It was hard to imagine that the same girl I had talked with at Margate Manor was underneath all that defensive armor. When her and Elmo left, someone in the radio room, possibly Jim Allewelt or Kaiser made some mood lightening remark about the temperature having gotten uncomfortably cool, which along with the collective sigh of relief from the 2 or 3 others in the room, convinced me that I wasn't just imagining things.

Now I was all too familiar with the phenomenon of friends and acquaintances reappearing after a period of lost contact only to go out of their way to behave as if I was now a complete stranger. What I had never encountered before was this kind of retentive paranoia, which manifested in bull bating EAT and stirring up the sibling rivalry between Elmo and Donna. I am 100% certain that there was a causal relationship between Elmo's dating Brenda and the change from the happy open loon into the more guarded serious guy he became later on. Perhaps I owe Elmo an apology for introducing this bane of entrapment into his life. He never mentioned Brenda any of the times I saw him after high school, and I'd always hoped that he had gotten rid of her. He certainly deserved better.

BRIAN HELMS

One of the three major figures in my 8th grade group of friends that also included Steve Tennant (AKA Good) and David Bracken (AKA Stills as a Nickname, or "Stills" for short). Although Tonny was my closest friend at home and on the bus to and from Luther Jackson, I don't recall crossing paths with Tonny too often once inside the school, where-as I shared a gym class, homeroom (which was oddly enough in the cafeteria) and numerous classes with the aforementioned three.

In the great high school break-up of 1971, my entire circle of friends was sub-divided into different schools throughout the region. Steve Tennant, who would have and later did attend Oakton High, was forced to attend a private school for a year. Tonny went to Fairfax High for his freshman year, and Helms and Stills went to Woodson. Though my contact with Tennant and Stills would dwindle to naught by the summer of

1972, Helms and I remained in relatively close contact until the summer of 1973.

One post Luther Jackson event saw the reunion of the fearsome foursome - the Alice Cooper concert at the Alexandria roller rink on the night of a very frigid March 12 1972. Mitch Ryder's Detroit was the opening act, and Alice's "Killer" era show came complete with decapitated baby doll heads, a well dramatized hanging of Alice on a fake gallows, lots of creepy atmospheric dry ice, and of course an appearance by Alice's pet boa constrictor. Despite the fact that I noted a strong presence at the concert from Oakton's freshman class (most notably Scott Machercher), this was really the last hurrah of my Luther Jackson days. Beyond this point, I would continue to periodically visit Brian Helms at his house in Mantua for about a year and a half, and then that chapter of my life ended.

Helms was my main musical cohort during the early 70's. I'll never forget that it was at his house that I first heard Atomic Rooster and Deep Purple, and albums like Jefferson Airplane's "Long John Silver," Jethro Tull's "Thick as a Brick," and King Crimson's "Lizard." Male adolescent suburban bucolic is how I would describe afternoons spent at Helms' house listening to albums. Oh! And lest I forget to mention, the Ard twins, Abbey and Amy, lived right around the corner from Helms. As I regarded the Ard girls as the epitome of pulchritude at Luther Jackson, the thought of being in proximity to their actual home added a little spice to my Mantua visits. Helms did bring to my attention the fact that all of Luther Jackson's budding young beauties resurfaced at Woodson, as if to wryly imply that us Oakton guys had gotten shortchanged. I must say that during my freshman year at least, it appeared as though we had.

Helms was one of those people that I (even into the early 90's) made a habit of running into. As Tonny and I were walking across the Pickett shopping center parking lot, on our way to the February 1973 Woodson basketball game that would confirm for me every tale I had ever been told about Woodson having more than its fair share of lovely ladies, we would meet Brian Helms and a small group of his friends. I would converse briefly with Helms before Tonny and I would be on our way. Helms would make his first post high school appearance sitting two rows in front of me at the fall of 1976 Ted Nugent/Black Sabbath concert at the Capitol center, where I would again speak briefly with him (and no doubt swap a few tidbits of info on whatever music the two of us were into at the time). Joining Emmette and I on the first of our excursions to Christ United Methodist Church for an insanist recon mission was the only brush Helms would have with my Oakton world, although a diary entry dated May 2 1972 talks about a phone call with Helms where he shows some interest in the "Walk for Ratkind" idea I was trying to pull together at that time.

Curiously, when Tonny moved into Margate Manor late in the summer of 1972 and began attending Woodson his sophomore year, he came to know Helms (it's safe to say that with the names of Helms and Hetrick, the two of them shared the same homeroom).

Brian Helms is remembered fondly for being one of my best friends during my 8th and 9th grades, and perhaps more importantly, for being a pivotal figure in the development of my musical tastes, making his influence a thing that I will carry with me to my grave.

BRITISH INSIPIDS

How Tonny and I referred to ourselves during the first year of our friendship. Having no exposure to the Bonzo Dog Band or Monty Python (if they even existed at this point), Tonny and I nonetheless somehow managed to pick up and adapt a dialogue steeped in the traditions of English absurdist humor. Bereft of any finite inspiration, I would say that "Madcap" is the word that best describes our 8th grade muse. There was certainly no conscious assimilation that I can recall.

Affecting an exaggerated English accent that vibrated with the loosening of the old "Stiff upper lip," Tonny and I co-created a mode of behavior I can best describe as silliness seeking to temper itself in a society governed by convention and conformity, which (now that I look at it) is exactly how the English seek comic relief. Of course, we weren't in England. It was 1970. We were in the 8th grade. There were no bullets flying around the neighborhood. We could be as silly as we wanted to be. It was; however, the pretense that our silliness wouldn't be tolerated or might cause us embarrassment that gave our silliness added entertainment value, as well as an air of excitement. This point is made with the fact that sometime a month of two into our 8th grade year, we began referring to ourselves and our behavior as "insipid."

Any dictionary definition of "insipid" will include the word "tasteless," and that was the definition we were working off of. Insipidity only has meaning, however, in a situation where taste accounts for anything, and if you have an inkling of what life was like as an 8th grader at Luther Jackson Intermediate School in 1970, you can see where I'm heading with this. What little passed for good taste, etiquette and fashion sense was nothing Tonny and I couldn't have gotten away with ignoring completely. If we had thought at the time that our jokes and skits about farts, butts, and toilets made us stand out as particularly insipid, we were only kidding ourselves.

Approximating the same perverse pleasure the English take in reveling in their own manufactured tastelessness, Tonny and I dubbed ourselves The British Insipids. From that point on, however, our expressions and mannerisms were increasingly in a language that was all our own. Our affected speech pattern soon mutated into something barely recognizable as an English accent, and our pronunciation of certain words and phrases was often skewed beyond the point of comprehension. Though practically none of these words and phrases were in usage beyond this period (Fall of 1970 - June 1971), they collectively form the basis of the loon lexicon. Here are all of the ones that I can recall:

Oau kau (O.K.)
Mu du buey (My dear boy)
Sau stewpid (Sooo stupid)
Quite!
A minute fart (it seemed as though we were capable of none other during this period)
But of course! (As this expression was borrowed from the cartoon character Pepe La Pue, a French accent was employed, furthering the mutation of the original English accent).

As the insipidity joke wore off, it was quickly replaced with insanity (which better describes the spirit Tonny and I would take with us into high school anyway). Our accent was further modified. New terms and phrases arose. The Insanist movement was born. Insipidity and the term British Insipids became a relic of our Luther Jackson/Merrifield Village days. Early in 1973, during the From Under a Log sessions, we recorded a song entitled "Insipid Soul," but aside from that, the term Insipid was not used much after 1971.

BUS STOP

Most people with any memory of their high school experience will recall their bus stop as being a world unto itself. It was certainly true of me to the extent that I tended to not even see the people at my bus stop once inside the walls of OHS.

I moved into the Fairlee subdivision a month before the end of my 8th grade year, so I had already met some of the people I would be shivering with throughout the mornings of my four years at Oakton. For an isolated subdivision of two short dead end streets, there was an unusually large amount of students around my age or slightly older. The class of 75 prevailed at our bus stop with Thomas Ring, Paul Nevitt, Kelley Maddox, Larry Laufer, Jennifer Husky, Terry Fullen, and myself. Rusty Siron and Lindsay Trittipoe represented the class of 76, with the upper-classmen consisting of Robin Siron, Patty Maddox, Sam Molinas, Pat Carrico, and Glenn Ring. As these people either got drivers licenses or graduated, our bus stop, with few underclassmen to replenish it, had by my senior year, shrunk to a third of the size it was my freshman year. Even at its numerical peek (which would have been my sophomore year), my bus stop was a bland affair by loon standards. Still! While no loon prospects or allies existed there, my bus stop was also conspicuously devoid of any elitist jocks or antagonistic ruffians who might have made waiting in the frigid morning air a more unpleasant experience than it already was. And as for waiting in the cold, I had, by my senior year, trimmed that to a minimum with a system that would have impressed any fireman. I would set my alarm for 6:50 AM, jump out of bed, hop into the shower, wash and condition my hair, shave, get dressed, grab my books and any records I might be playing if I happened to have a radio show that day, and run up to the corner of Maple and Fairlee to catch the bus between 7:15 and 7:20. That's how freakin' psyched I was about school. It took 12 years, no gym class, and a radio show to get me that excited, but there I was.

For as often as I had timed my arrival at the bus stop to coincide exactly with that of the buses, I missed the bus completely only twice during my four years at Oakton. There were many close calls though, adding to the adrenaline rush of my morning ritual, and it WAS as much an attempt on my part to start the day with an energy surge as it was an attempt to save myself some quality sleeping time.

My first task upon entering the school my senior year was to visit the always-empty bathroom in the guidance/administration hallway to comb the mane of long hair that I was fairly proud of. Being as my run to the bus stop occurred only minutes after stepping out of the shower, there was many a clear winter morn that found me standing in front of the mirror in that bathroom combing snow out of my hair. It seemed as though the bus would take its sweet time getting there on the coldest mornings, and I can now imagine that it took some work to crank those old yellow workhorses. I can remember times, especially in my earlier grades, where the shivers and grumbles of the half frozen Fairlee bus stop would turn into a collective cheer at the sight of the bus turning off of Lee Highway onto Fairlee. It is a sight that, for better or worse, will be burned into my mind forever.

CA COADJUTOR

A term widely bandied about over the course of my junior year. It was an all too common adjective used in the loon parlance of the day to describe any female who was seen interacting with Cheri Allen. Being tagged a CA coadjutor meant that you were someone to keep an eye on, though not so much as a person who might throw more water on my already doused hopes of winning Cheri's affections, but as a possible conduit for more information on what made Cheri tick. It was mainly exchanged between

Elmo and myself in hushed tones of intrigue that percolated with the excitement we both felt over the ongoing discovery of girls. It wasn't until the circulation of erroneous gossip my senior year that the term took on its more sinister implications.

CARLTON THOMPSON

Part of the Flip Anderson/Bill Dye/Ray Denk group of acquaintances, and though normally a fairly matter-of-fact, even tempered young man, something drew Carlton into being a major player in the Paying folly, leaving me the impression that under the right circumstances, the little devil perched on Carlton's left shoulder could be appealed to. Curiously, although Bill Dye was in my view the biggest music enthusiast from that group, Carlton became a regular customer of mine at Record World in the mid-80's, often with wife and child in tow. He then gave me his phone number and we proceeded to have the type of conversations I would have imagined having with Bill Dye 10 years after the fact. Despite having even more of the appearance and manner of walking life's straight and narrow path, Carlton's musical tastes (which included Throbbing Gristle, if you please) often veered into the exotic, making conversing with him on the subject of music that much more interesting. It was often when Carlton seemed the most disinterested in his own life that he would suddenly surprise you with some observation that revealed his underlying complexity (and sense of humor). Wherever he is, I wish him well.

CAROL BELL

That memorable 8th verse from Tonny's "Life in PA" went -

A certain girl in my class had a ring to her name
Carol Bell was the name of that dame
That name shall live in the hall of fame

Tonny's tuneful forecast has turned out to be accurate inasmuch as this book is as close as we've come to a "Hall of Fame." Carol Bell was as close to being Tonny's CA as any girl got. He mentioned her in at least one of his letters from Punxsutawney, but what I didn't know (or connect with) until recently was that Carol Bell was a girl in Tonny's junior year sociology class. As CA was a girl in MY junior year sociology class, those archetypal tales of psychically connected friends following similar paths come to mind as the coincidences here begin to stack like firewood.

Though Tonny never acted upon the feelings or desires he had for Carol, her name still came up fairly frequently during my trip to Punx'y in July of 1974. In looking at this, it's clear to me that while Cheri had made a much greater emotional impression upon me than Carol ever made on Tonny, their periods of influence followed concurrent timelines.

I must read the 6th verse of Tonny's Life in PA, because it illustrates how far away we were from the thin-as-sexy ideal that has recently all but revolutionized our countries beauty aesthetic. Keeping in mind CA coadjutor Devon Brown's third party appraisal of my fat chance in hell of attracting Cheri – "He's too thin, and his hair's too long," I'm fascinated to read Tonny's off the cuff reference to his own thinness as being reason enough for not approaching Carol.

Well there was other gals, many to be seen
I was sitting near, and I was clean
But I was green, I wasn't mean
I was lean, not fit for a queen

Now Tonny was not nearly as "lean" as yours truly. Still, like cattle to the market, an ample amount of meat on the bones made one more desirable in those days. A certain amount of stockiness was even allowed for if one was well proportioned. If there was another law governing the process of natural selection, Tonny and I had yet to see it. Cheri said I was "Too deep." Devon said I was "Too thin." Hmmm! We seem to have a discrepancy here.

CAROL GALANE

My earliest memories of Carol were of the plain Jane that sat three rows up from me in my 7th grade ESG class. Few transformations into womanhood were more spectacular than Carol's (and believe me, I tracked the path of many down that golden road). Throughout high school, I would catch passing glimpses of Carol, and at one point somewhere in the midst of my junior year Cheri Allen haze, it finally struck me that Carol was no longer the plain Jane I remembered from 7th grade. Along the way, I had increasingly seen the casual nods of approval from my fellow males turn to jaw dropping gapes. But it was the phenomenon of Carol worship that caught my attention before I took a good hard look at Carol myself and thought – "Man! Oh Man!"

During the early 70's, heft had its place in the heart of the American male, and at Oakton, I recall the term "Built like a brick shithouse" being used to describe females who were in fact, larger than your average shithouse. Carol Galane, on the other hand, had one of those sleek Bo Derek-type of bodies, a divinely crafted figure of the female form that absolutely screamed to be sculpted in bronze or marble, or painted at the very least. And if anyone could be said to have beautiful brown hair, it was

Carol. In my senior year 2ⁿᵈ period government class, I sat directly behind Carol, marveling at (among other things) her long straight earth-tone locks that complimented her skin tone in one of mother nature's seemingly purposeful uses of color. Carol was blessed (unlike her siblings, as their yearbook pictures would indicate) with a perpetual tan, and though I never had the pleasure, I can only attest to how silky smooth her skin surface appeared to be.

While sitting behind Carol in government class afforded me the mental pictures I use now to detail her numerous charms, I was a little apprehensive about engaging her in conversation. Truth be told though, enough of my heart's attention was yet focused on the Cheri lost cause as to make Carol a beautiful blur. It was after Peggy had taken Cheri's place as my heart's lost cause that I really began to notice Carol, or should I say, that Carol began to notice me. Carol apparently knew Peggy well enough for Peggy to confide in her. I don't recall how much Peggy told Carol, or if Carol had actually obtained part of her information from a third party source. Whatever Carol had uncovered, it was enough for her to turn around in class and begin to console me. As Carol and I had probably not exchanged word one beforehand, she was doing this out of the blue and out of the goodness of her heart. I will never forget the gentleness with which she interjected herself, taking a nurses care in dressing wounds that were at this time only days old. She spoke softly and reassuringly about the feelings she was sure Peggy still had for me.

From this point on, Carol and I spoke daily, if only to exchange greetings, but her continued assertions that everything would eventually work out failed to raise a glimmer of hope above the finality Peggy's rejection seemed to have. I had apparently written something to Peggy that really affected Carol, for I remember her saying, "I saw what you wrote to Peggy. I think you have a really good heart, and I think in time, Peggy will see that you really care for her, and she'll come around." If by now, dear reader, you are asking yourself, "Why was this guy even thinking about Peggy Wallace with this beautiful angel of mercy removing the proverbial thorn from his paw?" Well, aside from the excuse that love is the most blinding force in the universe, I think that around this time, I probably felt that this "Good heart" of mine which Carol spoke of wasn't worth a plugged nickel on the Oakton market, despite how reverently girls spoke of such things.

After graduation, Carol's graceful form flashed across the screen of my life for one last fleeting moment in the summer of 1976, when driving around Fairfax Circle, I saw Carol crossing the circle on foot. I noticed her just in time to catch her waving to me, a wave that would turn out to be a wave "Goodbye."

Carol tops my list of people from Oakton whose kindness and inner beauty I am only now coming to appreciate fully. And while Cheri will always be my unfulfilled cheerleader fantasy, and Peggy will always be the unrequited love of my life, both maturity and hindsight lead me back to Carol as the girl I would most like to turn back time and have a passionate love affair with. Carol wins my Miss Oakton award for being the most complete package. They don't make 'em like that anymore.

CEREMONIAL CRUSHING OF HAMBURGERS

Taken from a misinterpreted David Bowie lyric from the song "Sweet Thing." Sweet Thing was a song from Bowie's "Diamond Dogs" album, and as such, was akin to being a chapter from the New Testament for EAT and I. Unfortunately, holy document or not, Diamond Dogs was also the album that screamed the loudest for the inclusion of a lyric sheet of any album I can recall from that era, and as often as EAT and I would quote passages from this determinably oblique LP, mix-ups like this were bound to occur.

The actual lyric (which I never would have known had I not been driven by curiosity to thumb through a music tablature book of the Diamond Dogs album at Giant music) was "Turn to the crossroads – hamburgers." However, EAT and I were thoroughly convinced that he was singing "Turn to crush those hamburgers." Whatever concoction of cocaine and spur of the moment genius wrought this lyric was rendered unimportant by the genius of the formalization of our misinterpretation.

It happened during the Morty Sneaky show on December 4 1974, with me sitting in. In between songs, EAT made some form of announcement, turned completely around, produced a softball size glob of raw hamburger from a plastic bag he had brought from home and began to mash it to bits with his hands. As the ceremonial bit catcher, I held my cupped hands underneath so as to prevent any bits of meat from falling on the floor. EAT, whose microphone patter was as dry and as John Page influenced as my own, was in a state of obvious glee as he "Turned to crush those hamburgers," knowing full well that to his listening audience, it just sounded like 20 seconds of dead air.

This ritual had already taken place a few weeks earlier outside of the Capitol Center after the David Bowie concert, with Elmo present for the ceremony. What did it mean? Well, if you step back and examine what our little ritual had in common with many rote religious practices performed weekly, you will find at the core of it man's unquenchable desire to take nonsense seriously. What separated EAT and I from most religious practitioners was that our misinterpretation actually made more sense than the original text.

CHEERLEADERS

The mystique around those pom pom wielding oracles of young womanhood, which dates at least to the mid-50's, was alive and well in the mid 70's. Helped along by a uniform that flattered the attributes of even average looking ladies, this mystique eventually filtered down into the core circle of loons.

There was no avoiding it. Even if you were one who attracted well refined patrons of the arts like Melody Rouzer or romance novel ingenues like Peggy Wallace, there was no way you were getting through four years of high school without falling in love (or at least into some degree of sexual fascination) with a girl in uniform. Even EAT's little angel of music, Hunk, eventually ditched her braces and glasses, and joined the corp.

Trying out for the privilege of wearing the uniform of this or that squad opened up avenues to greater involvement in the preservation of school spirit, as well as greater visibility and prestige. Making the squad was enough to push a theretofore attainable catch like Hunk well out of EAT's firing range. I fell in love with a demure little bobby-soxer named Cheri Allen, but upon joining the Cougar Corps, Cheri's sexiness and popularity seemed to grow exponentially on a weekly basis. By our senior year, Cheri had become part of the mystique, and absorbing the light that she radiated only made me feel more and more like an outsider. This is what EAT and I could have viewed (if we had examined it closely) as the spirit-crushing effect of a practice that was intended to RAISE school spirit.

Though this noble service to the cougar cause may have been partially blamed for putting us another world away from the apples of our eyes, the mystique was never tarnished. While I speak from experience that being infatuated with a mystique can be painful and demoralizing, it was exactly this infatuation that would for me make the cheerleader's uniform forever a symbol of feminine purity, as well as being sexier than all the leather and lace on the planet. Actually, the root of this association of cheerleading with feminine pulchritude predates my Cheri infatuation by two years. As a freshman at Oakton High, I suddenly found myself in proximity to girls who were, despite the classifications of law, actually young women. Exposure to ladies like Jamie Machercher and Rae Ann Johnson at the tender age of 15 summoned forth the biological forces of attraction. That these ladies were cheerleaders was significant. That 90% of all the Oakton cheerleaders throughout the 1971-75 period were not attractive to me in the least was insignificant. The connection had already been made in my young impressionable mind. You see, the memories of men will always hold a special place for those ladies who first stoked the fires of manhood. This simple fact of life insures the continuance of the cheerleader mystique.

CHERI ALLEN

More commonly referred to in loon circles as CA. Cheri was not my first crush, but she was the first crush I would have that would last long enough and go deep enough to be life defining. And although I can attest to the rewards of marching to the beat of one's own drum, Cheri made me long for the ability to remain apart from the crowd while selecting at will my relationships from within the crowd. My attempt to foster a relationship with Cheri was further proof that, especially in high school, things do not work that way. I could never be anyone but myself, and that was always my downfall in situations like this.

And Cheri Allen? God! She was a piece of work. She had that distinctly American way of being virtuous and coquettish at the same time, like Annette Funicello with a Mid-Atlantic twist (sans the sun and surf). Cheri was in look and manner much closer to the teenage feminine ideal of the 50's than she was to anything twirling a baton in the brave new world of Fairfax county in the 90's, and it saddens me to think how archaic her unabashed femininity and organic beauty might seem today. Cheri reflected the times by wearing her hair long and her dresses short. She was the unaffected, unadorned, picture of cheerleader charm, and all the more desirable to me in retrospect when compared with some of the dyed and pierced androgens one might find walking the halls of Oakton today.

It was September 1973, in Mr. Wargo's Sociology/Psychology class, that I first took notice of Cheri. As I picture myself in that class with the good and evil dichotomy of Cheri Allen on my right and Fausto Bengochea on my left, I'm struck by the Sociology/ Psychology study Mr. Wargo hadn't realized was staring him in the face in his own classroom. For starters, what first attracted me to Cheri has yet to be defined, and if ever identified, it may render all those topics of class discussion meaningless. She was just there one day, and then she was really there, and a few weeks later, she was so there that 25 years later – she's still there, and I am belatedly doing my homework for Mr. Wargo's class.

Sometime in early October, I made the decision to contact Cheri via the old letters in the locker exchange, a communication system that I felt best allayed the awkwardness of the period between being total strangers and knowing each other well enough to exchange phone numbers. After doing some detective work, I located Cheri's locker upstairs on the eastern wall of the math department. I did not wish to reveal my identity too quickly, so I set up a system where Elmo would deposit my letters in Cheri's locker (lest she had her locker staked out), and all of Cheri's return correspondence would be handled by Laura Bombere. I must pause here to comment on the conspicuous heroism of Elmo and Laura during this period. It's the sort of thing one never says Thank You for until the wisdom of adulthood causes them to pause and reflect. I know that both Elmo and Laura were to some degree caught up in the youthful exhilaration of being secret agents for cupid, but it was the fact that they were with me psychologically that made a romance with Cheri seem to be not quite the long shot it actually was. My hotline to Laura, who seemed to be wiser in matters of the heart than the lot of us, was in full use months after Cheri's rejection. Hers was the needed voice of reason at a time when the spirit of insanity was being dealt its first major blow.

Cheri's first return letter came within a matter of days, and was basically a plea for me to reveal my identity. Cheri had a secret admirer and it was driving her nuts trying to figure out who it was. Her initial reaction to the contents of my first letter was that it was some sort of joke, which Laura had to convince her it was not. This left Cheri in such a state as to have nothing much more to say in her letter than to exclaim – "I REALLY REALLY wish you'd tell me who you are because I'm going crazy trying to figure it out. Come on, PLEASE tell me." Cheri was courting more direct contact, which was only days away from coming. My second letter was more of an introduction proper, being forthright enough to engender another prompt and sincere reply from Cheri, who signaled full speed ahead with the passage – "I really would like to talk to you (and also to get to know you). And the reason I don't talk to you in class is because I don't know you and I don't know what to say. I just don't want you to think I am a big snob or something."

The next move was mine, and it was clear that that move was to acquire Cheri's phone number and make the call heard round the world. I can't recall exactly how I obtained her number (though I suspect that Laura was instrumental in its acquisition). I do recall, however, that at the moment I found myself on the threshold of picking up the receiver with number in hand, I was at my uncle Jack's house on Cottage street in Vienna - with my cousins, Linda and Betty egging me on like a couple of victory driven cheerleaders. I remember stretching the receiver cord of their kitchen phone into my cousin Jackie's adjoining bedroom for privacy, and once there carrying on a conversation with Cheri which left me floating around in a haze of head-in-the-clouds elation.

Whatever had drawn me to Cheri in the first place reasserted itself during our first phone conversation, and from a sense-of-smell attraction came a genuine affinity. The more she prattled on in that little girl voice about her stuffed animal collection, the further I drifted beyond the point of safe return. When Cheri told me that I was thinking of "Somebody Better," I almost fainted. A lady of such charm, beauty, and grace, imbued with the virtue of modesty as well. She was just too good to be true. When my confidant Laura Bombere informed me that Cheri was not going with anyone at this time, and that my chances of winning her were quite good, I must have forgotten my station completely. I forgot all about us and them and was focusing completely on her and I.

In successive weeks, enchantment would turn to love, but for the

moment, I emerged from Jackie's bedroom bathed in the light of this special person. And of course! My cousins were like Mexican jumping beans in their demand for a full briefing. If I was nowhere near my first girlfriend, my first kiss, or even my first date, it was not for lack of moral support. Even Scott Merrill, brother of the Midnight Cackeler, insisted that I give him Cheri's number, that he might speak to her on my behalf. Scott was a loon from the get-go, and there was no denying him the number or dissuading him from such a brash act. Though I cannot recall the substance or the information gained from their conversation, one amusing instance does come to mind of Cheri looking at me in the middle of class and innocently proclaiming – "Oh! Your friend called me." This drew some quizzical looks from the surrounding students, who I'm sure were not aware of any pre-existing line of communication between Cheri and myself. Indeed! This may have been the first time that Cheri actually spoke to me in class.

The Merrill's would move unexpectedly shortly after Cheri's rejection, but for the time being, Scott, as well as Linda and Betty, Elmo, Laura Bombere, and even Tonny via the US mail, expected regular progress reports. The news was all positive - up until black Friday, December 4 1973, when I would make the fatal mistake of uttering the unspeakable. If there is one thing that I DID learn in my four years at Oakton, it is that "I Love You" is NEVER NEVER NEVER to be spoken to a female unless she's your mother.

I recall my frame of mind that night with crystalline clarity. I by this time had several warm congenial conversations with Cheri on the phone, and had seriously over-estimated her knowledge of and ability to accept my feelings. The unspeakable was not unspeakable at this time, it was the simple expression of those feelings. It was not exactly spoken in a grand or glorious context, but Cheri's response to it was absolutely Shakespearean, crying "NO!" in a tone that more resembled the reaction to being told that her cat had just been run over. I was more shocked by Cheri's reaction than she was by my confession. I was also surprised by the sudden change in Cheri. I had apparently really done a number on her mind, because she became noticeably quiet and uncommunicative, as if I had interjected an element of danger into our conversation. I asked her if she reacted this way to every boy who professed his love for her. At an obvious lose for words, she stammered out a tentative "No." More curious than hurt at this point, I inquired what she did do, how she normally handled this sort of situation. She said "I just try to let them down easy."

The greater visibility and involvement of EAT in early 1974 dulled the pain of Cheri's rejection to a great degree, but summer vacation lay ahead, and with it time to brood and ponder. The two weeks I would spend with Tonny in Punxsutawney PA that summer were among the most fun filled times of my life, though at odd moments, my desire for Cheri and the pain over her rejection seemed to be especially acute at this time, a full 7 months after the fact and hundreds of miles away. There was a valuable lesson to be learned from the summer of 1974. Unfortunately, I did not possess the foresight to see how such a pain might linger beyond graduation, where the rest of my life lay like one long open ended summer vacation dragging on indefinitely. If I had had the presence of mind to examine how the sharpness of such a pain might intensify in the absence of high school's continuous diversion, I would have demanded some form of resolution from Peggy and buried all hatchets before graduation.

I would have no classes with Cheri during my senior year, but our paths would cross frequently. Her ever-blossoming beauty would add a discomforting physical element to my longing sufferance. Strangely, it was during this time period that I became aware of something happening on my side of the fence. While Cheri and I were growing further apart in terms of popularity (which is the truest measurement of distance in a world where no one is ever more than a few hundred yards from anyone else), I began to sense the presence of anti-Cheri sentiments encircling me. The leader of the charge to convince me that Cheri's proper place was about a foot beneath my gaze was newcomer to the camp, Melody Rouzer. Melody's dislike for Cheri went beyond simple jealousy. Cheri was all the things that made intelligentsia elite's like Melody's skin crawl.

On November 6 1974, Melody and I had a most interesting conversation in the school library. Melody, who had made a valiant attempt to seduce me at her Halloween party only days earlier, seemed to have more knowledge of my feelings for Cheri than I felt comfortable in her having, and flatly refused to divulge where she obtained this information. "I have my sources" is all she would say, with a devilish glint of satisfaction in her eyes. And as our conversation progressed, Melody would vacillate between belittling Cheri and refusing to give the identity of her "Sources."

Now I would probably have forgotten this incident entirely if Melody hadn't brought up the subject of Cheri in a manner that made me feel as if my privacy had been violated. Melody had obvious designs on me, and while I took precautions not to encourage her advances, I had long since made it a point not to refuse the friendship or the company of one as intelligent and interesting as Melody. That Melody had done her own romance background check on me was not surprising. The thoroughness of her investigation was only mildly disconcerting. It was those mysterious "Sources" that had passed from Melody's lips through my mind like unidentified radar blips. My first thought was to suspect that there was a direct link between Cheri and Melody - a nightmarish thought. My reason for suspecting this was the fact that about a month earlier, I had given Cheri some papers I had written over the summer detailing the feelings I still had for her. Though long lost, I cannot actually recall if Cheri was mentioned by name in these musings. Cheri, being her sweet self, graciously accepted, read, and returned the papers to me a few days later. But who had Cheri shown the papers to in the interim? I cared not one whit about any of Cheri's immediate friends reading those papers. Gayle Alcorn, the Davis sisters - all were fit to know the depth of my feelings for their friend. The thought of Melody reading those papers, however, was enough to send me to the edge of panic.

Melody would neither confirm nor deny obtaining the information directly from Cheri, though the more I thought about it, the harder it became to even imagine Melody sharing the same space with Cheri for any length of time. Unseen third-party speculation aside, the only acquaintance that EAT and I could conclusively determine Melody and Cheri to have in common was none other than Hunk. This was significant as Hunk had rejected EAT only four days earlier. EAT and I went immediately to Defcon 3.

I must say here that while Melody had planted the seed of paranoia in EAT and I, and while Melody would continue her attempts to wean me off my fondness for Cheri Allen right up to the eve of graduation day, her arguments were neither illogical nor without precedent. What Cheri wrote on my junior yearbook was longer than either of her letters, and while it stands as further proof of the kind of understanding person she was, it does end with an unfortunate choice of words that took Cheri down a few notches in the eyes of EAT and Elmo, particularly EAT. "If you think I don't like you, or avoid you sometimes, don't worry about it. If I do, It's just because you're rather deep for me." This reads like a confession of shallowness, and it was interpreting it as such (rather than as an insult directed at me, which it clearly wasn't) that made Cheri really seem like one of THEM in the eyes of EAT and Elmo. But here's the rub; hindsight has revealed my attraction to Cheri to be nothing that could be explained intellectually, hence my reluctance to discuss it with intellectuals like Melody, Emmette, Fausto, or Kaiser. On the other hand, I could go on about Cheri into the wee hours with either of my cousins, EAT, or Laura Bombere. I WAS following the rules of selective communication, even If I lacked the conscious understanding of them. Cheri had unwittingly hit a loon nerve, and I can recall wincing myself the first time I came to the "You're rather deep for me" passage.

In the final analysis though, Cheri was such a great sport about the whole thing. Early in the fall of 1974, I dedicated one of my Queen Viper radio shows to Cheri. I had to play "I Wanna Make it With You" by Bread because Bread was Cheri's favorite group, but the concessions ended there. I couldn't resist playing that dreadful song by Frankie Valli & the Four Seasons which bears Cheri's name. Cheri (and probably 90% of all the Cheri's in the world) absolutely hated that song, but when I called to inform her that I had played the song in her honor, her chastisement of me was loud and long, but thoroughly unconvincing. This brings to mind the Friday December 20th 1974 radio show that EAT and I would do together. Billed as a special A lunch presentation of The Morty Sneaky – Queen Viper Show (and apparently with Elmo and Emmette in the station room looking on), EAT and I kept our holiday spirits high by running through an a capella chorus of:

We Wish You a Cheri Christmas, We Wish You a Cheri Christmas
We Wish You a Cheri Christmas, And a Happy New Year

to which I'm sure the A lunch crowd in the cafeteria interpreted as a simple holiday wish from the gang down in the radio room. It's doubtful that anyone's attention was grabbed quickly enough to turn both ears towards the speaker in time to catch the fact that we were not wishing them a "Merry" Christmas. Though I don't recall phoning Cheri directly after school to inform her that we had done this, I'm sure if I had, her reaction was one of mild girlish embarrassment, accompanied by an admonishment that was tempered by the knowledge that she was addressing someone who obviously still thought and cared about her a lot.

65

One of my last encounters with Cheri was another example of her gentle and tolerant nature, yet it also bore the ominous undertones of being a passing of the torch. EAT and I were having a conversation downstairs near the stairwell that led up to the confluence of the math and language departments, across from room 124. I had stopped EAT specifically to describe my third sighting of Peggy Wallace in the school cafeteria, when suddenly, Cheri appeared. We had apparently been standing only a few feet from her locker, and she was making a pit stop. To lighten the mood, and to wave the tattered flag of insanity for EAT's benefit, I walked over to Cheri and quoted a lyric from Jobriath's "Creatures from the Street" album. Getting in her face, I purred "Cheri, you know, you make the best girl, the worst boy, but the best girl." Oddly enough, this lyric leads into a song entitled "Liten Up," the very song that was appropriately playing in the radio room when EAT would break the news of Diana Malone's rejection. Cheri just gave us one of those "Oh! You guys!" kind of smirks and went merrily on her way.

My last memory of Cheri Allen was bittersweet to say the least. I was serving one of my self-imposed detentions upstairs in room 210, which partly overlooked the front of the school. I was sitting next to a window with a snipers view of the student body as it filed into the waiting buses. Instantly, I caught sight of Cheri walking with her boyfriend, a nondescript fellow who I'm sure I did not know, yet from an earlier glimpse of him at a football game EAT and I had attended, he seemed to be an appropriate match for Cheri. They turned and kissed each other goodbye, a gesture that pierced me with its dark finality. I remember mentioning this to EAT on the phone. His response was "Aw Bob! It's really over." I shall never forget the pain in his voice, because it represented a camaraderie of shared experience that has been lacking in my life in recent years.

And what of my feelings for Cheri Allen? Has maturity dragged me into the realization that it was all a wrongful waste of emotion? Not on your life! For beneath the apparent incompatibility, Cheri possessed certain qualities that I felt were lacking in my life, to the level that even listening to her describe her cheerleading routines gave me a sense of completion. Those who still do not understand this do not understand me.

I'll take it a step further. Were I to encounter Cheri today, she would have to have husband in tow to stop me from whispering inappropriate things in her ear. My darkest fantasy? How about persuading Cheri to don her Cougar Corps uniform (assuming it would still fit her), sneaking up some night for a candlelight dinner on the Oakton football field, and then a little something special behind the bleachers. Now that would be the absolute height of suburban kink. But then again, suburban was always something that I was defiantly proud of being.

COATI MUNDI

Or the "Mundi," as she was more commonly referred to. The daughter of J. Courtney Sheffield, the pastor of Christ United Methodist Church during the time of the greats (1972-73). Her real name was Co Co, and her nickname was derived from a TV special I had recently seen about a Coati Mundi named Co Co. Emmette was especially curious about her from my description of her, as she seemed to exhibit some (if not all) of the characteristics of the Peterson Syndrome, suspicions that were all but confirmed by Emmette during the first of his two visits to the church. Co Co was a pleasant and attractive young lady, but aside from Emmette's interests in the name of science, she was of little significance in the grand scheme of things, and was barely even present during the increased loon activity in the church in the fall of 1973.

COLONEL HASH

A true on-air personality, and part of WOHS's vaunted B-lunch triumvirate of Queen Viper, Colonel Hash and Doctor Sal. Here is an endearing character if ever there was one. The Colonel (AKA Ken Wilt) was never far from flashing that rural Virginia grin of his. It almost brings a tear to my eye to recall that silly hat he used to wear on the air, with the pot-leaf pin attached to the front of it. He called it "The Hash Hat," and like Linus' blanket, it was always on his person. He was at a loss to do his radio show without it.

His taste for tom-foolery showed itself in the cafeteria during the final folly, providing an extra bodily presence for our mock press assault on Peggy Wallace, but the truest summation of the Colonel is what he wrote in my yearbook. He drew a pentagram with a circle around it, and beneath that he wrote – "Bob, have fun (usual opening) and destroy WOHS. Ken Wilt, Colonel Hash," and underneath that he drew a smoldering hash-pipe and a caricature of himself. You may have seen attempts by modern TV and film producers to capture the essence of the 70's stoner dude, but this here was the genuine article.

CONNIE UNDERWOOD

Peggy's B lunch companion, as well as "The Little Southern Girl" in EAT's English class. If we were talking about any other girl in that school, I would say that her coincidental (and synchronized) appearance in the attention fields of both EAT and myself put her smack on the chart for VOT collusion. But to sit with Connie for two minutes was to realize that here was a teenage female who was too nice to give or receive malicious gossip.

Somewhere there's an encyclopedia that has a picture of Connie's face next to the term "Southern Hospitality." And when I say Southern, I'm not talking about the administration and Phys Ed teacher holdovers from the days when Fairfax County was 2/3 pastureland. I'm talking about Pecan trees and Peach orchards, and a disposition and outlook that came from a slower moving part of the world.

One of my greatest regrets in the whole Peggy affair was not taking Connie into my confidence. Only through hindsight have I realized what a stabilizing force Connie could have been, there in the crosswinds of two emotional typhoons like Peggy and myself. At the very least, talking to Connie outside of the cafeteria would have given me an inside track on exactly what I was dealing with in the evanescent Miss Wallace.

Looking at what Peggy and Connie wrote in my senior yearbook is an almost humorous peek at the antithetical sensibilities of these two ladies. The cryptic and soul ensnaring question mark in Peggy's "Always" in the front of the book, and in the back of the book, Connie's very down to earth (almost Cheri-like) parting:

> Hey Bob!
> I don't know you too well, but you seem like a pretty nice guy. I guess you're a guy who does his own thing and acts himself. Those are good qualities!
>
> See ya, Connie Underwood

The bottom line is that I should have ended my days at Oakton as both Peggy and Connie's friend, but Peggy and I were too self-absorbed to have had the presence of mind to use Connie as an intermediary, and Connie was too polite to have even offered an opinion unless asked to. Few aspects of my Oakton experience are more soaked in irony. Peggy and I, two romantics caught up in a grand sweep of emotion, and the one person who could have calmed things down long enough for some real communication to take place was the least looked at in the entire cast of characters.

Was Connie even mentioned in song? Well, curiously enough she was, in a rather oblique (and to my knowledge unrecorded) EAT composition entitled "Lepreconic Mystic." Now aside from the fact that Connie could have been the offspring of a union between a Southern belle and a leprechaun, I wasn't totally sure when I discovered this lyric recently that it was inspired by Connie Underwood until I got to the following line -

Lepreconnie hick girl, speaking with the death maid

Hmmm! Who could the "Death Maid" be, I wonder? Peggy? Hunk? No connection existed between Hunk and Connie that I was ever aware of, but Hunk sang in the chorale and Connie played French horn in the brass and percussion ensemble, so their extra-curricular activities WERE tied to the same department. I particularly like the stanza that follows the Death Maid line.

Metallic mommies do not regard the seasons
Always coming up with nice and friendly reasons

And then an earlier passage intimating that EAT might have been a little sweet on Connie is borne out (along with EAT's predilection for the musically inclined) in the final passage -

Artistic little green girl, afflicting with a bleacher
Thrilled for hello and always told to reach her

Ah yes! Oakton's little mint julep. Connie, I'm sure you are remembered fondly by all who knew you. In the 76 yearbook, under Connie's radiant senior picture, her favorite saying is listed as being – "Take to the wind and fly to the height of your destiny.
Find your goal, for I have found mine – Love." (Sigh!)

CONVERSION ATTEMPT

A conversion attempt was signaled to begin on a particular person if that person was noted as having a propensity for committing insane acts and/or had a personality that would allow them to be guided in that direction. Attachment to a particular clique or to the student body cognoscenti as a whole was the usual spoiler or disqualifier in any given conversion attempt. Actually, conversion attempts rarely bore fruit as intended. I mean, you were either with us or you weren't, and to be with us for more than the commission of a folly or two required a special caliber of individual, as well as a certain degree of isolation from the social mainstream. Where conversion attempts were beneficial to the cause was in uniting us around a singular goal, and in keeping allies to the cause such as Don Frank, Jeff Long, and Rick Judd aware of our presence. They made us more visible.

CRACK EM' BUTT AND SMACK EM' GOOD

No loon lingo was used as long or as often as this innocuous phrase. The fact that even at its inception there was no meaning attached to it made its usage all purpose. Depending on the situation or prevailing mood, it could be a rallying cry, or as most often was the case, supplanted into lagging phone conversations where neither party had anything relevant to say at that particular moment. In other words, it was used extensively to plug up the silent holes in-between topics of discussion. It would occasionally find its way into our song lyrics as well, owing to the fact that most of our songs were created on the spot. When one of us was at a loss for words in the middle of a vocal line, the old stand-by was there to be invoked in just such an emergency. The words – "I'm gonna crack your butt, I'm gonna smack It good" may have been loosely suggestive (as were many early rock 'n' roll lyrics) of some sort of hanky panky, but as I intimated before, its greatest definitive meaning for our purposes was in its lack of any meaning.

I did say that it was also used as a rallying cry. At some point, an "Ahooo!" was added as an optional front and back to the root phrase, making it resound more like a call to action. "Ahooo! Crack 'em butt and smack 'em good 'n' Ahooo!" This variation, like the bipartite call and response phrase Crane a Po and Hide your Ho, was derived from a Tonny utterance during a Follies recording session. The difference in the two phrases is that Crane a Po and Hide your Ho are actually two separate phrases, and very often used separately by themselves, whereas it was extremely rare not to follow Crack 'em butt with Smack 'em good. Smack 'em butt and Crack 'em good was a commonly used variant.

CRANE A PO

A term taken from an unintelligible lyric of Tonny's in the Bonneville Follies song "I Had a Little Girl." It eventually evolved into an informal greeting among core loons circa 1973-74. The usual call and response reply to "Crane a Po" was "Hide a Ho," or if a special air of camaraderie was present –"Hide your Ho."

DAMARIS BONNELL

Usually referred to as "Number 2" in my writings of the period, Damaris was an inspirational figure in my break from Christianity. I would say this makes me indebted to Damaris, but considering the fact that she broke my heart soundly, I'll just say it leaves us dead even. Sometime late in the summer of 1974, during one of my Sunday visits to the Fairfax Assembly of God, the winsome Damaris caught my eye.

Far too physically and emotionally mature for her age, Damaris was strangely detached from everything sufficient to lead scores of heart struck schoolboys to their doom. My cousins Linda and Betty, in observing my growing attraction to Damaris, began to discreetly pass me the smiles and winks of the blessed little matchmakers I knew them to be. They were at my side, as they had been during that fateful first call to CA, eager to be of any assistance in guiding romance to its fruition. They (or at least Betty) may have had a hand in setting up the following ice-breaking incident. It was during one of the evening social gatherings at the church. Everyone was milling around downstairs with plates of food in their hands, when I happened to see Damaris slipping upstairs to the chapel, with Betty gesturing me to follow her. It had all the markings of a set-up, and I was all too delighted to find Damaris sitting by herself in the front pew of the half lit chapel. Only candlelight or moonlight would have provided a better ambiance for the work at hand. Having been acquainted with Damaris long enough to make such an act seem not so obvious, I took a seat next to her. We chatted amiably for about 20 minutes before I suggested that we exchange phone numbers.

Damaris was utterly charming, and though only a girl of 13 or 14 at the time, she was possessed of the ladylike aloofness of a flower awaiting pollination. She certainly was devoid of the type of girlish immaturity's that would chase away older guys. She was also blessed with a pair of legs that sparked an impure thought or two to dance through my head there in the house of the lord. Even her voice, though effeminate and coy, was a good octave below Cheri's baby soft birdsong. Be that as it may, my first private conversation with Damaris was encouraging in a way reminiscent of that first phone call to Cheri. Similarly spiced with the flavor of déjà vu was Betty's inability to contain her excitement for me as I returned to the gathering downstairs and produced a piece of paper with Damaris' phone number on it.

Betty, Linda, and a few other young people at the church soon showed me that I once again had my own cheerleading squad. I'll never forget riding around the suburbs of Vienna one night with Linda, Betty and 2 or 3 others, when that horrendous Grass Roots song "Sooner or Later" came on the radio. As if cued by Cupid himself, Linda and Betty both turned around and serenaded me with a rather loud chorus of "Sooner or later, love is gonna get ya, sooner or later, love is gonna win." At this time, a successful relationship seemed to be the natural outcome of the events that were unfolding.

My subsequent conversations with Damaris, though short of the rarefied walk through the clouds I took on the phone with Cheri, were promising nonetheless. The biggest fence separating Cheri and I did not exist in the Fairfax Assembly of God. In fact, on Sunday mornings, Damaris found herself surrounded by people closer to my age who had in confidence allied themselves with my hopes and intentions. In other words, everyone that had knowledge of my feelings for Damaris was secretly rooting for my success. It had also occurred to me that my being a few years older than Damaris was perhaps another point in my favor. That and the bashfulness underlying Damaris' maturity combined to lull me into a state of over-confidence. Still! I was taking things slow enough to gauge myself at 2 to 3 weeks away from making any serious moves on Damaris, when I called her on the evening of Friday December 6 1974. It was almost a year to the day since Cheri's rejection (which was on the eve of the first Friday of December 1973).

Damaris was intently withdrawn on the phone. In a display of passive rejection that all but ended with Damaris asking me not to call her again, it was clear by phone call's end that Damaris had suddenly and inexplicably made a decision against having anything further to do with me. After the Sunday service on December 8th, my attempts to re-establish a friendly dialogue with Damaris were met with expressionless eyes and a tightly closed mouth, making it clear that this was more than just a mood she was in.

Although the first Peggy sighting was only three days away and Damaris would be a distant memory by mid January, the pain I was feeling at this time was extreme. There was also the added ego-crushing element of Damaris' relative youth, which raised the question of whether or not her parents had interceded on her behalf to put a stop to our relationship before it started. Despite being an easy and obvious explanation, its going against the grain of the facts as I knew them made it a stretch to believe. For one thing, her parents (who appeared old enough to have conceived Damaris in their early 40's) gave off no disapproving vibes to me at church. Her father, who usually answered the phone when I called, could have made things easy on his daughter (and me as well) by calmly explaining that he and his wife felt that Damaris was too young to have a relationship with a boy, a decision I would have sadly but dutifully accepted, and that would have been that. The impression I got from others in the church (if not from Damaris' parents directly) was that romances within the church were approved as being a way to insure that both young people involved remained in the church. As neither of us drove a car, our only face to face contact occurred inside the church itself, so how out-of-hand could things have gotten? Also, if Damaris' parents had forbid any further contact with me against her wishes, I believe some trace of regret (or at least a glimmer of frustration) would have shown up on her face. I have a hard time believing that anyone could so forthrightly engage in passive rejection as she did under even the partial command of someone else's determinism.

As of December 6th, Damaris' energies were directed towards fending me off without explanation, so I conceded defeat without ever finding out what really happened. Both Linda and Betty were as much at a loss to explain the sudden change in Damaris as I was. The real clincher though, came the following Sunday, December 15th. Reverend Keller's sermon dealt with the dangers of dark depressing people and how sharing too much space with them can drag one's spirit down into a sympathetic vibratory parallel of emotion. It was unusual, as it was more in the form of a common sense friendly advice type of sermon, instead of the normal scripture based rants that were more his style. Now despite the fact that I can now appreciate the logic of his sermon, at the time, I felt the accusatory fingers of all the angels pointing directly at me. With every gesture laden urge to "Push these people away" and to "Cleanse these people from your life," I felt more and more the object of Keller's sermon. He was warning his congregation about energy vampires, but at that particular time, I certainly fit his description of the dark and depressed soul. In fact, experience has born out that nothing will put an 18-year-old guy in a dark and depressed state faster than being rejected by a girl, especially a guy whose heart was still looking for first contact.

In the vestibule after the sermon, Damaris avoided me like the plague again, which did little to raise my spirits, but outside in the parking lot, I got the same cold shoulder from Tom Casey and Rick, two buddies of mine. These were the same guys that only weeks earlier had demonstrated their fellowship and loyalty by cheering me on to success with Damaris. And now! As if cued by Keller's sermon, they were giving me the social pariah treatment. If there is a God in heaven, these two will have some explaining to do. Needless to say, I never returned to the Fairfax Assembly of God, and have since distanced myself from the Christian church. This is a decision I have made not to dishonor the Christians who were truly deserving of my love and respect. No! This vow was made to celebrate the overdue love and respect I had come to show myself, and the truly divine revelation that I was not put on this earth to put up with bullshit like this.

DAVID OLSON

A lab partner of mine (along with Kirk Foster) in my Freshman year science class under Mr. Neal, whose ruffian tales of drinking so much alcohol that he was completely blind and the like made an otherwise boring class somewhat bearable. Olson was the type of colorful character that left me with a more romanticized view of the ruffian than Emmette's instantaneous shudder of disdain. I will never forget Olsen's practice of waiting until Mr. Neal's attention was diverted elsewhere, leaning under the lab table and spitting phlegm up on the bottom side of the table. After months of this practice, the underbelly of the table looked like the stalactite covered roof of some underground cavern. It was an unusual sight, and a horrific future discovery for some unfortunate maintenance worker. He either dropped out, or was snatched away by the great Chantilly High assimilation, but I never saw David Olson after my sophomore year.

DAVID ZOUTES

My freshman year was a static transitional year filled with daily phone calls to Emmette in order to keep the loon spirit on life support. The Luther Jackson crew became the scatterlings of Fairfax County. Tonny went to Fairfax High for a year, Good went to private school for a year, Helms and Stills went to Woodson, and Emmette was still in Luther Jackson. It is true that I went into Oakton High School on my own, without friend one.

Although Eduardo Alonso was my closest friend inside Oakton that year, it was David Zoutes whose loss I would come to mourn the most. During two separate field trips that year, one to a farm in the country, and one to the Smithsonian Institute, Zoutes displayed such a madcap jollity that it became one of my greatest regrets that he was not with us for the rise of imperial insanity. I can only imagine what a great loon he would have made and how much his spirit would have aided the cause.

One event during the Smithsonian institute field trip bears mentioning, as it was the undisputed highlight of my freshman year. Zoutes and I were walking around the American History Museum. We came across a canon (circa war or 1812). We tilted the barrel down slightly, when suddenly a slot machine rush of pencils, pens, gum wrappers, and other refuse that museum patrons had been dropping down the barrel of that cannon for what must have been months came crashing to the floor. Zoutes and I dropped the barrel and instinctively ran, laughing all the way back to Virginia over that one.

Our second field trip together was to an agricultural research center in Maryland on May 8 1972. Some of the highlights of this trip are given in a diary that I was keeping at the time. I brought a squirt gun (which I recall Zoutes and I having immense fun zapping people with on the bus ride over). I had to bum a dollar off of Tim Paulett for lunch, which I distinctly recall doing while our group was moving through some particularly odious stalls, where I remark on one bull which had a hole in its side (which made me wonder about the nature of the research going on there).

Zoutes and I made up songs on the way over, and it was just one of those magical times where I recall basking in the delight of complete silliness. We ate at Burger Chef (there's a blast from the past), and I've no doubt that I had a three course meal on that dollar I borrowed from Tim

Paulett. After eating, Zoutes and I ran across the street to a Dart Drug to buy Zoutes a squirt gun, so that the two of us could be fully armed, but we were unsuccessful. It is truly a shame that David Zoutes moved after my freshman year.

DEATH BY HANGING

As much as a chronicle of the Bonneville Follies would read like a chronicle of the early days of my friendship with Tonny, so too will the evolution of Death by Hanging read like a companion to the evolution of my friendship with Elmo. Though I probably have it on tape somewhere, I'm not quite sure when our first recording together took place. I'm fairly

sure that it was in the fall of 1972. I remember one of our early reel to reel recordings having a version of Pink Floyd's "Careful with that Axe, Eugene" entitled "Careful with that Blade, Elmo," with Elmo handling Roger Water's screaming part (and trying not to bust out laughing in the process). A mention of a "Blade" or a "Knife" or a "Weapon" was a sure sign that Elmo was involved in the recording. In fact, early in 1973, Elmo and I started mass-producing Death by Hanging albums that were recorded with the expressed purpose of presenting songs with a particular (and rather narrowly focused) theme. The first one of these theme albums was entitled "Knifey Songs" and was all songs about knives.

Moving through the spring and summer of 1973, at least five more of these albums would be recorded by Elmo and I, with more memorable non-thematic recordings occurring in-between. The most memorable of these theme albums was "Shed Songs," and was so only for the fact that it was recorded in Elmo's shed. It was a rather small shed at the back of the Zarin property, just barely large enough to fit Elmo, myself, and a cassette recorder. I can recall Donna Zarin being totally perplexed to find her brother out in the shed assisting in the recording of an album's worth of songs about sheds.

This tradition of theme albums (and I use the term lightly) existed up until the early days of EAT's involvement with the group. In fact, the last one of these theme albums was the very first recording of EAT and myself together entitled "Room Songs," which was an album of songs about various aspects of EAT's room, his wall, his door, his bed etc. This took the Bonneville Follies idea of drawing lyrics from the immediate environment to a greater extreme, and it's astonishing how rapidly these theme-based sessions were rattled off, as if the tunes were coming to us as fast as we could pick out a new way of looking at the thematic subject of the session.

As Death by Hanging's early days overlapped with the final (but most productive) days of the Bonneville Follies, it's not surprising that the two sounded similar to one another, despite their stylistic differences. Elmo would blow notes into this long cardboard tube that came to be known as the "Elmoaphone," but for the most part, the same instruments were being used by both groups. I encountered the same air of merry abandon recording with Elmo as I did with Tonny, so my approach was not altered significantly. A pivotal event in the history of DBH was one in which the two groups actually interconnected for one recording, becoming a trio for the first time in the history of either group. In July of 1973, Elmo and I went over to Tonny's apartment for the recording of "Live at Margate." This was a recording that an unusual (for us) amount of preparation went into. I wanted everyone to contribute equally in the vocal department. Perhaps I felt that becoming a trio put us into the size category of an actual band, and so a modicum of direction was called for, but it meant that everyone had to have something prepared or be prepared to wing it during the actual recording. Tonny and I were old pro's at winging it, but Elmo was one for having his lyrics all written out, so he was forced to do a little homework.

For much of 1973 and 1974, I was preaching Live Album to anyone that would listen. I wanted to actually make a recording in front of an actual live audience (of our choosing, of course), but I could never get anyone I was recording with to get up the nerve to join me in undertaking such an endeavor. The bone I was thrown, and the closest thing we would ever get to an actual live album was Live at Margate. Instead of recording

in Tonny's room, as we would have normally done, the three of us made the recording on Tonny's balcony, probably to the wonderment of a neighbor or two of Tonny's, and to anyone who might have been walking by below, but certainly not to any audience in the traditional sense. It's possible that some people down at the pool could have caught some of our more boisterous moments, but you get what I'm driving at here.

Although some Follies tunes were covered in the 10 song set, the fact that we opened with DBH's "Hang Me Tonight" was a tip of the hat to the era we were entering. We then launch into Elmo's short but intense "Baby Crackin' Blues," the first of the two songs that Elmo composed just for the occasion (the second being the show closer "I Don't Know What to Do"). Tonny's "Life in Virginia" and "I'd Love You, But" were both rendered faithfully, as well as my handling of "By the Beachside," complete with identical lengthy scream during the break (which saw Tonny's dad giving me a "You call that music?" half-grin of mock disgust through the patio window). My spur of the moment composition "Living in His Neighborhood" came off as one of the afternoon's highlights, and all of our jams flowed extremely well, an outcome that was more common in the Bonneville Follies than in the relatively young Death by Hanging. All that would soon change.

With Tonny's move at the end of August, my musical preoccupations were cut from three to two, and DBH's direction came into sharper focus. As in the evolution of the Bonneville Follies, DBH had reached a point where recording sessions were becoming less of an excuse to screw off, and more of a purposeful mission toward the goal of creating finite bodies of work. During the month of September 1973, perhaps as the result of finding himself in some sort of study hall with a pencil, paper, and lots of time, Elmo wrote a profusion of new lyrics. 10 of these songs would make up the body of the early October "Crane and Crack" sessions, which concluded with an 8 minute jam misleadingly entitled "The Birth of the Elmoaphone" (though it's possible that this was Elmo's premier as a soloist on the instrument that bore his name).

Though most (if not all) of the lead vocals were handled by yours truly, the lyrics were all Elmo's. Composing and/or improvising on the spot to fit someone else's pre-written lyrics was a challenge for me, especially in light of the fact that Elmo's lyrics were so unabashedly Elmo. Despite achieving mixed results, our loose ends were clearly tightening up. More pre-composed material meant that more of our output was sounding as if we had actually intended it to sound that way, and though the spontaneity and fun factors had been compromised a bit, Elmo's legacy within the group had been secured, with "Russian 2 Blues" and "Hot Wash, Tumble Dry" going on to be considered classics.

More successes in a session had the effect of raising our confidence level going into the next session, as if we not only had a greater reputation to live up to, but possessed a greater ability to live up to our own heightened expectations of DBH. It was with the same cocksure attitude Tonny and I carried with us into Smackin' Crackin' on a Sunday a year earlier that Elmo and I were sporting as we convened at his house to begin work on "Worlds You Never See." Despite the fact that only 6 songs were recorded (less than 17 minutes of music), this was a landmark recording session, marking the beginning of DBH's golden age. My pre-composed "Bleeding Murky Dreams" went off better than planned, and Elmo's vocal on "Outer Mongolia" stands as (in my opinion) his greatest and most definitive vocal performance on tape. As an album though, Worlds You Never See would not see completion until early 1974. In the meantime, Elmo and I would take an artistic detour, and in the process, record our finest work together.

Sometime in the fall of 1973, Elmo and I had both purchased electric guitars. On December 28th 1973, we convened in my basement to record our first plugged-in session. Utilizing the dual cassette delay method for the entire session (a time consuming process), Elmo and I painstakingly put together "We were Promised a Female, but got Stuck with a Pillow." All through the recording and subsequent re-recording process in order to achieve a suitable delay effect (I.E. not too little, not too much), Elmo and I were somewhat surprised at what we were creating. Aside from the obvious differences in the texture of our sound that electric guitars and an applied delay effect were bringing out, both Elmo and I seemed conscious of the muse that was guiding this session. Despite the fun Elmo and I had in making it, We were Promised a Female, but got Stuck with a Pillow marked the death of innocence in both tone and subject matter. Despite the fact that only one track, "The Immortal No!" (The shortest and only tongue-in-cheek track on the album) would in any context refer to the rejections Elmo and I had recently suffered, the title of

the album left no room to ponder where our heads were at. Despite the fact that our mood over the course of the two days we worked on these recordings (Elmo slept over for this one, as attested to in the song –"The Floor, Like I Slept on Before") was as light as it had always been, I distinctly recall the oppressively glum state Elmo showed up in. Dragging his guitar case downstairs under the weight of something I could not see (but by this time knew all too well), he was clearly not himself. As soon as the tape was rolling, however, our romantic misadventures were either forgotten completely, or as my impersonation of Cheri Allen on The Immortal No attests to, made light of under the reigning spirit of our lunacy. We were

Promised a Female was the artistic exclamation point of my Oakton experience, a dark melange of undulating gray-noise and delay-created poly rhythyms. It had more the sound of something one would have expected to come from EAT and I circa the spring of 1975. References to Beelzebub in the lyrics further underscore this point.

As if EAT's place in DBH wasn't just a matter of time after the success of our first recording together as a duo – Room Songs, Elmo played EAT a tape of We were Promised a Female, which had him clamoring to get in on the fun. In February of 1974, the three of us convened in Elmo's basement for the recording of the "My Baby Knifed Me" sessions, an albums worth of music, half of which would complete the theretofore unfinished Worlds You Never See, and the other half would make up the first side of the "Uawau!" album, which curiously derived its title from an expression that EAT made popular around this time. Songs about knives, blades and weapons dominate this session, making it stand out as the final major statement of the Elmo era. EAT would make his mark, however, on the song "Hunks," the first original composition of his that DBH would perform. A smile will always cross my face to recall EAT's over dramatized death scene in "The Death of Ezrin." The three of us would also record a track from Room Songs – "Lampshade Yeah."

Elmo's "She Thought I was going to Rape Her" recalls an incident where Elmo came across a girl (while walking around his neighborhood) who reacted with noticeable paranoia upon seeing his approach. Having had similar encounters with females in the past, the pangs of irony would never allow me to simply view this sort of thing as females reacting to the fear they sensed in us. I wanted our side of the story to be heard (or at

least recorded), and I can recall expending the minimal effort it took to convince Elmo that this incident was song material. Our mocking falsetto on the chorus demonstrates the lengths we would go in order to avoid taking it seriously.

Though long since consigned to the role of lead vocalist, my inflection on "Whip Out Your Blade" and "Breaking the Bread" demonstrated how Elmo's subtle influence had wormed its way into my singing style. And something that not even We were Promised a Female could escape from, no session from this period was complete without at least one song with the word "Pay" in the title. As Worlds You Never See began with the strangely forthright "The Burper," the My Baby Knifed Me sessions would conclude appropriately (I suppose) with a track called "The Chewer."

The next chapter in the DBH saga is a tale of what might have been. In January of 1974, it was announced that at an indeterminate date sometime around late March/early April, Christ United Methodist Church would be hosting a talent show in the large reception room downstairs, which was conveniently equipped with a large elevated stage at one end, making it perfect for this sort of thing. Having attended 2 or 3 church suppers there in the day of the greats, and being perpetually intrigued with the idea of making an actual live recording, I started to get ideas. Despite how controlled and tame an audience for such an event was likely to have been, Elmo and EAT could not be sold on the idea. I persisted, but to no avail, and in retrospect, it's amazing to consider how psyched up I was to take the three of us up on that stage and perform Bleeding Murky Dreams, Whip Out Your Blade, The Immortal No and God knows what else to the wonderment of those terminally ordinary young people. Still! It would have no doubt made a great tape, and that's really all I was after anyway.

The short-lived trio of Elmo, EAT and I would, however, make a recording inside Christ United. Having gotten permission to frolic around in the very cavernous chapel, we were able to take advantage of the intensely reverberant acoustics by recording a set of songs I don't believe I've heard since the day we recorded them. Setting the recorder somewhere in the middle, the three of us fanned out and began banging, blowing and wailing at a volume level somewhere near waking-the-dead. I'm not sure our little experiment with natural reverb was quite the success we hoped it would be. As always, failure to produce a classic did not dampen the fun of the event itself. Later in 1974, when DBH had become the duo of EAT and myself, reverend Keller agreed to allow us the use of the chapel at the Fairfax Assembly of God for recording purposes, a recording that for some reason never materialized. Keller's "Why sure!" Response to my inquiry as to whether we could use the church organ in our recording really left me with the impression that churches as a whole were unusually lenient about such things. Perhaps it's just that I was not used to anyone giving me any degree of support or encouragement to make the music I was making.

Following shortly after our un-live recording at Christ United was a recording session that marked the beginning of DBH as the duo of EAT and I that would prevail throughout the spring and most of the summer of 1974. We recorded an album and a half's worth of music that was so successful that Elmo may have gotten the mistaken impression that he was no longer needed (although his intensifying relationship with Brenda is the reason I'd prefer to give for his sudden departure from DBH recordings). Half of this recording session went to complete the theretofore-unfinished Uawau! album, and the rest of the session comprised the entirety of "Living Minds, Dying Hearts." Containing polished up versions of three songs from the almost completely plundered vault of material that Room Songs had become ("Blue Rug," "White Wall," and "Bed"), Living Minds, Dying Hearts had, nonetheless, set the course for the EAT inspired glitter esthetic that would follow in its footsteps. It was a transitional recording

to the degree that it stood on its own, and though a stylistic harbinger of things to come, in some respects (specifically in the area of doing longer multi-sectional pieces with a more serious lyrical content), it picked right up where We were Promised a Female left off. Having gotten Room Songs completely out of our systems, Blades, Knives and Paying would be replaced with Satan, Christ, Moobunga, exaggerated English accents, EF Sly, and EAT's life/death quandary all floating on a bed of oblique Bowie-esque nonsense. I mean, what more can be said about a song that starts off with the line – "He hangs by a chain, and clutches at thoughts of secretions"?

The spring of 74 brought DBH hard into the EAT era with the incredible "Peachbottom and a Pickle," and the audaciously haphazard "Bunga in the Halls of Life." "Silver glitter, black leather" became the chant that would define this period of DBH, with our vocals often veering toward an affected shrillness that was one part David Bowie, one part witch being burned at the stake, and one part our own mutation of the former two. As composed as some of this material was, the end product came off as loose and abounding with wild youth as anything the Follies had done to date, and listening to it now recalls the relatively carefree early days of my friendship with EAT (Cheri not withstanding).

Moving beyond our glitter era, we come to DBH's swan song "In Name of Panic Karen," which was really a collection of recordings made throughout (and in a few cases, after) my senior year. Actually, about a third of it was taken from an August 1974 session that saw the return of Elmo. Tonny was also in town at the time, and so this session stands as the only recordings of DBH as a quartet. Elmo brought his electric bass over, and EAT brought over his newly purchased electric guitar. Elmo and EAT were actually involved in some side project around this time called "The Rods," though I don't know who else was involved or if any recordings were made. We recorded one track utilizing the old dual cassette delay, and the result was a track that not surprisingly sounded like a We were Promised a Female outtake. We also finally got around to recording Elmo's "Kill Them All," his final contribution to a DBH recording. An actual drum kit (albeit a toy drum set) was employed on a couple of tracks, and one bizarre instrumental featured Tonny playing my electric guitar on his lap, going up and down the fretboard with a slide.

Despite the dire reference to EAT rejecter Karen Cockrell in the title, In Name of Panic Karen is conspicuously devoid of references to anything that was happening in our lives over the course of the 74/75 school year. Failing as a chronicle of events that year, it nonetheless sported two of EAT's greatest songs, "Kill and Forget" and "Broken Spheres and Powder Puffs." I was busy recording Time is the Murderer, 9, Black, and Creepers, and putting the beginning touches on Valentine Trashcan Rain, three projects which were rife with references to current events, and perhaps in light of my compulsion to "Get the observations and write 'em down." DBH had become a catch-as-catch-can project. The strength of some of the material could not disguise the fact that DBH was losing its direction, and would very soon lose its reason for existing. That is not to say that a reunion recording is out of the question. As will always be the case with DBH, any successful reunion session could only stave off the encroachment of old age.

DEBRA SHORTRIDGE
A girl whose face I recognized from my recent yearbook culling as being familiar enough to say "Hi" to through some forgotten affiliation with either Elmo or EAT. At first, I theorized that she might have been an earlier pre-Brenda flame of Elmo's, but recently in a letter from EAT, he confirmed that she was in fact an earlier (possibly pre-Hunk) girlfriend of his. From a point after EAT's arrival on the scene until graduation, Debra remained a recurring but peripheral presence.

DENISE WATSON
Though it's not what I remember most about her, Denise was a ranking CA coadjutor, and out of the lot of them, the one I would have felt most comfortable confiding in, had I not had Laura Bombere's ear to bend. In

Miss Heeter's English class, Denise sat in front of me and next to the mother of all CA coadjutors, Gayle Alcorn. Although I tended to lump Cheri's friends into a single group, Denise and Gayle were opposites in a way that I found most entertaining. Gayle was a very literal A to B Christian girl, whose pleasantness has become a sublime thing of beauty in my memory, but in person was actually a wearisome impenetrable mass. I couldn't put my finger on it at the time, but I think it was Gayle's lack of an attending sense of humor that left me wanting to keep our conversation brief (even on the subject of God). Denise, on the other hand, could speak volumes with a smirk, and though I doubt we exchanged more than 50 words between us over the course of the class, her often-wordless displays of personality and humor have left a more profound impression upon me. By some of the looks she would turn around and give me, I could tell that Denise did not take me seriously, and as well she shouldn't. In fact, if certain other females could have seen me through Denise's eyes, certain rumors about me would not have been taken seriously enough to be circulated.

Believe it or not, though I never saw enough of a sense of humor in Cheri to credit her with having one, it is in Cheri's senior will that I find the greatest example of the kind of humor I saw in Denise Watson. After finally getting around to reading Cheri's will in the summer of 1998, I at last came to understand what the two of them had in common as friends. In Denise's senior will, she left Cheri (among other things) their "Possibility List." This was a list that I can assure you I was not on.

DER KAISER (JEFF KAISER)

Known affectionately by Elmo, EAT, and myself as "Kaise." In varying capacities, Kaiser was never far removed from my center of activity while within the walls of OHS. As my freshman homeroom was located in Mr. Sachs' biology class, the students sat at laboratory tables for two (so to speak) instead of conventional desks. I was paired with Kaiser, and will always remember Jeff as being the first person I would make the acquaintance of at Oakton.

Kaiser was a gangly spectacled honor roll inductee with a penchant for telling grotesque jokes (I still remember the one about the huge pimple). As a first contact, the brainy science-minded Kaiser seemed like a safe bet. Gradually throughout my freshman year, however, the devil-may-care side of Kaiser's personality began to reveal itself, giving rise to the idea that he might be loon material. An entry in an old journal dated May 4 1972 mentions an incident in my third period gym class involving Kaiser, Jeff Long, Steve Larsen and myself. While the rest of the class was playing murder ball in the main gym, the four of us snuck off to the corrective gym to have "Battles with the rubber dummies." I can't for the life of me recall what we were doing exactly, but as I've no doubt that either or both Kaiser and I incited this little diversion, it demonstrated our preference for making up our own games. It wasn't the idea of sports per se that Kaiser and I were dismissing. It was the creativity stifling adherence to rules that were often centuries old. I know that none of the four of us were big, strong, or athletically inclined, but the thing that eventually brought Kaiser into the fold was his ability to make a game out of anything he saw a fun potential in. That alone defined him as a loon.

Having a last name that was as alphabetically close to mine as you could get assured that Kaiser would remain in my homeroom class throughout my four years at Oakton. It was during my sophomore homeroom class, under the supervision of the quietude obsessed Mr. Cupelli, that our strange relationship was solidified, and a clearer distinction existed between Kaiser and fringe spectators like Jeff Long and Don Frank. Kaiser was quick to take his place at the loon lunch table. He henceforth discovered the first loon oracle (The Kaisey Module), had the largest hand in the invention of Leaf Biting, and was instrumental in gathering votes for our man Rick Judd during the Fleming-Judd election.

Though Kaiser was never christened with a loon name (a bizarre oversight), and 2 or 3 phone calls would be the extent of our contact outside school grounds, Kaiser continued to be an important figure throughout my junior year. He had a major role in Paying and in the receiving label folly, and it was the latter of these wherein lie my most precious memories of Der Kaiser. I became rather proficient at plastering those labels around the school on the sly, but Kaiser's brazenness at slapping one on a bare wall in a crowded hallway was truly inspiring. One of my most endearing memories of OHS was the sight of Kaiser taking a running leap and slapping a receiving label on the ceiling of the music hallway. While the lockers, fire hydrants and walls of the school were promptly cleaned off, that one label that Kaiser planted in the music hallway remained defiantly out of reach of the schools maintenance men at least until the end of the school year. That little orange sticker was a reminder to all who passed through that hallway (which connected the history/sociology wing with the main gymnasium) that we had been there.

Kaiser was not only learned in the sciences, but had a knowledge of electronics that approached Elmo's. This, along with the fact that he had been Rick Judd's assistant at WOHS the previous year, made Kaiser the most likely candidate to replace Rick Judd (the same fellow he helped elect to the student government two years earlier) as the head of WOHS. Elmo was the logical choice as Kaiser's technical assistant. While this assured EAT and I of DJ spots, it had the unforeseen effect of causing a schism

between the loons that EAT and I still were, and the no-nonsense sticks-in-
the-mud that Kaiser and Elmo were becoming. While the stultifying
influence of Elmo's girlfriend was an understandable (if disheartening)
explanation for the change in his behavior, Kaiser was a different story.

I suppose I had an air of rebellion about me, but a rebel for rebellions
sake was not what I was at heart, and I mistakenly trusted Kaiser to know
me well enough not to treat me like one. Elmo was cozying up to a catty
vindictive bitch who didn't like me. OK! I could put 2 and 2 together
there. But the criticism Kaiser began handing me about playing too much
David Bowie was difficult to even take seriously. In fact, I didn't take him
seriously at all until his pressure to conform to this nebulous arbitrary idea
of a "Balanced format" became almost a daily thing. What really began to
yank my chain was the fact that neither his criticism nor the criteria for this
balanced format of his held an ounce of water.

Q: Did Kaiser want us to play more commercial top 40 music?
A: No! If that were the criteria, David Bowie would have been a lot closer
to fitting that criteria than most of EAT and I's format, and much of Elmo
and Kaiser's as well.

Q: Did Kaiser accept the findings of our survey that showed that the
student body overwhelmingly preferred album tracks to top 40 singles?
A: Yes he did, but only with the appended qualifier that certain people had
stipulated their preference for hearing album tracks by groups they were
familiar with – "Like the Carpenters."

Q: Never mind who was going to supply us with these albums, which of
the 9 MALE DJs did he think was going to happily volunteer to play the
Carpenters on his show?
A: I'd love to have heard him try that argument out on Elmo.

Q: Because the student body preferred album cuts by a whopping 7 to 1
margin, did Kaiser use this data to pressure Doctor Sal (who had a standard
top 40 format) to play more album cuts in order to have a "Balanced
format?"
A: No! He knew Sal wouldn't take him any more seriously than I did.

Q: Did Kaiser have enough knowledge of independent and college radio's
tradition of playing everything from free jazz to bluegrass, giving their
listeners a diversity of programming that EAT and I's comparatively puny
record collections could not even approximate?

A: No! Kaiser's reaction was that by playing a Bowie track on every other show, EAT and I were pushing the limits of acceptability.

Q: Did Kaiser stop for a moment, look at the big picture (which would include the fact that Oakton was an institute of learning), and realize that EAT and I's shows balanced out the otherwise mainstream programming of the station?
A: Apparently not! Kaiser was acting as if WOHS was market driven, and that he had advertisers and corporate sponsors to answer to, which was patently ludicrous. His attitude towards the student body seemed to be that in regard to musical programming, they were to be placated rather than educated.

Q: Did Kaiser give any specific guidelines as to what a balanced format was, or offer any coherent explanation as to why he felt that my show was not balanced?
A: Not one that made sense. Given the music lover that I was, my record collection was probably larger and more diverse than the other DJs. Kaiser even seemed oblivious to the fact that the David Bowie track I played this week was stylistically different from the one I played last week, leaving the impression that Kaiser was not objecting to WHAT I was playing as much as WHO I was playing.

Q: Do I presently have any theories to explain why Kaiser was acting like this?
A: Yes! But none that I'm satisfied with.

However! I hashed this out with EAT on the phone a couple of days ago and he had a thoroughly plausible (if hard to accept) explanation for the change in Elmo and Kaiser. He fully remembers how tense the air in the radio room got at times. He posits that Elmo and Kaiser were holding some unexpressed resentment towards us over the degree of fun we were having. Out of reverence for the first three years of my friendship with Kaiser and the first two years of my friendship with Elmo, I didn't want to believe that this could be true, but the more I thought about it, the more it made sense.

There's no denying that the amount of fun EAT and I had during the 74/75 school year did not seem to be in any way contagious. There's also no denying how fraught with seriousness Elmo and Kaiser became, as if overburdened with the responsibility of operating this radio station. But EAT takes it a step further by claiming that Elmo and Kaiser were resentful of the radio personalities EAT and I may have seemed to be coming on as, a sort of "They do all the work and we take all the credit" scenario. This still doesn't explain why the two of them didn't seize the opportunity to have the same fun EAT and I were having, because the Elmo and Kaiser that I knew would have done so.

The irony in all of this was that EAT and I took the greatest care in the programming and delivery of our radio shows. It really meant something to us. I look at all the praise I'm receiving now for the pacing and the patter of my current radio show, and I can trace the developmental roots of these qualities back to the Queen Viper show, and the emulation of WGTB jocks such as John Page.

Though this tension that EAT spoke so truthfully of led me to not include Kaiser in my senior will, Kaiser did bequeath to me (of all things) "A balanced program, a prayer, and a never ending appreciation for the gorgons of the world." His senior will concludes amusingly with – "To Oakton itself I thank for giving me the opponent needed to fight the good fight." This parting message was given with the humor and personality (not to mention the impertinence) of the Jeff Kaiser that I'd like to remember. It is also a reminder (lest this entry lead you to believe otherwise) that even during our senior year, Kaiser and I were on good terms more often than not. If indignation over Kaiser's attempts to censor the Queen Viper show ever threatens to overshadow my fonder memories of Der Kaiser, I'm drawn to his inscription in my Junior yearbook – "It happens to be Bobney: Arch of Arpochney, felicitations, remember the Alamo, the Main, Andrew Jackson, Millard Fillmore, and me, Jeff Kaiser." A request that will certainly be honored.

Despite the fact that much of the tension that escalated during the latter half of my senior year had nothing to do with Elmo or Kaiser, my 4 year friendship with Kaiser ended with a whimper. It's all water under the bridge now, and Kaiser would be welcomed back to any insanist roundtable that would be convened. He was a great loon in his day, and though the commonality of his name makes tracking him down through the Internet an impossible task, a toast should be made in his honor in lieu of a reunion. He was last seen through loon eyes by Howard Koretz at the "Library" nightclub in Fairfax sometime during the Christmas season - 1978. Wherever you are tonight Jeff Kaiser, I hope the world never conned you into taking it too seriously. Oh! And by the way, I'm still on the air.

DEVON BROWN
A friend of Laura Bombere and at least a casual acquaintance of CA. She also knew EAT, and it was her rather hurtful comment to him that prompted me to remember her in my senior will. Knowing of my interest

in CA, her two cents worth was to tell EAT "She'll never go out with him, he's too skinny and his hair's too long." Though the reality that CA would never go out with me had long since been established, it was with no small amount of relish that I left Devon Brown – "My corpse, as a constant reminder that I was too skinny and my hair was too long."

DIANA MALONE

A rather tall, big boned, leggy, and fairly attractive freshman blonde that EAT dated for a short time in January of 1975. In a recent letter from EAT, he proved what a small impression Diana had left on him by getting her name wrong. He then went on to prove that he was still the same EAT I knew and loved by giving his clearest memory of her as playing Queen's "Loser in the End" on his radio show after she dumped him. Diana figured into the Peggy Wallace timeline, as her rejection of EAT took place on January 22 1975, smack dab in the middle of my push to get something going with Peggy. Despite what EAT may have forgotten about his fling with Miss Malone, I will never forget the disconsolate look on his face when I entered the radio room that day. He didn't say a word, and he didn't have to. I knew exactly what had happened. Strangely, the Jobriath song "Liten Up" was playing at that moment, the same song that I quoted from to CA in the hall in front of EAT a little over a month earlier.

DID YA' FINDER

Tonny was coming back from a trip to Punxsutawney PA with his family (I would date this as sometime in the latter half of 1972). They were still in Pennsylvania when the call of nature forced them to stop at a gas station out in the middle of nowhere. The attendant was a grizzled old man of the country, who pointed Tonny in the direction of the restrooms. Later on, when Tonny was returning to the family car, the old man reappeared and inquired "Did ya' finder?" The accent and inflection of the old man's words as retold by Tonny are impossible to convey here on paper, but Tonny and I were so amused by it that "Did ya' finder?" became an instant loon cliché, spawning other clichés that complimented the rhythm and meter of the original.

Here's an example of what a Did ya' finder inspired call and response dialogue between Tonny and myself might have gone like in 1973 -

Me: Did ya' finder?
Tonny: I founder
Me: Well, Put 'em asunder
Tonny: I'll take a gander
Me: I'm in a binder

Tonny: Just as a reminder

That's a little more stream of consciousness and a bit more longwinded than we'd normally take it, but each one of the aforementioned phrases was used hundreds of times at odd junctures by Tonny and I throughout the remainder of the 70's.

DOCTOR SAL

The WOHS on air name of James Salyer, who was part of the B lunch triad of Doctor Sal, Colonel Hash and Queen Viper. Sal had ambitions of pursuing a career as a top 40 DJ, and his on air style was clearly influenced by the vociferous bark of the AM jock. Even by 1974 though, AM top 40 radio was on the wane, bowing to the more listener friendly FM stations, with their soft spoken DJs and expanded hipper formats. Sal was a junior, a member of the class of 76, and I've often wondered how he adapted to the changing face of commercial radio, or if he gave up the idea altogether. Sal and I represented the opposite extremes of AM vs. FM delivery and format, and we often joked with each other about our differences. I remember sitting in on one of Sal's shows, and one of us had the idea to not only co-announce the show, but to switch personalities as we were doing so. In other words, I would announce a song in the Doctor's clamorous AM huckster cum car salesman delivery, and he would announce the next song in my pensive breathy John Page-Abstraction Show inspired style. The result was humorous and memorable, and recalling it now brings to mind how even the sanest among us was occasionally game for wackiness in those days. I overdid it a bit with the volume on my impersonation of Sal, peaking the meters and bringing Jim Allewelt running. It didn't occur to me that AM jocks might have to maintain a good foot between themselves and the microphone (well out of breathing distance).

DON FRANK

Few of the friendships I made during my freshman year would last much beyond my freshman year. People would either move out of the area or gradually drift away from contact, becoming lost in the vastness of a 2000+student body. But that does not diminish the brightness of freshman stars such as Don Frank, who kept things interesting until Emmette arrived with the cavalry my sophomore year.

I met Don Frank in my room 112 economics class, and from early in our relationship (and for reasons that were never made clear to me), Don nicknamed me "Zigfreid." He would often address me in an abbreviated form such as "Ziggy" or "Zig," but the basic nickname stuck. I recall him saying something to the effect of "You look like a Zigfreid," whatever that meant.

Don and I were drawn together by our love of music, and I suppose one could consider Don my Oakton replacement for Brian Helms as an in-school contact for discussion on the attributes and deficiencies of various groups and albums. Don and I probably had a good 4 or 5 knockdown drag-outs about the merits or lack thereof of this or that album before it was apparent that the two of us had become friends.

Through Don Frank, I would meet Steve Larsen and Fausto Bengochea. With the mind expansionist Steve Larsen's appraisal of rock albums guided by how much sitar music was included, Fausto extolling the hippie hedonism of Jimi Hendrix, and Don's constant pressure to get me to admit the greatness of Pink Floyd's "Umma Gumma," it was clear that I had found myself in the middle of some psychedelia appreciation society. The Grand Funk, Led Zeppelin, Alice Cooper hard rock coalition that had held my 8th grade group of friends together so well was dissolving, and in its place was the reality that I was going to be musically challenged, whether I wanted to be or not.

This was a period of great musical discovery for me, and Don deserves some credit for this. It's fitting perhaps, that when I got my reel to reel recorder in August of 1972 and began writing and recording my own songs, my first composition would be called "Don Frank's Song." Oh! Don and I did not agree nearly as much as Helms and I, but that just made sweeter the victory of turning Don on to something he hadn't heard before, and visa versa. I remember Don bringing over the latest Pink Floyd album, which at the time was "Meddle." I also remember the "What am I going to do with you?" grin on his face as it was becoming clear that the music was not moving me. It was such a seemingly small and immediately indiscernible gesture, but think about it. Most people my age probably couldn't remember the first time they heard Pink Floyd. Despite my lukewarm reaction to Meddle, Don's continuous raving about Umma Gumma got the better of me. No matter who was doing the talking, when they described a particular album as "The best thing I've ever heard," it was time to take them seriously. I bought Umma Gumma in early 1972, and I must tell you that much of it was way over my head. Gradually over the next 17 years, more and more of the album would reveal itself to me, until one day in the spring of 1989, when I listened to it and realized it WAS the masterpiece that Don claimed it was.

Don was trying to blow me away with Umma Gumma. He failed (at least at that time), and now it was my turn to bring out MY secret weapon - Alice Cooper's "Easy Action" (which as it so happened, was as psychedelic as anything Don or Fausto had thrown my way). March 22 1972, 10 days after seeing Alice Cooper at the Alexandria roller rink with Good, Helms and Stills, I set out on foot for the Bedford Village townhouse complex next to Fairfax hospital, determined to turn Don on to Easy Action. A journal entry, written the day after, chronicles every hardship and wrong turn taken during this ill-fated trip.

I left my house at approximately 2:48, carrying a large paper grocery bag, containing 4 cassette tapes, 2 LPs, 6 45's and a small tape player. I cut across the woods towards route 50, but when I broke out of the woods, I found Lee Highway instead, and realized I had gone in a circle. Walking was a bit uncomfortable, because I had twisted my ankle slightly on the acclivity of our driveway, which should have been an omen of what a bad idea this was, but I trudged on with youthful determination.

My watch stopped at 3:10, which reads in my journal like something I panicked over. That and the line "My lung hurt from running" indicated that Don was meeting me at a particular time, and to lose track of time and miss him would mean that I was stranded there. As I was passing the elks club on route 50, it started to rain. When I reached Bedford Village, Don didn't show up, so I went looking at mailboxes for the name "Frank." After searching fruitlessly for Don's townhouse, the bottom of my bag started to give away. I then got the idea to look for Woodburn Road in order to find Steve Larsen's house, as I knew that Steve and Don shared the same bus stop. What I didn't know was that Woodburn Road was not in the Bedford village complex at all.

Desperate and tired, I began heading down Gallows Road in the direction of Jeff Aman's house. Not knowing the exact house, my one lucky break of the day was hitting it on the first try. His mother answered the door and told me he was at the 7-eleven across the street. He was not there. Disheartened and at my wits end, I headed back towards Bedford Village. Somewhere along the way, the drizzling rain became a torrential downpour and I was forced to seek refuge in one of the village's laundry rooms. After slipping and falling on the wet floor of the laundry room, I became so vexed that I ran down Anderson road screaming "Don Frank! Where are you?"

At this point, it was getting dark and my fear that my mom might be thinking of calling the police was growing. I was supposed to call my mom as soon as I got to Don's to let her know I'd made it safely and to give her directions there so she could pick me up later. It was now at least 6:30, and with no money to use the pay phone at the 7-eleven, and blisters on my blisters, the only end I could see to this ill-planned expedition was to start knocking on doors and ask people if I could use their phone to call home. I knocked on 9 doors (Yes! 9! Casting a doubtful shadow on the idea that people were more trusting back then) before some kind soul let this drowned rat of a kid into their home to call his mom. It was 7:40 PM. Thankfully, my mother (who simply surmised that I had arrived at Don's and had forgotten to call her) was not too concerned. But you can bet that I had learned an important lesson about traveling long distances on foot to meet someone.

Limping into school the next day, an amused but slightly guilt stricken Don Frank offered to come over to my house the following Saturday (March 25). He came over with a bag of records and we listened to the Yes album "Fragile" while I creamed him at table hockey. It's worth noting here that while it would take me another 15 years to really get into those classic early Yes albums (Despite Elmo's attempts to convert me), as I will explain later, Don Frank would have a major role in introducing me to progressive rock. I played Alice Cooper's 1968 debut album "Pretties for You," and like a bee to honey, the psychedelic enthusiast began to overcome his skepticism. Don was forced to at least admit that it was better than the "Killer" album (which had apparently left an impression on Don that Alice Cooper was not to be taken seriously). However, my second attempt at utilizing my secret weapon also hit a snag, as the batteries in my cassette player were low, and the copy of my prized Easy Action was a holdover from my 1971 fascination with pre-recorded cassettes. So Don and I walked up to the Dart Drug at Fairfax circle to get batteries. There I bought batteries and a copy of Frank Zappa's "Chunga's Revenge" (I was going through a Zappa phase at the time).

We were back at my house in time for Don to be fairly impressed with Easy Action before his ride came to pick him up at 3:10, giving the game to me. A month or two later however, the match would go to Don. Getting detailed directions, I made my first successful journey to Don's townhouse for what would be one of the revelations of a lifetime. Don played me an album he had just acquired - Van Der Graaf Generator's "Pawn Hearts." About 30 seconds into the opening track, I was mesmerized by the room-filling aura of the music. This was my first exposure to Peter Hammill (who would become my favorite artist throughout the remainder of the 70's), and in a very real sense, it was the checkered flag for me to delve further into progressive rock. The main reason I took the plunge on Genesis with "Selling England by the Pound" was that they were on the same label as Van Der Graaf Generator, the famous Charisma label. As Tonny and EAT would both become fans of Peter Hammill through me, they too owe Don Frank a debt of thanks.

Having no classes with Don my sophomore year, our relationship gradually died down to the occasional phone call and messages passed back and forth through Fausto Bengochea, who I would continue to have a class with until his graduation in 1974. By my junior year, I would hear about

Don from talking with Fausto more than I would have actual contact with him (it WAS a pretty big school).

His name will likely come up more than once in this book (if it hasn't already) in the context of being a failed conversion attempt. I felt compelled to keep the pressure on with Don until he realized his potential for lunacy. Fausto told me once that he saw Don drink an entire bottle of whiskey in one long chug and end up instantaneously drunk off his ass. You'd think such a person would have no trouble adapting to insane behavior, but Don was in many ways a quiet reserved individual, whose appreciation of all things strange was not reflected in his manner or appearance. But appreciate them he did. Umma Gumma and our friendship was all the proof anybody needed of that.

DONNA ZARIN

Elmo's little sister in both age and physical stature. During my sophomore and junior year visits to Elmo's house, I detected a rivalry consistent with siblings of the opposite sex. At times, Elmo exhibited an aversion to his sister, often accompanied by that form of embarrassment peculiar to male adolescents. The two of them argued, of course, but nothing seemed out of the ordinary, and truth be told, not all of the contention was provoked by Elmo.

I liked Donna though, and found it distracting when Elmo would shoo her away as she was relating something interesting to me (which on later visits included any casual mention of Tanya Herrell). About three months into my senior year, I began to suspect that the delicate balance of familial disharmony in the Zarin household was being tampered with. As Elmo was increasingly distancing himself from EAT and I under the guise of maturity, so followed a gradient decline in the relationship between Elmo and his sister. Toward the middle of that school year, my phone calls to Elmo grew increasingly brief, as a pattern was starting to develop. If Donna answered the phone, she and I might end up talking for as long as two hours before she would hand the receiver over to her brother (who was always a man of few words on the phone) for a five minute conversation filled with gaps of silence, if I was lucky.

Donna needed a sympathetic ear to air her concern over the fact that Elmo was treating her with less and less respect, a state of affairs which belied the maturity he was attempting to affect. Now I knew Elmo was a good and decent guy, but as Donna made perfectly clear, we were not looking at Elmo. We were looking at Elmo under the evil influence of his girlfriend, Brenda Paris, a paranoid sociopath who was actively working to alienate Elmo from all who were close to him. That this included his own sister infuriated me. Donna disliked and distrusted Brenda as much as

EAT did, and with good reason judging by the length of some of our conversations. Elmo, as one might imagine, did not like me talking to his sister. I'm sure he felt that I was slowly beginning to take her side in the Brenda issue, and I'm sure he did not trust Donna to speak well of him or Brenda in his absence. You can imagine (and I can still hear) Elmo's grunts of disdain as I began to call his house and ask specifically to speak to Donna. By the end of my senior year, the change in Elmo made it impossible NOT to take Donna's side in the matter. It was no longer just the idea that Elmo was not fun to hang with anymore.

Despite having avoided any involvement beyond being a shoulder for Donna to cry on, I could not resist expressing where I stood on the matter in my senior will. To Donna Zudinski Romanoff, I left "The title of Grand Duchess in the Viper Queen's court, and the decision of whether or not to exile the usurper Elmo for insurrections against her ladyship." I further emphasized my position by leaving Elmo "The honor of Knighthood, should the Lady Donna deem him worthy."

Now my friendship with Elmo died a very quiet death, and it is to his credit that we never came to words over this. I still liked Elmo, and whenever our paths crossed after high school, he always had a smile for me. I never inquired about Donna, but it was always my hope that Elmo's relationship with his sister had mellowed with age.

DORIS DICK

Another recipient for the medal of kindness beyond the call. I must admit to having formed my opinion of Doris based on the company she kept. Until she sat next to me in class, I knew only that I had on earlier occasions observed her consorting with ruffians. But in the short time I was graced by her company, I was touched by a naturalness and a gentleness that had I known how rare these qualities would become later on, I would have asked her for her hand then and there. The distance between the long-held impression and the soul of the actual person was greater in Doris than in any other person I had encountered at Oakton, and by this time, I had encountered quite a few.

Doris, like Carol Galane, did not interact with me under the cloud of anything she had overheard or been told about me. When she looked at me, I felt that she was watching the light of goodness glowing within me, and when she spoke to me, it was this light she was addressing. Even her voice had a hush-a-bye mistiness that seemed to be beckoning me to slow down and calm down, a call that wild youth often refuses to hear. As I look at her yearbook pictures now, all I see is that same angelic expression of acceptance beaming up at me from the page, as if she was yet exuding and extending some measure of inner peace across the years and miles. I'm filled with the most peculiar desire to find Doris Dick and make sure she is healthy and happy, to thank her for her kindness to a near total stranger, and to convince myself that the milk of human kindness hasn't soured with age.

DRUGS

This entry is given primarily to dispel a few reigning stereotypes about the early 70's, for drugs were not so much a part of my life, as much as many people I've met in the ensuing years feel they must have been. I would love to proudly proclaim here that I had the strength of character to resist all this temptation and peer pressure that the TV and radio adds were warning parents about, but the truth of the matter was that I experienced absolutely no temptation or peer pressure whatsoever, and had not the slightest inclination to experiment on my own.

It wasn't until my 8th grade year that I even became more than vaguely aware of the fact that things like Marijuana and LSD existed, or even that one's perception could become seriously altered through the consumption of large quantities of alcohol. It was during this time that I was getting closer to knowing people who were not only partaking of these substances, but were telling stories about their side effects in such a way that I was given the impression that alcohol and drugs were things that had to be survived rather than enjoyed. Bottom line – It didn't strike me from afar as being a lot of fun. You mean if I drink that entire bottle of Boone's Farm, I too can get violently ill, throw up my entire stomach contents, and have a raging headache in the morning. Hand it over here immediately!

It was in my 8th grade shop class that I saw a guy holding what I was informed was a nickle-bag, in other words – 5 dollars worth of pot in a plastic bag. I remember thinking – "So that's what that stuff looks like." It was not long after this that I began to measure money in 5 dollar increments. From a point somewhere during my freshman or sophomore year throughout the remainder of the 70's, 5 dollars would equal 1 album. 10 dollars would equal 2 albums, and so on. Or put in context here – 1 album = a bag of what most resembled someone's lawn clippings. In viewing this period as the point in my life when my love of music was really blossoming, the equation would have looked something like this – 1 nickel-bag minus 1 album = 0 temptation. Stack my aversion to my Mother's smoking habit on top of these economic considerations and stories about the negative side effects of over-indulgence and the overview of my Oakton experience shows an increasing aversion to the idea of imbibing in drugs, with the benefits side of the ledger remaining at a flat zero.

The beauty of high school was that I did not have to go to parties to make friends or to meet girls. All I had to do was just go to school and there they'd be. After high school, that all changed. Toward the end of the 70's and increasingly into the 80's, I attended parties in an attempt to either find my soul mate and/or meet the type of interesting people that would fill the social void left after my graduation from Oakton. While I was lucky enough or enjoyed myself often enough to not become totally disillusioned with the promise of the party, what I was more apt to find was people in such a state of intoxication that my attitude towards drugs would gradually move from neutral abstention to wanton disdain.

Though I could see the beneficial effects that moderate amounts of alcohol and pot could have in helping certain older people relax from a hard day's work, moderation was not a practice that people closer to my age group were as proficient at. Also! My partying years coincided with the period where cocaine had become the hip drug among suburban 20-somethings, and this was one drug that certainly did not encourage moderation.

The paradox of drug use was that what young people did in the late 60's to distance themselves from the social mainstream they were now doing in order to fit in with an accepted social norm, and it was just the thought that I too might be conforming in such a way were I to take a hit or snort of something that added a determination to resist drugs onto any ambivalence I may have previously had. I was particularly confounded by the air of elitism that surrounded cocaine use. It was a never ending source of bewilderment to me that such an air of elitism could have grown up around the use of a drug that reduced its adherents to such sniveling servitude. During those periods where I was in-between girlfriends, parties were my principal avenue of meeting girls. Imagine my frustration when I would find myself conversing with an interesting young lady, only to have her lured away from me to a vacuum sealed back room by some seedy low-life carrying a bag of nose candy. After this had happened to me on 3 or 4 different occasions, I was left with the sense that any effort I might expend mastering the art of conversation would be wasted on this generation of females. I had also gathered that cocaine was something that people preferred doing in privacy, perhaps out of elitism, but mostly out of paranoia. I so enjoyed arriving at a party teeming with people, only to watch the bulk of them disappear quickly into cloistered sniffing parlors. My view of adult life from the perspective of the party was that the service to the social animal that was high school's saving grace was not being served.

Equally annoying was how drugs, particularly cocaine, could fake you out. While the stupefying effects of alcohol and pot made those assembled for the purpose of socializing that much less interesting to socialize with, I would occasionally be drawn into conversation by the light of someone who was going against the prevailing mood by exhibiting an abundance of insanist-style enthusiasm. Thinking I had discovered a kindred soul, I would engage the person until their conversation had accelerated to such a stream-of-consciousness pitch that I would find myself in the unpleasant role of attempting to worm my way out of a conversation with someone who was obviously "on something" before that person's ramblings began to enter the creepy realm of paranoid delusions.

It's true that I did meet many interesting and beautiful people, and that I proceeded to have another book's worth of adventures. It is also true that during this period, I discovered the true meaning of loneliness. It was not simply being alone. I was an old pro at amusing myself. It was the measure of the distance between myself and others, and the level to which I was experiencing that distance. It was arriving at a party and watching people I knew slowly turn into people I didn't know and saw no point in attempting to communicate with. At this point in my life, even showing up at a party where I knew most of the people present was no guarantee that my thirst for socializing would even come close to being quenched. A strange post high school gradient decline in spirit-sustaining insanist style camaraderie coincided with a gradient increase in the amount of phone numbers in my little black book. By the end of the 70's, I had 10 times as many friends, none of which was as close to me as EAT was 10 minutes into our first conversation, and all I kept hearing during this period was how useful drugs were in aiding the process of socializing. In my experience, drugs thwarted the pursuit of socializing in every way imaginable (and in some ways I wouldn't have imagined). What was the point of having a deep philosophical discussion or plotting some grand design with someone, I thought, if that person would have no memory of it the following day?

I've retained enough of my individuality that people are quick to comment on the fact that I "must have done a lot of drugs in high school." Never mind that the drug culture that I experienced preached its own brand of conformity, or that the effect I witnessed most in excessive drug use was an erosion of the person's individuality, let this entry stand as my answer to certain stereotypes concerning drugs and the early 70's. It will unfortunately also serve as a lead-in to the following entry.

DWIGHT PICKETT

I was saddened to find out recently that Dwight was murdered in a drug deal gone wrong a few years after graduation. Dwight was one of the friendly freaks of Oakton, possessed of the same marijuana-mellowed temperament as the Hockmuths. Dwight was apparently also given to partaking of hallucinogens, as one humorous incident demonstrated. I was walking down the main hall, which runs the length of the school. I was coming from the direction of the cafeteria, and the mad rush of scurrying in-between class students was on. At one point, Dwight passed me in the oncoming surge. Upon seeing his approach, I said "Hey Dwight!" His reaction, which I caught in the flash of passing, was one of mild surprise followed by a nervous snicker and a slight shake of the head. This odd response to a casual greeting was explained the following morning in Mrs. Leech's English class (the same class, by the way, which contained Carrie "Smile Bob" Hines). Dwight, who sat behind me in the class, said "Hey Bob, you know when you said Hi to me in the hall, your voice was really booming, like the voice of God." I immediately took this as a sign that I might be assuming some sort of ministerial role in Dwight's life, and henceforth chose my words to be of a more uplifting nature while in his company. It's telling how normal this sort of thing appeared to me at the time, and it must be understood that drugs were so far removed from my day to day routine as to be the last thing I would suspect as the cause of unusual behavior. Of my friends at the time, only the Hockmuths (by far the most normal of the lot) were weekend pot smokers. And of the core circle of loons, none to my knowledge had even been on the staggering side of tipsy, and theirs was the source of some truly unusual behavior.

Dwight Pickett, despite his stoner appearance, was a fairly focused intelligent young man, with an accompanying finite delivery of speech that made even casual conversation with him memorable. As I now look back on the hallway "Voice of God" incident, and review Dwight's genuine surprise and apparent lucidity at the time of the incident, I believe that Dwight was not high at the time, but was experiencing some sort of flashback from some previously ingested chemical substance. That this flashback happened at the exact moment that I (of all people) passed Dwight in the hall probably ended up confounding me more so than him.

Dwight and I talked about music on occasion, and it was from Dwight's lips that I first heard the name "Lynyrd Skynyrd." I remember him explaining to me that every song on their second album was good, and while the bulk of their first album was sub-standard, it did contain this one song called "Free Bird" that Dwight went on animatedly describing the greatness of. While I would never become a fan of this group, or own any of their records, the ubiquitous Free Bird would on odd occasions send my mind racing back to the impression it left on the face of Dwight Pickett - himself now a "Free Bird" as well. He was a real nice guy, and I'm sad he's gone.

EAT (EZRIN AMPHITRON TALUS)

Though EAT would arrive and depart like so many transient friends throughout my life, the fact that he was my closest friend throughout my pivotal senior year at Oakton makes us something akin to Vietnam war buddies. It's that shared experience that will forever bind us. But unlike the nightmare and syndrome inducing memories of a wartime experience, our last year at Oakton would provide us simultaneously with the enigmas of life and the psychic signposts that would eventually lead us towards the unraveling of those enigmas. Aside from that, the fun and excitement of this time period has never been matched by all the promising parties, concerts, and beautiful girlfriends I've gone through since then.

EAT appeared on the scene as a freshman in the fall of 1973. Strangely, as with Emmette, my first impression of EAT was not a good one. EAT would issue these low-key taunts in an apparent attempt to get some sort of reaction out of me. This was rather brazen behavior I thought, for a freshman, particularly one as small in stature as EAT was. As EAT was also a close friend of Elmo (my closest friend at Oakton at the time), his behavior was more baffling than it was intimidating. Two incidents, in particular, drew me to ponder the motivations of this strange newcomer. I was walking down the main hallway, heading in the direction of the cafeteria. I was wearing my Peters jacket at the time (a freshman and sophomore year fashion stalwart that I was only months away from physically outgrowing). Sometime after the life changing experience of seeing the movie "Willard," I had affixed this patch of a rather happy looking rat on the back of my jacket. The unusual thing about this patch was that it was heavily strawberry scented, and like those original copies of the first Raspberries album you'll occasionally come across in a used record store, bringing my nose close enough to the patch alerts me to the fact that traces of the scent have survived to this very day. At some point, I became aware that EAT was walking behind me because he began making snide little jabs at the "Mouse" on the back of my jacket. What struck me about these little barbs he was throwing at me was that the lack of volume in his voice seemed to indicate that he wished to attract my attention, but no one else's.

I did not turn to confront him or acknowledge him in any way, because like the more easily explainable provocative remarks thrown at me by various jocks and ruffians, there was no force of delivery that demanded my attention. I wasn't fat, didn't have acne, was not particularly self-conscious about my appearance, and while remaining an outsider, engendered only the most generic taunts that were always devoid of anything I could take personally, as if the person was addressing me, but was really speaking to someone else. That this might have been the case with EAT was evident in a further incident that occurred when I rode Elmo's bus to hang out with him at his house after school. The bus had

stopped on Gallows Road, and EAT, Elmo, I and the 3 or 4 other Oakton students that lived in this tiny subdivision filed out. As Elmo and I were walking together towards his house, which was about three houses down on the right, I became aware that once again, EAT was walking behind me and issuing me these low volume taunts. I was a little more conscious of him at this time because Elmo was walking with me, but aside from the fact that EAT was kicking pebbles up at my feet periodically, if his intention was anything beyond attracting my attention, he was going about it rather half-heartedly.

On the phone with Elmo a few days later, I would receive a clue to the mildly antagonistic behavior of this impish upstart. I happened to mention EAT in passing (who was then referred to by his sane name - Doug Lay, if I had known his name at all by this point). Elmo's reaction was to rather quietly say "That guy's a hey." Aside from being a rather non-committal put-down phrased in the loon vernacular of the time, I detected in Elmo's voice the solemn dejection that appeared to be accompanying some recent falling out, as if to even bring up the subject of EAT was to remind Elmo that he had just lost a friend. I had already sensed some sort of tension between the two, and was now beginning to wonder if EAT had either blamed me in part for this falling out or had become so disgusted with Elmo that he had come to view any friend of Elmo's as no friend of his.

Only days later, however, it appeared as though Elmo and EAT were on speaking terms again, as quite unexpectedly, EAT, who sat two rows over from me in my second period Russian class, suddenly blurted out "Bob! Bob!" as if hurriedly trying to attract my attention. Half expecting EAT to hurl some sort of challenge at me, I turned to be instead greeted by the icebreaking line – "I heard you liked David Bowie" (which was information he could have only obtained by speaking with Elmo). "Yes" I replied, to which EAT enthusiastically inquired "What do you think of his latest album?" (Which at the time would have been Aladdin Sane). As I was in the process of answering EAT's query, he moved to take a seat next to me, and our friendship began with our first, but by no means last discussion of our mutual inspiration - David Bowie.

The apparent unlikelihood of any friendship blossoming over a mutual appreciation for David Bowie must be viewed in the context of the time. Fans (or admitted fans) of David Bowie among suburban high school kids in 1973 were scarce enough to make it a pleasant surprise when one encountered another. Guys were quick to distance themselves from the transsexual elements in his make-up and costuming, and females were generally creeped out by the graphic imagery in his songs, as well as his cadaverous persona. It's stating the obvious to say that no such an enigmatic figure exists in rock music today. I can remember turning around in my senior year English class and treating Cindy Delancey to a rather dramatic recitation of Bowie's "Future Legend" - complete with Bowie's English accent. Cindy's quizzical look turned to a shudder of

horror when I explained that I had just given her a reading from David Bowie's latest album. "OOOOOOH! He's so weird" she exclaimed with a shiver of morbidity. This is the type of reaction I cannot even imagine a Trent Rezner or a Marilyn Manson instilling in an 8 year old today. Yet not only did this type of thing qualify Bowie's mystique in our minds, it was also the sort of reaction that EAT and I had come to identify with by simply being at Oakton High.

At any rate, it was no more than a week after EAT's unforeseen decision to join the circle of loons (which I would date as sometime in October of 1973), that Doug Lay had christened himself "Ezrin Amphitron Talus" (or EAT for short). The impertinence that was only days earlier buzzing around the back of my head like a bothersome bee had

101

suddenly become one of the most endearing and influential elements in the inner circle's life force. EAT's acclimation into the flow was swift enough that he had a role in every major folly undertaken during my junior year. His youthful exuberance was a needed shot in the arm at a time when a number of things were signaling the decline of the Insanist movement.

1. Boniface Ignacious was no longer with us in body or in spirit.
2. Emmette was slowly drifting away from us throughout the course of the year.
3. Tonny had moved to Punxsutawney PA, making him less of the spiritual catalyst he had been in the early days of the movement.
4. Elmo and I had both suffered heartbreaking rejections in early December of 1973, and were experiencing the warning pains symptomatic of the onset of adulthood.

The willingness of this cocky freshman to evoke and/or provoke for the sheer madness of the moment kept the clock on my childhood ticking for one more year. Addressing our overstarched Russian teacher Mrs. Bryan in class as "Toots" is but a small example of what I'm talking about here. The Emmette-Tonny pool of inspiration that fed my desire to perpetuate the group through my freshman and sophomore years had become the Elmo-EAT pool, with bi-monthly letters from Tonny exhorting all loons onward to greatness. This was not so much a shift in identity or personality as it was merely a raising of the importance of music within the group. Despite the plethora of music that Tonny and I recorded, Emmette was too grounded in his obsession with Richard Wagner to join in the fun. Like so many lovers of classical music I have known since, Emmette may have held that only those trained in classical forms should attempt to create music. On the other hand, both Elmo and EAT were enthusiastic followers of music, and took naturally to the spontaneous creation of it.

If EAT's acceptance into our high order hadn't yet been finalized, the announcement from Elmo that EAT had written and recorded his first song made his membership official. I remember the pride with which Elmo first relayed this information to me, as if preparing to unveil the first composition of his musical protégé. And one could describe EAT as having been exactly that, for it was through Elmo that EAT was exposed to the early DBH recordings, and so, the idea of recording itself. I also remember how impressed I was with the "Already there" quality of EAT's first offering – "My Baby Left Me." It would fill a room with a sound reminiscent of an infant's first attempt to form words, yet contrastingly, the shifts in mood and tempo alone were enough to convince me that EAT was ready to join Elmo and I for future Death by Hanging recordings.

For a short period (circa February-April 1974), Death by Hanging became a trio, and mostly thereafter, the duo of EAT and I. This brief trio period was highlighted by the eponymous My Baby Knifed Me sessions. Recorded in Elmo's basement (and prone to the intrusions of a demonstrably bemused Donna Zarin), these recordings still bore Elmo's stylistic stamp, with all their references to blades and weapons, Paying and biting, not to mention the loosely effusive Bonneville Follies-like atmosphere of the songs themselves. However, it did give EAT a chance to premiere his second composition, "Hunks," wherein EAT makes his now famous proclamation -

You're a Hunk and I'm a Hunk
And Susan Clark is the biggest Hunk of all

The historical significance of this song actually eclipses that of My Baby Left Me, for it is one of the earliest examples of the name of Susan Clark rearing its ugly head, (aside from an earlier letter to Tonny where I mention Hunk as EAT's bid to bring a female into the ranks of the loons). EAT had mentioned Susan on a number of occasions, and I gathered that he had hopes of someday moving beyond the stage of casual acquaintance with her. EAT knew of my feelings for CA, of course, as he had arrived on the scene in time to watch me go down in flames over that direct hit. What hadn't been discussed was any connection between Hunk and CA, as indeed, none may have existed at this time. Hunk was already heavily involved with the choral department, but as a four-eyed freshman, her self-confidence may not have been up to the level of wearing a cheerleader's uniform, and so she would not have had occasion to cross paths with CA. Hunk had entered the music world of Oakton (which was at least closer in spirit to our world), but she would not enter the world of Oakton sports until the following year, at which time EAT would develop a greater understanding of the hopelessness of my situation with Cheri. For the time being though, and for all the good it did EAT, Hunk might as well have joined the revelations club. There was still the gulf of us and them between the manifestations of Hunk's love of music (if indeed she had one) and the manifestations of our love of music. We were Death by Hanging. They were the choral department. If any songs were going to be written, they would be written BY us ABOUT them. Shunning school participation for the freedom of self expression was both our joy and our curse, but what really separated us from them was when it did become a curse, that's very often when the joy of inspiration would flow.

And then there was this David Bowie thing. I remember phoning EAT from Howard's apartment at Circle Towers to relay the exciting news that I'd just seen an advertisement for the new Bowie album – "Pin-ups." Despite being nothing more destructive to the fiber of American society than a cover album of some of David's favorite British invasion tunes, Elmo (and others I either knew or overheard) stood firmly on principle, as if defending themselves against this encroaching threat to their sexuality. But let's get one thing straight! Despite the impression that EAT and I had been given by our Oakton surroundings that David Bowie was some kind of underground fringe artist, the world at large had already accepted Mr. Bowie. If EAT and I had been pleasantly surprised to find Bowie on Don Kirshner's rock concert singing "I Got You Babe" with Marianne Faithful in November of 1973, we could have (and did) pass it off as a lucky find. I mean! Carmen and the Troggs performed on the same show that night, and who were they?

EAT and I were similarly surprised in the fall of 74 by American popular music's ultimate stamp of approval - Barbara Streisand had covered Bowie's "Life on Mars" on her latest album "Butterfly." This was no less of a surprise to us because despite a pair of hit singles from 1974's "Diamond Dogs" album, the heat that we were taking for playing David Bowie on our radio shows during the 74/75 school year was indicative of his increasingly controversial place in Oakton society. It was not so much the music of David Bowie that Kaiser objected to (for God knows, EAT and I both regularly played music that was far less listener friendly than anything Bowie had ever recorded), it was the idea (or ideas) of David Bowie that Kaiser had to protect the student body from. True, Diamond Dogs was a significant step forward in Bowie's rise to pop stardom, but as for the acceptance of mainstream America, Bowie would have to wait for the FM radio explosion of the late 70's and the release of the "Changes" greatest hits album. Diamond Dogs was, if anything, a step backward in that department. You see, the post-apocalyptic Orwellian imagery of Diamond Dogs hit just a little too close to home for some people. Growing up in those times, I can say that the inevitability of world war 3 was at the back of a lot of people's minds as the only possible end result of our cold war with Russia. A lot of people were also wondering if maybe George Orwell really was some kind of 20th century prophet. Big Brother, 666, Armageddon, all these things were taken a lot more seriously in the mid 70's, and though EAT and I joked about these things with macabre relish, it was obvious from others that I spoke with that most believed it likely that the world as we knew it would end before the millennium would. This could of course be the overstatement of their own disgust at the direction they saw mankind was heading in, but nonetheless, despite the relative innocence of the time, and the productive citizens these students were preparing themselves to be, the future (oh, say, from 1984 onward) was a sore spot.

I remember seeing an interview of Angela Bowie on TV sometime in the early 80's. She said that David was living in LA during the Diamond Dogs period, and was doing so much cocaine that he began to insist that he was being watched by Satanists. He was absolutely convinced, she related with a tone of maternal sympathy for her former husband, that Satanic forces were working to control him. I could only think of the field day the Oakton rumor merchants (who were spreading stories about EAT and I being Satanists) would have had with this had this been common knowledge in 1974. The bottom line here was that in 1974, even pop stars like David Bowie took this shit seriously.

On a lighter note, in February of 1974, EAT, Elmo and myself went to see Black Oak Arkansas at the Kennedy center opera house. I'll never forget clowning around with EAT and Elmo in an opera house lobby filled with long uncombed hair and buckskins. Later in 1974, we almost caught Lou Reed and the New York Dolls at the opera house, but it snowed the day of the concert and we couldn't get a ride from any of our parents.

Then there was the time EAT and I had the bright idea to invent our own language. We spent an afternoon in EAT's living room making up words, only one of which I remember – "Fonsvefgeshe," the meaning of which is now long forgotten.

And then there was that pygmy familiar of EAT's invention - Arvin Moobunga. I could describe Arvin as EAT's alter ego, but I believe he was more of an extension of the wild free spirited little pygmy that lived in EAT. I would hear Arvin's voice in the joyous chimpanzee-like hootings EAT would make in moments of heightened frivolity. Arvin's mythical homeland – "The South African Peoples Republic" was evoked by EAT and I in a send up of Bowie's "Panic in Detroit" entitled (what else?) "Panic in the South African Peoples Republic." The sound of EAT's voice blurting out "Bunga! Bunga!" around the area of my junior year locker (which for my alumni readers was next to the door of the planetarium) will no doubt startle and frighten the Oakton janitorial staff for ages to come.

EAT and I were at our silliest during Mrs. Bryan's second period Russian class. Aside from the fact that EAT and I sat next to each other, there was something about the atmosphere in that class that really brought out the mad jester in both of us. As I recall, the rectitude of our teacher, Mrs. Bryan, was matched only by the inconspicuous studiousness of the predominately female students in the class. In the midst of such straightlaced environs, EAT and I may have felt the subconscious urge to turn the juice up in an attempt to ensure that neither of us ever got close to dying of boredom.

I recall letting some silent but extremely odorous wind loose on the girls who sat behind me (one of which was Bonnie Tuggle, if my memory serves me). The class was silent in its collective effort to study and/or solve some kind of problem, when from two desks behind me, I heard the ever scowling Erin Cejka let out a gasp of disgust. I then remember looking next to me and finding EAT with his head down on his desk, buried in his arms as if taking a nap (which I can imagine might have been a welcome sight to Mrs. Bryan, knowing what a disruption the wide awake EAT was in class). I then peaked beneath EAT's left arm and saw what he was concealing from the rest of the class. He was silently laughing his ass off. He knew that I was responsible for cutting the cheese, but didn't want to arouse suspicion. Even funnier is the fact that this exact same incident happened again sequence for sequence on at least two other occasions, with poor Erin getting the worst of it.

Also among my fond memories of that Russian class were EAT's proud unveilings of the lyrics to some of his early songs, a few of which I still possess on the yellowing sheets of paper they were written on. One particularly topical number was entitled "The Art of Slaying Dragons." Printed below in its entirety, the genesis of EAT's genius is apparent even here.

Life - We live it in a court
We die without retort
Give a synthesized snort
I'll put you on report

Your brain – can't just let it sit there
Oh Cheri, put it somewhere
He's peeking at your underwear
Oh Cheri, your quite a snare
Dead heart – can't just let it sit there
Oh Cheri, put it somewhere
He has no time to spare
Oh Cheri, your quite a snare

Death - we died from over-snort
We live without retort
Try and sell us short
And you'll be put in court

Now in the words of this early EAT composition, we can see that all of the ideas in his writing were somehow tied to the polar opposites of life and death. The first DBH album proper with the duo of EAT and I was entitled "Living Minds, Dying Hearts," a title seemingly drawn (though unintentionally) from the lyrics to The Art of Slaying Dragons. Sometime in the spring of 1974, EAT wrote "Life/Death in the Circle," one of his most successful compositions, and one in which DBH later recorded. In fact, I liked the song so much, I recorded my own version of it that year. Every third line in the song became an oft-repeated cliché of the sort that Bowie and Steve Harley would engender, but EAT really states his case with the lines:

I'm dressed up in black and all shiny glitter
The humanoids about me are oh so bitter

EAT goes on to bemoan that he can't be what he wants to be - a rock and roll monster, though in the process of writing this song (as the lyrics go on to bear out), he had become exactly that. Aside from the furtherance of EAT's artistic credibility, this song also prompted the standing joke about the life and death thing EAT had going on in his lyrics. The joke lasted long into the 74/75 school year, as evidenced by the then rare attempt of mine to interject a little humor into one of my solo recordings. It was on "Death by Slow Girl (Including the Four Testimonials)," during the testimony of Morty Sneaky (EAT's on-air radio nickname) when the joke resurfaced. The testimony of Morty Sneaky (which on the actual recording was read by Mitchell Robinson) was intended to be EAT's poetic personal account of his own "Death by Slow Girl."

The Testimony of Morty Sneaky:
So long have we waited for death, allow us to explain. It was sometime in November, I believe. Pakistan had just covered my body in a fine veil of gloom, which was not only my resistance, but the epoch of my soul's long awaited freedom from the death that dies to live in the love of my life, and you can quote me on that.

As you can see, the temptation to end off on a rib of EAT's life/death lyrical propensities was more than I could resist. EAT's recollection that "It was sometime in November" was in reference to the November 2 1974 Hunk rejection, but the line - "Pakistan had just covered my body in a fine veil of gloom" recalls EAT and I's early 1974 discovery of the wonders of Georgetown, and in particular, a clothing store we frequented called EF Sly.

In Georgetown, EAT and I discovered pockets of glitter culture that our life at Oakton High had trained us not to expect to find in our area. Recent trips to Georgetown have depressed me, because I remember what a truly wondrous place it was in 1974. The record stores were well stocked with Cockney Rebel albums. Clothing stores like EF Sly specialized in the type of black clothing that won EAT and I the fear and loathing of our fellow students, and even the subs at Blimpie's sub shop tasted better.

In the mid 70's, I resented the references to Georgetown as being a place where strange people congregated, because EAT and I blended into the fabric of Georgetown to a degree we could never have dreamed of doing at Oakton. There really was this feeling that one could get away with wearing just about anything in Georgetown during this period. The punk fueled factionalization of DC's youth hadn't occurred yet, and the Love is Everywhere communal atmosphere of the late 60's/early 70's hadn't dissipated completely.

In EF Sly, EAT and I had finally found a store that sold clothing to fit the aesthetic we were aspiring to. The EF Sly logo that was printed on their black plastic bags (and on their black T-shirts, of which EAT and I both wore regularly) was a skull and crossbones with the verse – "Too fast to live, too young to die - EF Sly" printed underneath. But it was those Pakistani made black shirts that covered our bodies "In a fine veil of gloom." One of those shirts (which I still own and wear occasionally) was made by a company called "Billy Whiskers," whose product logo on the inside back of the shirt bore the likeness of an equally Satanic (but well dressed) goat-man. Hell! Maybe it wasn't us after all. Maybe it was our clothes that were putting out all those menacing vibes. I'll tell you this much, aside from the blood red lining of a beautiful black velvet vampire cape I saw on sale there once (which was a little out of my price range at $75.00 - a nice chunk of change in 1974), if it wasn't black or silver glitter, Sly didn't sell it. My clearest memory of EF Sly was our December 30th 1974 pilgrimage there. We had been there at least twice before earlier in the year and knew to expect something special, but there were two things that made this visit particularly memorable. One was the fact that on this particular visit, I purchased the infamous silver mylar shirt (which you will read more about later on in the Ray King entry), the second was the beauty and charm of the black girl who waited on us. I think EAT will vouch for the fact that this princess had skin as pure and as dark as the richest chocolate mousse, as well as the kind of sweet smile and curvaceous 20 year old body that could (and did) turn a couple of Northern Virginia white kids like ourselves into a standing mass of tapioca pudding.

To fully appreciate why EAT and I would be dreamily recalling this young lady for weeks afterward, one has to realize how rare black ladies were in Fairfax county in 1974, much less black ladies this beautiful. Despite my boyhood fascination with Nichele Nichols, Dianne Carroll, Diana Ross, et al., I had probably not seen 10 black females in the flesh even up to this point in my life. Being waited on by such a creature (who was quite impressed with my decision to actually own such an outrageous shirt) simply added to our already formed impression of Georgetown as being a beautiful exotic place.

A more humorous clue that we were no longer in the suburbs of Northern Virginia came as EAT and I were hanging out near the corner of Wisconsin and O Street (possibly waiting to be picked up by our chaperon, my mother). Near us were two very glitter looking young men, one of whom was speaking into the receiver of a pay phone that was on the corner. As he put down the receiver and the two men walked past us, we distinctly overheard the man say to his companion – "Well, it doesn't look like I'm going to find a husband today." I'll never forget the look of surprise on EAT's face. It's the clearest mental picture I have of this particular expression of his, making this an EAT memory as much as a Georgetown one.

September of 1974, and not more than a week into the school year came the news that Kaiser had landed the position as head coordinator for Oakton's radio station, WOHS, and that Elmo was lending his technical support as Kaiser's assistant. As to all concerned, things were just picking up where they left off at the end of the previous school year, EAT and I were assured of DJ slots for this, the second year of operation for the fledgling radio station. The room which housed the radio station (which was an ancillary room within a room adjacent to Mr. Williams electronics class) was to become the spiritual center of my friendship with EAT, as well as the center stage around which many of the scenes of our lives would revolve during those extraordinary 9 months.

That the shop/electronics wing of the school was separated from the school proper by a long hallway was no doubt by design a consideration of the possibility of an electrical fire or explosion. This prudent design measure also provided EAT and I with a sense of getting away from it all within the confines of the school itself, a place to relax while remaining close enough to selectively tend the little home fires we each had burning. Strangely enough, while the radio station served to keep the core loons of the previous school year together in one place, in practice, the radio station caused (or widened) the schism between the assumed responsibility of Elmo and Kaiser, and the perceived recalcitrance of EAT and myself. I use the word "perceived" because neither EAT nor I produced our radio shows with the slightest intention of creating a controversy. But it was during my second show (after playing the song "Watch That Man" from the Aladdin Sane album) that Kaiser came to me with the complaint that EAT and I were playing too much David Bowie. Kaiser then went into what was to become his ongoing thematic plea for a balanced format. While Kaiser never put his foot down far enough to actually forbid EAT and I from playing David Bowie or anything else, the pressure to conform to this nebulous balanced format of his remained constant.

Over the course of two 25-minute radio shows, I had played three Bowie songs. EAT had probably played 2 or 3 Bowie tracks as well. Over this, we suddenly found ourselves becoming rebels within our own group, a development that was not solicited nor was it anticipated. At the risk of beating a dead horse, I'd like to vent a little more indignance over the illogic that led EAT and I to ignore Kaiser's balanced format rants altogether. First off, my memory of walking in on Kaiser's show while he was playing "Ladies" from Jethro Tull's "War Child" album brings to mind my impression that Kaiser's own radio show was hardly the top 40 utopia he condoned in DJs like Doctor Sal, Jim Allewelt, and Wolfman Jeff. Elmo's favorite group was "Yes,", and I dare say he probably played all 18 minutes of "Close to the Edge" on his show a time or two. Now I could really split some hairs here and point out the fact that by this time, David Bowie had more American radio hits than either Yes or Jethro Tull, but like Kaiser, I'd be comparing apples and oranges.

I still contend that Kaiser's balanced format admonishments were more a personal reaction to his own perception of David Bowie than his feigned concern for musical diversity. Shit! The format of EAT and I's show (and to some degree, Elmo's as well) were the ONLY balancing factors in the overall content of that radio station. Everything else was at or close to being the same goddamn thing. That Kaiser chose to ignore this and go wig out over the possible repercussions of playing the thin white duke over the cafeteria speakers confounds me as much today as it did then.

About half way through the school year, Kaiser and I conducted our own individual polls, asking students what they would rather hear from us - radio hits or LP tracks. I took some care to get a good cross section of people, including jocks and regular Joe's like Michael Jackson and Dan Pernell. Out of the 24 people I asked, the tally was:

LP tracks - 21

Radio hits - 3

But while Kaiser admitted that his findings were almost identical to mine, he used them to support his original position by pointing out that some people qualified their responses by adding that they preferred to hear album tracks from groups they knew – "Like the Carpenters." The Carpenters????? When he handed me that, I gave up trying to appeal to his sense of reason, because it was obvious that any further discussion on the subject would bring us straight back around to apples and oranges. The point to keep in mind here is that by simply being the same people we were the previous school year, EAT and I found ourselves in the hot seat by September's end, a condition which set the tone for the entire year. Really! It's amazing how little EAT and I had actually changed in relation to how differently we were now being treated by those who not only knew, but appreciated us before. This drew EAT and I closer together, and at the time, was perceived by us as simply more of the fickle ever shifting alliances that so many years in the public school system had conditioned us to accept.

However, while Kaiser was quick to fall from loon brethren to the intrusive patronizing father figure I never had, Elmo's fall from grace was slower in coming. In fact, late in October of 1974, EAT came to me with the surprising news that Elmo was joining us for the November 11th David Bowie concert at the capitol center. This was surprising to me because despite the fact that Elmo's second in command reinforcement of Kaiser's anti-Bowie balanced format crusade was rather half-hearted, he was not shy about expressing his personal displeasure in all but a handful of Bowie's songs. While it's probable that the greater exposure to Bowie's music that Elmo was now receiving through the radio station had warmed him up a bit to the idea of attending the concert, this really was the last expression of Elmo's wonderfully adaptable spirit, asserting itself against the attention demands of a manipulative girlfriend. Elmo had very admirably wrangled another night out with the boys for one last hurrah, and while some of the camaraderie the three of us carried with us to the Black Oak Arkansas concert earlier in the year was gone, it was, as I said, an admirable effort on Elmo's part. Just how admirable can be gleaned from the fact that while Elmo did not join EAT and I in donning the full make-up and vampire cape glitter regalia, he did approximate the spirit of the event with a pair of glow in the dark orange pants (or shirt, I can't remember which). Elmo probably thought, as I'm sure EAT and I did as well, that we were making ourselves targets for ribbing and cat calls from the rest of the concert patrons. Imagine our surprise when surveying the crowd on the way to our seats, it became increasingly evident that the three of us were among the most understated fashion statements in the whole arena. Sequenced top hats, multi-colored wigs, a glowing gold tuxedo, you name it. It's unfortunate that this concert audience turned costume party was treated to such a mediocre performance. For one thing, I know EAT and I had paid 9 dollars to see the Diamond Dogs tour. We expected a show, with costume changes galore. Unfortunately, David was already into his disco-chic "Young Americans" phase, single-handedly signaling the death of the glitter era by wearing a gray pin-stripped suit for the entire evening. I remember screaming "Do Sweet Thing" until my voice was hoarse, but the two hits "Rebel Rebel" and "1984," along with the title track (sans the Future Legend intro) would be all he would give us from Diamond Dogs. Really! Outside of the 4 or 5 new tracks performed with his soul revue of Luther Vandross and company, Bowie was giving us the "Changes One" tour. I felt particularly slighted that he did not do anything from "The Man Who Sold the World," a fact that made me feel doubly bad for Elmo, because I know that a crunching rendition of "Width of a Circle" would have reconciled the evening for him somewhat. To make matters worse, the sound was close to being about the worst I've ever heard at a concert. I've been told the acoustics of the capitol center were to blame, but I saw Ted Nugent and Black Sabbath there in 1976, and the sound was fine.

The most telling thing about the concert was afterward, as the three of us were roaming the hallway of the capitol center in search of the exit where we came in. We happened upon this young man who was dressed from head to toe in the same shade of light pink. Not only his clothes, but his hair was dyed, and his face and hands were painted this same color as well. He was talking to a group of his friends, and I can recall EAT and I being absolutely transfixed by his monochromatic appearance. We had seen some oddities in Georgetown, but nothing like this. After conferring briefly with EAT and Elmo about the idea, I decided to walk up to him and ask him for his autograph, with the explanation that he was much more entertaining than the concert we had just attended (an understatement if there ever was one). He thanked me for the compliment and graciously signed the back of my ticket envelope. Jackie Darlington's autograph now resides in the book of artifacts, a truer memento of the spirit EAT and I brought with us to the concert than Bowie's own autograph would have been, for truly here was a person who was unafraid to assert his individuality. While Jackie was also no doubt expressing his own homosexuality, his employment of make-up and hair coloring to distinguish himself from the rest of society made him seem like a kindred spirit of EAT and I at this particular time. EAT reminded me recently that his father at first refused to drive us to the concert because the three of us were wearing make-up (yes, even Elmo had put a little white eyeliner on). It was only after his understanding mother put her foot down that his father agreed to undergo the indignity of driving the three of us in our glitter regalia.

Once EAT and I put on make-up just to walk up to Fairfax Circle. The two of us were hanging around my house, when our glitter emulation and our youthful aversion to boredom melded in a rather memorable walk to the circle. Nobody actually said anything to us, but I do remember getting a couple of befuddled looks, and a double take or two.

While much of EAT's involvement in the rush of events my senior year is chronicled elsewhere throughout this book, one event does bear mentioning as being another shovel full of dirt on the grave of our friendship with Elmo. Sometime in early 1975, EAT's family moved from their house on Sandburg Street in Dunn Loring to a house in McLean. While this thankfully did not prevent EAT from finishing out his sophomore year at Oakton, it did mean that he no longer lived just a minute's stroll from Elmo's house, an untimely communication breach any way you look at it. Elmo was hired to drive EAT home, but after a while, what small part of this job that wasn't a job to Elmo disappeared, and I'm sure that near the end of the school year, Elmo came to look at this task as time spent away from his precious Brenda (and perhaps not even worth whatever he was being paid).

After June of 1975, Elmo was out of sight and out of mind, while EAT and I's friendship continued on under more natural (and infinitely more relaxed) circumstances. Though Tonny had returned to Northern Virginia, and I had the greater freedom of being able to drive, and I began dating young ladies and making new friends along the way, my contentment was tinged with the feeling that I had left part of my life force behind at OHS. I was too young to be pining for the glory days I had left behind, but despite the beckon call of the future all around me, that's exactly what I was doing. I was not being challenged by the people or the circumstances in my life the way I had been during those incredible four years at Oakton. Despite the fact that there were things about high school I will never miss, and despite the fact that the harmony and balance loving Libran inside of me was happier, my life lacked the fun and excitement that I had grown accustomed to throughout my Oakton years. There was also the specter of unfinished business in the guise of Peggy Wallace's memory. Only the growing inner sense that I had kissed off my soul mate back in June of 75 could explain allowing my late 70's relationships with such beauteous ladies as Cindy Martens and Angela Sheble to rot on the vine the way I did.

Two interesting things happened in the summer of 75, however, that illustrate how my friendship with EAT went sailing right along on auto-pilot. One was the release of the first Patti Smith album "Horses." I have a very clear memory of EAT calling me up and excitedly exclaiming "Bob! I just got this new album by Patti Smith, you would not believe how great it is." When he called me "Bob" instead of "Bobney," I knew it was serious, but as this Patti Smith's album was produced by John Cale, and EAT was a devout follower of Cale's, I received EAT's rave review with tempered optimism. Several days later, though, upon entering the Vienna Penguin Feather record store, I was instantly struck by the stark picture of a woman staring down at me from the cover of an album on their new release bulk wall. Forgetting what I came in for, I walked immediately over to the album to discover that it was in fact, Patti Smith's Horses album. Now EAT had gone on and on about how beautiful this woman was, but it hadn't quite prepared me for the shock of discovery that broke like a wave on top of me as I stood there staring at the album cover in my hands. One has to consider how EAT and I's taste in beauty ran towards the exotic and weigh that against the fact that in 1975, women, at least female recording artists, did not look like Patti Smith. There was no way I was leaving the store without that album. I don't think I've ever been so blown away by an album on first listening, and the reason for that is what makes this story worth recounting. You see, I (and I firmly believe that this was true of EAT as well) was anxiously awaiting the arrival of a female recording artist that I could relate to on any level. Oh yes! There was Nico, but Nico was - well, something else altogether, and aside from how much EAT and I revered Nico's "The End" album, it was obvious that this masculine voice of hers was emanating from a cocoon of sexual and spiritual anonymity. You couldn't put her in a category with other female recording artists. And relate to her music? Forget it! If you had, she'd have been the first to tell you that you were fabricating something that wasn't there. No! Despite the fact that she got ordinary after a couple albums, EAT and I will remember Patti Smith for being the first female recording artist that we could look up to AS a female recording artist.

Before Patti, and all through our days at Oakton, EAT and I had to satisfy our thirst for some expressed form of female aesthetic through the various male recording artists such as David Bowie, Freddie Mercury, Steve Harley and Jobriath, who could gender bend creatively. What made Patti Smith stand out from the female artists that preceded her was the aggression in her music. It's the sort of thing that is so passe today that it would be difficult for many young alt rockers to imagine how sexy it made Patti Smith in 1975. It certainly got EAT and I's juices flowing, and despite the fact that Patti was dating Blue Oyster Cult's fair-haired keyboardist Alan Lanier at the time, she soon had major rock hunks like Mark Farner and Bruce Springsteen sniffing around her door. The sex symbol status that Linda Ronstadt had spent 10 albums and a number of revealing album covers cultivating, Patti Smith pulled off with one album, dressed rather androgynously, all because she gave the legion of Iggy, Bowie, Harley, Hammill fans like EAT and myself the emotional and physical sock to the gut we had come to look for in our music. Not to mention how reassuring any demonstration of female sexual aggressiveness must have been to EAT and I after our experiences with the Linda Ronstadts of Oakton High.

One of the most tangible remnants of this period is our recording of the EAT composition "Be My Lenny Kaye." Lenny Kaye was Patti Smith's guitar player, and the song penned in his honor was (along with the EAT classic "Broken Spheres and Powderpuffs") one of the three songs that comprised what would turn out to be our final recording session.

The second song-inspiring incident of the summer of 75 occurred only a week or two after graduation. I was spending the summer helping Meemaw and Poppy with their cleaning and yard work, when Poppy asked me to take a break and accompany him to Springfield mall. This was my first trip to Springfield mall, and quite a memorable one it would turn out to be. We established a designated time and place to regroup for lunch and then the two of us split up. So while my grandfather was off tending to the business that brought us to the mall, I was wandering about with the same wide-eyed wonder that years later would come to symbolize our culture's relationship between teenagers and malls. Eventually I happened to stroll past a clothing store called merry-go-round that was obviously catering to the hip young suburbanite during this post-glitter/pre-disco fashion void. While my general state of mind was that of a kid in a candy store, what really drew me into Merry-Go-Round was the invitation of an absolutely ravishing brunette, who addressed me with some term of endearment such as "Honey" or "Sweetie." I could probably pull her name out under hypnosis, but her warm friendly face I never will forget (along with the fact that underneath her jeans and tight fitting sweater was the body of a future month's centerfold). Once inside the store, she lavished me with seductive sales tactic attentiveness, while maintaining enough of a cheerful people-person attitude to make me feel right at home in her store. I knew, or at least supposed, that the world outside of Oakton High school could not possibly be this radically different, but despite her obvious sale driven intent, the newness of the experience of having a woman this beautiful paying this much attention to me made me linger awhile to soak up as much of her friendliness as I could.

I don't recall purchasing anything on my initial visit to Merry-Go-Round, but what made it that much easier to justify planning a return visit was the fact that they did carry some clothes to fit the tastes of EAT and I. It wasn't EF Sly, but it was the closest thing to it I had seen in the Northern Virginia suburbs. After I obtained my driver's license in February of 1976, I was able to drive anywhere at will to do my clothes shopping. By this time however, glitter was dead, and without a particular fashion movement to drive it, EF Sly disintegrated into a preppy casuals one-stop for Georgetown university students.

After the summer of 1975, aside from the antique clothing and old stage costume castaways one might find in those upstairs holes-in-the-wall,

Georgetown at large ceased to be an interesting place to shop for clothes. Indeed! As of the summer of 1975, my personal focus for clothes shopping shifted to Springfield mall, and although the mention of a particular upstairs hole-in-the-wall Georgetown costume clothier would lead EAT and I into hungrily discussing the attributes of a black girl who worked there, the store itself was more geared towards costume rather than practical wear.

After returning from my two week vacation in Sarasota Florida, I planned a pilgrimage to Springfield mall with EAT. We would get there by Metrobus (an adventure in itself). Sometime during the morning of Thursday August 14th 1975, EAT and I met at the intersection of Lee Highway and Gallows Road to begin a three-hour Metrobus odyssey that at one point had us running the streets of Oldtowne Alexandria to make one of our many connections. We could have probably walked to the mall in less time, but as I said, our Metrobus vision quest was an adventure in itself, and made sweet victory out of our final arrival at the mall. This was my third visit to Merry-Go-Round, but I felt that EAT needed to experience it for himself. And the bountiful co-eds of Merry-Go-Round did not disappoint us. I was whisked away by my usual brunette, while EAT was being gobbled up by an incredibly suggestive blonde. I'll never forget the look on EAT's face as this girl addressed him as "Honey" and started coiling her arm around his shoulder in a snakelike manner that in these litigious times would be considered child molestation. At this point, EAT knew that the stories I had given him about my two previous visits to

the store were not exaggerations. I also recall EAT being somewhat impressed with the fact that Merry-Go-Round did stock a modicum of black clothing, which was some consolation for two disaffected glitterheads like ourselves. Having no Satanist rumors flying around us may have taken a bit of the fun out of wearing black clothing, but our tastes were nonetheless fairly set by this time, and aside from the standard corporate dress suit, black clothing for adolescent males was a little harder to come by in this area with EF Sly out of the picture.

Other post-Oakton memories involving Eat were largely centered around his house in McLean. I remember lying on the floor of EAT's dining room listening to WGTB. EAT was lying on the floor as well, on the other side of the family dinner table near the door to a very oddly designed kitchen. Shafts of light from the mid-day sun crisscrossed the room from the edges of barely drawn curtains, as WGTB took us into the aether with a set that included Tangerine Dream and what I would years later discover was a track from Gong's "You" album. Although EAT and I waited like whaler's wives for the barely intelligible announcement of what had been played (always a hit or miss endeavor with WGTB), what makes this memory significant is that it was my first exposure to electronic music, which became a fascination of mine that grew steadily throughout the latter half of the seventies.

Music continued to be the tie that binds for EAT and myself. I remember walking with EAT into McLean shopping center where EAT bought Pavlov's Dog's "Pampered Menial" and I purchased the latest Aerosmith album "Toy's in the Attic." Aerosmith was a group that EAT and I had discovered together almost two years earlier. EAT and I's reaction to the first few lines of David Surkamp's voice on the Pavlov's Dog album he had just purchased was, as I recall, similar to the reaction we had upon hearing Bryan Ferry struggle with "Smoke Gets in Your Eyes" (which had us on the floor for a good minute).

It was at EAT's house in early 1976 that I heard the first Ramones album, which was a sneak peak into the punk/new wave movement that would consume my attention (as well as significant portions of my paychecks) in the late 70's. I remember my unsuccessful attempt to turn EAT on to Sweet's "Desolation Boulevard" and his unsuccessful attempt to get me excited about Silverhead's "16 and Savaged."

Aside from the good times we would continue to have, EAT would periodically bemoan his lot in life at McLean High. His remaining two years of high school appeared from the onset to be disappointingly unremarkable. As is true of all high schools, McLean High had its fair share of attractive young ladies, one or two of which EAT found worth mentioning. Generally however, EAT, like me, seemed to be suffering from a case of anti-climactic post 74-75 school year blues.

After receiving my copy of the 1976 Paragon in the spring of 76 from my man on the inside, Rick Hockmuth, I took the yearbook over to EAT's house for his perusal. It was with no small amount of reverence that I pointed out what swans clucking hens like Tanya Herrell and Sherry Hogge had become, as well as the continuing beatification of Peggy Wallace via that poetry inspiring senior picture of hers. For EAT and I, the book was like a tonic that eased the difficulty of self-inspiration in the absence of outer stimuli, as well as a reminder of the people we had left behind.

1976/77 was EAT's senior year, and during this period, the change that had been so slow in coming began to creep into both of our lives. I became preoccupied with the dramas of the Burley family, and then the Cindy Martens, Tom Kilbey, Sher Weston NOVA affairs later on in the first half of 1977. EAT began dating a girl named Samantha, and upon meeting "Sam" for the first time, which was probably sometime in the fall of 1976, I can remember being struck by what a perfect match she seemed to be for EAT. Aside from the fact that she matched EAT in height, Sam also had the quality of having an appreciation for the same sort of music that once symbolized EAT and I's ostracism. Even more of an anomaly was the fact that Sam shared EAT's interest in the creation of original music, which eventually led to their forming a group together called "Rhoda and the Bad Seeds." Could EAT and I, in our wildest dreams, have imagined even the musically inclined ladies of Oakton (such as Hunk or Peggy), who once courted our attentions, sitting in on a Death by Hanging session. It's amazing that the idea, as preposterous as it was, did not cross our minds for even a nanosecond. I mean, Connie Underwood played the French horn, Peggy played the piano, and Hunk sang. Jesus! We could have just composed the music and let them do most of the work.

As it turned out, EAT would have to achieve a certain degree of distance from Oakton High for someone like Sam to come into his life. Sometime in the summer of 1977, EAT's family (as many had before them) moved to the more affordable town of Manassas. From this point onward, my communications with EAT became markedly less frequent. I do recall two communications from EAT in 1978 that curiously recalled old times. From out of the blue, EAT phoned me at the Annandale Penguin Feather, where I was employed at the time, all abuzz over the release of Steve Harley's first solo album "Hobo with a Grin." As Harley had been the one recording artist that EAT and I had collectively most identified with during the 1974-76 time period, EAT felt compelled to seek out the one person in all of Northern Virginia whom he could share the joys of a new Harley album with.

Our next communication was under more dire circumstances. I came home from work one Tuesday to find a note from my mother saying "Call EAT Tomorrow (Wednesday) at 11:00 AM." As Wednesday was my day off, this was no problem, but my mother's in person recounting of EAT's phone call made it sound like an urgent matter, requiring my immediate attention. I phoned EAT straight away and discovered that Samantha had ended their relationship. EAT had gone to the one person who could appreciate the gravity of his situation from a historical perspective. This phone call would begin a long tradition of old friends (even old girlfriends) digging out my phone number when the need demanded a confessor for their romantic woes, as if my experiences qualified me as the patron saint of failed relationships. I recall that there was such the tone of the old EAT in his voice, as if he had just woken up to the fact that he had become the unwitting victim in the VOT's most elaborate plot.

Well, time bore out the fact that EAT and Sam had just had a tiff. When contact was re-established with EAT in early 1979, he was living with Samantha in a townhouse in Washington DC atop a performance space called the "Hard Art Gallery." I visited EAT at his new residence on a number of occasions, and for a period during the spring and early summer of 1979, our friendship enjoyed a brief restoration. It was apparent from my first visit with EAT in that gloomy gray tenement that the world had taken some of the sparkle out of his eyes and out of his

smile. A telling moment came on the phone with EAT when he suddenly let out with a startled cry and then told me to hold the line for a moment. I thought he had just discovered that his building was on fire, but when he came back on the line, he told me that he had just seen a huge rat crawl by his bedroom window. Knowing how

dangerous an animal an urban rat of that size could be, I certainly could empathize with how shaken EAT obviously was. It underscored my opinion that EAT was now living through some of the things he once wrote about from a comfortable (and safe) distance in his house in Dunn Loring.

My last artistic endeavor that involved EAT was a poetry reading/performance with Hank Lowman at the Hard Art Gallery in the summer of 1979. EAT had some minor involvement in the performance of both Hank's reading and my own. What I first conceptualized as a straight poetry reading, was in its preparation phase guided by Hank more in the direction of performance art, a shift in direction that I would have to adapt to in order to keep pace with in subsequent readings. Despite the impressive turnout of friends and fellow "Penguins," and despite the fact that both "From Far Away Beauty" and "Psychodrama" can trace their origins back to this single event, my first and last public performance with EAT was a rather ill-rehearsed and amateurishly executed affair. As I think back on it now, I can't help but think that if EAT and I hadn't been so bitten by the maturity bug, we might have thought to treat that too kind audience to something a bit more memorable by ending the evening with a DBH set, but that was something we had already left behind.

I called EAT a couple more times after that, but the next time we would talk face to face was an accidental meeting in the lobby of the Ontario Theatre after a U2 concert. This was in the fall of 1981, and though we quickly came to that loss for words that besets once close friends whom time has transformed, I was consoled by the fact that EAT did appear to be somewhat happier.

The last time I would hear of EAT was months later at a party held at the apartment of a former girlfriend of mine, Mimi Baumann. Somehow the name of Doug Lay was mentioned and Mimi's boyfriend (and future husband) Danny Frankel said "Yes, I know that guy." While not in immediate contact with him, Danny told me that the last time he saw EAT, he had gone almost completely deaf, a story which had more than the ring of truth to it. All through the 1973-76 period of our friendship, EAT was being treated for some sort of chronic ear problem. Knowing EAT's love of music, this bit of news saddened me greatly. I feared for more than the future of Rhoda and the Bad Seeds.

I was happy to discover in December of 1997 that Danny's description of EAT's deafness was somewhat overstated. EAT, apparently picking up the psychic vibes I was giving off through the tremendous amount of past recall needed to write this book, called me out of the blue. EAT seemed to be his old self, calling me Bobney and exclaiming that there was not a day that passed that he did not think about "Those Times," a confession that led not only myself, but others connected to the writing of this book, to conclude that mystical forces were at work here shaping some glorious revival. While EAT had lost a portion of his hearing, it was not enough to prevent him from continuing to produce music on his own under the name "Lay." And Yes! We have discussed the eventuality of some sort of Death by Hanging reunion. EAT has claimed to have many memories of the old days, and I've no doubt that some of those memories will find their way into the final draft of this book. This book was written to ensure that the past will always be ours, but EAT's return heralds much in the future that will also be ours.

EDUARDO ALONSO

Here we have the strange and baffling case of Eduardo Francisco Alonso, who was one of my closest friends during my freshman year, and thereafter became a completely reticent stranger to me. Our friendship, as many had before it, grew out of the sheer chance of classroom seating. Eduardo sat next to me in a rather progressive English class, which had the unusual feature of having a pair of teachers, a man and a woman. The woman, a late 20's pale and perky homemaker type (who nonetheless had a great pair of legs) named Mrs. Petry. And the man, a bald rotund motivator who used wit and enthusiasm to breath life into the classroom (the same classroom that I would serve my volunteered detentions in during my senior year) named Fritz Smith. The relative youth and enthusiasm of both of these teachers established the most positive rapport with a class that I had witnessed up to this point, and their teaching techniques were often unconventional. Once the two of them got into a mock argument that was so convincing that it brought a traumatized Julie Dargush to tears. It was Julie's tears that brought the two of them to finally confess that the whole thing was staged. I forget what point exactly they were trying to make (although being an English class, I suspect it had something to do with modes of communication), but this teaching through dramatic example style of theirs made this the most interesting English class I would have at Oakton, if the least adherent to the lofty goal of making us better writers, readers, and speakers.

It was in the more open atmosphere of this classroom that my friendship with Eduardo was allowed to rage on unchecked. While Mrs. Petry's rosy disposition was at times mixed with a "Come Now, Boys!" primness, the boy-at-heart Mr. Smith was just as apt to join in our boyish banter as admonish us for disrupting the class. One thing's for sure, with the possible exception of my junior year Russian class with EAT, there has been no other class in which I spent so much time laughing. Eduardo and

I were cutting up constantly, and in fact, my clearest picture of Eduardo is of Eduardo laughing.

The following story illustrates how unflappable the two of us were together. We were hanging around Eduardo's locker in the upstairs math hallway when the emotionally disturbed Robert Beach happened to walk by. Unable to repress the sourness of his own existence, Robert felt compelled to get in my face and issue invitations for me to fight him (as he was often given to do). On this particular day, the frustration over my placid, often silent refusals to engage him must have been more than he could endure, for he knocked my books out of my hands and proceeded to kick the papers that fell out of them all over the hallway. I looked straight at Eduardo, who by the growing smirk on his face had already anticipated the light I would make of this incident, and said to him – "And this started off to be such a good day." The two of us then began cracking up over the absurdity of the moment, escalating our rib-splitting merriment to the point where I had difficulty steadying myself as I went about picking up my papers. Eduardo had the type of sense of humor that lent itself to almost any situation. On this particular day, that sense of humor defused the aftershock of a moderately tense situation.

Strangely enough, Eduardo seemed to be much more serious on the phone, and the 3 or 4 times I called him, I sensed a more guarded Eduardo in regards to his family and home life. The same guy that could take anything I said, make a joke out of it, and milk that joke for a good half hour at school, was hurrying me to get to the point on the phone. While I never entertained the thought of visiting him at his home, at the same time, I felt I dared not ask. The perimeters of our friendship seem to have been established within the walls of Oakton High.

It wasn't until my post graduation yearbook perusals that I discovered that Eduardo had an older brother in the class of 73 named Pedro, and a younger sister in the class of 76 named Maria (who I vaguely recall EAT later mentioning had been in one of his classes). Now believe you me, I would have loved to have been introduced to Maria. None of my other friends had sisters this cute, or this close to my age for that matter. The logical assumption would be that Eduardo was guarding his sister's virginity, but I don't think this was the case at all.

What perplexed me even more was how Eduardo and I went from being the comedy team of the freshman class to being total strangers our sophomore year. It was the totality of the transformation that drew another delineating line between my freshman year and everything else that followed it. The few times that our paths crossed during our sophomore year (granted, simple geography made or broke many friendships in a school that size), Eduardo looked through me as if I wasn't there.

Avoiding eye contact, he had apparently transformed completely into that guarded serious young man on the phone.

My last memory of Eduardo was another wordless near miss a month or two before the end of my sophomore year. I can remember wondering if the rumor mill may have swayed him into distancing himself from me. Experience had trained me to accept the ephemeral nature of friendship, so I easily brushed the whole thing off.

The rush of events that followed my freshman year pushed my friendship with Eduardo further and further into the forgotten corner of my memories attic. It has only been through the writing of this book that Eduardo's memory and these observations have been brought back to life, where they belong.

EF SLY

A Georgetown clothier that became a fashion Mecca for EAT and I during the 1974/75 school year. Sly boasted vampire capes, silver mylar shirts, and an extraordinary amount of black clothing for those pre-gothic days, when much of an impressionable America still equated black clothing with Satanism. "Silver Glitter, Black Leather" the two of us chant near the close of EAT's classic composition – "Black in the Boy of Silver," but the final verse reveals how Sly inspired the song actually was:

You've gone to Lord & Taylor
And bought pretty clothes
Now you're heading for Sly
Still you're only human in body
So you climbed the ladder to the top
Anton will be displeased

As a chant, "Silver Glitter, Black Leather" was a bit like EAT and I petitioning the fates for more of this kind of clothing. Unfortunately, as if cued by EAT and I's departure from OHS, Sly began its slow descent into disco yuppidom in the summer of 1975, and in the process making the words on its shopping bags and T-shirts read like a prophecy -

Too fast to live
Too young to die
EF Sly

ELMO ZUDINSKI ROMANOFF

Emmette's greatest contribution to the Insanist movement was bringing us Elmo. Elmo was a made to order loon, in the respect that prior to our meeting in September of 1972, Emmette had been grooming him for acceptance into our group. As Elmo lived only the next bus stop down (about the same distance from Emmette as Tonny), rode the same bus, and possibly had a class or two with Emmette, the two got to know each other their 8th grade year at Luther Jackson intermediate, which was my freshman year at Oakton. Emmette spent much of the spring and summer months of 1972 hyping his new prospect to me in preparation for our eventual meeting in September when the two of them would arrive at Oakton as freshmen.

Emmette sat next to me in Mrs. Bryan's Russian class, and Elmo sat behind him. On the first day of school my sophomore year, Emmette's first order of business was to introduce Keith Zarin to me as "Elmo Zudinski Romanoff." Yes! Elmo even came complete with his own ready-made insanist name, making his assimilation that much smoother. Smooth? Hell! Emmette introduced him as someone who should join our movement. I asked him "Do you want to join us?" He said "Sure, I'll join you," and that was that. I'm assuming that Emmette spent some of their time together at Luther Jackson hyping me to Elmo as well.

Within a month's time, the quiet soft spoken Elmo was out of his shell and in like Flint. Despite being thoroughly adaptable to lunacy, Elmo, like Tonny, had that regular guy quality about him that made it easy for us to become buddies, whereas Emmette was not like that at all. Also like Tonny, Elmo took immediately to writing and recording music. I would record my own versions of two of Elmo's songs, "Bite One" and "Russian Class Blues") as early as late 1972. Throughout 1973 and into early 74, I would record other Elmo compositions ("Bite on by Tonight" and his classic "And I Freed Them"). Unlike Tonny, however (or at least the Tonny of this era),

Elmo was himself a musical enthusiast, which throughout much of 1973, put him in the role of picking up the slack from my waning contacts with Brian Helms and Don Frank.

I remember my first view of Elmo's sparse but meaty record collection, which lay on a shelf that overlooked his bed. He only had about 20 titles (at least half of which were the Led Zeppelin and Yes catalogues up to this point), but as he was only a freshman, he would acquire many more albums through the influence of EAT and I over the next two years. Although we never corrupted Elmo with our unwholesome David Bowie, you can throw the book at us for Iggy and the Stooges, the first three Queen albums and the Black Oak Arkansas catalogue. It was at the Dart Drug at Merrifield shopping center (of all places) that Elmo picked up Iggy's "Raw Power," as well as Johnny Winter's "Still Alive and Well." I remember walking there with Elmo, and upon returning to his house listening to my two

acquisitions of the day - Edgar Winter's "They Only Come Out at Night," and Donovan's "Cosmic Wheels," dating this little excursion to the summer of 1973.

Elmo's up for anything attitude put him in the middle of any folly that was going down, but what really bound us together was the shared experience of discovering new music together. Add to that our passion for composing and recording songs at will, and you have two guys who were having the musical time of their lives.

So when did Elmo stop having the time of his life and begin to have the time of somebody else's sad life? That's right! When the specter of seriousness moved into the picture in the form of his girlfriend - Brenda Paris. When I scan the overview of the three years at Oakton that I knew Elmo, a rather tragic before and after picture emerges. Girlfriends are the inevitable consequence of life (I kept telling myself), and though the impulse to maintain some degree of fairness and impartiality has me resisting the urge to blame Brenda 100% for the "After" Elmo, I'm drawn back to the fondness of my memories of the "Before" Elmo. This was a guy who took very little seriously, making EAT and I take notice that much quicker when the specter of seriousness did arrive. To drive the point home, my clearest memory of the Before Elmo was that face-wide smile that seemed to be always on his face, which was often followed by a hardy "Hey, Hey, Hey."

Without even really trying, Elmo's speech, mannerisms, and unique way of interpreting loon slang was a major influence on our little group. The opening two lines to an EZR song entitled "Words," dated September 12, 1973 went:

Crane & Crack are words we know
Tell us how to Crane A Po

Without really saying anything an outsider would have understood, these two lines speak volumes about the purity of Elmo's insanity. Those pages of song lyrics he left me with are a treasure trove, because they really were written by Elmo Zudinski Romanoff, a cheerful gun-ho unique individual who lived for two years (give or take a month) after the disappearance and before the return of a dour quiet Keith Zarin.

Did I say unique? Indeed, I did! For instance, Elmo had a way of pretending to be macho that was so obviously an anti-macho parody. His way of challenging one to a mock fight is not only something I have a picture of, but is something that can actually be heard in progress at the end of the DBH song Whip Out Your Blade, (an Elmo-ism if ever there was one). Elmo's obsession with singing about blades, knives, and weapons is but another manifestation of this bizarre machismo. Now Elmo did lift weights, and he definitely had a guy's taste in music, but underneath that blue shirt jacket with the leopard spotted lining he wore continuously, beat the heart of an aspiring non-conformist.

Contained in the book of artifacts is a letter written by Elmo, which he stuck in the vents of my junior year locker. It is quite simply one of my most prized possessions, because of the simple way in which it captures what was a very special time in my life. It reads -

Hey Bobnee:
Crack, I have to stay after today for Sach's test, in rm. 109. If you still want to bite, stay after and we could ride the late bus, but it's crowded as all crane.

Hadinaho, EZR

Obviously, Crane and Crack weren't the only words we knew. But you see what I mean about the purity of Elmo's lunacy? He really used the loon dialect to this extent (or greater) whenever he addressed me.

Elmo had that certain something that made him a perfect loon. Call it "The power of going along." Emmette became fascinated with the behavior of this girl in our Russian class named Karen Peterson, thus formulating a syndrome that codified her patterns of behavior - Elmo went along. I suggested we get together and record our own songs - Elmo went along. Kaiser invented this game called Leaf Biting - Elmo went along.

 And he didn't just play along, he perfectly assimilated and mirrored the absurdity of any folly that was cooked up, in exactly the spirit in which it was put forth. I'm sure that somewhere in this book is a definition of insanity (as it pertained to the Insanist movement) as "The ability to take absurdity seriously." Elmo had this ability in spades, and though he began developing his own quirks and colloquialisms shortly after settling in, Elmo's "Power of going along" was so instantaneous that it's impossible for me to separate Elmo's going-along with any hand he might

have had in fomenting the original folly. Hell! For all I know, his input might have help to shape Emmette's ideas about the Peterson Syndrome.

While Emmette (despite his unabashed crush on Wagnerian diva Birgit Nilsson) disguised his fascination with females fairly well, Elmo held his own in the non-committal middle ground, vacillating between Emmette's empiricism and emotional detachment, and my heart-on-my-sleeve romanticism, though openly leaning more towards the former. Underneath it all, Elmo was (like most of us) just a regular guy, with regular guy aspirations like getting laid, getting married, settling down, and all the security normally associated with this racket. But Elmo (also like most of us) felt that bitter self-defeating feeling that no girl he would ever find attractive would in turn find him attractive. He had acne, and I'm sure his sister calling him "Pizza Face" did little to bolster his self-image. This is one thing I think we loons had in common with the average guy. With me, it was my thinness, or my long hair, or my personality. Everyday it was some new damn excuse. But whatever reason Elmo was using to explain why girls weren't paying attention to him, it wasn't worth settling for Brenda Paris. No amount of security or companionship he thought he was getting was worth the death of Elmo Zudinski Romanoff.

And it wasn't just the return of that quiet shy Keith Zarin fellow. The bone hard square-jawed look of veiled contempt I saw on Brenda Paris' face was proof enough that the specter of seriousness had come to break up the party. I have a few regrets about my high school days, but doesn't everybody? The only thing that I can honestly say shamed me into learning a valuable lesson was introducing Elmo to Brenda. I was having these enjoyable, but overly long phone conversations with this rather clingy girl who I was beginning to want to get rid of. So what did I do? I introduced this girl to one of my best friends, and later paid for it with the loss of that friend. Woe is me.

Ah, Well! There are plenty of good times to recall and write about. If my senior year was the most exciting and influential year of my life, then my sophomore year was certainly the most fun, largely due to one Elmo Zudinski Romanoff. Emmette has passed on to that big insane asylum in the sky. EAT has already come home, Tonny's on his way, and Howard apparently never left, but we've still got one more lost lamb to bring in.

EMMETTE OPHASSE

One night in August of 1997, I got my hands on a 20th year reunion alumni book for the class of 1976. In the front of the book (which was really more of a pamphlet) was a page with five names under the heading – "In Memoriam." One of those names was Tim Kulik. It took a couple of days for it to really sink in - Emmette was dead. Never again would I respond with a spirited "Emmie! Baby!" to the triumphant cry of "Bobney Baby!" Gone were my chances of ever reminiscing with Emmette about the Peterson Syndrome and a hundred other things, some now lost to my memory. If I had only begun to write this book, and had not yet made the resolution to see it through to its conclusion, seeing Emmette's name on that page solidified my resolve. Moreover, it also pulled from me the assurance that the completed version of this book will find its way into the proper hands, lest the name of Emmette O be forgotten. It should go without saying, that it also filled me with the sudden desire to re-establish communication links with many of the people I have written about in this book lest I see some more familiar names on the In Memoriam page of the 25th anniversary alumni book.

Emmette's road to glory actually began in the late 60's at Timberlane apartments in Falls Church. It was here that Emmette met and built a friendship with Tonny around their shared interest in baseball. Sometime just prior to the beginning of Tonny and I's 7th grade year at Luther Jackson intermediate (which would have been the fall of 1969), Tonny's family moved to Merrilee apartments and the Kuliks moved into the adjacent Merrifield Village apartments. In May of 1969, I moved into an apartment in Merrifield Village, perhaps only weeks prior to the fateful moves of the Hetricks and the Kuliks.

Tonny and I's friendship developed throughout 1970, but as Emmette was a year behind us, I did not become aware of him until he started attending Luther Jackson in the fall of 1970. Curiously, as with EAT's shaky entrance into my ongoing friendship with Elmo in the fall of 1973, my first view of Emmette was as a potential trouble source. A journal entry written sometime in early 1971 puts my concern in perspective.

There has been a new addition to our bus stop, a friend of Tonny's from years ago named Tim Kulik. It doesn't look like we're going to get along. I don't think he likes anything I do, and I'm sure he'll get in the way of our recording.

Aside from my worry that Emmette might interrupt (or cause the cancellation of) a Bonneville Follies recording session, Emmette's studiously serious vibe appeared to dampen the goofing off code of conduct that Tonny and I observed around each other. Yes! My first impression of Emmette was that he was a bit of a wet noodle. The first time I actually interacted with Emmette was in March of 1971 at Tonny's apartment. Tonny and I were engaged in a recording session in Tonny's bedroom when his mother knocked on the door, announcing Emmette's arrival. Now despite the fact that my fears of Emmette disrupting our recording sessions had now been realized, the Tonno-Bobney spirit of music and insanity squared off against the Emmo-Tonny baseball alliance, and Emmette was the one left outside of his element. He had probably walked over to Tonny's apartment that Saturday morning expecting to spend the afternoon conferring with Tonny over baseball statistical data. Entering Tonny's room, Emmette found not only a strange new presence, but a spiritually altered Tonny. Tonny, now caught in the middle, toned his insanity down to a point in-between the two codes of conduct he had theretofore observed separately for Emmette and myself, but it was not enough to put Emmette at ease. On the surface, Emmette appeared to be focusing his energy and attention on adapting to the situation, taking a slightly defensive posture in declining our invitation to join us in a recording. An inspiration seized me, and somehow, I got the tape recorder turned on and the microphone into Emmette's hands, forcing a few moments of air clearing spontaneity out of him. Emmette went into his "You stink, you stink, you stink, you stink, you stink, you stink, you stinky" rap, followed by his now famous "Norm Cash is Great" soliloquy, making history out of what probably would have been an otherwise uneventful session. If Emmette harbored any unspoken objections to the spirit of jollity and lunacy that had descended upon our apartment complex (as Tonny's behavioral adjustments would indicate), he had now unwittingly contributed to the furtherance of that lunacy.

The next time I had to deal directly with Emmette was late in the summer of 1971, after both Tonny and I had moved to Fairfax. I went over to Tonny's new house on Country Hill Drive to discover Emmette and Tonny engaged in some sort of Baseball card trading session. Someone (I can assure you, it was not I) suggested that the three of us go out to Tonny's front yard for a game of Wiffle Ball. Though I went along with the idea, I recall groaning inwardly. Playing catch with Tonny was one thing, but I was in no hurry to demonstrate my athletic ineptitude for someone who took sports as seriously as Emmette appeared to. After striking out Emmette and Tonny in succession, and whacking a couple of Emmette's pitches out of the yard, my attitude (if not my lack of enthusiasm) changed. I recall Emmette at one point summing up his and Tonny's surprise by exclaiming to the effect of – "Boy! We were worried about Bob not being able to play, and here he is making US look bad." For the record, no one was as surprised by the fortuity of my success on the mound and behind the plate as I was.

Once again, as if fate was trying to tell me something, my initial fears of Emmette putting the damper of boredom on an afternoon with Tonny turned out to be unfounded. I'll stop short of saying that this was a turning point in my relationship with Emmette, but it was the last time I saw

Emmette before his sudden (and to this day unexplained) conversion to insanity, which could not have been more than a month or two afterward. With Emmette gone, there is no way of confirming the importance of this strange Wiffle Ball game in shaping the future of the Insanist movement. I personally believe that shortly after this game, Tonny said something to Emmette about me that impressed him enough to want to join our club, so to speak.

The very next time I saw Emmette, (which would have been around or shortly after the start of my freshman year), he was a completely different person. Seemingly overnight, he had transformed from Tim Kulik - cautious outsider, into Emmette Ophasse - Wagnerian madman. And as with EAT two years later, once Emmette was with us, it seemed like he had always been with us. I don't know what Tonny told him, but at some point, he decided that I was some sort of guiding light, and from that point onward, he spoke and behaved like the Emmette O I will always remember.

Since Tonny and I were the founding loons, Emmette was our first conversion, and the first to take part in the loon initiation rites. In late summer/early fall of 1971, Tim Kulik donned the ceremonial underwear and christened himself - Emmette Ophasse. I didn't know it at the time, but recently, Tonny informed me that this name was derived from ancient Egyptian mythology, of which Emmette had an interest in at the time. I was not aware of his Egyptology predilections, but I was, however, quickly made aware of his obsessive fascination with Richard Wagner. In fact, the first time Emmette came over to my house, he brought over some records that were part of Wagner's massive "Ring Cycle." I recall Emmette going on at length during our phone conversations about the characters and sub-plots of the voluminous saga told in this series of opera's. Emmette knew the Ring Cycle word for word and scene for scene. I distinctly recall Emmette raving on about the magnificence of Birgit Nilsson, the portly Scandinavian diva whose performances as Brunhilda had made her the only woman in Emmette's life. The epic grandeur of Wagner's music was mirrored in Emmette's spirit and mannerisms. He would gesticulate with wide sweeping motions, and in fits of fancy, issue pronouncements in a declarative operatic tone. Things that truly excited Emmette became monumental in scope, no matter how trivial the item.

Despite the fact that Emmette's insanity was now irrefutable, the three of us did not develop into the triumvirate of loons that one would have imagined. For one thing, the three of us were split up during the 1971/72 school year. Tonny was now attending Fairfax High, Emmette was still finishing his term at Luther Jackson, and I was attending Oakton. Strangely, two separate loon alliances now existed, the Emmo-Bobney alliance and the Tonno-Bobney alliance, with Emmette and Tonny's friendship in a state of gradual dissipation. No falling out between the two had occurred, but increasingly (and especially so once Emmette had joined me at Oakton) his reaction was to guffaw whenever I would invoke Tonny's name for the glory of the cause, as if Emmette considered Tonny a milquetoast loon (a rather cavalier attitude considering Emmette's initial reaction to Tonny's developing lunacy). Make no mistake, Tonny was at the height of his insanity during this period, but his relationship with Emmette never evolved beyond the baseball oriented friendship they had forged in grade school, and so withered in its obsolescence.

Tonny may have felt it inappropriate to reveal his loonier side to Emmette. As Tonny was not attending Oakton with the rest of us, he had only heard me speak of Emmette's involvement with the movement, but he was in no position to see for himself just how much Emmette was involved. Even so, it's really bizarre that neither Emmette nor Tonny sought to align themselves together under the insanist umbrella, because there were definite similarities in their styles, even down to some of the colloquialisms they shared.

Now let me try to recall some of Emmette's more oft quoted sayings. Ah Yes! There was "Live Dangerously, Live Dead," and "Yaw Boob," which he alluded to as having some deeper mystical meaning, though I was never privy to what exactly that was. His cry of "Bobney Baby!" was usually given during one of those moments of triumph or excitement that would bring Emmette to make this rally gesture with his arms that became the unofficial loon salute. It was pure spirit, and it will always bring a smile to my face to recall the look of mad glee that crossed his face whenever he gave it.

I knew that things were going to get more interesting at the start of my sophomore year with Emmette's arrival at Oakton. Emmette sat next to me in my Russian class, a class that was to become a springboard for bigger and better things. The first order of business for Emmette was to direct my attention to the fellow sitting directly behind him. After introducing me to Elmo Zudinski Romanoff, our duo had become a trio, with Kaiser, Howard, and Boni coming on board in a matter of weeks.

For the next two school years, the core group of Emmette, Elmo and myself (flanked by Kaiser, Howard, and various other allies) congregated daily at the loon lunch table. Days after the start of my sophomore year, the lot of us staked out a tactically secure table at the Northeast corner of the cafeteria - nearest the tennis courts. I probably had a hand in picking out the spot, as it was the same place I had sat with Don Frank my freshman year. This table was a hub of activity, planning, and merriment during this period, but by the start of my senior year, shifting schedules and dissolving alliances had reduced the loon lunch table aggregate to just Howard Koretz and myself, lunching together at the lonely Southwestern corner of the cafeteria. After Peggy's rejection and the buzz of whispering rumor merchants had made the cafeteria a little too hot for me, Howard ended up as the lone survivor.

It overwhelms me a bit to contemplate everything that grew out of my sophomore Russian class. Emmette, whose Russian name in the class, was "Nicolai" (Mine was "Boris," and Elmo's was something like "Vladin"), had delivered Elmo on a silver platter. He would then go on to single out for immortalization a female in that class named Karen Peterson, whose behavior so fascinated Emmette that he began keeping notes on what he called The Peterson Syndrome. I personally found Miss Peterson completely unremarkable, and was initially at a loss to explain Emmette's fascination, but the more he stated his findings to me, a clearer picture emerged. Emmette apparently sat near Karen Peterson in another class of his, later relaying things he had observed her saying or doing to me. As I've posited later in this book, bridge club psychobabble might pin Emmette down as having had some suppressed desire for Miss Peterson, and accompanying feelings of inadequacy that he was coping with by reducing her to the level of a lab specimen. However, everything that happened there in that time and place must be viewed from that perspective. As that would be a near impossibility for an outsider, I'll attempt to clarify. At this particular time and place, Emmette and I harbored a disdain for those whom we looked upon as the "Sanes," those unduly given to conformity and convention. More often this tainted mass was mocked collectively, rather than singled out individually. It was the sheer ordinariness of Karen Peterson that I now believe was at the heart of Emmette's fascination. I recall a number of occasions in our Russian class where Karen Peterson would make a seemingly innocuous observation and Emmette would burst into a laughter that was restrained only in its volume, as if Karen was proving the validity of his syndrome every time she opened her mouth. Whether Emmette found Miss Peterson attractive or not is immaterial. He clearly could not take her seriously. Again, the things we inner circle loons took the most seriously were the jokes we perpetuated. Add to that Emmette's penchant for pulling great schemes and grand significance's out of the most static blandness, and you have the Peterson Syndrome.

As fun as it was for Elmo and I to have Emmette on our team, all that really mattered was that Emmette considered these things important. His spirit was such that Elmo and I were empowered just playing along with him. But this spirit would dissipate, as throughout my junior year, Emmette would move further and further away from the group. In many ways, EAT was Emmette's spiritual replacement. During my senior year, Emmette had, by all accounts, "Gone Sane." He had taken to wearing flannel shirts, drinking beer with quasi-redneck pseudo ruffians, and raving about Dixie Liquors in Georgetown and Hank Williams in some bizarre attempt to sport a rougher image. I may have at the time lamented Emmette's selling out to run with the crowd, but looking at it now, it appears to have been just another one of Emmette's phases, no less an unforeseen reinvention of himself than the one I witnessed back in 1971. My final encounter with Emmette on the grounds of Oakton High pretty much bears this out. It was during my September 1975 post-graduation return visit to Oakton (which wouldn't have been complete without a trip up to the radio station). Entering the radio room, I found a slightly modified set-up, and 3 or 4 people in a flurry of activity, one of which was a less than excited to see me Elmo, and another was Emmette O, who happened to be the on-air DJ at the time. Emmette was still in his back-to-the-heartland mode, raving to me about the greatness of the album he was putting on - Leon Russell's hillbilly treatise "Hank Wilson's Back." While Russell's honky-tonk whine made the radio room seem all the more like a place I had no business being in, I kind of regret not playing along with what would be my last glimpse of the old Emmette. I can recall thinking at the time that Emmette was irretrievable, and aside from this final mad rant over a Leon Russell album, perhaps he was. The operative word is "Rant," and on reflection, he was ranting like the old Emmette, just not AS the old Emmette.

It was in the summer of 1976, that I last saw Emmette. Curiously, this was also the only time I would ever visit Emmette's apartment and get to see for myself the old boy's room, his bench press, and his record collection (close to half of which were the massive box sets that comprised Wagner's Ring Cycle). I also saw his many books on baseball, Wagner, and all the other ingredients that had made up all the Emmette's past and present. Even stranger than finding myself in this museum of Emmettian history, was the fact that Tonny was with me at the time. We had been delivering the Fairfax Mirror at Merrifield Village, when we came upon Emmette's apartment (which Tonny had remembered from his 1969-71 days at Merrilee). Five years had passed since Tonny had walked the couple hundred yards to that apartment building, but we decided to try our luck anyway and knock on his door, and sure enough, Emmette answered the door.

While this was the last time I would have any contact with Emmette, Tonny recently told me that his friendship with Emmette saw a brief renaissance in the late 70's with a number of phone calls from Emmette, wherein he would rave at length about the greatness of the TV show

"Happy Days." Tonny said that Emmette considered it to be great wholesome American entertainment, and would chat on at length about the various characters and their foibles and predicaments. Never mind how much this recalls Emmette's earlier expounding on the characters in Wagner's Ring Cycle, what made this story quintessentially Emmette was the fact that Happy Days was the last thing one would expect Emmette to become fixated on. His predictable unpredictability had shown through to the very end.

In a recent phone conversation with Howard, he related what was probably the last eyewitness account of Emmette-O. It was in December of 1978, at a Christmas party held at the townhouse of a bowling team associate of Howard and Emmette's in Annandale. It was on recounting this final memory that Howard remarked about what a good bowler Emmette was, and indeed, this was a pastime of Emmette's that I had all but forgotten about. As Tonny had attested to Emmette's failures in little league baseball, it was comforting to know that Emmette had found a sport that he could personally excel in. Wagner, Norm Cash, Bowling, and the TV show Happy Days. All of these things (among others) will forever remind me of Emmette O. Rest in Peace old friend.

THE EMMOLIN
A musical contrivance (I hesitate to call it an instrument) of Emmette's. The Emmolin was basically a yardstick bowed across the strings of my two string acoustic guitar. It was used only once during the one and only piece of music where Emmette agreed to sit in on a recording with Tonny and I. Emmette had, for some reason, found himself with Tonny at my house with instruments strewn and tape recorder light on in session mode. It was mid 1974 and I suspect we were celebrating Tonny's temporary return to Virginia. Emmette, who at first emphatically refused to join in the session, agreed conditional to his appearing on an instrument of his own invention. His terms were agreed to and the Emmolin had its brief but glorious footnote in musical history.

FAUSTO BENGOCHEA
A sociology/psychology classmate of mine during my first three years at Oakton. Fausto and I came to know each other through our mutual association with Don Frank. Aside from our fairly straightforward discussions on music, it's difficult to retrospectively pin Fausto down, but I'll try. In the unholy Bedford Village apartments triumvirate of Steve Larson, Don Frank, and Fausto Bengochea, Larson was the obvious odd man out by virtue of his unrelenting pursuit of other planes of consciousness. Less obviously, Fausto, in his own way, and by his own

design, was an odd man out in any situation or group you were likely to find him in. This made our pairing off in class almost an inevitability independent of our Don Frank association.

If I had started imbibing in various mind-altering drugs, Fausto and I would have undoubtedly become the best of friends, but I just wasn't interested. Confounded as he was by my continuing refusal to be "Turned on," there nevertheless remained between us an unflagging respect for the other's individuality. In fact, I'll make the shocking assertion here that Fausto was even more of an odd man out than me. There were too many contradictions in his nature for him to fit easily into any hole on the Oakton pegboard. Larson's data spewing sci-fi constructs were the eggheaded opposite of Fausto's Mediterranean cool, but Larson had an affinity for psychedelia, and had an IQ well within Fausto's level of acceptance, so on those two points, their association clicked.

Fausto once rated Don Frank's IQ in the 180's and mine in the 160's, which told me that Fausto valued root intelligence and one's knowledge acquisition potential as a determining factor in who he would associate with. Despite being well groomed, well dressed, and generally well spoken, Fausto's personality was that of the outsider-ruffian, whose time on the grounds of OHS would be as short as he could possibly make it. Fausto's own high IQ would have lead him to avoid suffering the company of Oakton's ruffian rank and file, so again, we're looking at a square peg in a school full of round holes.

I'd love to have some of our classroom discussions about music on tape, with Fausto arguing the case for Jimi Hendrix, and me waving the prog rock banner with exclamations of the greatness of ELP's "Brain Salad Surgery." As a face off between psychedelic and progressive sensibilities, this particular discussion didn't progress very far, but when I put forth Brain Salad Surgery as a glimpse into the future of man's battle to maintain parity with the encroachment of technology, Fausto nodded affirmatively and gave me one of those facial expressions that said – "OK, I'll accept that." You see, I knew the perceived rocking up the classics aesthetic of Emerson, Lake & Palmer would never pass Fausto's coolness test, but I also knew that I could always appeal to Fausto's intellect to achieve some level of agreement.

I'll never forget going over to Don Frank's townhouse, hanging out there for awhile, and then walking over to Fausto's townhouse. Fausto greeted us at the door and showed us to his room. His sisters and parents appeared not to be home at the time. While the three of us hung out there, Fausto, in one final attempt to convert me, walked over to his turntable and put on Hendrix's "Axis: Bold as Love" album. After 2 or 3 songs,

Fausto looked at me and said something to the effect of – "Not into it, huh?"

Well, in the last five years, I've grown to have quite an appreciation for psychedelia, which has occasionally brought me to wonder what ever became of Fausto Bengochea?

FEMME FAMILIARS

The cat, the crow, and the chicken all had special connotations for EAT and I during my senior year. Each of these three animals were linked by association to a specific female in our lives. The cat was linked to CA, owing to her love of cats, the crow to Hunk by virtue of her strikingly black hair, and the chicken to Peggy. I honestly cannot recall how such an unaesthetic creature as the chicken could have become an instantly recognizable reference to Peggy. The cat and the crow were definite references to CA and Hunk, but when Peggy arrived on the scene in early 1975, the chicken became at once a reference to Peggy and her coadjutors, and to the whole of womankind. I remember snapping a photo of a couple of chickens at jungle gardens during one of Tonny and I's visits to Sarasota Florida. I showed the photograph to EAT, who upon seeing the chickens quipped "Ooooh! Girlie pictures!" The association was rarely addressed, but was apparently well ingrained.

The obliqueness of all three familiars is best characterized by how each is mentioned in my last will. Now leaving EAT a "Hunk of my crow hatred" may have been an obvious enough clue to be picked up by a friend of Hunk's, or Hunk herself, but then we'd have to assume that said person would have known who "EAT" was. We have to remember that outside of the dwindling circle of loons, EAT was still known as Doug Lay, cousin of the more popular Carol and Gerri Lay. The other two familiars, the cat and the chicken, appear in such obscure references that I to this day wonder if anyone other than EAT has gleaned an inch of meaning from them. For starters, they appear not in my will, but in the will of Howard Koretz. After submitting my own will, and upon seeing Howard working on his own, I became thirsty to leave a few more tokens of my esteem. Howard agreed, and so the lengthy introduction to his will closed with – "I wish it known that numbers 2,3,4,5 and 6 are bequeathed by request of Bob Karnes, and the rest are of my own contriving" (an explanatory line that I recall penning for Howard). It is apparent now from reading these cryptically charged lines that I felt that my will did not go far enough in expressing certain feelings, or that given the chance, I could have written a book. Entry number 2 reads – "To Bob Karnes, a thunderstorm on the anniversary of chicken delight (God save the Queen)." Now "God save the Queen" was an oft-used rallying cry by (or for) Queen Viper, but "A thunderstorm on the anniversary of chicken delight" refers to February 1st, the date of Peggy's rejection. I was leaving to myself, in effect, the charge of observing this dark anniversary in a manner befitting the emotions it would revive. Now thunderstorms in February are rare indeed, but the symbolism was two-fold – may dark clouds appear in my soul (if not in the sky itself) in solemn remembrance of this date, and may the fire that was in my heart on that February 1st always be of sufficient amplitude to light up the night sky.

A thunderstorm was an apt description for my feelings at the time, and the Chicken Delight Peggy reference reflects my growing bitterness over the realization that there would be no finality to any of this. This bitterness was more directly expressed in entry number 6 – my final parting shot, if you will, "To the Miss Loonies of our minds – The chickens we choked and the cats we were too deep for." Now "Miss Loonies of Our Minds" refers to a song written by Howard, and my inclusion of it was an attempt to tailor this entry to fit the vernacular peculiar to Howard himself. The chickens we choked and the cats we were too deep for were the real life embodiments of Howard's poetry – Peggy and CA. They were the miss loonies of MY mind (of whom Howard's lyrics were admonishing me to "Get the observations and write 'em down").

To the Miss Loonies of OUR MINDS was an all-encompassing invocation directed – To all of you, from the major heartbreakers on down to the nattering gossip-mongering third parties – I leave the chickens we choked (a reference to Peggy's infamous "You're choking me" line, and not what you're thinking) and the cats we were too deep for (a reference to CA's immortal parting words in my 1974 yearbook – "If you think I don't like you or avoid you sometimes, don't worry about it. If I do, It's just because you're rather deep for me").

Bitterness of this sort exists when no clear adversary or object of anger exists. I was stuck in the middle of a mystery with no clear point in which to direct my emotions. I had been given no reason to harbor any ill will toward Peggy or CA, and as such, had no anger I could direct toward either one of them. Neither CA nor Peggy had really gotten to know me, and I had gotten no closer at the end of it all than to refer to them in the guise of these femme familiars, as if they were some sort of mythological beasts. To me, they are part of what I would call Oakton mythology, as the word mythology connotes some degree of distance in time and space from the actual truth of something.

Interestingly, other fowl such as the vulture, the swan and the dove were invoked in Peggy's name in my last will, reminding me that it had become all too easy to paint the miss loonies of our minds in the guise of our fine feathered friends.   Maybe it was their propensity for suddenly flying away.

FIELDTRIP TO LANCASTER PA

On October 30th 1973, I went on a fieldtrip to Lancaster Pennsylvania with Mr. Wargo's Sociology class to observe (at least from the view of a passing school bus) how the Amish people lived. This is a bittersweet memory for me, because outside of the classroom, I got my first long look at Cheri Allen as she interacted with others. In the more relaxed atmosphere inside the school bus that transported us to and from Lancaster, there was no teacher that I had to pretend to give my attention to. I could give my full attention to the light surrounding Cheri, and it was here on this trip that I truly fell in love with her.

Two busloads of students went to Lancaster, so I assumed by some of the unfamiliar faces that I saw that all of Mr. Wargo's sociology classes were included in the fieldtrip. Of course, whenever a stop was made, I took great care to reboard the same bus as Cheri. Unfortunately, Fausto (who was probably taking a trip of his own) did not attend this trip, leaving me feeling rather detached in the center of the bus, while Cheri radiated her girlish charm for a circle of friends at the front of the bus. It's prolonged periods in this type of situation that can really ground a sense of hopelessness into a young man.

After this trip, the inevitability of black Friday (Cheri's rejection) was written in the stars, an event that might have been delayed a few weeks had Fausto been there to distract me. When our caravan stopped at an Amish operated gift and souvenir shop, I purchased a ceramic figure of a rat dressed in a Dickens-like top hat and overcoat, a tie to something familiar. Back on the bus, however, this tie to something familiar was severed rather quickly by the sight of Cheri, reminding me that things and ideas would only temporarily feed the greater hunger for female companionship.

Despite the dire picture I've painted of this fieldtrip, I've really only been singling out those impressions that were eerily precognitive of my future broken heart. In actuality though, I found the trip as a whole quite fascinating, and can recall upon returning home thinking how much fun I had that day. It seems worth noting, however, that the themes of Cheri and Pennsylvania resurfaced the following summer when I visited Tonny for two weeks in Punxsutawney. Despite being one of the happiest times of my life, the specter of Cheri Allen was ever present. Watching Amish people riding through town in their horse drawn carriages further connected the Punxsutawney trip with the fieldtrip to Lancaster. The alienation of the Amish from the society that surrounded them, and my

139

alienation from the world of a girl I was falling in love with is a correlation that has only now made its way to the forefront of my consciousness.

FLASH FRANNY

AKA Christina Rose. Flash was one of the few fans that EAT and I could claim to have as radio personalities. The fact that she is pictured in the 1976 yearbook as playing a woodwind in the symphonic band indicates an interest in music that, like Paula Pippert, may have been what attracted her to our little corner of the school. As she was a sophomore in 74/75, it's most likely that I first heard of her from EAT, though I distinctly remember Elmo mentioning her on one occasion.

Flash arrived on the scene too late to become a part of it. In fact, when I finally got to meet Flash, I had her sign my senior yearbook, which was probably no more than a week or two from graduation. She had slipped into the picture just in time to immortalize herself with a genuinely nice parting gesture. I'm glad she did, because being reminded from time to time that there once existed a girl who called herself Flash Franny keeps me in touch with what I liked best about Oakton high. It's just a shame she didn't come forth sooner.

FLEMING-JUDD ELECTION

During my sophomore year, there was some sort of election between the perennially involved junior Rick Judd and fellow sophomore Quentin Fleming. I knew both of them, and considered both to be likable and capable. Rick was the bearded longhaired intellectual whose activist proclivities had been channeled into working constructively within the system. Quentin was the slickly-dressed politico, who, despite his bow-tied car salesman look, was an equally earnest young man. As both were courting my vote, I was in a quandary over how to decide between these two equally qualified candidates. Despite their differences in physical appearance, there was nothing else about them that swayed me either way.

Then I had the brilliant idea that made me as integral a part of the American political process as the two candidates themselves. It suddenly occurred to me that I was the de facto leader of a special interest group - The Insanist movement. I then decided to query each candidate on whether they would recognize the insanists if elected. Whichever candidate gave me the most enthusiastically positive response would be the man that I would throw my support, and that of the entire movements behind. Rick Judd, upon hearing my terms, gave me an affirmative and forthright response - saying, "Yes! I will recognize your group." Quentin, surprisingly, gave me a simple and just as forthright "No." When I told Quentin that his decision left me no choice but to throw the weight of my group's support over to Judd, he jokingly wrapped me on the top of my head with his biology textbook. When I pretended to be addled by the blow, Quentin seriously thought that he had hit me too hard and apologized rather nervously. He really was a good guy, the type of guy you would at least like to give a verbal "Good luck" to, if not the validation of your actual vote. Nevertheless, my position was clear. I now had to spread the word that Judd was our man.

The Insanist movement was numerically at its apex during this period, and on any given week, I could have swayed 20 to 30 votes in either direction. As it turned out, my subsequent campaigning pulled in exactly 25 confirmed votes for Rick Judd. Beyond that, it's impossible to say how many other students may have been influenced by my expounding on the selling points of the Judd platform when Election Day finally came. Rick Judd did win the election, a victory for the Insanist movement, though not because any of us had the slightest intention of worming our way into Oakton student government politics. That was never the point of the whole exercise. It was the exhilaration I got from mobilizing the group around a unifying goal. The way I looked at it, anything that got this disparate group of misfits to act as a singular unit strengthened its solidarity.

One interesting conclusion could be drawn from this election, that despite how the appearance and demeanor of the two candidates would lead one to suspect otherwise, it was actually Rick Judd who better understood what it takes to be successful in politics.

FLORIDA
"27th state admitted to the Union" as Tonny sang on the opening track to "Fading Out with Glitter." Tonny and I would accompany my parents for three consecutive summers (1973-75) to the sunshine state, and have numerous adventures there. Fading Out with Glitter was actually, in part, a chronicle of our first Florida trip. These trips will be examined in greater detail in Tonny's entry (and elsewhere in this book), as well as my first trip to Florida in the summer of 1972 with my stepfather's son Kevin Hans.

FOLLY
An act committed for the sheer ridiculousness of having committed it. A folly could be planned in detail beforehand or thought up on the spot. It could be a one-time event or something repeated to the point of becoming a ritual. It was insanity in practice.

FREAKS

Everybody who attended high school in the 70's knows you had your jocks and you had your freaks, and everybody else was somewhere in the middle of these two poles. On the surface, the Oakton student body of the early 1970's seemed to exemplify this formula, but from one who tended to dwell below the surface, let's examine these stereotypes a little closer, shall we? The freaks - those 1970's successors to the hippie freaks of the 1960's, were identified by their long hair, their blue collar thrift store dress, and their propensity for indulging heavily in marijuana (alcohol was the jocks drug of choice). An occasional acid trip was almost a rite of passage, but my understanding was that the LSD that was going around then was not as pure as it was in its 60's heyday. Oakton seemed to have a lot more pot-mellowed stoners than serious mind-expansionists.

Whatever identified the freaks, the point is that they could easily be identified and tagged accordingly. The paradox of the freaks is that (despite the name they were given as a group) they now fit in perfectly with the accepted order of things. They weren't making a nuisance of themselves by protesting anything, and by and large, they were an affable group, who made friends easily. No! The real "Freaks" of Oakton high fell squarely into that unclassified mass in the middle of the freak/jock spectrum, and were, for the most part, fairly inconspicuous in appearance.

Then there were people like me, who confounded my order loving fellow students by mixing up the formula. I did have long hair, but I didn't dress like a freak, didn't partake in drugs, and was vibrating at an intensity level about a jillion gigawatts above your average freak. And jocks, I'm afraid, despite their inclination to travel in packs, could also be difficult to pin down individually. I don't want to sound like I'm putting forth the idea that freaks (or "Heads" as they were also called) were any less colorful or were lacking in identity as individuals. They simply seemed to be the most consistent and well-adjusted group among the 70's Oakton panorama. We called them freaks, but they really did fit in.

At times, the mellowness of these people (along with all the James Taylor and John Denver music that was being pumped out over the airwaves) was a balancing force against the volatility of all the teenage energy conduits surrounding me. Despite the fact that mellow was not a word that would ever have been used to describe me in high school, there where times when I was glad to have some of these freaks around.

FREE FARE

Occasionally, the student body was called to an "Assembly" in the auditorium. These assemblies usually took place during 5th or 6th period, and though attendance was mostly optional (due to the fact that most assemblies were entertainment oriented), most students viewed them as a welcome relief from the grind of their afternoon classes. Though I spent most of my 5th and 6th periods safely ensconced in the radio room during my senior year, EAT and I did put in an appearance at one bizarre (and rather sparsely attended) assembly which involved the showing of music videos by T. Rex, Jim Croce, and Sparks.

Those of you who attended high school in the early 70's may recall escaping 6th period to be treated to the music of your school's "Jazz Lab," or some visiting Jazz Rock group that barely met the minimum hipness requirement of the time. I don't know why, but these groups seemed to always have at least two horn players, and take at least one break during their set for the lead singer to tell the audience what miracles the Lord had accomplished in his life (I kid you not!). Sometime during the first half of my Freshman year, one such a group –"Free Fare" played during an assembly at Oakton High. Being as the hippest group I had heretofore seen perform was Luther Jackson's Jazz Lab, I was mildly impressed by the fact that "Free Fare" had an electric guitarist who took a few baby steps into rock n' roll by treating us to a couple of all too short solos. I was nonetheless impressed enough by them to come back later in the evening and pay one dollar to see their entire hour and a half set that their 6th period performance was merely a taster of, and in fairness, without the faculty breathing down their necks, they did stretch out a little bit.

Interestingly, page 24 of the 75 Paragon is devoted to what was the very first assembly of that school year (and one which I missed, I hasten to add). It was the appearance of a "Rock Group" from Florida called "First Gear," who looked so much like Free Fare it's uncanny. Yes! As the photos on page 24 bear out, they had two horn players, something that was that much more uncool in 1974. At least Free Fare could have claimed to be riding the last wave of the Chicago, Blood, Sweat and Tears fueled brass-rock explosion, even if most guys my age never identified with that stuff in the first place. Surely by the end of my freshman year, it must have seemed as if the public school system were attempting (against every fiber of my being) to convince me that brass instruments had a place in all forms of music.

However, recent amazing tales of the national and international rock acts that played at surrounding high schools have convinced me that whoever was booking the bands at Oakton was better suited for employ at Oakton elementary school. I still find this hard to believe, but Madison High actually hosted Dutch prog legends Focus, whose music was about 6 inches over my head at the time. It would be years after becoming a full-fledged music snob before I would be able to fully take them in. I won't get any closer to looking a gift horse in the mouth. Free Fare came to my school to entertain and that's exactly what they did, which is more than I can say for my 6ᵗʰ period teachers.

GANZERAREUX AZZIAMEKIASSA

AKA Tom Henry, "Ganzer" (as we called him) bears the distinction of being the last person to wear the ceremonial underwear and be formally christened as a loon. It's perfectly OK to be a tad after the fact when you're from a small town like Punxsutawney, and as the most promising discovery of Tonny's 21 month stay there, Ganzer's lack of a rush to cast his inner child to the wind would have been greatly appreciated here in Northern Virginia.

At some point during our junior year, Tonny began bringing up Tom Henry's name in his written and telephone correspondence. The first real indication that we might have another loon on our hands came with a cassette tape Tonny mailed to me containing a few songs he had recorded with Henry. With such instant classics as "I Met Her in a Hog Trough," and "Football Frank,", and Tom Henry's accompaniment on electric guitar and backing vocals, I was forced to give some serious thought to this Henry character.

Tom Henry's principal loon qualifier (and according to Tonny, the very thing that defined him as a person) was his tendency to over-exaggerate his past and present successes, both in sports and with the fairer sex. Henry's claims didn't exactly jibe with Tonny's eyewitness accounts, but the more ludicrous Henry's claims would be (as humorously related by Tonny), the more convinced I was that Henry would make a colorful addition to our ranks. In fact, both Henry and I had been so predisposed to the idea of his induction into the Insanist movement that when I arrived in Punxsutawney for my two week stay there in June of 1974, his donning of the ceremonial underwear and recital of the insanist oath were mere formalities.

Meeting Tom Henry was like meeting someone I already knew, unlike Tonny's other big insanist build-up Al Early, who didn't seem at all like the person Tonny had described. Henry was so eager to be a part of the movement that I christened him "Ganzerareux Azziamekiassa" during our very first meeting. There must be something in the air up in those Pennsylvania hills, because I had never encountered such a gun-ho attitude in a convert before.

My vacation in Punx'y was marked by a number of follies that featured Ganzer. One was our famous rat hunt described in detail later in this book under the "Rats" entry. Another was Ganzer's participation in the filming of "The Hand," which you will be reading about shortly. And of course, some sort of recording session was destined to occur. At one point, Tonny and I found ourselves over at Ganzer's house. I distinctly recall the rust red carpet in Ganzer's room and the fact that Mott the Hoople's "All the Young Dudes" was on his turntable. I'm sure that the idea of a session utilizing Ganzer's talents on the electric guitar greatly appealed to me, and I'm sure it was due in part to my insistence on making a recording that the four of us (Ganzer, his brother Rick, Tonny and I) soon found ourselves in Ganzer's basement rehearsing a number that he and I had sort of whipped up on the spot. It was called "The Woman in My Death," and featured Ganzer on electric guitar, myself on percussion and lead vocals, and Rick and Tonny on percussion. 2 or 3 more improvised numbers were recorded, but after the semi-composed (and rather lengthy) The Woman in My Death, the session disintegrated into unfocused entropy. The tape has disappeared with time, and so the only way I have of assessing the musical value of this recording session is my memory of the session itself.

After my 2 weeks in Punxsutawney, any subsequent correspondence I had with Ganzer was through the mail. I still have in my possession a letter from Ganzer wherein he claims to "Have been trapped and caged by the female species in the personage of one Debbie. All I see is the old $ sign quickly fading out of my sight." He goes on to state his plans for going completely berserk in approximately two weeks from the time the letter was written, saying "It has the possibility of being the greatest one man exhibition of complete mental loss in the history of lunacy." His letter ends in a rousing Tonnian fashion, with the words "Remain Insane" written in large letters. Despite the relief that came with seeing the loon spirit alive and well during the later quarter of 1974, nearer to the end of my senior year, it was more than I could do to match Ganzer's enthusiasm, and so we lost touch.

Strangely, Ganzer would come back into the picture 2 years later in the winter of 1977. The rough draft of a letter I mailed to Ganzer in February of 77 under the letter head of "BIOLA" speaks of the revivalist mood that Tonny and I were in during this period, and as such, is quite an artifact. It was both a statement of our intention to foment a resurgence in the Insanist movement and an attempt to bring Ganzer back into the fold. I seem to recall that Ganzer was having girl troubles around this time, and that this is what may have prompted the letter. You see, January - March 1977 was the first period where Tonny and I both had girlfriends simultaneously. I was dating Cindy Martens and Tonny was seeing Romina at the time. The significance of this is borne out in this part of the letter:

Since we have now conquered that adolescent mountain, and have attained feminine companionship, it would seem an appropriate time to resume our battle with the forces of sanity, to which only partial success was achieved by the previous movement. BIOLA (the BobTonnian Institute of Loon Attics) was formed on February 18, 1977, and consecrated to the goal of reuniting and preserving the brotherhood of loons, which had crumbled under the nefarious circumventions of the Sanes.

Nothing much became of this particular insanist revival except to raise Tonny and I's spirits to the level where it was obvious that dwelling on the past would always make the trials (or the boredom) of the present a little easier to handle. Ganzer came to visit Tonny at some point in the late 70's, and the three of us dined together at Pico's restaurant in Fairfax before the last loon, Ganzerareux Azziamekiassa, went riding off into the sunset.

GARY GARLAND

Now here's an unusual story. Gary Garland was a rather mouthy ruffian who was in my 8th grade class at Luther Jackson intermediate. While I have no memories of Gary having the affront to get up in my face, I do recall that his brusque manner left no love lost between the two of us. When our paths crossed again at Oakton sometime during our freshman year, I recognized the face and the voice of Gary Garland, but his body seemed to have been taken over by one of Christ's apostles. That's right! Gary had become a Jesus freak - with an emphasis on the word "Freak." Even later on, during our junior year, when Gary and I became friends, I still couldn't get over the change in him.

While Gary was arguably the most outspoken Christian Oakton had ever had, he was very much his own version of a Christian, choosing the role of the outsider, and eventually engendering my respect to the point where I found myself in the unforeseen role of seeking out the fellowship of Gary Garland. While Gary seemed to be on good terms with the Kim Koan's and Gayle Alcorn's of Oakton's Christian establishment, you won't find him in any of the revelations club yearbook pictures. You would have been more apt to find Gary at a mall, or in the hallways of Oakton High, preaching the gospel of Revelations at a socially unacceptable volume, which I witnessed him doing on at least one occasion, much to my amazement.

Despite the generally positive change in the direction of Gary's life, his already formed personality could not be contained, and this gave Oakton the contradiction it will recall as Gary Garland. He still listened to his Black Sabbath records, still cursed like a sailor, and had let his hair grow to a length that more resembled the wise-cracking downstart he had left behind at Luther Jackson than it did anything I saw at any of the revelations club functions. This made Gary appear more Christ-like, which may have been his intention. In some ways, Gary had become, at least in appearance, even more of a ruffian. I wouldn't have blamed Kim Koan for not inviting him to any of her club parties, but the truth of the matter was that Gary had the confront and the aplomb to go out in the rain and do Christianity's dirty work.

My clearest memory of Gary is one that exemplifies both the courage and the craziness of the path he had chosen to walk down. One night, Gary called me up to invite me to join him for an evening service at this church on Braddock Road. Not having anything else going on, and still at an age where a Christian girlfriend seemed an attractive option, I agreed to go along, and so Gary drove over and picked me up. All through the service, and the car ride over there and back, the strangeness of the event was overwhelming. The defining element in the evening was the fact that Gary knew no one at this church. No one invited him there. He just read in the paper that there was going to be a service there that night, and he decided to go. Now picture this! He was a high school junior. If he had followed the path he was on at Luther Jackson, he'd have been driving to parties, or football games, or over to pick up his girlfriend. If he had been looking through the paper, it would have been to find out what bands were coming in concert, or what movies were showing, instead of following whatever impulse was leading him down this lonely road to the house of the lord. It's difficult to imagine anyone, much less Gary Garland, making such a solitary commitment at the age of 16. I suppose it was fitting that it was me who accompanied him that night.

The last time I would see Gary was at graduation. There's a picture of the two of us standing together, with Gary drawing attention to a button he was wearing. Though it's too small to make out in the photograph, I don't have to know what the button says to know that right up to our last goodbye, Gary was still crusading for Christ. If Gary ever reaches the age of senility, I can imagine him as one of those bearded long-in-the-tooth street corner evangelists, babbling on about how the day of judgement is nigh. Senility? What am I talking about? I can see him doing that now. Rock on Gary!

GAYLE ALCORN
A rather attractive, well endowed strawberry blonde who was a casual acquaintance of mine throughout my junior and senior year, owing to her friendship with CA and my brief involvement with the revelations club. Gayle was a devout Christian who demonstrated a concern for my soul on at least two occasions. As long as I live, I will not forget the look on Gayle's face when I told her I was going over to the other side. Her jaw dropped and with a horrified look, she exclaimed – "Bob, No!" It was in Mrs. Heeter's English class, and Denise Watson, another CA coadjutor who was sitting directly in front of me, turned around and looked at me with a wry grin that I shall also never forget. Denise, I believe, either sensed my lack of seriousness, or realized that humor was the only thing a third party could derive from witnessing such an exchange.

It was not my intention to be cruel to Gayle or to purposefully upset her, but the war between good and evil was a touchy subject for me at that time. I had drifted away from the revelations club, which is what prompted Gayle to engage me in Mrs. Heeter's class. Even before the great disillusionment of December 1974, the revelations club party at Kim Koan's house on that steamy spring day earlier in 1974 should have convinced me that I did not belong with these people. The party was, apart from myself, 100% female, and there was such an air of sweetness and light that it was absolutely twilight-zonish. If ever there was a party that screamed for the intrusion of a good loud fart, it was this one, and I was all too happy to leave, breathing a huge sigh of relief upon doing so.

Any serious interest I had in Christianity lasted only as long as I remained sold on the idea that Christianity could help me solve the riddle of good and evil. My primary reason for involving myself with Christian youth groups was to possibly find more truth seekers like myself, and on the more practical side of things, a non-judgmental girlfriend. The fact that I had found neither, but HAD found a certain amount of passive rejection, did not exactly leave me responsive to the soul saving pleas of a CA coadjutor.

Also, consciously or unconsciously, I knew by this time that the rumors afloat in the school about me were serving me to some degree, at least to the degree of warding off undesirables. Curiously, with the exception of my last will and testament that was published at the end of my senior year, this one ambiguous sentence spoken to fend off Gayle Alcorn was the only instance where I actually said something that might have supported these rumors. They were otherwise based solely on my black clothing and the vivid imaginations of certain students still in the throes of Excorcist mania.

Though I will always remember her best as being CA coadjutor no.1, Gayle was accorded her own notoriety by Emmette and Elmo, who came to refer to her as "Peterson 2," or with mock affection – "Petie 2." Gayle was in fact the inspiration for Elmo's song "Peterson 2," in which Elmo wrote woefully of Karen Peterson's transfer to Chantilly high in the great 1973 exodus, leaving Emmette and Elmo (temporarily) without a Peterson syndrome subject to study.

The original moved, who else could we find
Along came Gayle, strong and stable mind

Look ahead to the Peterson syndrome entry for further details, suffice to say here that for a time, Emmette and Elmo's scientific fascination switched from Karen Peterson to Gayle Alcorn, and though I knew and liked Gayle personally, I of course played along, calling her Petie 2 in their presence. Despite having picked the wrong time in my life to approach me as a Christian, she is remembered fondly.

GOOD MOURNING

A slightly morbid, but more versatile and less time-restrictive greeting co-created by Howard Koretz and myself (after all, one could mourn contentedly any time of day or night). Howard's dark humor was all over this one, and to hear him bid me a "Good Mooourning" in that low creepy Boris Karloff voice of his on the phone recently was the tonic I needed to deal with a world that now seems to take itself way too seriously.

GRADUATION

June 7th 1975 was a magical day, it truly was. It was a beautiful sunny day, albeit a bit windy, and a picture perfect day for having a graduation ceremony at Wolf Trap Farm Park. It was, amid all the pomp and circumstance, also an opportunity for EAT and I to make one last statement. EAT's presence at my graduation was due to the family obligation he had of witnessing the graduation of his cousins, Carole and Gerri Lay. As EAT was transferring to McLean high school the following

year, it was only fitting that EAT was also present with me to make a final impression together. And we did not waste the opportunity to leave a contradictory impression on those who thought the black clothing we wore was full of dark significance. Just for shits and grins, we decided to wear all white, as if to suggest that we weren't just leaving Oakton, we were ascending to heaven. And sure enough, as we were milling around outside before the ceremony, stray comments to the effect of "Look! They're wearing white now," would intermittently disrupt our conversation. Following the comment back to its source would always reveal a pair (or group) of females completely unfamiliar to either EAT or I, underscoring the point that we hadn't yet left Oakton High.

Another thing that makes graduation day stick out in my mind is all the people I would see for the last time, all the memory trails that would lead up to, and stop at this one event. I would see Jim Allewelt, Gary Garland, and Mitchell Robinson there for the last time. I will surely take to the grave my treasured last glimpse of Doris Dick's angelic smile.

If it hadn't yet struck me what was coming to an end here, one final opportunity presented itself to honor all those members of the Insanist movement (as well as later acquaintances like Ray Denk and Mitchell Robinson, who embodied its spirit). At some point during the ceremony proper, something was said that cued the graduates to the traditional cheer and the tossing of the caps. But while I tossed my maroon colored cap in the air, what came down in my lap instead was the white cap of a female graduate. Being as white better fitted EAT and I's adopted theme for the day, I decided to wear the white female cap as I crossed the stage to take my diploma. Though I did not receive as much applause as most of the students who crossed that stage to receive their diploma, I do recall Howard Pritchett giving me a fist in the air and an "Alright Bob!" as I stepped off the stage, as if I had just scored the goal that put our team ahead. I guess graduating from high school was an accomplishment of sorts, given the amount of F's that appeared on my report cards.

Above all of my teachers, I was happy to see and have the chance to thank Mr. Wargo at my graduation. I had Mr. Wargo as a teacher for various classes my freshman, junior, and senior years, but it was the fact that Mr. Wargo passed me in his government class despite my flunking the exam that made my "Thank You" and my handshake a little more heartfelt. I've always had the feeling that Mr. Wargo, like a few of my other teachers at OHS, knew that I was intelligent beyond my poor grades. Graduating from high school gives one an appetite, as I can attest to from the lunch my family and I had at the Roy Rogers restaurant at Tyson's Corner on route 7 before the ceremony, where I downed five roast beef sandwiches. Times were good.

GUTS THEATRE
Back in January of 1971, when Tonny and I discovered the joys of recording songs and skits, a twisted brand of juvenile vaudeville was created. But as any audience we would even pretend to be addressing was a listening one, our skits tended to reflect our limited knowledge of the golden age of radio that preceded us. My "It was a cold night" series, for instance, played off of what little I knew about old detective shows. After leading in with "It was a cold night" in my best low narrative gumshoe

voice, and perhaps a few details about a blonde or a dead body, the skit would usually degenerate into farcical Follies style mayhem pretty fast. My recovery technique was to simply go back to "It was a cold night."

Apart (though not completely) from our obvious radio show parodies was the completely original "Guts Theatre." A Guts Theatre performance appeared in our very first recording session, and we knew instantly that at least from the standpoint of self-entertainment, we had a hit on our hands. The basic premise of Guts Theatre was anything that would lead the slavering narrator on a mad romp through the bloody guts and slimy organs of whatever character happened to pop into his head at that instance. Strangely enough, one of my first victims was "Rodney Pumpernickel," whose miraculous recovery only weeks later would allow him to star in "The Undersea World of Rodney Pumpernickel." Some of my other victims included Frederic Von Poopindorf, John Filabarr (the bartender), John Finch, and Larry Laharinx (the sphinx), although they were more props for my rants about guts than actual characters in a play.

Before I continue to define what Guts Theatre was, I should clarify by stating what it was not. It was not intended to be, nor was it even inspired by, horror of any kind. If any effect was intended upon the would-be listener (and I'm not sure there was any), it would have only been the most puerile attempt to gross them out. Unlike most of our skits, which established a serious premise and then deteriorated into total silliness through our character interaction (or even the few like The Undersea World of Rodney Pumpernickel, which were almost entirely serious), Guts Theatre was, from the first to the final word, a complete parody of itself. The gruesome subject matter (as well as Tonny and I's apparent lack of anatomical knowledge) made it all the more humorous. With almost every guts rant (I hesitate to call them performances) concluding with either Tonny or I taking the victims guts and pouring them all over our nude bodies, it was evident that the same muse that had inspired the summer camp smash hit "Great Big Gobs of Greasy Grimy Gofer Guts" had a hand in Guts Theatre.

Actually, a great deal of time was spent during Guts Theatre performances giving grotesquely lurid advertisements for up and coming performances with such titles as "Open Gut." Bear in mind that as an early 1971 British Insipids era phenomenon, Guts Theatre was not only nonsense, it was tasteless nonsense. A year later, in the spring of 1972, I would revive Guts Theatre in a solo performance that closed the book on Guts Theatre, while at the same time moving it as far as it would ever get from the nonsensical tastelessness of its heyday.

Whatever possessed me to attempt my own version of Guts Theatre so long after the fact is beyond me. Even stranger (and just as much of a step back in time) is the fact that I give the performance in the style of my old It was a Cold Night skit, even opening the piece with the line – "It was a neat-o cold night," delivered in that same pensive detective voice of mine. Now, despite the fact that I'm clearly mixing genre's here, and unlike any previous Guts Theatre performance, Neat-O Guts follows our 1972 trend by being semi-composed, it does have all the ingredients (if not the spirit) of the original Guts Theatre. That and the fact that Tonny was kind enough to type it up for me make its inclusion here essential. As one must really hear Guts Theatre to really get the sense (or the nonsense) of it, its inclusion may also fall short of explaining itself.

Neat-O Guts

It was a neat-o cold night. The smell of guts was in the air. The stench of rotting bodies was everywhere. The smell attracted guts fiends from neighboring towns and villages. One was me. Guts McCoy they called me at the old school. I was the number 1 guts consumer in all Devonshire. I was running a stroke of bad luck until that neat-o cold night when I met Randy Rectal. I followed him for awhile until I couldn't stand it any more. The delight of ooking my hands through greasy organs and watching the blood fill through his blechy cavity that I couldn't bear it any more. I just had to have his guts. Oaah! Ha! Ha! Ha! Meaough! With this I took my dagger and threw it into his eyeball. He screamed, "oh," and said to me, "Is this yours?" I said "Why yes! Pulling the dagger from his empty socket and licking the optic materials which oozed over the knife blade. Blood gushed from his socket into my mouth. I tried to get every drop, but it was futile, as the blood came out in a spraying fashion. I squeezed his neck, forcing the blood to gush faster, gush, gush, gush. Finally, after his head had shriveled to the size of a prune, I plummeted the knife into his butt."

Guts fiend gets the urge. The urge grows until the fiend makes some Poe-ish maniacal pronouncement to the effect of "I can't stand it anymore!" A flurry of Insipid era terms such as "Blechy cavity," and "Optic materials" are bandied about. Yep! All the ingredients are there.

HADINAHO
Another loon expression brought into heavy usage throughout the 1973 Elmoian era. It was just another solidarity affirming way of saying "Well, hide your hoe."

THE HAND

Tonny and I's ersatz attempt at a horror film, and another fond memory of my two week stay in Punxsutawney. While the bulk of our movies were filmed at Margate Manor during the spring and summer of 1973, Tonny still had his super 8 camera when I went to visit him in Punx'y in the summer of 1974, so we decided to try our luck at something different. We decided to attempt a horror film, built around a laughably unoriginal premise entitled "The Hand." The scope of the production itself was further limited by the fact that the entire cast and crew numbered only four, Tonny, myself, Ganzer and his brother Rick.

The four of us walked up to Punxsutawney High's football field to begin work on the film. The first scene showed Ganzer jogging around the outer track and then suddenly collapsing dead in a fit of over-acting. The second scene showed Rick Henry's hand reaching up menacingly from the

adjoining bleachers, intimating the presence of some disembodied (and all too familiar) evil force. By the next scene, Tonny was experimenting with camera angles and I was brainstorming right and left on possible directions in plot development. There was definitely the sense (at this point at least) that we were more than half-serious about this project. The next scene showed me approaching the field carrying a briefcase (the significance of which I've long forgotten, save to say that it was to be revealed later in the movie). About halfway across the field, I suddenly became agitated and disoriented, eventually collapsing into motionlessness. Once again, Tonny pans to the bleachers and the insidious hand makes another appearance.

This was as far as we got, and while Tonny and I would always regard The Hand as an unfinished work, one has to wonder, with Ganzer and I dead, Rick Henry playing the part of the Hand, and Tonny operating the camera, how much further could we have taken this? Our ideas HAD taken shape far beyond this point. This much I do remember. As the conflicting schedules of the Henry's and other factors brought production to a halt at this point, I feel nothing short of regressive hypnosis or returning to the Punx'y-High football field with Tonny and Ganzer would jar loose the memory of what we had intended The Hand to be. Whatever it was, I'm sure that our ideas exceeded our resources, and the realization of this hit us shortly after the first days filming. The film itself (or what there was of it) has since been lost in Tonny's travels around the world.

MR. HERNDON

The only member of Oakton's administration who was visible enough to be able to acknowledge many of the school's students (myself included) in the halls by name. Mr. Herndon came to be known, feared, and respected as the school's enforcer. I honestly believe that he inherited this dirty work by virtue of his thin wiry build, which made him most suitable for chasing down truants and breaking up pot parties in the adjoining wooded areas. In fact, Mr. Herndon won himself quite a reputation for being able to run after (and overtake) students who were a third his age. As I did not partake of any activity on school property that required me to seek the privacy of the woods, I thankfully never got to see this side of Mr. Herndon.

I personally liked the man, and I occasionally went out of my way to engage him in the halls. I found the dry wit through which he filtered many of his observations endearing and reminiscent of both of my grandfathers in equal parts - one part folksy, the other more urbane. Despite his thinness of stature, Mr. Herndon had a retired navy man look about him that would never allow one to forget his job there was to maintain a standard of discipline. My only dealing with him in this regard was to seek him out weekly, and report to him that I had once again skipped my Russian class (a practice during the latter half of my senior year necessitated by my desire to continue doing my radio show). I would usually approach him outside his office near the center stairwell, and simply say "Mr. Herndon, I skipped Russian again," to which he would calmly reply "OK Robert, detention." Then I would cheerfully go to the detention room upstairs and make use of my time there by writing lyrics, poetry, or even a little VOT mapping.

Now I'm sure that handing out detentions was one of Mr. Herndon's more mundane tasks, but I always sensed a smile of incredulity just beneath his thinly stoic veneer, as if his job did not allow him to react inappropriately to how easy I was making his job. He was so used to seeking out (if not actually running after) students to give them detention. It must have struck him as odd that finally one of those students was now seeking him out to volunteer for detention out of conscience. It was, in fact, out of some strange sense of duty that I did so, for shortly after disappearing completely from my 4th period Russian class, I was issued another schedule sheet, which had my 4th period adjusted to show that I was now a teacher's assistant (which I actually was in the context of my radio show). The radio station's administrative head – Mr. Williams, was now listed as my 4th period teacher, underscoring the point that I could have probably coasted through the rest of the year with only that easily explained away "Incomplete" on my report card. I recall that EAT considered my volunteered detentions to be silly and unnecessary, but I nonetheless wanted to keep the whole Russian class affair above board, despite the fact that my true allegiance was to the Queen Viper show.

It was the sudden appearance of Mr. Herndon that cut short the Ray King interview during the final folly on June 3rd 1975. As I was hawking questions at Ray King at the center intersection of the two main hallways, Ray Denk happened to spot Mr. Herndon walking into his office, prompting Ray to guide our little group in that direction. I stood at the doorway to his office and called him out for an interview that turned out to be classic Mr. Herndon. I asked him what he thought of our student body, and whether he considered it particularly "Restless" in comparison to that of surrounding high schools such as Madison or Woodson. His straightfaced reply was "In a word, raunchy." I asked him – "Does this make your job more difficult?" He answered "No, it makes it simpler. Simple predictable results for simple raunchy people." Again, my take on Mr. Herndon was that he was not an innately serious man, though his job demanded that he project a degree of seriousness. On this occasion, he demonstrated an ability to express himself humorously, seriously, and truthfully all in one breath. It's funny, but as I find myself now approaching the age he was back then, the joke that Mr. Herndon was almost good at keeping to himself is finally revealing itself.

HET THE THREAT

The nickname given to Tonny by two of his Punx'y friends - John Lee and Scotty Rigden. It was a good natured ribbing invoked whenever Tonny displayed a pronounced lack of athletic ability.

HOLES IN TRUE TO LIFE FANTASY

Despite being mired in excessive Poe-like gothic mumbo-jumbo and hyper-inflated neo-Shakespearean verbiage, this short story paints a clear picture of where my head was at in February of 1975. The story begins with me sitting alone in my room, listening to the cracks and creeks of my empty house, and as was my want at this age - thinking way too much. Gradually, the extraneous noises of my house begin to take shape and I begin to draw impressions from them until I find myself having a conversation with the devil that only a playwright could make any sense out of.

What fascinates me about this story now is how it captures the convergence point of the two adolescent quandaries that choked the life out of the Insanist movement. The first one was good vs. evil (as personified by God and the Devil), and the second one was to pursue love and marriage over the lure of protecting one's emotional security. Although I had broken from the Christian church in December of 1974, the Christian view of life as a constant battle between good and evil was considerably more difficult to break from. Though I left the church viewing myself as a good guy protagonist caught between these two opposing forces, my view of myself as a social outcast was thematically more aligned with the story of the Devil being cast out of heaven. The overwhelming feeling I received during the last church service I attended in December of 74 that the pastor and a couple of theretofore friends of mine were casting me out of the church only furthered this thematic alignment. Add to this the rumors of my involvement with Satanism that were cycling back to me around this period and you have one grade A adolescent quandary.

But the real indecision over which side of the fence I belonged came with the bitterness over the rejections of Cheri, Damaris and Peggy. I felt as if I were being cast out of the Garden of Eden, not by God, but by Eve. I began to feel betrayed by the very romantic visions of love and marriage that had led me through my childhood like a dangling carrot. Throughout the story, the Devil is trying to persuade me to abandon these visions altogether, as in this wonderfully infernal passage -

Senior prom indeed! I know not why you waste your mentality on such indescrepancies when I have offered you title and distinction as Lord of the Rats, to command the creatures of my service and liken unto me in the honor of my office.

Aside from my song lyrics, which were concise by necessity, the other writings of my late high school period were fraught with rambling circumlocutions, and Holes in True to Life Fantasy was no exception. It stands alone, however, as being the first opportunity I gave to my dark side to express its rising doubts over this normal life of marriage and a family I had planned out. I may have over-dramatized the Devil a bit, but after we get into it, it's amazing how the story takes on the form of a dialogue between two of my own viewpoints. When contradicted, the Devil becomes testy and authoritative, and his constant referral to himself as "Your Earthly Father" suggests that this might have been my stronger half giving the guidance that my weaker (or indecisive) half was seeking. When he attempts to gain my trust by saying things like – "You know well that I have adopted numerous socially-outcasted unfortunates as proof that I accept that which man rejects," he sounds like the part of me that always accepted myself unconditionally.

The flaw of the story, as seen through hindsight, is that I end up chasing the Devil away without realizing what I had uncovered, as if the point of every story must be to lead up to an obligatory battle between good and evil, with good reigning triumphant. Although I end up choosing love over bitterness, any attempt to hide a portion of myself was done so in order to gain acceptance from a person or institution resembling one that had previously spit me out like a mouthful of sour milk. In the story, it is the Devil who is willing to except me then and there as-is, but I persist in my faith in a magical self-transformation under the healing powers of love. Without denying the existence of those magical healing powers, the unwritten moral of the story remains:

1. Love is Ok, as long as you do not depend on receiving it from others.
2. Companionship is OK too, as long as you do not depend on females and church groups to provide it.
3. That little voice in your head that sounds like the Devil just might be common sense talking.

Yes! The story has holes, but I prefer to think of it as merely living up to its title.

HOWARD KORETZ (see SASATIOUS VON CANON)

HUNK

A winsome elfin brunette named Susan Clark, who was the apple of EAT's eye, and a shadow that would haunt him for much of his stay at Oakton. Hunk was EAT's CA, a pretty pom pom wielding member of the cougar corps (of which CA was also a member). Although Hunk's involvement with such activities as the choral department and the cougar corps drew constant comparisons between her and CA, other factors suggest a Hunk-

Peggy comparison may be a more logical one. EAT's interest in Hunk, like mine in CA, dated from the fall of 1973. Both ran concurrent time lines, making comparisons between the two inevitable. Both were the fair-skinned brunette in a cheerleader's uniform that we couldn't have. Both would shadow us for most of 1974, until the color of their hair became the predominant color of clothing worn by Eat and myself - black. Where they differ is that the tragedy of CA was in what could have been, but not necessarily what should have been. Although I will always feel blessed for having gotten to know Cheri Allen, I can now see how such a relationship was all the better for not having taken place. Peggy was a different matter altogether.

It is the tragedies of what SHOULD have been that leave holes in men's souls. Hunk, like Peggy, was a tragedy of what should have been. At least I feel this was true from EAT's perspective. EAT knew Hunk, and there may have been a point where they had come close to having a relationship. Hunk, a vivacious intelligent sophomore beauty, was well on her way to greater popularity and greater involvement in school activities by the fall of 1974, while EAT and I dwelled evermore amongst the shadows of WOHS. The widening gap between expanding and contracting spheres of influence precipitated Hunk's rejection of EAT on November 2 1974. This single event sent EAT and I on a five month long emotional roller coaster where some form of shit was hitting the fan almost daily. By late January 1975, the VOT had been identified and many of its members linked to Hunk. Indeed, at one point after Karen Cockrell's rejection of EAT in late February, all roads seemed to wind their way back to Hunk.

Hunk's appearance on the scene was innocent enough, and in fact, EAT first brought her up to me as a loon prospect, citing the following story as evidence. EAT had apparently been lunching with Hunk in the cafeteria, when she suddenly stood up, threw her roll across the cafeteria and shouted - "That's It! I've had it with these school lunches." She then stormed out of the cafeteria in what I'm guessing was a mock fit of anger. I agreed with EAT, and although nothing came of it, I thought it was enough of an admirable insane act that I recounted it to Tonny in a letter shortly afterward. In my senior last will and testament, I left EAT a "Hunk of my crow hatred," a rather oblique parting shot to the young lady who left EAT with a pain that by this time I knew all too well. The pain of still having a piece of yourself attached to something that should have been.

IGGY POP'S BIRTHDAY

I remember thumbing through the albums at the Pickett shopping center Giant Music and being instantly struck by the cover shot of Iggy Pop on the Iggy and the Stooges "Raw Power" LP. I remember turning the album

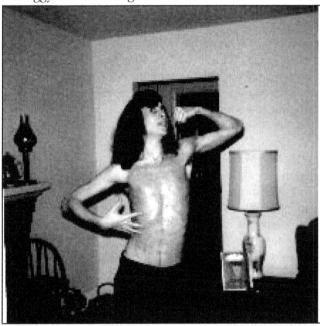

cover over, looking at the photos on the back cover, and thinking to myself "Man! That is one evil looking fucker." The cover photos, along with song titles like "Death Trip, and the fact that the album was mixed by my hero at the time - David Bowie, made its immediate purchase essential. I would date this purchase as sometime in the summer of 1973. By the fall of 73, Iggy Pop, on the strength of the Raw Power album, had grown to iconic stature among Elmo and I, and as well with EAT shortly thereafter.

Curiously, Howard Koretz developed a more unlikely fascination with the "Ig," which manifested itself rather amusingly during the course of our junior year music class. Apparently, Howard had decided that Iggy Pop's birthday should be celebrated as a national holiday, and upon entering Mr. Curtis' music class, he would express this desire by writing on the blackboard how many days were left until Iggy Pop's birthday. As the school year progressed, and the actual date (which was sometime in late April) was approaching, Howard got a bit more technical in his daily ritual by listing how many shopping days there were left until Iggy Pop's birthday.

If our classmates thought of Howard as a trifle odd, I'm sure his persistence in this practice did little to dissuade them, though most seemed to view it with a level of good-natured amusement. Mr. Curtis, who was greeted with this message every day upon entering room 145 for his 5th period class, would probably have an easier time recalling the countdown to Iggy Pop's birthday than he would recalling any of the faces and names of the students in that class.

As Howard had done such an excellent job of making an event out of the arrival of Iggy Pop's birthday, when the day did finally arrive, EAT, Elmo and I decided to celebrate at EAT's house by listening to Stooges records and smearing peanut butter all over our naked torso's (as Iggy was known for doing in concert). While I was the only one of the three of us who took the observance of this holy day seriously (or unseriously in this case) enough to actually take my shirt off and coat my top half with the ceremonial peanut butter, a good time was had by all, and that's about all one needs to do to appease the gods of rock 'n' roll.

THE INSANIST MOVEMENT

OK! You've read so much about this thing called the Insanist movement. What was it exactly? - you might be wondering. Though your best answer will come from reading this book through 2 or 3 times, I will say here that it was (or became) my attempt to preserve our camaraderie by figuratively institutionalizing that element which kept us young, which had been pre-defined as - our insanity. Even when it was just Tonny, Emmette and myself, I began referring to our little group as a movement in order to make it sound more substantial, as if we now owed it to this bigger thing to remain friends. Calling something a movement instantly makes an institution out of an idea, but beyond this initial trumping, little conscious planning went into the development of the movement's personality, as defined by its members. A limited amount of planning did go into expansion. Conversion attempts, follies, and recording sessions all required some degree of planning just to get them going, before the elements of improvisation would be allowed to take their course.

What we called "Insanity" grew out of that element in Tonny and I's friendship we had identified as "Insipidity." We were in the 8th grade at the time, and in the 8th grade, one is not apt to plan much of anything save new ways of having fun. Marrying whimsy and frivolity with mock decorum brought us things like the golden hoe - the symbol of imperial insanity, the underwear over the head initiation ceremony, the eulogizing of Areteus the Cappodocian, and the oracles (the Barnacle Clavicle and the Kaisey Module). It was a fraternal order that uncharacteristically insisted upon the individuality of its members. In the context of the movement, individualism and insanity were synonymous. We could have just as easily called it "The Individualist Movement," but that would have been a presumptuous declaration of what we already were by the scantest of design, whereas the word "Insanity" defined the quality of our deeds, words and actions, as well as freeing us from the restrictive bonds of logic.

Individual and group are mutually exclusive terms. There has to be some degree of commonality in a group of individuals. I suppose our commonality was our sense of the absurd. If I had to define the movement in a single sentence, I'd probably call it a haphazard group of young people who lived for the thrill of the ridiculous.

IN THE GAME TODAY

A baseball expression adopted by Emmette and put into common usage during the 1971-73 period by Emmette, Tonny and I. Basically, if anything or anyone was thought to be quantitatively or qualitatively superior in any way, that person or thing was said to be the biggest (or the best) "In the game today." An example of how this term might have been used back then by me on the phone to Tonny is – "CA is the biggest beauxkya in the game today." Emmette, during one of his Wagnerian rants, might have said to me "Birgit Nilsson is the greatest Brunhilda in the game today." The "Game" he would be referring to would of course be Wagnerian opera, and not baseball.

The formalized loonspeak of the early 70's was rife with baseball terminology. "Laid one down" was used if someone had (or was suspected of having) just passed wind, as in – "Bob, Did you just lay one down?" "We have got a ballgame!" was our enthusiastic exclamation whenever the condition of becoming a game entered into whatever we were looking at. Or put more simply, we "Had a ballgame" whenever something interesting occurred that had the potential of putting us into a game situation. I wrote a note to CA, but if Tonny had been present when I received her reply, my first words to him would have likely been – "We've got a ballgame." In this regard, our commentaries on the events of our lives mirrored that of the play by play announcer giving his commentary on the episodic life of a baseball game. The term "In the game today" was our tongue-in-cheek way of addressing the reality that even inanimate objects, by their placement and position, could become pieces in the game of life.

JEFF LONG

Although being the irreverent but brainy sort that would cinch his friendship with Kaiser, I don't think Jeff knew quite what to make of me. Despite frequenting the loon lunch table, I think he believed me to be a bit too left of center to become involved in any group that I was a major figure in. Personality-wise, Jeff Long had a lot in common with Jeff Kaiser. So why then did Jeff Long refuse to even confess to insanity, while Kaiser was so "in" from the beginning of his development that no confession was necessary? The answer lies not in any differences in personality, but in a difference of alliances. Put simply, Jeff Long was a non-athlete whose thirst for involvement led him into the student government, and then into maintaining propriety for the sake of his alliances, whereas Kaiser's lack of alliances led him to us. I do not speak disparagingly of Jeff Long in this regard, but it has shortened the length of an entry that should have been at least as long as Kaiser's.

In my junior yearbook, Jeff wrote – "To the biggest rat I know, from a cat." Aside from being a rather off-handed way of expressing himself as a cat lover, Jeff alludes to having lived through a number of my preachings on the greatness of rats. Though primarily a sophomore year crusade of mine, apparently I was preaching rodentia superiority well into my junior year, for moving my eyes from Jeff's signature to the opposite page, I find Joe Gorsuch's drawing of a rat next to the words "Joe Cool." Jeff signed my senior yearbook with another one liner that encapsulated the general perception of me that many peripheral figures had – "To my favorite vampire, good luck." That I was his "favorite" vampire speaks of the good terms that Jeff and I remained on during our four years at Oakton. That his signature appears in both of these books is also a testimony to his omnipresence. However, our mutual friend Kaiser would remain our strongest tie. Jeff Long was not an involvement junkie like busybody Doug Hart, but he had spread his contacts thin enough that he and I would remain just casual acquaintances.

JIM ALLEWELT

Part of the A lunch triumvirate which also included Elmo and Morty Sneaky. With a format that made him A lunch's answer to Doctor Sal, Jim was something much closer to Kaiser's ideal. He was a super nice guy, but his reaction to EAT and I's format revealed how musically challenged he was. Even at this age, I realized how understandable this was given what he had probably been exposed to up until this time.

JOCKS

One thing that could always be counted on was that in the locker room, on the playing field, and at parties, jocks would always behave like jocks. This has led to the misnomer that this is what all of them are like, all of the time, and at Oakton High, that just wasn't the case. Oh! I would agree that in their element, they tended to live up to their stereotypes, but one has to consider that there were pressures as well as advantages to being on the upper rung of the social ladder, inner and external pressures to act a certain way. Once out of their element, surprising glimpses of humanity could be seen.

Oakton did have a few quintessential jocks. Thor Kritsky, John Lee, and Curtis Jackman come to mind as prime examples. But moving away from this small group, the picture of the rank and file jock gets fuzzier. You had your high IQ weight lifter types like Don Frank. Then you had this bizarre longhaired pot smoking jock/freak hybrid (of which my friend Jeff Bolton claims to have been one of). Then you had your cocky class-clown types like Ray King. Then you had your small of stature third string more enthusiasm than athletic ability sports nerds. And you even had your total goofball types like Mark Watts, who on a good day could have cut the mustard as an insanist. I could go on here, even subcategorizing by different sports, and the only thing that would be getting any clearer would be the distance between the locker room stereotypes and the classroom realities.

Oh! I know what you're wondering. Why is this guy defending jocks? Wasn't he harassed by them in high school? Well OK! Let's take a look at that. Ask me that question a few years ago and my knee-jerk reaction would have been – "Yes they did! Those God damn jocks." But I really would have been answering for all the people who've inundated me with high school horror stories over the years.

Looking back on my own experience, I'm impelled to separate the harassment I received into two distinct categories. Firstly, there were the open challenges to fight, as in "Come on Karnes, let's fight." This was mainly an 8th and 9th grade phenomenon, exhibited by such non-jocks as Robert Beach, Liam Mcgranahan, and Bob Deitz (the latter two of which would become good customers of mine at the Penguin Feather after high school), and jocks by association like Ray King. The second form of harassment was the obligatory locker room/gym class taunting I had to endure, but even that came primarily from toady blowhards like Jim Nichols and Mark Crenshaw, and not true jocks. The only jock I can remember really giving it to me good was Bob Matich, and that was in my freshman year gym class. From that point on, he did not say word one to me. Actually! After my sophomore year, and the bane of gym class embarrassment, it became clear that all I had to do was not screw up in some sport or exercise in physical coordination in front of these guys and I was OK. From that point onward, and particularly into my senior year, the world of the Oakton jock seemed progressively further away from my own, as if we were attending two separate schools. The bigger the jock, the further away they seemed, entrenched as they may have been in the demands of their football world.

There's another reason why I'm playing the Devil's advocate for the jock that aside from the truthfulness of everything I've given here so far, has been building up inside of me for some time. All through my years in school, the jock was perceived to be the guy who had the best chance of getting the best girl. Regardless of reality, that's remained the lovelorn teenage guy's major beef against them (though for the record, the guy that landed CA was clearly NOT a jock). Progressively, over the last decade, quite a few of the young ladies I've worked with (some of whom were still in high school) seemed to have a universal disdain for jocks that was rooted not in who the offending jocks were, but in WHAT they were, a lifelong sore spot with me. As I would listen to them go on, the irony of it struck me, and I would ask myself – "Has the world turned completely around on itself?" So much of what was natural is now unnatural, and vice versa. It's apparently fashionable now to look down on jocks or jock stereotypes I should say, as the bulk of this derision seems to come from these ladies intolerance of jocks, and not the other way around.

All this jock bashing has led me to go back and look at my own life experience to find out if the jocks I've known fit these stereotypes. And in the process of doing this, I've been quite surprised to discover that they did not actually fit into their stereotypes as much as I had been predisposed to fit them into those stereotypes.

JOE GORSUCH

The only ruffian to crossover and join the ranks of the loons. His involvement with lunacy was brief but glorious - even participating in a couple of follies. Though never given an insane name, he did don the ceremonial underwear and profess total insanity. The additional spirit of this madcap ruffian at a time when our ranks were approaching double figures made the fall of 1972 a great time to be a loon. Alas! Oakton was a big school, and I would see little of Joe after our sophomore year, though he did reappear in my junior year history class, and may have even participated in a folly or two before disappearing completely. He was the inspiration for my song "To Get My Mind Out of the Gutter."

JOHN FOWLER

Actually a 7th grade friend of mine, who nonetheless may have had some influence in shaping the tenor of the folly. In facial expressions and overall manner, it's uncanny how much like EAT John was, a fact that in and of itself might be sufficient to label John THE prototypical loon. Grade school had conditioned me to look at each school year as a separate time cycle unto itself in the respect that just because someone was your best friend last year wouldn't stop them from treating you like a complete stranger this year. Such was the case again in 8th grade when John Fowler gave me the ol' more-mature-than-thou/I've-outgrown-you shrug off (in front of Tonny, no less). It's literally been in the last couple days that I've thought back on our 7th grade friendship enough to reassess his importance.

Most of the timeline perspective of the Insanist movement in this book stretches back to my 7th grade year only because I met Tonny that year. It's now clear to me that some of the stuff John and I did that year stands as the earliest form of the loon behavior that would manifest itself during my sophomore and junior years. For instance, something about the way motion was portrayed in comics struck our fancy, and so for a time, John and I would go through periods where every time one of us spoke, he had to become motionless, even to the point of keeping his mouth as rigid as possible when mouthing the words. If this meant that one was running down the hall at the time, one had to stop all motion, while affecting a pose that had one's legs out and body tilted forward, as if one were modeling motion rather than engaging in it. During these periods, it was like we had entered into our own comic strip that was brought into existence whenever one of us said something. What made it almost impossible to keep a straight face at times was the fact that we were compelled to use exaggerated facial expressions and body language, because as the comic strip artist well knows, when motion is being portrayed in a series of still frames, one may have only one frame to make his point, so subtlety may have to be compromised for the sake of communication. It was the over-exaggeration of the expressions and poses of these characters that we were really engaging in a parody of.

This is my earliest memory of involvement in something that my fellow insanists and I would have called a folly. It is distinguishable from all previous silly behavior of mine in a number of respects. Firstly, there was this paradoxical adherence to established rules of execution of something for the sheer absurdity of it, as if knowing John Fowler either brought me up to a full appreciation of absurdist humor, or at least made me realize the possible applications of it. This is not to say that John and I didn't spend most of our 69/70 school year engaged in good old-fashioned grade school style goofing off – we did. It was those periods where unity, spontaneity and creativity combined to produce a more developed "Insane act" wherein I believe the seeds of inspiration were planted.

Along with the insane logic that characterized this stylized behavior of ours, the unity factor was equally important, because when the grade school urge to form a group returned my freshman year at Oakton, it undoubtedly led to the subconscious correlation that the charge I got out of engaging in insane behavior in unison with one other person would be magnified exponentially if 6 to 8 people were involved.

I'm even more certain that John's brazenness was an influencing factor upon me, that his willingness to practice his insanity openly in a crowded classroom, hallway or cafeteria set an example for me to be as much the fearless leader as I could be for the group I later assembled. And having been inspired to go along with John, I was thereby introduced to the thrill of interjecting insanity into an atmosphere of practiced conformity. Although admittedly, illogical behavior was not as out of place in a classroom of 7th graders as it was in high school, where the delights of the folly led me to romanticize non-conformity and (as it came to be known) our "Battle with the forces of sanity."

As John Fowler never crossed my mind in high school (outside of the handful of times Tonny brought his name up), any influence he might have had on me remained on a subconscious level. Still, I felt the parallels here were too great and too many not to grant John his place as an inspirational forefather of the Insanist movement.

THE KAISEY MODULE

My sophomore homeroom class was in Mr. Cuppeli's shop class in the industrial arts wing of the school. Though Kaiser and I had met and became friends during our freshman homeroom in Mr. Sachs biology class, it was in our sophomore homeroom where our casual acquaintanceship mutated into a loon alliance. As Kaiser's lunacy progressed, this homeroom increasingly took on the quality of being a home base for the movement.

Much to Mr. Cuppeli's displeasure, many plans were discussed here between Kaiser and myself, with Howard's occasional input. You see, Mr. Cuppeli had this fanatical insistence upon absolute silence in the room (which was rather odd for a homeroom teacher). He was constantly admonishing the class to silence, at times in blood vessel popping anger. What gave his anger a measure of hollowness was that he tended to address the class as a whole, and rarely, if ever, singled anyone out. As Kaiser, Howard and I sat in the back of the room, I can recall being impressed from afar by Mr. Cuppeli's forcefulness, but can recall it causing only momentary delays in our discussions. Mr. Cuppeli, I suppose, was becoming increasingly frustrated with his face to face encounter with the reality that no one took homeroom teachers seriously.

At any rate, during a period of particular laxness on Cuppeli's part, Kaiser discovered and christened the first loon oracle – "The Kaisey Module." The module was a semi-circular piece of hard plastic, cut into the shape of your basic paperweight. The plastic was extremely cloudy, giving the module the appearance of a half crystal ball with a perpetually forming image in the mist. Sizewise, it fit snuggly in the palm of our hands. Kaiser's imagination wasted no time in proclaiming that the module had special powers, which I went along with for the sake of infusing as much positive energy into the movement as I could.

After an indeterminate period of time, I came into possession of the module, and have since lost track of its whereabouts. I'll stop short of saying it's lost forever, but just as I'm sure that I did not intentionally throw it away, I haven't seen the module in at least 20 years. Of course, I haven't really looked very hard for it either. But who knows? If this book doesn't partially revive the spirit of insanity, perhaps the discovery of the missing module will. Writing about it has at least revived the memory of the true Jeff Kaiser.

KAREN HAWKINS

Nicknamed "Hawkwind" by EAT and I, Karen was one of those mysterious peripheral figures whose VOT credentials were earned by association. She definitely knew Hunk and this was EAT's primary reason for pulling her into the picture. I didn't know Karen personally, but I have line graphs from the period which link her not only with Hunk, but with the Tanya Herrell/Tinker Bell/Peggy axis as well. There also seems to have been some significant revelation made concerning her in March of 1975, but the few notes of mine that have survived the years do not provide any specifics on Karen Hawkins. She apparently knew or had some relation to Donna Zarin, and had a sister, but again, the incompleteness of my notes fall short of even indicating why I felt these little tidbits of information important enough to write down. She was definitely EAT's baby, though I took seriously his consideration that she was one to keep an eye on.

Not only was Karen in suspicious company the few times I saw her in the cafeteria, her physical presence struck me in such a way as to give an extrasensory confirmation of EAT's apprehensions. She was a will-of-the-wisp brunette like Hunk, but as with other VOT members, her beauty lay not just in the lines of her face, but was more of an active ingredient in the air around her. Karen's ties to otherworldly beauties such as Theresa Bell, Tanya Herrell and Peggy Wallace might be more worthy of poetry than of a simple charted line on a 23 year old piece of paper. I'll tell you this much, any make-up artist would have an easy job convincing an audience that any of these ladies was an alien from another world. I've half convinced myself just thinking about them. Hmmm! Perhaps "Hawkwind" was a more appropriate nickname for Karen Hawkins than EAT and I realized.

KENNETH CASTLE

A character in the soap opera "Ryan's Hope" played by actor Ty McConnell. For some strange reason, EAT and I both got tuned into this particular soap opera (which was far outside the normal viewing habits of both of us). Our interest in the show peaked in 1974, when Pat Ryan's girlfriend Faith was being stalked by a hospital orderly named Kenneth Castle. It was the all too familiar Hollywood tale of the weirdo outsider turned bad guy that had served to warn an entire generation of young women to steer clear of young loners like EAT and myself. Naturally, EAT and I identified somewhat with this Kenneth Castle character. As the natural course of scripted events progressed, Castle kidnapped Faith, putting boyfriend Pat in the role of the hero/rescuer. A little ways beyond this point, things got too way out (or too predictable depending on your viewpoint), and EAT and I lost interest in the show, but not before I immortalized Ty McConnell's character in song on 9 Black And Creeper's "The Complete Kenneth Castle."

A strange addendum to this story is that in 1978, I waited on and spoke briefly with the actor who played Pat Ryan on the series in the Annandale Penguin Feather where I was working at the time. He told me that his parents lived in Annandale. Small world.

KENNETH "SPECS" DECKER

Although not actually having his own radio show, Specs Decker was, nonetheless, a recognized presence in the radio room. He was an associate of Kaiser and Elmo, and by virtue of his electrical expertise, a consultant in the overall maintenance of the station itself. Specs kept his sense of humor throughout the year and was generally well liked by all. Although Specs was obviously a guy who took things easy, what he wrote in my 75 yearbook suggests that through acclimation, a bit of the stations aura had rubbed off on him.

Bob,
It's been a very strange experience for me this year at WOHS. Thanks for all the fun. Good luck and don't work too hard.

Ken "Specs" Decker

KERRY HINDES

The army jacket wearing hippie girl in my senior year English class who, like Marcia Carter, took to telling me to "Smile!" A pretty blonde junior with a pot-mellowed smile, Kerry was more persistent than Marcia, as if something bad might happen to me if I didn't hurry up and smile that very second. I honestly appreciate it when perfect strangers show a concern for my happiness, but the party was already over for me. It was painfully clear that I would not be taking anyone to the senior prom. I don't want to sound ungrateful to Kerry, but when I would see her doting boyfriend coming to greet her after class every day, I was reminded of the reasons for the differences in our perspectives. I did, however, remember her in my senior will. I left to Kerry Hindes – "A photograph of me smiling, taken when I was three." But did I ever break down and give her that smile she at least deserved for her efforts to cheer me up? No, not even once.

KEVIN HANS

My stepfather's eldest son, who came to live with my mom, stepfather and I on January 28 1972. This date figures elsewhere in this book under the "Scotty and Kevin" entry, with an accompanying tale of fun and adventure that was unrelated to Kevin's arrival, save that the two occurred on the same date. As I kept a diary through much of his stay at our house, his otherwise brief footnote in loon history was documented up to the level of a very eventful (and anecdotal) chapter. January 29th has me noting that Kevin parted his hair in the middle. January 31st has Kevin confirming "My hypothesis of the ugliness of Fairfax chicks" (a hypothesis that a couple more years of high school and one Cheri Allen would cause me to rethink). On February 1st, the four of us ate at Wagon Wheel before going to Memco, which requires a trip back in time to even imagine. I also mention that Kevin spent the latter part of the afternoon making snowballs, indicating a vast temperature change from the 70 something summer-like conditions that had me sweating through a day of hard outdoor play just four days earlier on the 28th.

On February 2nd, I awoke to find that school was cancelled due to the sudden winter storm. At 9:30 AM, I went out back to begin working on a snow fort, with Kevin joining me to assist in its construction shortly after 10:00. Rolling bricks of snow, we had it waist deep by 11:00. We were padding in the sides when Mrs. Puglissi, our neighbor to the south, who happened to be in the backyard of the Tasselmeyer's, our neighbors to the north, suggested to the 8 or so kids in the Tasselmeyer's yard that they initiate an old fashion snowball battle with the two of us. They started firing on us, and anxious to get some use out of the fort we had just built, Kevin and I dutifully returned fire. Any attempt to paraphrase my account of the ensuing battle for the sake of clarity would mar a classic bit of early-adolescent literature, so I'll give you the unedited version below:

The smallest boy (Tommy) had a good arm. I was standing by the front fence while they insulted me. They called me "100 Years," and Kevin "Cockeye." While they approached I heaved the snowball I had, but missed. Once we caught them off-guard, and managed to get over the fence. Kevin chased Frank Howard (Tommy), Eric and Laryngitis across the street, where he plastered Frank. Meanwhile I hit Green Bitch at home base. We were running out of ammo about 12:00. This little one (Bob) was throwing snowballs at us from just beyond the fence. We neglected to hit him because of his size. When I did, his older sister (Terri) shouted at me. I plastered her in the face. Later, Eric, Laryngitis were heading home, so while Kevin held off the others, I smeared snow in their faces. Their mother called them in about 2:30.

Besides how much fun Kevin and I obviously had, there are two things that came to mind as I read this again. The first is how readily children will give nicknames to other children, even ones they don't know. "Laryngitis," for instance, was this boy who talked with a pronounced raspy frog in his throat, as if he did indeed have a touch of Laryngitis. "Green Bitch" was this nattery little complaint of a girl in a Christmas green coat, whose mouth I took great pleasure in silencing with a snowball square in the face. Frank Howard was still regarded as our area's quintessential hometown baseball hero, and any kid with a noticeable baseball-type skill might be given that nickname off the cuff. I suppose I was called 100 years because at 15, I may have been the oldest kid there. The second observation I made about this snowball battle is how it differed from the battle I fought with Scotty and Kevin only days earlier. Put in a world war 2 context, it was like fighting in the winter campaign in Europe AND in the steaming jungles of the South Pacific all in the same week. It certainly puts the unpredictability of the DC area weather into perspective.

On February 18th, it snowed again from second to fourth period. After school, Kevin and I began making a supply of snowballs to freeze overnight in preparation for another battle the following day. I discovered that plastic trashcan lids made excellent shields. Paul Nevitt brought over his new dog "Ray Charles." On the 19th, Kevin and I began work repairing the original fort, building a chest-high wall that extended from the fort (which was located in the middle of the backyard) to the Northwestern corner of the carport. Paul Nevitt came over again shortly after we began construction of the wall, and assisted us. We would shovel snow into the plastic trashcans and use them as molds. I actually used a few wooden logs to support the wall, and to cover up the gapping holes. As the children would not fight us, Kevin abandoned the project midday, while I carried on until 5:07, clearing the entire Northeastern corner of the yard and exhausting myself in the process.

On February 21st, Kevin took some photos of me simulating death. He climbed up on top of the shed with camera in hand, while I put ketchup on my face and lay against the south wall of the fort (which incredibly was still standing). Afterwards, we went to Peoples drug store, where Kevin bought the book "The Sensuous Man." After eating at Roy Rogers, we proceeded to Fairfax Music, where Kevin bought himself a snare drum. More moments in time of this nature were recorded until April 2nd, when Kevin began wearing out his welcome. Kevin and I had been dropped off at Meemaw and Poppy's with the intent of the four of us taking a trip down to the national zoo. We were probably less than a half-hour away from leaving, when I heard my grandmother upstairs screaming. Moments later, Kevin comes running down the stairs and does a frantic dance in front of me, excitedly asking me if he was on fire. I knew something weird was happening, but I didn't know what it was exactly until my near hysterical grandmother related that Kevin had accidentally lit himself on fire. Kevin later explained that he had spilled lighter fluid on himself, and in one of those moments where childlike curiosity overcomes good sense, he put a match to his pants leg to see if it would ignite. Well! It ignited all right, and though Kevin only suffered one minor burn on his hand, my grandmother (not to mention my stepfather) was not too happy. My grandfather and I went to the zoo by ourselves.

Would that this were the end of Kevin's troubles. On May 1st, at 4:41 PM, I received a phone call from an officer of the law, who related Kevin had just been caught attempting to steal an Alice Cooper cassette (of all things). When Kevin had failed to show up after school, I smelled trouble. At 5:56 PM, my mother and Kevin arrive. An unrelated event follows that again, is too classic not to just give you the entry exactly as I wrote it.

6:03, I conned Mom into driving me to Memco. Once there, I obtained "The American Heritage Dictionary" and "The Wit and Wisdom of Archie Bunker," two books I've had my eye on for some time.

Yes! I WAS a very unusual child. Anyway, May 2nd was not a good day for Kevin. He was booked, and was informed that he might have to go to a detention home. May 3rd, and Kevin was due to meet with an officer Paternoster, but the officer didn't show. I recall Kevin having to meet with officer Paternoster a number of times, but by summer vacation, things had calmed down, and Kevin's fat was out of the fire again.

Come late June/early July, and my first of four consecutive vacations to Sarasota Florida, and the only one to include Kevin Hans. Despite the two of us getting painful cases of sunburn, Kevin and I had about as much fun as Tonny and I would on our three subsequent visits to Sarasota. On our first trip to Jungle Gardens, Kevin and I became enamored with (and had our picture taken with) a lovely young lady named "Donna." Kevin and I convinced his father and my mother to take us to Jungle Gardens (Where Donna worked as the cashier) a second time, so that Kevin and I could bask awhile longer in the glow of this older woman (she might have been

18). Whether by accident or design, Kevin and I found ourselves on the beach with Donna and three of her friends, who we also photographed for posterity. It was nice seeing Donna in a bikini, and I'd hazard to guess that this might have been the afternoon that Kevin and I forgot about the sun that was baking us to a crisp as we gawked at these comely young women we were (sort of) hanging out with on Lido Beach.

Throughout the spring of 1972, my stepfather was having trouble battling moles in our yard. The little beasties had made a mess of our backyard, forcing him to put traps in the ground along the routes of the tunnels they had burrowed. After catching a mole, Kevin and I put the dead creature in a shoebox and buried him in the Northeast corner of our front yard, in an elaborate ceremony. We even dressed the gravesite up with gravestones, and I imagine some people in the neighborhood probably thought that the beloved family dog had been laid to rest.

Our 6-month experiment as a four-member household ended abruptly around the beginning of August, when Kevin's ruffian proclivities became too much for my mother and she demanded his ouster. While Kevin's personality was such that it was obvious that he and I would be walking down separate paths in life, he nevertheless would exhibit periods of jollity and loon-like inspiration. For instance, when he discovered that my insane name was Bobney, he began addressing me as such in an exaggerated English accent that more than slightly recalled Tonny and I's previous year antics as The British Insipids. He went so far as to refer to himself during periods of heightened silliness as "Kevney," and practically jumped at my invitation to be initiated into the order of loons.

Though I believe it was his willingness to indulge in the absurdity of the act itself, rather than any desire of his to be a part of our group, it is now a matter of historical record that Kevin Hans was the third person to don the ceremonial underwear (after Emmette O and Steve Larson). As Kevin was a year behind me, and was given the old heave-ho only a month before he was due to start his freshman year at Oakton, the true test of what kind of a loon he would have made was never given. Though it's difficult for me to imagine Kevin keeping company with the likes of Emmette or Boni, it's equally difficult for me to imagine him being able to resist participation in things like the receiving label folly and Paying. While I've no doubt Kevin would have hung with more of a ruffian crowd, his appetite for mischief (of any kind) was all too easy to appeal to. The fact that I had almost no contact with Kevin between the summer of 1972 and my graduation makes it that much more difficult to imagine how he would have fit into the picture at Oakton.

On a frigid night in December of 1976, Kevin had a rather memorable Christmas party at the apartment of him and his girlfriend in Maryland. I say memorable because joining me at the party were Tonny and his girlfriend Romina. Being the odd man out between these two couples, and Queen chanting "Find Me Somebody to Love" on the radio, it was one of those moments of detachment, where I would find myself rather lost and defenseless without EAT by my side. At some point during the party, Kevin and I stepped out to take a walk around the apartment complex in the crisp night air and have what would be our last and most memorable heart to heart talk on the subject of women. It left me with the impression that the both of us had grown up a lot in the interim.

KILLER KEATING

Another byproduct of Tonny's eventful sophomore year at Margate Manor, and another legend by association. Mike "Killer" Keating AKA "The Killer" came by his nickname in the same way that Tonny came by the nickname "Het the Threat," by being the qualitative opposite of everything the name suggests. His ineptitude at various sports was such that, true to form, his legendary status among Tonny and myself grew almost overnight. Though I hadn't even met him at this point, the Killer legend was soon expanded to include his (nonexistent) triumphs with the ladies. It was our attempt to build up one of our own, while at the same time having some fun in doing so. Tonny's ode to Killer from the early 1973 From Under a Log sessions succinctly sums up the Killer legend.

Well, my Killer Keating
was a mighty fine ballplayer
Best linebacker in the game today
He had a little Killer
Called him Killer Junior
A mighty fine ballplayer also
He could catch a pass, he could throw too
Well, Killer had a way
With them ladies, he could get 'em good
He had many a friend
Girlfriend that is
Well, Mike was so shy, you could take a pie,
Throw it in his eye, he wouldn't know where's the sky
With them ladies he was good
As good as wood

The session that this song came from began with a tribute to another member of the Keating family, Killer's sister Kathy. Though I had probably met him by the time of this recording session, my greatest memories of the Killer are a 1975 trip to his Margate Manor apartment with Tonny, and our Huck Finn-like adventures at Lake Accotink with Steve Riddle during the 1979-80 period. I can date this particular visit to Killer's apartment to 1975 because the ELO fan in Killer was exclaiming his displeasure over their latest album, "Face the Music." He was rather dismayed that one of his favorite bands was well on their way to selling out completely. I remember that the Strawbs were also one of his favorite bands, and that their 1975 album "Nomadness" was a bone of contention with him as well.

Aside from these scant few encounters, the Killer legend, via word of mouth from Tonny, shall proudly take its place in loon lore. One final word regarding Killer's sister Kathy, who I only met in passing once or twice. She seemed to be one-cup size, a hairdo and a year or two away from a Tanya Herrell-like transformation into a beauxkya. Tonny's hyper-excited Mitch Ryderesque vocal line on the song "Kathy Keating" suggests that he was even further along in anticipating this transformation than I was.

LAURA

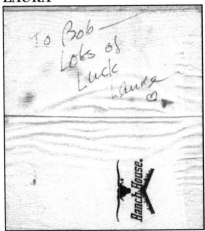

There have been numerous characters whose fame in the annals of insanity is predicated on the fact that some influential and timely crossing of paths had occurred. In other words, they were at the right place at the right time, and said or did something amusing and/or inspiring. Laura was such a character. She was a waitress at the Ranch House restaurant adjacent to the apartment building where Tonny and I stayed during our first trip to Florida in 1973. She just happened to be our waitress for one fateful meal, and exhibited such an air of whimsicality that I was moved to ask her for her autograph - which she cheerfully gave as if it was a daily occurrence. Her "I want a hamburger, you want a hamburger" dance became an instantaneous slice of loon lore, and the napkin which bears her autograph - signed "To Bob - Lots of luck, Laura" has been forever encased in the book of artifacts, gravy stains and all.

Asking waitresses for their autographs was to thenceforth become a semi-regular loon practice. But to this day, none has matched the spirit that Tonny and I possessed at that time quite to the degree that Laura did. If the act of asking Laura for her autograph, a folly in itself, should ever seem to me to be merely the folly of youth, I'm admonished to remind myself of all the genuine celebrities I've met since then who've failed to charm or entertain me as much as this waitress - Laura, deserving of her 15 minutes of fame. For Tonny and I, her place is in our hearts, and our history. Yes! A song was written about her, which I later adapted for inclusion on my "Futile Preaches."

LAURA BOMBERE

Despite her recent inability to recall my connection with Cheri Allen, I remember Laura quite fondly as the person who calmly talked me through the entire Cheri affair. Though actually a grade behind me, I respected Laura's understanding and maturity, having 8-10 marathon phone calls with her throughout the first 6 months of my obsession with Cheri. Laura's rational, yet compassionate approach to my dilemma did help to smooth things out, and I was glad to be able to finally thank her recently for her kindness.

How I came to meet Laura is a story in itself. Elmo was writing on his desk to some female (a not uncommon way of breaking the ice with strangers). This female turned out, as luck would have it, to be Laura Bombere, who sat in the exact same seat as Elmo during another period. He obtained her locker number, and they began exchanging notes. This all was going on while I was hatching my plot to make contact with CA. That Laura was a friend of Cheri's, and happened to come on the scene at this particular time was coincidental in itself, but that she would come to us through almost the exact same mode of communication as Cheri makes her arrival appear to be an even stranger quirk of fate.

Despite being Cheri's friend (and quite unlike another friend of Laura and Cheri's - Devon Brown), Laura was in my corner 100%. She seemed to have this rosy view of human nature that permitted her to believe that a romance between Cheri and I was never out of the question, exhorting me to keep the faith well into 1974. The strangest thing about this fairly important figure is that I have no memories of actually meeting Laura in person, and though I'm sure I must have met her at some point face to face in the halls of Oakton, I have only the memories of those phone conversations. Laura was the poetry and music loving articulate intellectual whose kind my own maturation would have been accelerated knowing more of. She was quite simply years ahead of me in her discernment of many things, while maintaining a positive attitude that occasionally had me thinking her capable of lifting me up to her level through the power of the spoken word. A true jewel.

LEAF BITING

During the fall of 1973 and 74, leaf biting became the sport of loons. Matches were held at my house, Elmo's house, and even once in the faculty parking lot of Oakton. The players usually consisted of Der Kaiser, Elmo and myself, with EAT joining Elmo and I for one memorable match in my backyard.

Wryly referred to as the November Classic, the nature of leaf biting made it a seasonal sport. The idea was simple - each player would attempt to bite a falling leaf before it hit the ground. Every leaf bitten and held in the mouth was counted as a point. Any leaves swallowed were counted as half-points. The thick woods next to the Oakton parking lot, and the large trees that overlooked the backyards of Elmo and myself assured there would be no shortage of falling leaves, and kept the action brisk. It was all good clean loon fun.

LESLIE CHESSMAN (AKA "CHIKA")

Now here is a ghost that I fully expect to be haunting the halls of Oakton's music department a decade or two from now, if she doesn't walk them already. Really! The fact that I have never come across a picture of her in any of my yearbooks, and the fact that nobody I knew had even heard of her leads me to suspect that she was even then a ghost haunting me throughout my junior year. Even Howard, who was in Mr. Curtis' music class with us, does not recall Leslie Chessman. I have only a drawing of a totem pole head with the inscription "Leslie Chessman's work of art" in the book of artifacts as proof that she did in fact exist.

Leslie was a winsome creature, with the kind of pretty blemishless face that would escape the watchful eye of jocks on the hunt (and everyone else's, apparently), a face kept hidden behind a pair of oversized glasses and ever closed curtains of light brown hair. Leslie was a girl who gave the impression that she did not want to be noticed. Throughout my junior year music class, I was flanked by Leslie on my left and Howard on my right. The seating was of a converted bleacher type, meaning that Leslie and I sat a lot closer to each other than we would have with normal classroom seating.

I made repeated advances towards Leslie throughout the year, advances which were less of a romantic or sexual nature, and more of a nature that reflected the nagging feeling I had that we should have been good friends. True! I did find her attractive, but even a heart-on-his-sleeve pin cushion for cupid such as myself would have been hard pressed to nurture any closeness with one as distant and elusive as Leslie was. It just seemed to me that Leslie was too unusual for it to be happenstance that our paths crossed. Though through it all, Leslie sat quietly aloof at my side, as if waiting for me to adopt some psychic form of communication to properly plead my case. I did manage to get her to tell me that she lived in one of the newly built townhouses across Blake Lane from Oakton, and in a discussion on drugs, she revealed her preference for "Chemicals." Indeed! Leslie's peculiar behavior should have given me the clue that she had already ingested enough chemicals to make it undesirable to allow any sudden noises in her presence, but I was much more interested in the end product than I was the means.

Not far into my junior year, I began addressing Leslie in person, and referring to her in the third person, as "Chika." Leslie would spend what amounted to many class hours drawing little hash marks that would end with her softly saying – "Chika." Sometimes the marks would form recognizable pictures, such as the totem head that resides in the book of artifacts, but sometimes they were just a series of random lines, whose sole purpose seemed to be the perpetuation of her classroom mantra. And while Mr. Curtis was going on about music theory, all I would hear was "Chika…Chika…Chika…Chika," as if some 4th dimensional stapler were folding and stapling the fabric of space around us. Leslie comes to mind whenever I hear the song "The Bogus Man" from Roxy Music's "For Your Pleasure" album (which was released only months prior to the start of my junior year). The song ends with Bryan Ferry making the exact same sound in synch with the beat, "Chika…Chika…Chika."

At one point, I began joining her in this ritual. I would lean over and put my pen to the nearest corner of the page she was drawing on and we would have our own one word call and response dialogue going. It was at this point when I began to mimic-answer her Chika mantra that I believe any initial nervousness Leslie had in sitting next to me was absolved. But we would get no closer, and the 2 or 3 times I encountered her in the halls outside of class (which was always in the hallway that led to the entrance to the music department), her passing greeting was tentative and guarded, as if I were to suddenly, out of curiosity, double back and follow her, I might catch her disappearing into a wall, or discover her secret hiding place. Ah Leslie! Tell me there is a place somewhere that hasn't changed since the early 70's, where they still make young ladies like you. I don't quite know what you were, but you were something special.

LINDA AND BETTY KARNES

Two cousins of mine who lived almost within walking distance of me on Cottage street in Vienna. Linda was in my grade and Betty was in the class of 76, but due to the mad logic of the dyslexic person who drew the school boundaries, they attended Madison High, which is presumably where Peggy Wallace and a host of other North Vienna folk spent their freshman and sophomore years. Living in South Vienna put Linda and Betty in the same subdivision as a sizable chunk of the Oakton student body, but as both Madison and Oakton were situated equidistantly from this area, placement anomalies like this were bound to occur.

We had such fun together as kids, but as we began to enter adolescence, our relationship (and the nature of our fun) began to change accordingly. Linda and Betty began the normal maturation process of dating boys, going to football games, and preparing themselves socially for the families they would eventually be raising. I, on the other hand, was evolving down a path of selective social isolation, and happily too I might add. Our isolation from each other at separate high schools may have helped to preserve our childhood camaraderie, but the simultaneous occurrence of two things in the fall of 1973 brought about an intense renewal of our friendship.

1. I fell in love with Cheri Allen, and
2. I began attending the Fairfax Assembly of God with my cousins, becoming increasingly involved with the youth group there.

My relationship with Linda and Betty had always been predicated on and perpetuated by the various Karnes family reunions where the 3 of us were in attendance, so jumping into a regimen where we saw each other once or twice a week was bound to bring us closer together, as well as ensure them of an entry in this book. Be that as it may, I say that reason number 1 (falling in love with Cheri) was of equal or greater importance because it put the three of us on the spiritual common ground that would give the adolescent phase of our relationship meaning, as opposed to simply seeing each other more often.

Let me explain this. From my earliest memory, I would share with my cousins a fascination with romance, though as a boy, my role would be to maintain a healthy distance from such a fascination by playing war games, collecting baseball cards, and watching TV shows like Combat, Lost In Space, and Star Trek. Nevertheless, the incident I shall now recount will read like an early ancestor of that spiritual common ground I spoke of. I must have been 8 years old at the time, because I distinctly remember Betty being 7. It was during a Karnes family vacation at a beach house in Nagshead North Carolina, more memorable for my marathon games of Monopoly with Linda. There was a convenience store next to the beach-house, and at one point, the three of us strolled over to the store and purchased (of all things) a romantic comic book, which we pored over in our room later that evening. It had illustrations of couples kissing, and I distinctly remember getting quite a buzz off of our ringleader Linda's mischief-tinged search for the forbidden fruit, while at the same time being closer in spirit to Betty's appreciation of the lighter romantic aspects of the book.

All three of us were filled with childlike awe and wonder over this thing that we would later confront in our adolescence. This scene picks up again in the fall of 1973 in the kitchen of Linda and Betty's Vienna home. I was right in the thick of my quest for fire with CA, with my hotline to Laura Bombere following me wherever I went. I had just gotten off of the phone with Laura, who had given me Cheri's actual home phone number and I was preparing to make the call heard round the world. The pleasure we derived as children from dwelling on the promise of love was now at fever pitch, with Linda and Betty urgently pushing me to make the call. It's doubtful that I would have made the call so soon after receiving Cheri's number had I not had these two romance junkies barking at me for a fix.

Well! As stated earlier in this book, my first phone call to Cheri was an extremely positive and promising one, leaving my cousin's appetites quenched, and me somewhere up in the ionosphere. It is quite invigorating and spiritually nourishing for me to recall this magical evening, as much for the glow of my pro-romance cousins as for my first full dosage of Cheri at her sweetest. Linda and Betty had (I'm assuming) already had their share of romantic successes, and were a bit giddy to be on hand for what had the earmarks of being my first romantic success.

Though Linda's well wishes were heartfelt, I could see in dear sweet Betty's smile that she knew exactly what I was experiencing. Betty and I were of one mind in matters of the heart, and the strangeness of this is that I've often pondered what good friends Cheri and Betty would have made. This idea prompts a most intriguing question. How different would things have been if my cousins HAD attended Oakton High? It's a forgone conclusion that the two of them would have gotten involved with the revelations club at some point, and though Linda might have been tempted to cavort with the likes of Valli Hess and Stephanie Hill, I've no doubt that Betty would have at least befriended the Davis's and the Alcorn's, if not Cheri herself.

Having Betty on the inside pleading my case would not have changed the outcome, but it would have made the game more interesting. Then again, perhaps it's a good thing my cousins weren't put through the blood-is-thicker-than-reputation test that they might have undergone at OHS. Losing a friend because they don't have the guts to stay your friend was an acceptable high school hazard, but losing the trust and sisterly love of my cousins would have really pulled my faith in the fairer sex down to a low point.

Aside from their uplifting attitudes, Linda and Betty served an even greater purpose. At this point in my life, having two females of the equivalent pulchritude and popularity of the Alcorn sisters who enjoyed my company and not only liked, but respected me was an essential reminder that I hadn't suddenly become some thoroughly unlikable person overnight. I saw myself as likable, but experience had taught me that third party opinion could adversely effect how certain people viewed me, and could at any time effect a negative shift in another person's attitude toward me. I didn't go around worrying about it, but the knowledge of it trained me to behave more guardedly in group situations such as parties were I was hopelessly outnumbered by attractive females and braying jocks. Strangely, this was exactly what I was apt to encounter at the parties I attended during my high school years. Linda and Betty held a number of parties at their house in 1974 and I was in attendance for at least two of them. I remember one particularly surreal evening in early 74, with a small but imposing mix of hotties and studs in my cousin's basement/party room, and me in the middle of it all. As nice as Linda and Betty's friends might have been, I couldn't for the life of me relax. The music that was coming from a radio behind the bar was constantly threatening to suck up what little attention I hadn't already turned in on myself. The greatest challenge for my attention came with the broadcast of "Fracture," a piece from the latest King Crimson album "Starless and Bible Black," at which point I recall thinking - I better get up and circulate before I become completely fixated. It's worth noting that aside from the revelations club party at Kim Koan's house, and the various youth group gatherings of both Christ United Methodist and the Fairfax Assembly of God, the only parties for party's sake I attended during my Oakton years were Madison affairs.

A part of me (though probably the part that was want to remind me that I was the cousin of the hostesses), wanted to make a good impression. At one point in the evening I found myself in the company of and later conversing one on one with a very attractive girl. She was impressively tall with long strawberry blonde hair, and wore one of those Daniel Boone style buckskin jackets that was part of 60's fashion carried over into the fashion vacuum of the early 70's. I took an instant liking to her gentle aura and curiously soft-spoken manner, though at the risk of appearing anti-social, I soon ventured upstairs to the living room and the less stressful company of my Uncle Jack. Oh! Half of me wanted and waited for the young lady to follow me, because as I stressed earlier, I was much more comfortable with the authenticity of one on one communication. The sudden wave of calm that overcame me and the perceptively consoling words of my uncle implied that what the other half of me wanted was written on my face - blessed relief from an atmosphere thick with young men who reminded me a little too much of Ray King.

We would talk again one or two more times before evenings end, but any subtle messages she may have been trying to convey were held in doubt until Betty related that after I had gone upstairs, the young lady turned to her and asked "I wonder if I should follow him upstairs?" Silly girl! Of course you should have followed me upstairs. We should have taken a stroll through the neighborhood and gotten to know one another, but that sort of thing seems to only happen in movies that are filmed in small towns.

Amazing! I thought. My first appearance at a Madison party and I've already caught the eye of an attractive girl, something that hadn't happened in almost three years of attending Oakton. Yes! I was distractingly out of my element, but I was beginning to see the positive side to this. I could have been anyone to this girl, so she had to accept me at face value. Encouraged by what Betty had told me and the idea of dating a girl who was safely removed from the rumor mills of Oakton High, I procured her phone number from Betty and called her up. She was less than responsive to me on the phone, and after several unsuccessful attempts to get a date out of her, an empathizing Betty confided that she wasn't interested. Though I suspected I had fallen victim to the dreaded return of the old boyfriend shrug-off, I did learn (or begin to learn) 2 important things from this experience.

1. Women are fickle.
2. A man is always more attractive walking away from a woman than he is walking towards a woman.

Having been in weekly contact with me throughout the months that followed Cheri's rejection, Betty felt bad for me and henceforth assumed the role of an aspiring cupid. When I never even got to square one with a girl who was a good friend of Betty's, the grim specter of failure hung over our relationship for a week or two. But Betty never gave up, God bless her. She (and occasionally Linda as well) would point out girls to me in church. And there were other parties, some church related and some not. One particularly memorable affair was the birthday party for Linda's boyfriend Billy Bean.

Billy was quite a character, and one that I've yet to figure out. With an actor's good looks, Billy's quiet persona balanced out Linda's out-flowing exuberance. It wasn't with a Bogartian arrogance or a dullard's lack of wit that Billy kept such a low profile, but what it was exactly I was never able to ascertain. His birthday party was a small gathering of no more than 10 people, and I dare say, most of them seemed to be there at Linda's invitation. Despite having nabbed quite a Madison babe in my cousin Linda, Billy had a lost soul aura about him that I really identified with. Though he was a Madison jock, Billy seemed even more out of place in a party atmosphere than I was, and for much of his own party, we conversed as two people with very little in common who suddenly found themselves as the two outsiders at a party. In this atmosphere, Billy's attitude strangely recalled my Uncle Jack's "I know how you feel" sentiments expressed at the previous party. Having said all 'this, Billy's party was a much more easy-going and enjoyable affair.

The sugary spiked punch concoction we all were drinking went straight to Linda's head and she was reduced almost to jabbering in baby talk at one point. I'll never forget the "Yes! That's my sister" look of embarrassment on Betty's face as Billy attempted to contain and revive Linda from a state that seem to come over her in a second. The humor of it suddenly struck Betty and she began to giggle at a subdued volume. When it was clear that

Betty was giggling a little too much and just a little too long, one of the girls who was present turned to Betty and said "Oh No! Not you too!"

As someone who had never felt the effects of alcohol to this degree, I found the whole thing rather entertaining, especially in light of my birthday present to Billy. In what both my cousins and my Aunt Janet would herald as something in-between a good idea and divine inspiration, I gave Billy his choice of two presents, a bottle of whiskey and a bible. The part of the story that my aunt may not have heard was that after Billy did the right thing by choosing the bible, Billy and I celebrated with a shot of whiskey at my insistence (Hey! No sense in letting good whiskey go to waste).

By this time you might be wondering, did Linda and Betty's path cross that of any of the other insanists? The answer to that is yes, on two occasions. One was the time EAT joined us for the Sunday service at the Fairfax Assembly of God, which was truly an otherworldly experience. I'll never forget watching EAT kneeling at the alter with 5 or 6 hands laid upon him and that many more hands raised towards heaven, as if to funnel down some of the holy spirit into his soul. The other instance of a Linda and Betty incursion into loon space was on a much lighter note. How this came about I don't recall, but Betty and her current boyfriend ran into Tonny and I at a night football game at Woodson High. I'm assuming that Woodson was playing Madison that evening, and that was her reason for being there, but whatever the reason, Tonny commented a number of times on her bubbly nature. He henceforth referred to her as "Bubblin' Betty Beauxkya." In fact, appended on to the factors which govern female behavior (which was a chart that Tonny and I drew up and added to periodically throughout the 1974-77 period) was something called "The Bubble Factor," which in truth - Betty DID personify.

I will most remember Betty for being such a terrific sounding board whenever my romantic misadventures threatened to get the better of me. Even by 1974, so many of the people I'd known had a cynically jaded view of love and romance, making it that much more of a joy to talk with Betty on the subject. One particular meeting of the minds stands out in my memory. My grandparents owned a cabin up on one of the mountains that overlook Front Royal. During a family get-together at the cabin, Betty and I found ourselves walking down the gravel road that led from the cabin. Walking about a half-mile and back, our shared viewpoints on the trials and wonders of boy/girl relations were augmented strangely by the quietude of that mountain road. Betty expressed some dismay over Linda's less than idyllic (though perhaps more functional from Linda's perspective) relationship with Billy Bean, and probably for the first time, I opened my heart up to Betty about the whole Cheri affair. Stopping to sit on a bridge that overlooked a small stream, Betty's "You'll find your angel" optimism really made me feel that had I been surrounded by people such as herself back at Oakton high, I would have gotten over Cheri Allen by this time.

Linda and Betty were both pulling for me (and occasionally even pushing me a little) throughout 1974, and into the approaching emotional storm of the winter of 1975. A large part of me wanted to join Linda and Betty as a participant in the game of romance. I didn't enjoy my increasingly set role as a bellyaching shoulder-crier, and as one who was raised on TV shows where the good guy always won, I fully believed that my true love was just a year or two away. Damaris Bonnell's rejection in December 1974 put a damper on that idea. For a refresher on the last romantic failure that I would suffer my cousins with, and why I disconnected from the Fairfax Assembly of God (youth group and all), it might be best if you stop here and read through Damaris Bonnell's entry once again. Lest anyone (least of all my cousins) have any misunderstandings on this point, let me lay this issue to rest once and for all. Reverend Keller's sermon of December 15th 1974 was a pivotal event in my senior year. It was a powerful and characteristically well delivered warning to his congregation not to allow themselves to be spiritually brought down by the sadness and the gloom of others in the world around them. Now picture this, not only had Damaris rejected me 9 days earlier, but this was the second consecutive Sunday where Damaris put on her Maybe if I ignore him, he'll go away act. This was a new and particularly painful twist of the dagger that was sticking in my heart, and one that I was not prepared to confront. Cheri and I had no problem staying on speaking terms. Neither one of us viewed her rejection as any kind of falling out.

So here I am sitting there in church feeling about four inches tall, and the more the reverend warned his flock in wild gesticulations to avoid those whose despair might suck the spiritual life out of them, the more I began to feel the finger of the almighty pointing down at me. Apparently Rick and Tom Casey, two of my friends in the youth group, were also of the opinion that I was the subject of the sermon, because the both of them were unfriendly and distant towards me afterwards. In the state I was in at the time, I took their actions that spoke louder than words to heart. I recall standing in the parking lot after the shrug-off from a normally gregarious Tom Casey had confirmed my worst fears about Keller's sermon and thinking – "Maybe he's right! Maybe Rick's right! Maybe Reverend Keller's right! Maybe Damaris is right! Maybe I don't belong here."

Now at this point, I didn't really care about any of these people. But I'm sure that in my not-so-subconscious mind was the consideration of what effect all this doom and gloom I was carrying around might have on the two people I did care about - my cousins. Despite the fact that I had interiorized into self protect mode over Damaris' rejection, Linda and Betty were (like Cheri Allen) people I deeply cared about, and whose happiness I would have fought to protect. But my station in Oakton society made me feel isolated from Cheri, and despite how far my cousins and I went back, Damaris' rejection ultimately led me to think that maybe my place was with EAT, Howard Koretz, and the great unwashed. Any lingering doubts I might have had of this were put to sleep with Peggy's February 1st rejection. EAT, Howard Koretz, and Rick Hockmuth were the only three people from Oakton that I kept in touch with after graduation. That speaks volumes about who I felt I belonged with. Mitch immediately moved to St. Louis to live with his new bride, and while it pained and saddened me not to respond to his letter, something within me was urging me to comply with the decision I had made the previous December. Everything inside me after the Peggy affair was telling me to pull in, suck up, and close down.

The last time I saw Linda and Betty was a couple years ago at our granddaddy's funeral. They both are married with children and I wish them all the happiness they so richly deserve. They are among that special group of people whose compassion and loyalty shown through at a time in my life when trust was becoming something I rationed out in thimbles.

LISA RENTSCHLER

A spunky displaced Rhinemaiden, who would have looked just as natural dressed as "Heidi" and carrying a basket of tulips as she did bounding through the halls of OHS in the burgundy and gold of her varsity cheerleader's uniform. In response to a long forgotten quote of Lisa's related to me by an equally forgotten third party, I concluded my December 1974 letter to Santa by requesting Lisa Rentschler's thoughts on the likelihood of intelligent life in Fairfax County, to which Peter Chapman would later take exception to in his senior will. As obscure as this reference is likely to remain, it does bring back the short-lived fascination I had with Lisa.

Far from being as appreciative of her alpine looks as many young men I knew, I was nonetheless amazed by the degree of unbridled happiness she exuded. Lisa's walk was more of a bounce, and though she would always be walking by herself at the point where I would encounter her in the halls, her pink face was ever-glowing with the sort of perpetual smile that 2 years earlier would have sent Emmette O scrambling for his pen and notepad. If determinate outsiders like Emmette, EAT and I hadn't been so predisposed to remaining on the outside of Oakton society, it may have been easier to view the joy we took in our lunacy and the joy that Lisa Rentschler publicly displayed as variations on the same theme - the song of youth. It's a paradox though, for the improvisationary nature of this tune as we outsiders played it made revelations of this sort nearly impossible to come by. The lesson I have learned from this is if anything is holding your fascination, take a good hard look at it, because chances are that something or someone is trying to tell you something.

And the fall of 1974 was the period in my life when I needed to take a good hard look at what Lisa Rentschler was exuding, because not long into 1975, things like friendship, love, romance and other interactive building blocks of happiness began to sour for me. I'd soon learn enough of the bad lessons in life to make distance between myself and the likes of Lisa Rentschler desirable. I was becoming the anti-Lisa, and had her presence persisted in my thoughts up to the time of the writing of my senior will, it's a good bet that I would have given Peter Chapman something to really get incensed over. And had I prior knowledge of her involvement in the revelations club, my disillusionment with Christianity, on top of everything else, would have made Lisa a tempting target for my poison pen. As it turned out, Lisa, Gayle Alcorn, Kim Koan, and all the other revelationettes were out of sight and out of mind by the final weeks of my senior year.

It's taken 24 years worth of distance from that group for me to be able to separate them from their blind faith and their social affiliations, and appreciate them for their purity of essence. "Social Affiliations" you say??? Well, Yes! Despite the compassion and sincerity that Gayle Alcorn exhibited, it was difficult to overlook the fact that she was, at that time, dating Bob Matich (the same beefcake bully who taunted me unmercifully in my freshman gym class). It was little contradictions like this that would always come up to clobber me whenever I felt that my soul needed saving.

I feel truly blessed to have finally received some of the messages I was apparently meant to receive in high school. I'm not complaining that it has taken 24 years to sort a lot of this out. Most people (if ever) are well into their golden years by the time they've slowed down enough to allow the joys of adulthood to be reunited with the joys of childhood. Wherever Lisa Rentschler is today, I hope that she hasn't surrendered her childlike enthusiasm to the apparent seriousness of life. Evidently I owe her that much for her belated but affirmative answer to the question of intelligent life in Fairfax County.

LITTLE GUYS

One of the follies of Tonny and I's first trip to Florida in 1973 was to spot and photograph "Little Guys." Little guys were the personifications on business signs that Tonny and I would spot along the road. Little Guy status was granted on a certain degree of charm being present in the sign's detail. A smile was pretty much a guarantee of acceptance. A smiling spoon, a smiling sandwich, a smiling liquor bottle in a tuxedo, any product that smiled down on the road we happened to be travelling was photographed and thusly immortalized. The little guys that were captured on film were Shane's, Mickey Cakes, Royal Castle, Maryland Chicken (more commonly referred to as "Piece of Chicken"), Mr. Sandwich, and our favorite and unofficial leader of the Little Guys –"Foremost" of Foremost Liquors in Sarasota, an establishment I'm sorry to say was no longer in business when I visited Sarasota for my grandfather's funeral in 1988. A Little Guys comic strip was drawn by Tonny for one of the issues of Insane Illustrated. The little guys were also immortalized in song on the Tonny composition "Little Guys of the World."

Pictures of the Little Guys appear on the next two pages:

Foremost, unofficial leader of the "Little Guys"

Royal Castle

Maryland Fried Chicken

Mickey Cakes – taken from inside my stepfather's car, at a point where it was evident to Tonny and myself that another trifling inconsequential aspect of our surroundings was about to be aggrandized.

Mister Sandwich

Pizza Hut (little Italian Guy)

Shane's (first spotted Little Guy)

LIZ DAVIS

With a sensuous pair of lips that Julia Roberts would envy, and a beguiling sparkle in her eyes, Liz was among the most natural, if less touted beauties of Oakton. Though after such an introduction, I'm embarrassed to say that my reason for including her here is a bit fuzzy. I'm quite sure that the song "Come! Come! Elizabeth" was inspired by her, but my memory is not clear enough, and the lyrics are not specific enough to reveal exactly what they are referring to. The first verse reads -

Cotton Mather knew obsession, What do you know?
Increase Mather is your expression, "What Do You Plead?"
I refuse to be your Satan any longer
Superstition in the faith is often stronger

This appears to implicate a Christian source for the rumors (or at least the spreading of the rumors) that I was a Satanist, but I'll be damned (no pun intended) if I can recall what tidbit of information I had come across that would have led me to this assumption, or how it relates to Liz Davis. The second chorus of the song is the clearest in terms of the amount of memory it jars loose -

I'm not going to speculate on what was said
Come, Come, Elizabeth! How much have you read?

I do seem to recall that something was said about me, but as the lyric indicates, the specifics of what was said were never revealed to me. The only thing that was apparently obvious to the person who relayed this information to me was that what was said was not positive, and was probably more bunk about me being a lackey for old scratch. Perhaps beyond the fact that so much else was happening at this time, my memory might be hazy because the content of what was said was not so important as the source of the gossip and its negative repercussions. Gossip, like the passive rejection of Damaris Bonnell, and the active rejection of the Midnight Cackeler, would have been that much less palatable coming from a Christian source. I naively believed that these people were above this sort of thing. That's why I freaking sought them out in the first place.

The line "Come! Come! Elizabeth How much have you read?" could refer to the Bible and/or the papers I loaned Cheri. It could be a reference to both, in which case the song would be saying - Elizabeth! If you had read between the lines of the papers I loaned Cheri, it would have been obvious that while Cheri may have had a claim on my soul, the devil would have more than likely found it too steeped in sentiment to be a fit habitat.

And Elizabeth! If you truly held to the tenets of the bible, you would be busy praying for the reclamation of my soul, instead of being such a bloody schoolgirl about the whole thing.

My view of this now is to harvest the understanding that we ARE talking about schoolgirls here. When Cheri wrote, "You're rather deep for me" in my junior yearbook, I knew that she was really saying, "You're too deep for me and my friends." One had to consider their station in high school. I realized this. It was true for me. Why wouldn't it be true for Cheri and her cohorts? I thought Cheri was the cat's meow. There was nothing that her friends could have known about me that was truer or deeper than this.

The jury can only deliver a unanimously "Innocent" verdict to Liz Davis. I never had any direct contact with her, and all the evidence I had that she was a source for the Satanist rumors came from uncorroborated second or third hand sources. Really! I'm the one who should be brought up on charges here, for not being able to recall every minutia of detail about someone who had such an incredible pair of legs. It's telling how quickly this incident went from being the inspiration for a song to being another blur in the rush of events. And few things speak of the pace at which I was living at this time as well as the fact that it wasn't until my post-graduation yearbook browsings that I came to appreciate what a knockout Liz was. And joy of joys! Liz had a twin sister named Helen. Now THERE'S a birth date that must have surely seen Venus shining down from the heavens.

MARCIA CARTER

I had already lived through a pre-adolescent sexual fascination with black female celebrities such as Nichele Nichols, Marilyn McCoo, Diana Ross, etc. But here in Marcia was my first face to face encounter with an actual black woman of comparable pulchritude and grace, and I don't mind telling you, when she started addressing me in the halls, my insides turned to mush. Unfortunately, as Marcia chose the month of January 1975 to make her sudden appearance, I found myself wondering – "Could anybody this beautiful really be trusted?" Her strange visit to the radio station with Suzanne "Zanders-Lavey" (described in detail later in Peggy Wallace's entry) did little to allay my apprehensions.

A sultry sinuous beauty given to wearing long glamorous gowns to school, I suppose it's possible that I might have taken notice of her sooner, but my earliest memories are of passing her in the science hallway between the planetarium and the front door. This was the very hallway (and the exact spot) where my first face to face encounter with Peggy took place. Changing my route in order to pass Peggy at that spot every day had also put me in Marcia's path, which explains why her presence dates from January of 1975. It corresponds with my first usage of that hallway in attempting to track down Peggy.

Marcia got my attention by smiling at me, and in a sweetly admonishing tone saying –"Smile!" as she sashayed past me. Around the end of January, this had become a regular practice with Marcia. Reading my description of this period in the Peggy Wallace entry will give you some idea of why Marcia had picked the worst possible time in my life to be pulling this kind of shit. Dragging me into the planetarium and making out with me under the stars would probably have shocked some sense into me, or at least might have knocked me off the collision course with heartbreak I was on, but simply telling me to smile wasn't hitting any nerves. I mean, Carrie Hindes, the buxom blonde hippie girl in my English class, had already undertaken the task of telling me to smile every day, so addressing the redundancy here, my reaction to both parties was to resist smiling. Of course, a lady of Marcia's caliber wouldn't have to tell me to smile today, but we seldom appreciate things until there's a scarcity of them.

By the time things had calmed down a bit in March, I was exchanging greetings and pleasantries with Marcia in the halls, but she was still way out of my league. After I got my drivers license and started making semi-regular trips to Tyson's Corner mall in the summer of 1976, I found Marcia working in Up Against the Wall, a sort of slimmed down Mall-friendly version of EF Sly. I ran into Marcia there twice. The second time I was with my mother and stepfather, and was rather self-conscious about what my hormones were doing in the presence of this attractive black girl that I obviously knew.

Marcia, being a member of the class of 77, had only just finished her junior year, but every aspect of her manner and appearance (not to mention her height) spoke of someone older. I was joyfully intimidated and boyishly smitten with Marcia's mixture of the Afro-American home girl hipster she was at heart and the glamorous Oakton debutante her surroundings (not to mention her own beauty) had drawn her into being.

Class President, Homecoming Queen, you name it. On beauty and grace alone, this thoroughly likable lady was deserving of any honor bestowed on her by my high school.

MARGATE MANOR

The apartment complex that sits in-between the Mantua subdivision and Pickett shopping center. Aside from the fact that Tonny and family lived there from 1972-73 and again from 1975-78, Margate Manor was home to many important figures in our lives, collectively and individually. On Tonny's side, there were such illustrious figures as Peter Brichant, Al Early,

Killer Keating and Rusty Gibson. Collectively shared in our mutual acquaintance were the Burley's and the infamous Sam Kaiser (both post-Oakton drama's here- we're talking another book's worth). I would have two girlfriends come from the manor, and my friend Debbie Bradshaw lived there during the first three years of our acquaintance. And lest we forget, Brenda Paris was also discovered there.

I have many fond memories of this place, like walking up to Pizza Cosmos (later Pizza Gaezano) at Pickett shopping center with Tonny and chowing down on one of their excellent shrimp pizzas, playing catch with Tonny, or Whiffle Ball with Tonny and Rusty Gibson, of making recordings in Tonny's room, and of recording Death by Hanging's Live at Margate out on Tonny's balcony. Margate Manor was the scene of a lot of fun times in my life. I will always remember this place.

THE MAUGHAN GIRLS

I have followed the trail of a pretty girl down some dark corridors in my day, but the significance of the Maughan girls (and the reason for their inclusion in this book) is that they were the direct inspiration for my 1972-74 involvement with Christ United Methodist Church. This links them through association with the resulting God vs. the devil/ good vs. evil quandary that further fragmented my already confused adolescence. This is how it happened. At the invitation of my grandparents, I attended an evening holiday service at a church on Leesburg Pike in Falls Church. It was a chilly night during the thanksgiving holiday, 1971. There, at this service, for the first time, I saw the Maughan girls.

I had previously met Colonel Maughan and his wife, and knew them to be friends of my grandparents. Upon seeing the beauty of their two daughters, I immediately decided that I should begin attending Christ United Methodist Church. My grandparents never knew that the Maughan girls were the catalysts behind what would eventually evolve into an honest quest on my part for knowledge concerning the spirit of man. I had forgotten myself until coming across their pictures recently in the 1972 Christ Church yearbook. After making the connection myself, I felt that surely they deserved an entry here.

Strangely, outside of shaking their hands in a greeting line one Sunday morning, I would have no direct contact with them at Christ United. I never came across them in the youth lounge, which I began frequenting around March/April 1972. Indeed! They were not involved in the church's youth group in any way that I could see. The couple of times that I was present during parties at my grandparents house on Buffalo Ridge where the Maughans were in attendance, they were not accompanied by their daughters. Keeping one ear cocked for any mention of them proved unfruitful as well. They did continue to make periodic appearances at the regular Sunday morning services, and that was enough to keep me attending. An occasional smile of recognition from one of them was enough to send my spirit soaring a couple hundred feet above the steeple.

I was in absolute awe of them. The younger of the two looked to be a year or two older than me (which is a measurable difference in age when you're 15). She had a darker complexion than her sister, favored her father, and was extremely well developed. The older sister, who appeared to be a good 2 to 3 years my senior, was tall and willowy, favored her mother, and was quite simply one of the most beautiful young women I had ever seen. From their differences in height, build, complexion and facial structure, it would be difficult to imagine them as sisters, were it not for the obvious resemblance's to their respective parents.

While the path they were, by happenstance, instrumental in leading me down makes their role in my life a small but important one, the more I think about it, it was the beauty and grace of these ladies that really qualifies them for as much praise as my pen can bestow here. In fact, as soon as I'm done writing this entry, I'm going to stand up and salute the colonel (and his wife) for a job well done.

MELODY ROUZER

I feel that some sort of award for good taste should be given to Melody for being the first female who actually attempted to seduce me. I wouldn't say that Melody was the first girl to ever take notice of me, but she was the first girl to take THAT MUCH notice of me, and for that she deserves whatever pedestal of quality and distinction I can give her here.

It's clear now that Melody fancied non-conformists. No female could have an eye for both Ray Denk AND myself and claim otherwise. The reason this was not so apparent at the time was that Melody seemed hell-bent on capturing me for the purpose of leading me down a more socially acceptable straight and narrow, as if she was itching for a chance to cultivate the potential she saw in me. Here, my friends, was a raving example of the maturity gap. I won't argue the axiom of human nature that states that women mature emotionally much earlier than do men, but often that left EAT and I making fun of these disapproving matrons of good sense as the only option for including them in our fun. The thing that maintained a level of endearment in our gibing of Melody (as opposed to the serious distrust we held towards the likes of others) was the knowledge that underneath it all, Melody was every bit the non-conformist we were. She admitted as much to me in a recent phone call, and went much further with the surprising revelation that she had very few friends at Oakton, the implication being that she felt intellectually stifled in high school. Melody was a very intelligent and cultured young woman, and I can now imagine the frustration she must have felt at already being above it all, but at the same time, it saddens me to think of the fun I had that she apparently missed out on. Even though, at age 41, I can finally appreciate the lady Melody was at 16, the adolescent boy that lives on inside of me would still, even today, rear its ugly head to drive a woman like Melody nuts.

At the time, part of me was always on guard around this Germanic towering figure of a woman. An amusing example of this was Melody's Halloween party, held on the afternoon of Saturday, October 26 1974, at Melody's house on Cedar Lane. Ray Denk and Melody's sidekick Mary Schaaf were among those in attendance, but I was the first to arrive. I remember Melody showing me her room. I also remember looking at pictures of Melody in a bikini on a beach with some friends, and being struck by what the clothes Melody wore to school hadn't quite revealed - that Miss Rouzer was as developed physically as she was intellectually and emotionally. Despite this eye opening (literally) discovery, I took care not to get too comfortable sitting on Melody's bed, lest Melody's suggestive comments transform into physical assertiveness. I have this wonderful memory of Melody and Mary bounding around the front yard, their capes flying in dramatic sweeps, once the party had got going.

I was also the last person to leave the party, and by this time, truly walking the line between enjoying Melody's company and feeling unnerved over what she might do or suggest next. Near the end of my stay there that evening, Melody made her grandest pitch. We had adjourned to a room that was basically an enclosed porch on the side of her house. Melody was reclining on a couch at the front end of the room when she, in so many words, offered herself to me. I remember looking down at Melody's "Come Hither" grin, and then following her form down to an even more summoning pair of legs, sparkling like jewels in panty hose that reflected glimmers from the overhead light. More than a few of my hormones were well aware that this was my first glance down the road to heaven, but in the next instance, I was roundly refusing Melody's invitation. You see, while Melody was well prepared to march headlong into womanhood, I was still naively holding on to the romantic notions of my first sexual encounter resulting from some great love affair, and the eventuality of marrying my soul mate.

To her credit though, Melody kept things cordial, while at the same time remaining unabashedly Melody. During a phone conversation some time after her party, I happened to mention that I had recently purchased some black satin sheets and matching pillowcases. I was attempting to explain to her how the sheets and pillows sliding off the satin mattress cover almost on contact rendered them absolutely useless to me, but I had forgotten who I was talking to. "To entertain your lady friends?" she purred suggestively, as if to paint me as some sort of lothario. Again, it was naïve of me to not imagine how it would appear, but during my late teens, I thought things like black satin sheets were cool simply because they were black. Where girls and sex were concerned, (and Melody would have cringed at the very thought of this) I grew up and fell in love with the last woman who could be referred to as "America's Sweetheart" - Annette Funicello, first as a Mouseketeer, and then in a succession of beach movies with Frankie Avalon. Annette's presence in my formative years may have made falling in love with Cheri Allen inevitable.

This brings us to the next chapter in the Melody Rouzer saga. On Wednesday, November 6th 1974, Melody and I had a conversation in the school library in which Melody brought up the subject of Cheri Allen. I spent much of the rest of our discussion attempting to find out how she knew about my affinity for CA, and she spent much of the rest of our conversation berating Cheri. Melody took the moral high ground by asserting that Cheri was sooooo beneath me, and how in God's name could I fall for someone like Cheri Allen. "CHERI ALLEN??" "CHERI ALLEN??" I recall Melody posing incredulously, as if the mere knowledge that I HAD fallen for Cheri had put a damper on some of Melody's high hopes for me. It was not out of any vision-blurred jealousy that Melody expressed these feelings towards Cheri. She truly disliked her intently, and treated me as if I was spurning an angel of virtue to go chasing after some demon of frivolity. This complicated an already hopeless situation, and would eventually cast VOT suspicions on Melody's undisclosed motives.

It was in my second period government class that Melody first made herself known to me. From a point early in my senior year, I felt her keeping an eye on me in class. "I have my sources" was the only answer I ever received from her to repeated queries on who was divulging details about my feelings for Cheri. It wasn't any big secret I was trying to keep, but it also wasn't anything that Cheri and I would have discussed with but our closest friends, more for the simple fact that it never amounted to anything. So WHO told her, and why was Melody being so secretive about their identity? This two-pronged question was perhaps the inaugural entry into the pool of mysteries that EAT and I would come to know as the VOT.

Beyond this point, there was just more of the same from Melody. What she wrote in my yearbook was both proof of how little she had changed her tune, as well as a lifelong memento of Melody's essence.

Bob -

You WILL write me in Charlottesville at the University of Virginia. I shall completely disown & abandon you as my cause if you do not. I intend to keep up with you. I will see you this summer. You have my phone number. Don't hesitate to call as you have in the past. Don't disappoint me, for I have high hopes for you.

Melody Rouzer

To the side of her message was an addendum, which read -

Am I a female of your "Conflicting Fancies?" I would hope this to be the case.

- Mel

This was in reference to a passage in the story I wrote (and obviously loaned Melody to read) - Holes in True to Life Fantasy. The sentiment was appreciated, and so was Melody, all the more for NOT having been one of the "Females of my conflicting fancies." As for the "High hopes" Melody had for me. I'm afraid they probably included someday having a drink together and reminiscing on what a vacuous twirp Cheri Allen really was, which I can state for the record, ain't gonna happen. I am sorry that I neglected to write to Melody in Charlottesville, but I'm afraid I would have only continued to be a disappointment to her.

The last time I saw Melody was during the final folly on June 3 1975. It was near the end of the day, and Tonny, EAT and I had discovered her working alone in chemistry lab (room) 108. Melody was dutifully performing what were probably her last few tasks as a lab assistant when the three of us burst in, cameras and tape recorder a-waving. Little of any consequence was actually discussed, but upon discovering the tape again, my heart was truly warmed to hear the sound of Melody's voice after all these years, and to revisit that unusual rapport the two of us shared. Melody exclaims that someone (there was too much ambient chatter going on for me to make out who) had just been chasing her around the lab with a carrot, as if to exact sympathy from the lord above for now having to contend with us. She then tells me that she didn't like what I wrote in her yearbook, saying – "You make it sound like all I do is subjugate you." I don't remember what I wrote exactly, but judging by her reaction, I seem to have hit the nail on the head, as even in our final moments together, Melody was doing grandmotherly things like correcting my diction.

How's this for a time capsule? Melody asks us what our recorded interview of her is for, and EAT comes back by telling her that it's going to air on "Panorama" (which was a daytime talk show hosted by Maury

Povich). Melody says – "Good! Because I know Maury Povich personally," which was actually something that she had told me before.

Now that she's married with children, it's far too easy for me to go on about how much I miss the old girl. When I told Melody that I was happily unmarried, her reply was –"Shame on you!" Hmmm! Maybe what I left Melody in my senior will should once again be my final word on the subject. "To Melody Rouzer - I leave well enough alone."

MERRY-GO-ROUND

An infamous Springfield Mall clothier that from the summer of 1975 through the summer of 1977 took customer service to new heights. By the summer of 1977, the store had developed quite a reputation among young men my age for the overly friendly service of the well-endowed co-eds that worked there. By this time, I had taken EAT, Tonny and Tom Kilbey there to savor the Merry-Go-Round experience, each with amusing results. Merry-Go-Round was the Russ Meyer free love aesthetic transplanted into the early disco-era Northern Virginia suburbs.

Actually, despite the sales intent behind their trained friendliness, I found none of the ladies who worked there overtly disingenuous, and a couple of them I found extremely likable. One such young lady made my first trip there with Tonny in the summer of 1976 particularly memorable. Her name was "Yummy," and I must say that her hair, her face, her body, her personality, and even her voice combined to make Yummy the most appropriate nickname imaginable for this person. Tonny and I were already half smitten-half bewildered by the bubbly quirky charm of this bouncin' baby girl, but when she hit us with her name, one or perhaps both of us must have lost it completely. I remember a brief expression of hurt crossing her face followed by an equally adorable explanation/defense of her name. Yummy instantly took her place alongside famed Ranch House waitress Laura in the annals of loon lore. What struck me as so amusing was not so much how fitting her name seemed to be, but how fitting it was that this girl named Yummy would come to find employ at Merry-Go-Round, as if her job there was an example of fate crossing the line and becoming destiny.

While actually a post Oakton phenomenon, Merry-Go-Round is connected through its function as being a successor to my senior year fashion Mecca - EF Sly. Along with Georgetown as a whole, Sly's descent into normalcy necessitated a shift in EAT and I's fashion focus briefly to Springfield mall. There upon EAT's initial Merry-Go-Round baptism at the hands of a fondling blonde, was also EAT's realization that Merry-Go-Round had picked up the slack a bit. In the right back corner of the store was enough black flared-bottom pants and black cotton shirts to outfit several whole covens, along with a few silver and gold glitter holdovers from the Diamond Dogs era that we were still connected to spiritually. By August of 1975, EF Sly was well on its way to Izod and blue denim functionality, so this was a welcome discovery. Like Sly though, Merry-Go-Round eventually changed its whole image and sales approach, sinking to the level of a Gap-type store by the end of the 70's, and not surprisingly, going out of business shortly thereafter.

Ah, but 'tis as much a fine memory for my body as well as for my mind to recall the glorious creature that first waited on me there. Her name was something like "Willie" or "Wendy," and she eventually became some kind of manager there. She was tall and well built, with brownish skin and a Cynthia Myers type of face, framed by luxuriously thick long brown hair. In short, she could have been one of Charlie's Angels.

THE MIDNIGHT CACKELER

(AKA Kit Merrill) - One of the first times I ever ventured into the youth lounge of Christ United Methodist Church, a strikingly peculiar looking young woman with long straight dark hair, thick dark eyebrows and a prominent birdlike nose emerged from the kitchen, looked straight at me, and in a shrill witch-like tone demanded "Who are you?" Without waiting for a reply, she turned and asked someone (the Combs boy, I believe) who was reclining on the couch directly ahead of her – "Who is he?" as if young Combs was better equipped to answer that question than I was. This was my first introduction to Kit Merrill, an individual destined for a special place in loon lore. In the months to come, I would become equal parts repulsed, fascinated, bewildered and (truth be told) duly smitten with Miss Merrill. While her tendency to condescend would never allow the part of me that was repulsed by her to ever submerge itself totally, I will say something in her defense. No one in the revelations club was as colorful an individual as Kit. She was intelligent (or maybe precocious is a better word) and intently strong willed. I think there's a chapter in the book of Revelations that describes what would have happened if I had taken Kit to one of the revelations club functions. With my own impression of Kit in mind, I can imagine what kind of three-headed beast she might have appeared to be to the Alcorn sisters.

Kit had a loud joyless cackle of a laugh that never let you forget that she was laughing at you instead of with you. It was this laugh of hers that inspired me to dub her "The Cackeler," or more formally – "The Midnight Cackeler." In late spring of 1973, I recorded "The Ride of the Midnight Cackeler," an album's worth of songs relating to this mythical character who would ride through the night Cackling and terrorizing the countryside with her ghostly cry – "Who are you? Who is he?" It was an attempt on my part to at least have some fun with a girl who would never accept me on my own terms.

As if duty bound to make something out of nothing, I made the Cackeler legend known amongst my fellow loons. At one point on the phone with her brother Scott, I let the cat out of the bag and told Scott about my nickname for his sister, and a bit about the Cackeler legend as well. I did this with full knowledge that Kit was in the room with him at the time, and that every word I was saying to him was immediately being repeated aloud for her benefit. I should add here that in relating these things, I had to make frequent pauses while Scott stopped to catch his breath from laughing hysterically. Scott told me (perhaps during this particular phone call) that he would follow his sister around with a tape recorder and get an actual recording of the Midnight Cackeler cackling, which I'm sure went over like a lead balloon with his sister. I imagine that Kit registered this sort of thing as further proof of what silly boys the two of us were.

In the final analysis though, I cannot recall being hurt or offended by anything Kit ever said to me, as unpleasant as she could be at times. Kit was one of those people who would jokingly condescend without any force of ill will behind it. I did manage to catch a glimpse of what was really beneath that brusque veneer of hers. I pretended once to be genuinely hurt by something she said to me. She looked mildly shocked, as if completely taken by surprise, and proceeded to be unusually nice to me.

Another incident that brings this point home was Elmo's one and only visit to an MYF meeting on the morning of Sunday, September 16 1973. When I introduced him to the youth group as Elmo Zudinski Romanoff, it brought on a predictable barrage of harassment from the Cackeler. She later exclaimed her total amazement to discover that she had hurt Elmo's feelings. "Didn't he know I was only joking?" she asked me in a pleading confessional tone. Feeling that a little atonement would do her some good, I didn't really answer her. "Was Elmo really hurt?" she asked, hoping to eke out a little absolution. Though I'm sure Elmo was not really bothered by the incident, I led Kit to believe that he was. Yes! I wanted to see her squirm a little bit, because I WAS bothered by the incident, being somewhat protective of my friend, and desirous of seeing a kinder gentler Kit Merrill.

While I got the distinct impression that my grandmother did not approve of Kit, I liked her. Kit would never let me live this down, but I thought she was kind of cute too.

MITCHELL ROBINSON

Words cannot express the amount of respect I have grown to have for Mitch. He had the courage to do what no one else did. He not only befriended EAT and I, but he chose to spend a lot of his spare time hanging out with us in the radio room. He did this despite the fact that he had a girlfriend and an assortment of more prestigious friends. EAT and I attracted a lot of attention with our very presence, but Mitch was attracted by the light of familiarity, and then hung around long enough to realize that he actually had more in common with us than he did with many of his other friends.

I don't even recall when or how Mitch appeared on the scene. Perhaps

 because the loon in him was such that it seemed like he had been with us from the beginning, through the conversion efforts of 72/73 and the great follies of 73/74. I would date Mitch's arrival around December of 1974, square in the middle of a period thick with fragmented hearsay, clandestine sources, and enough mysterious blondes to fill up a Mickey Spillane novel. What a contrast the boyish Mitch was in the midst of all this, with even his own variation on EAT's "Weirdly lab assistant" spasmodics. One day Mitch bumped his knee or his finger, or did something to himself accidentally that caused him to exclaim – "Aw! Fuck! Shit! Fuck!" In the next instant, he caught my gaze and our simultaneous laughter turned his outburst into an oft-repeated cliché (in good old loon fashion).

Mitch would occasionally bring some of his own records by the radio station, "Masters of the Airwaves," Frank Zappa's "Roxy and Elsewhere" and an album that Mitch tried unsuccessfully to get me to appreciate the merits of - Wishbone Ash's "Live Dates." Mitch also came over to my house to assist me on the pre-song narration for Death by Slow Girl from

"Time is the Murderer." But my greatest memory of Mitch was our March 7th 1975 trip to Georgetown. It gave EAT and I a chance to show Mitch our favorite clothing haunts, and as the three of us left directly after third period, we had the whole afternoon to wander around. We did the clothing circuit, ate at Blimpie's, and of course, stopped at a record store, where Mitch bought a copy of David Bowie's "Ziggy Stardust." Not

wanting to carry the record around with him for the remainder of the afternoon, Mitch went back and put the album in his car. Unfortunately, it was an unusually warm sunny day for early March, and when the three of us later returned to the car, Mitch discovered that his RCA Dynaflex unwarpable record had, in fact, warped, a slightly sour ending to an otherwise perfect day.

Unfortunately, Mitch would move to St. Louis shortly after graduation, so I would never see him again outside of Oakton. He got married that summer and afterwards wrote me a letter, which I did not answer, much to my later regret. Hindsight wishes that I had kept in touch with Mitch, but at the time I could see that he was starting life anew with his new home and bride, while I was still kicking around in the foothills of high school purgatory.

In my senior will, I left Mitchell Robinson – "My nuclear powered ax to aid him in battling the dreaded 'wingwongs' who would persecute him for his courage in befriending the little man of my schizoid manifests." Wingwong was a favorite term of Mitch's, used to describe everything from a dildo to an intellectually impaired individual. In an off-the-cuff way, I was even then paying tribute to the courage of one whose journey to the dark side was complete. Wherever Mitch is, I wish him happiness.

MORTY SNEAKY

EAT's on-air alias, taken from the Brian Eno song "Dead Fink's Don't Talk." As a name, Morty Sneaky really fit EAT's personality, as did the Bipperty-Bopperty hat he would don while shaking up the A lunch crowd.

NANCY KLEIGEL

The first female to admit to insanity. She was briefly my lab partner in Mr. Komars biology class my sophomore year (before Boni). Though Nancy's involvement with lunacy was virtually nil beyond her initial confession, the news that a female had confessed to insanity sent already high spirits soaring at a time when imperial lunacy was nearing the apex of its power.

NIGGERBUNCH

A nickname given to Tonny by his cousin (and Punx'y's only loon prospect by Tonny's initial assessment) - Bob Hetrick. Now I had as many nicknames for Tonny as fit the mood of the moment - Bunster, Butler, Bertrand, Cuthbert, Tonbooch, Tootis, Tanis, etc. But all of these on the spot appellations rolled off the tongue in that loon way. No! Niggerbunch, however much it may have fit Tonny (though I felt it more descriptive of the bowl over the head haircut he was sporting in those days), it was clearly someone else's nickname for Tonny. Though I hope Tonny will always appreciate that many people have someone who calls them "Friend," and many people have someone to call them "Sweetheart," but few ever have someone to call them "Niggerbunch."

NIGHTMARES

Here we take the darkest trip of the book, into a realm where control is relinquished. My theory on nightmares (and I'm talking about the really scary ones now) is that they tend to occur more in our youth, because that is when we tend to be less in control of our environment. What is fear, after all, but a perceived loss of emotional control. It's been at least 15 years since I've had a nightmare, so in practice, my life has borne this theory out.

I was never plagued by any recurring nightmare as such, but from my earliest memory, through to my early 20's, a recurring theme did crop up occasionally. My earliest nightmare, in fact, introduced this theme. How young was I? Well! The fact that my second nightmare featured my first grade teacher would date me as young as four for my first twilight baptism of fear. I found myself in a small closet size room with dark wooden walls and wrought-iron hinges on its door, which I could not seem to get open. Presently, I heard my mother outside the door, and being somewhat relieved, I excitedly called out to her to open the door. When she calmly refused and told me that I had to stay in there, I thought how odd and unlike my mother this seemed. I should say that as my mother spoke to me from outside the door, I received visual images of her standing outside the door. As I persisted in trying to convince my mother to let me out, I gradually became aware of the impression that this was not my mother at all, but something far more sinister, masquerading as my mother. Upon sensing this, I received another visual impression from the other side of the door of what I can only describe as a dark entity with no discernible outline and a pair of glowing eyes as its only discernible feature. The already dark room I was in grew still darker with the knowledge that I was in proximity to something evil.

Once the seed of suspicion began to grow within me, the deception collapsed, and I was able to see the entity for what it really was. This was, nonetheless, extremely disturbing to me, at least in the confines of the dream state. The recurring theme here that would not surprisingly resurface midway through my junior year was this - I would happily come across a female that I had some emotional attachment to, only to gradually discover that said female was not what or whom she appeared to be. Two other examples of this are worth mentioning here. The first of which dates from shortly after the Cheri rejection of December 1973. The setting was the upper level of 7 Corners shopping center, formerly Northern Virginia's pre-mall Mecca for one stop shopping. I was at the end of a large crowd of people who were clamoring hurriedly to make their way into Garfinkel's department store, as if in a mad rush to take advantage of some incredible sale. Turning around, I could see the outline of a lone figure walking slowly behind us, about half way towards the other end of the shopping center. I use the word "Outline," because aside from Garfinkel's, the rest of the shopping center appeared to be dark and deserted, save for this one figure. The figure was carrying a couple of books, and I could tell by its outline and the way it walked that the figure was none other than Cheri Allen.

I called out to Cheri, but she did not respond. Turning my attention back to the crowd clamoring towards the brightly-lit doorway to Garfinkel's, I could see Elmo at the doorway, jumping up above the crowd and enthusiastically motioning to me to join him. I was now torn between following the crowd and waiting for Cheri to catch up. As the forward motion of the crowd had slowed to a crawl in its attempt to cram through the doorways, I was able to stop and ponder my decision. What really began to creep me out (and what qualifies this as a nightmare) was the fact that every time I turned to look at Cheri, she was in the same place. She was getting no closer. Oh, she was walking towards me alright. She would even pass through the same area of diffuse sunlight that shown in-between the blocks of stores, giving her the illusion of forward movement. But the more my impatience turned to anxiety, and the more Cheri refused to acknowledge my now shouted pleas for her to hurry up, the more suspicious I became that, as with the dark entity that had impersonated my mother in the previous dream, this was not Cheri Allen. It was the soullessness of the ever-approaching figure that I believe was even more frightening to me than the evil presence of the aforementioned entity.

It was some weeks after graduation (possibly even as late as the fall of 1975) that I had a Peggy nightmare that fit into this recurring theme. Come to think of it, I'm sure it was after August of 1975, when Tonny and I had gotten jobs with the Fairfax mirror, because the dream was obviously inspired by that job. I was walking through a neighborhood that bore some resemblance to a neighborhood I had recently been delivering the mirror in. It was one of those times where a real life setting had been used as a template during the dream-state. I came to a particular house, and Peggy appeared at the door. Things got progressively bizarre and surreal from that point on, but throughout the remainder of the dream, I was attempting unsuccessfully to gender even the slightest emotional response from a cold and tight-lipped Peggy Wallace. It was as if some entity had agreed to portray Peggy in my dream, but was finding it difficult to conceal their contempt for me.

Retrospectively observing this, I'm brought to ask myself - What was my psyche attempting to convey, that appearances can be deceiving? My take on it today is to follow the trail of fear. In other words, what I was innately and continually wary of would hold any clues to any particular fear that might be playing itself out in my dreams. The resoundingly obvious answer was "Third Parties" or third party intervention. The root fear which keyed in on females that I had some level of emotional attachment to was not what the females themselves might say or do as originating from their own hearts and minds, but what the ideas and designs of unseen third parties might prompt them to say and do. This was the masquerading entity in my dreams, the thoughts, feelings, and perceptions of these females that were not their own.

Chalk these nightmares up to my fear of the unknown and you have a clearer picture of my suspicions concerning the role of the VOT, particularly in my aborted relationship with Peggy. On the other hand, if you were to view this fear as having the functionality of being a warning of some sort, then I must say that the warning was acknowledged, but misunderstood and summarily unheeded. I simply followed my overriding inclination to make light of everything and incorporated this element of danger into the game I was making out of my high school experience.

I really wasn't (despite Cheri's "You're rather deep for me" appraisal) deep enough to just sit down and contemplate what Cheri or Peggy thought or felt about me. If I had, I might have naively drawn my answers from the words and actions of Cheri and Peggy themselves, without separating them from their environment and imagining them forming an opinion of me devoid of external influences. Conversely, if Cheri or Peggy had wanted to know what I really thought or felt about them, they would have had to separate me from the influence of my own coadjutors, which wasn't going to happen. Keep in mind that there were dissenting third parties on my side of the fence as well. I could delve a lot deeper here, but to do so would be to step outside the purview of this book.

9, BLACK AND CREEPERS
Not just the title of one of my later solo albums, but a story unto itself. Rick Judd was amusing himself by applying one of those dime-a-dozen personality tests that were so popular in the 70's. They were fun for people of all ages, because you could give them to your friends and family, and draw up their psychological profiles based on their answers. He had just read about this particular test, and was eager to demonstrate its efficacy to his fellow students. This laughably simple diagnostic tool drew its conclusions from asking the subject three questions:

1. What is your favorite number (must be a single digit number between 1 and 9)?
2. What is favorite color?
3. What is your favorite flower?

My answer to the test was "9, Black and Creepers." A few days later, after consulting whatever criterion chart he had in order to give me the results of my test, Rick said to me – "You are a seriously disturbed individual." As I had been fearing for the future of the Insanist movement, I breathed a huge sigh of relief.

THE NODES
Two empty soda pop bottles that Kaiser discovered in our sophomore year shop class homeroom. As Kaiser had just discovered the Kaisey Module, he dubbed these two empty bottles "The Nodes." Their function, as I recall, was to act as a directional amplifier for the power of the module.

NORM CASH
Emmette's other obsession that predated his Richard Wagner fixation. Norm Cash was the first baseman for the Detroit Tigers throughout much of the 60's and early 70's. He was a stocky tobacco chewing power hitter who hit for a decent average, was a marginal fielder, and like other long ball hitters, tended to whiff a lot. Statistically Norm Cash ranks among the top home run hitters of all time. The lack of any further distinguishing talents

did not prevent Emmette from proclaiming that his hero was "The most underrated player in the American League."

The first words Emmette uttered into a microphone after showing up at Tonny's Merrilee apartment during one of our early 1971 weekend recording sessions was "Norm Cash is great,", after which Emmette went into his now famous Norm Cash soliloquy. While this was my first real exposure to the gesticulative manner of Emmette O, it would in time become one of the things I liked about him the most. For example, I shall forever know that Norm Cash wore number 25 because whenever the number 25 was spoken in Emmette's presence, his head would perk up and he would blurt out "25? 25?" as if even the most off-handed mention of the number was a summons for him to go into a discourse on the greatness of Norm Cash. Norm Cash was a character. Emmette was a character. There were some definite parallels between the unlikeliness of these two individuals. I cannot attest to the greatness of Norm Cash, save for the way in which Emmette utilized ol' number 25 to magnify his own greatness. That much I can attest to.

MRS. O'HARRISON
Howard Koretz and I saw this horror movie at the Fairfax Circle theatre called "Don't look in the Basement." The plot was about an insane asylum where the lunatics eventually take over, a story that one could imagine attracting a pair of loons like Howard and myself. There was an old woman in the movie that Howard developed one of his curious fixations with. As Howard could not recall her name in the movie, and certainly did not know the actress by name, he named her "Mrs. O'Harrison." This is interesting because recalling Mrs. O'Harrison has lead me to also recall Arthur O'Harrison, who like Alan Barksdale, was a haunting figment of Howard's morbid imagination. Howard delighted in ascribing situations and events to unseen entities such as Arthur O'Harrison. It was the horror movie aficionado in him divining his creative thinking processes. It was rather quaint of him to pull this old lady out of this movie and give Arthur a significant other.

OH YOU DO, DO YOU?
Punch line to a John Fowler joke about frogs amusingly retold by Tonny.

ORAL REPORT ON INSANITY
Here is another strange but true account from the memory files of my character molding junior year. It revolves around an oral report that counted as the final exam for Mrs. Sanford's English class. That year, we were rotating English classes every quarter, and the kids got to choose their

classes according to the subject matter that interested them the most. One of the quarters, I chose a class Mrs. Sanford was teaching which dealt with witchcraft, ghosts, Satanism, the paranormal, and in general all aspects of the unknown. What this had to due with the mastery of the English language, I haven't the foggiest. Nevertheless, it did sound more interesting than learning about conjunctives and superlatives.

Despite covering more than enough subjects to spark my eager and full participation in such a class today, such as I was, my attention was more often than not focused on the attributes of Pam Sherlock. I recall doing no homework, and being otherwise bored to distraction in class, much to the frustration of poor Mrs. Sanford. When the time approached for the giving of our oral reports, I probably greeted this idea with the same amount of trepidation that most my age viewed oral reports with. But then a sudden flash of inspiration hit me - I would do my oral report on insanity, a subject that fell well within the purview of the class.

And so, driven by my own identity as a loon, I made a rare series of visits to the library to collect data for my oral report. I say rare, for while I often enjoyed the pre-WOHS getting-away-from-it-all atmosphere of the library, I usually only went there on my own to study things I was personally interested in, and this was hardly an exception to that rule. I combed the length and width of that library for information on insanity, amassing a report that I actually now anticipated giving to the class.

When the day came, I walked up and took my place in the chair to face the class, carrying only some notes on a couple of 3 by 5 cards and some pictures up with me. At some time during the report, I know that I (with some pride and emphasis) quoted the words of Areteus the Cappadocian, words that were the idiomatic cornerstone of the Insanist movement, as well as the thematic thrust of my report – "Insanity is but an extension of normal thought processes." This premise was alluded to, if not forthrightly asserted, throughout my report, using source material readily found in Oakton's library. No small irony, if you ask me. Come to think of it, it was in Oakton's library (sometime during my freshman year) that I first came across that oft invoked phrase of Areteus.

I also discussed the case of the painter Louis Wain, with the added visual impact of showing the class pictures of Wain's cats to illustrate his descent into madness. What has since made expensive art objects (not to mention numerous psychological studies) out of Wain's cats was how much more vibrant and intense the colors in his paintings became as his madness progressed. The deafening day-glow colors used in his later cats (that were actually painted after Wain had been committed to an insane asylum) also foretold the Peter Max-ish psychedelic art of the 1960's.

But what really brought the Oooh's and Aaah's of fascination out of my audience was showing them pictures of Wain's cats as a demonstration of his developing psychosis, from the pale pastels and the monochromatic blandness of his earliest cats, through to the neon brilliance of his final works. His later cats pulsed with spectral waves of light, as if radiating luminous electrical energy. The eyes, as well, seemed to leer at the viewer with a wild mad look that said "Ha Ha! Yes! I have crossed the line into madness, and have done so by simply knowing too much."

While this was as much an insanist propaganda speech as it was an oral report, the subconscious message I was sending to my peers was – "Do not pre-judge those perceived as strange or different, for they may have talent and knowledge you do not possess." Apparently I came close to strumming the lost chord, for on the completion of my report, the entire class cheered and applauded, with a few even giving me a standing ovation. My reluctant sophomore racquetball partner Devin Hershey walked up to shake my hand and congratulate me personally, saying, "That was a great report, Robert." Rose Anne Sheridan also gave me a face to face "Well done."

After the applause had died down, I looked over at Mrs. Sanford, whose jaw was halfway to the floor. In amazement, she exclaimed – "My God! Robert, Do you know what you have just done? You have just given me this great report, and now I'm going to have to flunk you anyway because you've completed none of the other assignments." I nodded in acceptance, and it was true, the one assignment that I put the most work and research into in my entire 12 years in the public school system was done as a lost cause. I knew there was no way that I was going to be able to even salvage a D out of this class. Yes, I knew what I had just done. But to the artistically inclined outsider wanting of communication with and perhaps a little validation from his peers, the question remains, did Mrs. Sanford or anyone else in that class ever realize what I had just done?

THE ORGANIZATION

Tonny and I's friendship blossomed at a time when both of us were attending Luther Jackson intermediate school. Now that word "intermediate" is an especially appropriate description for my 7th and 8th grade years, and for more reason than being a trial run for high school. Oh, a great deal of acclimating did occur, but in the overview of my 12 years in the public school system, these "intermediate" years were a rest stop while I got my bearings. And what did I do after I got my bearings? Why, continue on with the business of forming a group. You see, while the roots of the Insanist movement date back to my 8th grade association with my new found friend Tonny, the root impulse to form a group dates back to my grade school years at Willston Elementary. Examining this impulse raises an interesting correlation between my 6 years at Willston and my four years at Oakton. As was the case with my freshman year at Oakton, my first two years at Willston were pleasant, but uneventful. Sometime during my 3rd grade year, I got the bug to form some kind of a group there. This yearning grew out of my friendship with Byron Howe, and was transferred into Willston through my fascination with a girl named Cathy Wilson.

That I was growing up as an imaginative only child in the midst of the secret-agent crazed cold war era of the mid 60's was evident in my friendship with Byron Howe, and the makeshift group that grew out of it. We were a part of something occasionally (and rather loosely) referred to as "The Organization." We had nerve centers, secret communication devices, carried toy weapons, led chases through the woods, ran from imaginary helicopters, ducked bullets, the whole 9 yards. What changed in 3rd grade was that my fascination with Cathy Wilson eventually led me to label her an enemy agent. Now we were battling "Wilson's Agents." If Lynn Kellum was one of Cathy Wilson's friends before, she was one of Wilson's agents now.

This was a conscious attempt on my part to spice up our adventures, at a time when my growing fascination with girls needed an outlet of expression. The equation became Danger + Girls = Fun, and boy, did we have tons of that. My enthusiasm was ratcheted up to the contagious level, and subsequently, Byron and I were joined by the likes of Chris Coulson and Clifford Pumphrey, among others, in a 4th grade explosion that would be duplicated in spirit my sophomore year at Oakton. During my 4th grade year, our chief enemy agent was a girl in my class named Jan Lutinski, and I will never forget the rush I felt when Chris Coulson came running up to me during recess with a frantic look on his face exclaiming – "Bob! Bob! Lutinski's here!" What had happened was Jan (whose recess normally followed ours) was let out for recess early. Excitedly, I gathered up Clifford and a few others for a conference in the northwest corner of the court. Now that's about all that happened, and despite how trivial this might seem, one has but to recall being 10 years old for the intrigue of this moment to become easier to imagine, especially if one considers how fresh and exciting a simple fascination with the opposite sex can seem at that age.

I can remember spending many recesses standing around while games such as dodge ball were going on around us, conferring with Clifford Pumphrey on various matters pertaining to the Organization. As I look back on it now, it was such an ingenious stroke of kid logic for me to take a fascination with females I didn't yet fully comprehend, and integrate it as both a tool for achieving solidarity within our all male group, as well as a means of keeping the excitement level high.

Another incident during my extremely eventful 6th grade year typified how high that excitement level had gotten. Our principal enemy agent was an attractive (of course) redheaded Jewish girl named Jeannie Morris. Byron Howe and I were walking down a street in our neighborhood when lo and behold, we see Jeannie Morris and another Jewish girl who lived in the neighborhood named Marcia Juneau walking towards us. This took us by surprise, as we knew Jeannie (who must have been visiting Marcia) did not live in the neighborhood, and while we nonchalantly offered our greetings to the 2 ladies as they approached us, shortly after passing them, we stealthily doubled back through the woods that lined one side of the road, in an attempt to keep an eye on our enemy agent number 1.

This was an extraordinary event, because our chief nemesis had shaken our little fantasy world by making an unexpected appearance on our home turf, and although the two girls eluded us by disappearing before Byron and I emerged from the woods, I will never forget the level of excitement as we raced through the woods to get a spies-eye view of the real thing – the genuine article. It was the type of thing that Byron and I did instantly and instinctively, without a prompt from the other. Just cue the James Bond music and we were off into the woods.

Now although all this fun and adventure preceded Tonny and the 8th grade birth of the Insanist movement, Tonny (like Byron before him) would become the primary catalyst in leading me towards the idea of uniting my friends around a central theme, an idea that by itself makes the Organization the ideological precursor to the Insanist movement. Strangely, the unity I strove for in both of these groups only worked in practice as long as I was immediately present and actively involved in coordinating the disparate entities within the two groups. Neither group stood alone as a collection of friends per se.

A more model cohesive unit was the 8th grade group that consisted of Helms, Stills, Good, myself, Neil Clouser, Jeff Aman, etc. Aside from the fact that this was much closer to being just your classic group of friends, this group's growth, unlike the Organization that preceded it or the Insanist movement that followed, was totally organic and devoid of purposeful direction. This was the only time in my life that unity on this scale just sort of happened on its own, and once inside Oakton, I wasn't about to just wait around for such a thing to happen again.

The more the merrier impulse to pull a group together all tied into my quest for fun against the constant incursions of boredom. The Organization grew not only out of my interest in secret agents (and the whole vistas of invented gadgetry that it opened), but my disdain for the imagination stifling routine of already invented games. The few times I was talked into playing football with a group of kids, I absolutely hated it. The Organization afforded me some creativity and brought me closer to the idea that in the public school system, scoping out girls was very much a clandestine operation.

For all their similarities, the differences between the Organization and the Insanist movement are perhaps more interesting. While the TV inspired fantasy world of the Organization may have been necessitated by my dismissal of the normal boyhood pursuits that were foisted upon me (yes, I hated those cub scout meetings and summer camp as well), the Insanist movement grew out of my reaction to the whole march towards conformity that the institution of high school seemed to be leading everyone on. I HAD to react against something now just in order to remain true to myself. The impulse to pull a group together and the quest for fun were still intact, but despite the fact that I've never considered myself a rebel in the true sense, I had discovered not only what a liberating feeling it could be breaking the mold that society was trying to make of me, but also what a good feeling one got from encouraging others to do the same. I had seen glimpses of how boring and droll the world could become, and I became determined to stave off the death and taxes mindset for as long as I could.

I should, before closing this entry, mention the one brief period during my 8th grade year when I did pull a makeshift group together (albeit one consisting of members of an already existing group). It began with an incident in March of 1971, in my first period class, and involved one of Luther Jackson's premier babes – Sue Cook. Good, who sat two desks behind me, was walking back to take his seat at the beginning of class one morning, when Sue Cook, who sat two rows over and one desk up from me, said something to Good that was so uncalled for that I was shocked into insisting that Good demand an apology. Sue, who obviously was not used to being challenged, addressed me with a long stream of conscious sentence that amounted to every obscenity she could think up on the spot, an attempt to put me in my place that nonetheless seemed to contradict itself, being issued in that sultry half-whispered voice of hers. Imagine being cussed out by Marilyn Monroe and you'll have an idea of what I was up against. Be that as it may, the contempt in her eyes, and her disrespectful treatment of a friend whose shortness had led me to be somewhat protective of brought an instant rebuttal containing every obscenity I could think of repeated 2 or 3 times, and with a little more volume. "Karnes!" Came the shocked response from my good buddy Stills, who sat directly behind me. Hey! There were few guys in that school who lusted for Sue Cook as intensely as I did, but even at this age when those hormones were really starting to kick in, when I saw this side of a girl, I didn't want to see any more.

A couple of weeks after this incident, Good broke up with a girl he was dating. This break-up was the final straw for me, in view of other recent incursions against my little friend, and so I concocted something I called "Tennantism," so named after Good's real name – Steve Tennant. The basic practice of Tennantism was incredibly simple. I would, as the opportunity presented itself, or the situation warranted it, gather a group of us around Good and exhort the group to salute Good with rhythmic (and rather loud) hardy hails and accompanying Nazi-like arm gestures. The idea behind the practice was to make Good appear to be the leader of a group that was actually larger than our immediate one. For that, ancillary group peripherals were employed to good effect in at least getting across the message that Good had a lot of friends, even if most of these guys were just going along for the fun of it. Being of such small size, it was easy for Good to stand on top of a cafeteria table, desk, or gym bench in order to appear elevated in stature, not to mention a prudent measure to insure that his ex (or whoever) could see who this gathered circle was saluting.

Tennantism reached its peak in mid to late April of 1971, with an incident that is described in a journal entry of what I would describe as a sparkling moment of unity. Good's ex and a group of about 6 female friends squared off in a cafeteria staredown with Good, Helms, Stills, myself, and about three other Tennantism practitioners. They were all lined up at one cafeteria table, like the front line of an advancing regiment, and I recall Helms (who had theretofore taken Tennantism as a complete joke) coming up to me and nervously asking what the lot of us should do next, as if some sort of showdown was imminent. Nothing of any consequence actually did happen, but as I watched this group of young ladies huddling together in watchful suspense, I knew that Tennantism had achieved some measure of success. I could see in their frightened little faces, along with the simple fact that they had gathered en masse, that the point that Good had a lot of loyal friends (whether true or not) had been made.

The buzz that I got out of all this was the almost Machiavellian thrill of uniting everyone under the pretext that an enemy of one was an enemy of the entire group. Key to my involvement in fomenting confrontations of this sort was the idea of uniting everyone. Even though our group was already fairly established, which may explain how easily I was able to rally everyone around Good in such a manner, I was in all sincerity operating under this idea of promoting greater group solidarity against perceived adversaries. Though short-lived (and completely forgotten until coming upon that old journal entry), Tennantism recalled the spark that would ignite and sustain the Organization throughout my grade school years, and what would continue to be the thing that motivated much of my activity during my first three years at Oakton.

The word Organization was used again my senior year to affix an organized-crime-like aura to the activities of the VOT. In my aborted cafeteria interview with a fleeing Peggy Wallace, I shouted questions about her involvement with .The Organization" In this context, the word became a cynical joke. The quest for fun, however, was still ongoing.

PAM MORRISON

On March 21st 1975, Pam Morrison became the fourth girl in almost as many months to reject EAT. Damaris and Peggy were about all I could handle for one school year, but the plucky EAT kept at it, though all successors dwelled in the shadow of Hunk. Pam's rejection came one day after Mr. Bradford denied my request for a public apology and retraction from Robyn Burchfield, so you can imagine that around this time, EAT and I had pretty much had it.

PAULA PIPPERT

The first evidence I would receive against the theory that it was a biological impossibility for a female to have good taste in music. It was sometime in early October of 1974. I was doing my radio show, with Elmo and Kaiser puttering about in the studio behind me. Both Elmo and Kaiser had already expressed their displeasure over my extremely radical format (I.E. too much David Bowie). So one can but imagine the tension in the studio that day as I pushed the envelope by playing Hawkwind's "Paranoia (part 2)" followed by "Seeing it as You Really Are," a full 15 minutes of creepy non-melodic space-rock. We were about 10 to 12 minutes into the melee, when something quite unexpected happened. There was a knock at the station door, which froze us for a couple of seconds. I say "Unexpected" because we had only been on the air a couple of weeks, and the general perception was that nobody knew we were there. Kaiser went to open the door, and there in the doorway stood the owl-eyed figure of a girl, bearing a sheepish look of inquiry, like a character out of Dickens. "E-Excuse Me! What is that music you're playing?" She asked in the tone of Dorothy as she approached the great Oz. I held up the cover of the first Hawkwind album, and as she entered the studio to examine the cover, I thought to myself – "Oh No! This girl has just had some negative psychological experience from this music, and she is about to hand Kaiser the I-told-you-so he has been so desperately searching for." But to everyone's amazement, she proclaims – "This is so wonderful" with a bewildered look that conveyed her astonishment at actually discovering such music on school property. She then asked if it was OK if she borrowed some paper to copy down the essential information from the album jacket. After doing so, she thanked us and left.

Once the door was closed behind her, Elmo let out with an "ALRIGHT BOBNEY!" Elmo's high fivin' smile and fist in the air was proof that he still knew a loon victory when he saw one. The loon (and the music lover) in Elmo must have surely appreciated the irony in the fact that the most radical piece of music that had been aired on WOHS up to this point was also now the first piece of music to have garnered such an enthusiastic (almost euphoric) response from a member of the student body. Kaiser, of course, had nothing to say, and while his paternal admonishing of EAT and I would continue throughout the remainder of the school year, amazingly, his main bone of contention would continue to be that symbol of anarchy and rebellion - David Bowie.

Curiously, I would have another format affirming encounter with Paula Pippert. I was walking down the main hallway, coming from the radio station, and heading back in the direction of my 4th period Russian class, when from behind me I overheard a voice exclaiming – "The music they played in the cafeteria today was sooooo wonderful." As I had just finished doing my show, my ears pricked up. I turned around to see Paula Pippert talking with her friend, and another of Oakton's fairyfolk - Stephanie O'Rourke. In the few scant seconds we had before branching off to our respective classes, we walked and talked about the music I played. I recall that "The Actor" from the Moody Blues "In Search of the Lost Chord" album had particularly caught her attention. Ah! Dear sweet Paula! To wherever you are right now, I shall put my pen down long enough to blow you a kiss.

PAUL NEVITT

At Luther Jackson, Paul was a member of a group that included Billy Robbins and Jim Schwab, and was a casual acquaintance of mine. When I moved into the Fairlee subdivision in early May of 1971, I quickly discovered that I had moved into Paul's neighborhood. Paul and I would visit each other occasionally, usually for the purpose of listening to each other's record albums (it was only a 5-minute stroll over to the Nevitt house on Fairlee drive and visa versa).

I'll never forget sitting with Paul on his front steps listening to the new Black Sabbath album – "Masters of Reality." It was a rather steamy day in the summer of 1971. I had never really given Black Sabbath a good ear up to this point, and I was having the adolescent male equivalent of a religious experience when lo and behold, the babe of the neighborhood, Patty Maddox, walks by. Paul calls out to Patty and she comes over and sits with us for a while. Paul wanted to introduce me, and I'm sure a part of him wanted to impress me as well, but a guy's first Sabbath buzz is a pretty hard thing to interrupt, even with Patty Maddox in a pair of shorts. All I remember registering is - pretty girl, older than me, way out of my league, a great pair of legs, not overly friendly. I'm sure I didn't leave a great first impression on Patty, but hey! Sometimes life's decisions are childishly simple.

Based on A: The fact that there was little hope of me ever dating such a creature. And B: The instant realization that I would probably own that Black Sabbath album until the day I died, what would you imagine me giving more of my attention to? Oh No! I wasn't rude. Patty and I did have a few cordial exchanges, but half of my attention and at least one of my ears was always tilted backwards towards the music that was emanating from Paul's open doorway. I will say that Patty reaffirmed the generally positive first impression I had of this neighborhood I had recently moved into.

My freshman year was speckled with memories of hanging out with people who lived in my neighborhood, like Rusty Siren, Pat Carrico, Larry Laufer and Paul Nevitt, with Paul being the most frequent guest at my house. I have a distinct memory of listening to music in my room with Paul under a black light. I also recall Tonny and I riding our bikes down Fairlee drive and encountering Paul, who was running a little motorized toy car around in the street. I remember Paul angrily pushing Tonny's bike out of the way when his toy car had accidentally run into the front wheel, so I can't imagine Tonny having a positive impression of Paul (if he has any memory of him at all).

I never had any classes with Paul at Oakton, and so after our freshman year, I had very little contact with him outside of his increasingly infrequent appearances at the bus stop. At some point, Paul got his driver's license and I rarely saw him after that. Paul, like Peggy Wallace, consistently addressed me as "Robert."

PAYING

An interesting folly that developed in the fall of 1973. Its principle participants were Kaiser, Elmo, Carlton Thompson, and myself, with several other ancillary players intermittently joining in. What it basically involved was 3 to 5 people, walking side by side down any particular hallway. One of us would countdown 3 - 2 - 1, and then all of us would shout in unison "PAY!" It was just one of those things that grew out of thin air, though at one point, the lovely Sherry Hogge seems to have become an actual target for our Paying outbursts. In one of my early letters to Tonny, I mention the lot of us making a point to "PAY!"

whenever Miss Hogge was spotted in the halls. What is interesting about this particular folly is how it attracted the involvement of non-loons, most notably Carlton Thompson and Flip Anderson.

Participants were gathered on the spot, making the impulse from thought to execution about as spontaneous as you could get. A couple of us would be walking down the hall, one of us would spot Carlton at his locker. As we would pass him, the closest would deliver the message "Hey Carl! We're gonna Pay." He would hurriedly finish up in his locker and run to join us. It was the gather-as-you-go manner of instantaneous collection that made it almost impossible for anyone familiar with the practice to resist participation.

Paying was never premeditated, and I doubt that the whole process, from thought, to collection, to countdown, to execution, to dispersal, ever took more than 10 seconds. Its appeal, I'm sure, was the thrill of the moment rush of causing a disruption that was too short in duration to bring teachers and administrators out into the halls, yet was of sufficient volume to indeed disrupt activity for about a 30 yard radius, if only long enough for people to stop and wonder - What was that? The anonymity of the participants was maintained not just by the brevity of the word itself, and the hit-and-run style of its delivery, but the acoustics of the hallways as well. I can recall a group of us Paying, and then watching students ahead of us lift their heads out of their lockers to look in the opposite direction for the source of the sound.

If you, dear reader, are yet pondering the point of such a seemingly pointless exercise, it might be time to examine how far you have drifted from the spark of your youth. Paying as a practice lasted for only about a month or two, but it was a shining example of how the best fun is the fun that one creates for oneself, which was a code that I lived by.

PEGGY WALLACE

There is no other person who has wrenched more emotion out of me than Peggy Wallace, which is an extraordinary thing to say about someone you barely knew, and had such a relatively small amount of actual contact with. I think it's accurate to say that Peggy opened doors within me that in many cases led to other doors, so while Peggy has vanished from my thoughts for months at a time, her influence will be with me forever.

Much of what I know about beauty I learned from Peggy Wallace, so needless to say, she has had a profound effect upon not only my own art, but my appreciation of art in general.

So how did this fleeting specter of enchantment wend her way into the darkest corners of Oakton mythology? It was Wednesday, December 11 1974, five days after the rejection of Damaris Bonnell that I first took note of Peggy in the Oakton cafeteria. I was sitting with Howard Koretz at our table of self-exile about 5 or 6 chair's length from the doorway on the southwestern corner of the cafeteria. Howard was sitting across from me facing the windows that overlooked the front of the school, and I, as fate would have it, sat overlooking the whole of the B lunch cafeteria crowd. Try as I did to ground my attention in the space between Howard and myself, I was continuously drawn by the feeling that I was being watched past Howard to a point four tables away. There I met the searching gaze of a less than discreet Peggy Wallace. Avoiding direct eye contact, I nonetheless registered the slightly unnerving sensation of being X-rayed, though at this point, I may have dismissed it as my own imagination.

The next day I would do my radio show, returning to lunch with Howard on Friday, December 13th. Once again, and that much less of a thing I could easily dismiss, I was under the watchful eye of this mysterious young woman, who now sat with her lunch companion - three tables away. On Saturday, December 14th, I call EAT up to tell him about this Jane Eyrish figure of a girl who stares at me in the cafeteria. EAT, for some reason, had his own story to relate about a little southern girl in his English class. This was significant, because we would later discover that Peggy's lunch companion and EAT's little southern girl were one and the same - Connie Underwood. EAT and I would go on to have a lengthy (and in the context of this book - historic) conversation about Hunk and CA, and how the popularity of both seemed to grow pending their respective rejections.

Monday, December 16th, and there was no denying it now. Sometime during our lunch, I called Howard's attention to this peculiar but winsome young lady who now sat - you guessed it! Two tables away. Later in the day, I would be conversing with Rick Hockmuth in the main hallway at the point where the hallway that runs from the administrative offices feeds into it. At some point during our conversation, I noticed that girl again, approaching us from the direction of the Admin offices. She moved swiftly passed us, hunched over slightly, as if protecting her textbooks, rather than simply carrying them. From the corner of my eye, I would catch her flashing a glance at me from the corner of her eyes as she passed. I mentioned this to Rick, and the following day, mentioned both sightings to EAT in the hallway, only to be curiously interrupted by the sudden presence of Cheri Allen.

Wednesday, December 18th, and I'm once again lunching with Howard. Though she was maintaining her distance at two tables, an incident occurred that finally convinced me that this girl's attraction to me (whatever it was) was something that I would eventually have to confront and deal with. It was near the end of the lunch period. I had just deposited my leftover trash in the large central trashcans provided, when my path crossed that of the girl and her friend, on their way towards the communal cans to perform the same ritual. Out of the corner of my eye, I caught a glimpse of her friend tugging on her arm to get her attention, and then pointing in my direction as if to say "Look! There he is." For some reason, this really made the hair on the back of my neck stand up. So much of what I had experienced over the course of the previous year had predisposed me towards a cautionary distrust of the fairer sex, and so the fact that this might simply be someone who found me attractive didn't even register.

Thursday, December 19th, and the clincher. In one of the most magical moments of my four years at Oakton, I found myself almost locked in direct eye-contact with a girl that at this point must have realized that she had finally gotten my attention. Quite involuntarily, a smile began to push up the corners of my mouth. As if responding to some permission granted, the corners of her mouth began to follow mine slowly upward. Our collective shyness had been overcome, and in one beautifully genuine moment of clarity, contact had been made. I must say this ranks near the top of all the precious moments of my life that I would love to go back and relive again.

December 20th and another radio show, and beyond that, a 16 day Christmas vacation. Never before or since have I so wished for the end of a vacation. As the days dragged on, her frequency in my thoughts became a portend of the four year long summer vacation that lay beyond my graduation. Anticipation increased by degree throughout the unending holiday to the point that when January 6th finally came, no decision had to be made about my next course of action. I marched into the cafeteria from behind Peggy's table with the full intention of taking a seat next to her and introducing myself. But to my dismay, I found only her little lunch companion dining alone. So I took a seat next to a visibly surprised Connie Underwood and forthrightly inquired – "The girl that normally sits here, where is she today?" I don't recall her response, only the shitting-in-her-drawers expression on her face, and of course, her adorable Southern accent and manner.

Peggy's absence was schoolwork related, rather than illness related, because I distinctly remember leaving the cafeteria hell-bent on accosting Peggy the next time I saw her in the halls, and at least getting an exchange of names. I didn't have long to ponder my approach (which was probably a good thing). At the end of 4th period, I found myself walking up the middle science hallway past the planetarium towards the front doors of the school. Since I normally went directly from my 4th period Russian class to the radio station, this was a deviance from my usual route. I vaguely recall knowing just enough about Peggy's daily routine to suspect that I might encounter her coming from the opposite direction down this hallway. And sure enough, about half way between the planetarium and the library, I spotted her approaching just a few feet in front of me, keeping her pace in the student stampede. Thinking fast, I reached out and grabbed her arm, bringing us both to a halt square in the middle of inter-period traffic. She had such the look of a frightened doe that I softened my voice almost to a whisper to ask "Hey Babe, what's your name?" "Peggy" came the reply in a voice that was diminutive and effeminate on the surface, yet conveyed the emotional depth of the speaker with such impact that it was all I could do just to give her my name before allowing her to continue on her way.

We had just exchanged about 12 seconds of soul swapping eye contact of the likes I had never experienced before, and I needed a good hour with EAT on the phone to snap my head back on. The following day, January 7th, and my 4th period Russian teacher Mrs. Bryan decides that we will be taking A lunch instead of B lunch. It does not interfere with my show, but I miss seeing Peggy in the cafeteria. EAT was doing his show, so I hung out in the station and discussed the current situation with him. EAT, as it turned out, was trying to work a little magic of his own on a bright-eyed freshman named Diana Malone. Later in the afternoon I asked both Bob and Rick Hockmuth if they knew of a girl named Peggy with blonde hair. Their inability to help me only further ignited my impatience. However, I did have one more chance in the evening to gather some shreds of information. The job that I had started the previous Friday as a telephone solicitor for the Washington Star was significant because I worked in the same office as Howard Koretz and Ray Denk, the latter of whom did have a few things to say about this mysterious Peggy. He could not provide me with her full last name, only that it began with a "W." He also showed me the sunset that she had embroidered on the back of his jean jacket. But when pressed for information on Peggy - the person, his only response was "Peggy is a troubled soul." That this was the primary impression she had left on an individual known for driving down Sutton road in excess of 100 MPH should have sent up warning flags, but this was curiosity, and I was the proverbial cat.

The following day, January 8th, and I have my radio show to do, so once again, I miss seeing Peggy in the cafeteria, and my first chance of having an introductory conversation with her. It was about this time that I started to carry my phone number around on a piece of paper on the off chance that I should bump into Peggy in the halls. At the end of 4th period, I searched for her in the middle hallway where our rather electrically charged introduction had taken place two days earlier, but no luck.

Thursday, January 9th, and Mrs. Bryan pulls the A lunch wool over my eyes again. I had already missed doing my radio show on at least one occasion prior to this, so I was becoming concerned, and while that did not happen this week, the effect was the same - no lunch with Peggy, and no phone number exchange. So the weekly recap on my efforts to effect the most rudimentary communication link with a girl that three weeks earlier seemed to appear every time I turned around goes like this -

Monday the 6th: Peggy does not, for some reason, show up for lunch in the cafeteria.

Tuesday the 7th: I have A lunch.

Wednesday the 8th: I have my radio show.

Thursday the 9th: I have A lunch again.

This time, Elmo was doing his show, so I decided to pump him for information. I asked Elmo (whose sane name was "Zarin") if a young lady fitting Peggy's description was in his homeroom. He assured me that she was not. As I knew that Peggy was a junior, this indicated that her last name was alphabetically near the beginning of the W's, and that the second letter of her last name was probably A. Peggy Watkins? Peggy Waldrop? Oh boy! Oh boy! Oh boy! I then asked Elmo where his locker was located so as to get a general idea of where her locker might be, figuring that if I made a detour to that area between every class, I was sure to come across her. But Elmo, like me, kept his coat and belongings in the radio room closet, and also like me, did not even know where his locker was located.

At about this time, my strategy of first introducing myself, then slowly and naturally easing into a regular dialogue with Peggy was out the window. It's hard to illustrate how frustrating this was for me without interjecting a few things here about how I was raised. Since my mother was a single working parent, I spent a lot of time with my grandparents and in the company of people from my grandparent's generation, to whom proper introductions were a point of courtesy. Every friend or acquaintance I had ever had up to this point, I had either been introduced to or had come to know through a process of acclimation. Even my introduction to Cheri Allen, though unorthodox, was nonetheless orderly and sequential, but with Peggy, my curiosity had far surpassed my rate of progress (with no sign of a kindly adult to intervene and give us a proper introduction).

By Friday, January 10th, the little light on my hold button was flashing about a million times a minute. I don't recall the specifics, but for some reason or another, Peggy and I failed once again to hook up during B lunch. This left me with the middle hallway scan as my last hope of avoiding carrying my phone number in an already burning pocket over what would surely be an interminably long weekend. Fortunately, I met Peggy at about the exact spot where we had quivered our way through a wide-eyed introduction four days earlier. I gave her my number, and breathed a sigh of accomplishment. I could now resume the flow of my one-step-at-a-time approach, or so I thought. Peggy did not call me that evening, as I felt sure she would.

Saturday, January 11th passed without a ring from Peggy, and by day's end, Monday's priority was clear - get Peggy's number. Sunday, January 12th, and time was grinding to a halt under the oppressive skies of an impending snowfall. By Monday morning, my hopes of securing a comm link with Peggy were dashed by the news that school had been cancelled due to snow. As the day crawled along like an in-extremis explorer through the Antarctic waste, I began to worry about not having heard from Peggy.

January 14th - Snow day, no call from Peggy

January 15th - Snow day, no call from Peggy

January 16th - Another Fucking Snowday!!!!!!!!! AAARRGGHH!!!!!!!!!!!

Now you dear reader may not be able to recall at what point snow ceased to be something fun that you play around in and build forts out of, and became an inconvenience, if not something you outright dreaded. I, on the other hand, know exactly where that shift in viewpoint occurred in my life. What really pissed me off was the fact that by Wednesday, the 15th, the snow had pretty much melted on the roads in my subdivision. The snow had never been bad enough to prevent my mom from driving me to my job for the Star. So I was shocked to discover that school was called again on Thursday due to snow that by this time was nothing more than steaming patches on the grass. I mean, I was dressed and had books in hand. But when I saw my sympathetic mother shaking her head in the negative, my only thought was "Those freakin' pantywaists are gonna sure as shit push this comm lag with Peggy into next week." One full month will have passed from the point where I first decided to befriend Peggy Wallace. I was by this point mired in worry over why she hadn't called.

The news reports indicated that Fairfax county schools were seriously considering scrubbing the week altogether, and picking up fresh the following Monday. So I was mentally preparing myself for four more days on the emotional rack, when again, the unexpected happened. Sometime late in the afternoon of the 16th, Peggy called, full of apologies and a lengthy story about how she had lost my number, and had to employ various services to obtain it. After Peggy's apparent ordeal, she was all too happy to give me her phone number. Finally! We could get on with whatever our relationship was to be.

Our first telephone conversation was definitely that important first step, but the real icebreaker came the following day, January 17th. On the evening of the 17th, Peggy and I would have our first long conversation by phone, beginning shortly after the dinner hour, and concluding at exactly midnight (which is lengthy even by teenage standards). The give and take of sharing and discovery were in full flow, and time just ceased to exist. Peggy apologized for staring at me in the cafeteria, which she certainly did not need to do, but it underscored my impression that Peggy was a lady of grace and manners.

Music was never far removed from our conversation, owing to Peggy's love of the piano. Not surprisingly, she expressed an admiration for Keith Emerson and the works of Elton John. Though, to quote Peggy concerning Elton John, "I don't like him personally, I just like playing his tunes." Peggy, as has been the case with many I have known since then with a passion for playing a particular instrument, did not compose her own music. The creation of music was not something that Peggy and I shared a common interest in.

As enamored as we were with the sound of each other's voice, little of what we said was actually retained by the other. All was accepted however, as if given by someone great and wise. It is the emotional tone, rather than the substance of those early Peggy conversations that has followed me through the years, and also the alpha-wave inducing lilt of that beautiful voice of hers. We were still feeling each other out, still ingesting our initial impressions of the others beingness rather than simple fact finding. I do recall at one point during the 100 year conversation on the 17th revealing to her that I was known to my friends as "Bobney." Though the Insanist movement was past the point of dissolution, we still addressed each other by our insane names (despite Elmo's faux-adult insistence on being called "Keith"). This was the deepest darkest insider secret I could have revealed to Peggy at this time, despite what she may have later been told by others.

Monday, January 20th was a magical day. On my way from the radio station to my first period English class, I passed Peggy in the main hallway. With a blithe smile that belied the haunted look in her eyes, she called me "Bobney" as she passed, a heart warming gesture, but one that I'm glad she chose not to repeat. What came so naturally from the mouth of Emmette, Elmo, EAT, and Tonny, seemed so foreign coming from the mouth of Peggy Wallace. I had pretty much given up the goose on my 4th period Russian class, in favor of doing my radio show, and for what was to become a tradition for the next two weeks, taking my lunch with Peggy and Connie. After school, Peggy called me, and we had our most memorable phone conversation, where-in Peggy went into detail about all of the things she liked about me - my hair, my eyes, my clothes, even the way I said – "Peggy." "I don't like my name, it sounds like a pegboard" was the famous quote of hers from this conversation that would later inspire the song "Stranded on a Peggboard."

During our last lunch together, I got to examine more closely the lost look in Peggy's eyes. It was her most distinguishable facial characteristic, maintaining itself through whatever the lower part of her face happened to be doing. However lightly and sweetly Peggy conducted herself in my presence or on the phone, Ray Denk's words "Peggy is a troubled soul" were the truth that would echo throughout the remainder of our relationship. And considering all the things, seen and unseen, that were building to a head around me, our mutual attraction may have been guided to some degree by the fact that we were vibrating on the same wavelength.

Tuesday, January 21st, and I had pretty much figured out all the necessary detours in my daily routes to achieve maximum Peggy exposure. On a couple of occasions during this week, we found ourselves walking together through the halls. Now there was no way that I could have had anything but the highest hopes for the future of our relationship during these walks. No lady had ever looked at me that way before. No lady had ever lavished such praise on me, and certainly none has since. The 21st was also significant for being the first time that Oakton siren Marcia Carter said "Hello" to me in the halls. My head was probably swimming with the idea that the opposite sex was finally beginning to notice me for reasons other than being an oddity (or perhaps they were finally beginning to appreciate me for that reason).

However! As close to perfect as this week may have been for me, Wednesday, January 22nd brought a sobering reminder of the company I kept, and to some extent, my own station at Oakton High. At the beginning of 4th period, I entered the radio station to find a disconsolate EAT, who had just been rejected by Diana Malone. As EAT was still nursing the wounds from Hunk's rejection, I felt bound to join him in cursing the damnable unpredictability of women, though this was the last rejection we could easily write off on some preconceived notion of female behavior. Clichés and axioms could no longer serve as signposts, for beyond this point, there was only the unexplainable.

On the 22nd, I gave Peggy a poem I had written entitled "Toms O'Bedlam." On the 23rd, I gave her another poem, and one that was written for her – "At Last a Swan and at Least a Buzzard." While I now consider these works artistically inferior to many of the song lyrics that predate them, and certainly to any poetry or song lyrics that I would write after them, Peggy was quite impressed and strangely moved by them. She would later become insistent upon me submitting them for inclusion in the 1975 Paragon, and became visibly distressed when I refused to do so. The irony of Peggy being so concerned with the development and the exposure of my art is inescapable, because it was that "Troubled soul" of hers that would eventually grow to be the defining element in much of my art.

Between Thursday the 23rd and Sunday the 26th, things were beginning to feel like they would grow on their own, with a minimum of watering and pruning from either party. At some point during a phone conversation with Peggy from this period, I suggested to her that we get together sometime, to which she replied – "Definitely!" This falls a bit short of asking Peggy for a date, and while a formal dinner date may have seemed inevitable, what I really had in mind was more like a walk through a park or around a lake, that sort of thing. This dated my expectation of such an occurrence as later in the spring, when the weather was more conducive to such activity. Two things must be considered here:

1. That I now felt a little more confident that our relationship would follow a gradient progression up to the point where we would take such walks, and-
2. The fragility of Peggy's emotions (or what I saw of them) demanded that I take things slow, which was fine with me, being such a novice at this sort of thing.

Monday, January 27th, and the news of Walt Robbin's death left me with the unnerving impression that something was going on beyond my five senses. The first chance I would have to speak to Peggy about Walt was over lunch on Wednesday, the 29th. Peggy was glum and listless, not at all herself, and while she knew Walt (though how well she didn't say), I got the distinct impression that there was a distance between Peggy and I that wasn't there four days earlier. But once again, it didn't smack me in the face, so I brushed it off. My next lunch with Peggy on Friday January 31st saw the mood of our lunch table down near the funeral home level. It seemed as though Peggy was keeping something inside. Her smiles were half-hearted and seemed to trail downward under the weight of something that had left a bitter taste in her mouth. There was a tension in the air that I just never expected to feel in the presence of Peggy Wallace.

It took me until the following evening of Saturday, February 1st to decide that drastic measures were called for. I called Peggy that evening to test the waters, and sensed the same pale tone of removal in her voice. Some sort of bad news seemed imminent, though she went on chatting the minutes away, forcing me to play my hand. At one point, the desire to reach out to Peggy and draw her close to me overcame good sense, and I blurted out the unspeakable. I said "I Love You" to Peggy, and while simple boyish naivete had as big a part as raw emotion in the utterance of those words to Cheri Allen, I was a lot closer this time to knowing exactly what I was doing, even if the sudden change in Peggy was squeezing it out of me. Unfortunately, Peggy's response would be the only time where she would remind me of Cheri on the phone, crying out "No!" in that identical horrified tone that left me feeling like I'd just said the worst possible thing at the worst possible time. I don't know about the state of romance in today's high schools, but in the early to mid 70's, these three words still carried a hell of a lot of weight behind them, if the reactions of these two ladies were any indication. I was even more shocked by this reaction the second time around, because I would have bet money that Peggy and I were on our way to bigger and better things.

Peggy followed with a few milder protestations before delivering her most infamous line "You're choking me!" Now I had not demanded any commitment from Peggy, nor had I demanded any great amount of her time, nor had I even pushed Peggy for a date, nor had there even been so much as a handshakes worth of physical contact between us. How in God's name was I choking her? I suppose I should have asked her, and maybe I did, but I had interiorized too far into my feelings of betrayal and dejection to be interested in anything else Peggy had to say. All I could feel at this point was that I'd been led down the path again, and that no amount of sweet nothings would get me any closer than this freezing cold stalemate with Peggy. And as with Hunk and CA, EAT and I were once again crying over the same spilled milk.

I gladly traded the unprotected openness of the cafeteria for the radio room's inner sanctum, but I was returning home empty-handed. My February 4th radio show was dedicated to Peggy, and while Peggy was down in the cafeteria listening, it was difficult to tell by her subsequent reaction to it how successful the words of the songs I played conveyed my own emotions as intended. Peggy was appreciative, and seemed to be moved, but it was difficult to tell how much of that was the conflict of emotions she was still dealing with.

Within the confines of the radio room, I now had time to ponder the questions that would loom ever larger in the months and years to follow. Firstly, who or what had interceded to transform the Peggy of January 20th into the Peggy of January 29th? I hadn't changed. Whatever light had drawn Peggy to me from halfway across the cafeteria was still shining, and shines down upon this page now as I pen these words. The change in Peggy was too sudden and too premature to convince me that she had just decided that I wasn't her type. This change had occurred sometime between the weekend of the 25th - 26th and our lunch on the 29th, which led me to focus on two seemingly unrelated events which occurred during that time period. The first event was, of course, the announcement of the death of Walt Robbins on the morning of the 27th. Was it nothing more than the shock of our first encounter with death, a sudden mortality reminder from one who had moved among us only days before? I have to believe this was the case. On the other hand, while I was nearly overwhelmed by a bodeful awe over the news of Walt's death, I found it somewhat disconcerting to find Peggy in a similar condition two days later. The dark cloud of Walt's death had hung over me for the better part of the day that Monday. But having lunch with Peggy that Wednesday brought the cloud back, as well as the added mood darkening presence of another completely different cloud.

The second event, and the one I think more deserving of serious consideration, was the mysterious encounter with Stephanie Hill in the library reference room during 2nd period on Tuesday, the 28th (see Stephanie Hill's entry). The incident suggested, if not plainly demonstrated, that Stephanie and her gaggle of friends were predisposed to the belief that I was involved in Satanism, the leading cultural scourge of the day. Now the practice of passing along information about someone you don't know should have been familiar enough to me to read the cue cards, and to stop and ponder the possible ramifications, but at the time, it seemed too far-fetched to even consider. A year or two later, hindsight would view the sudden change in Peggy as having all the earmarks of a third-party interference. Then, and only then, did I come to consider the possibility that Peggy may have slopped at the same gossip trough that Stephanie Hill had.

About midway through the month of February, Elmo's girlfriend Brenda Paris transferred to Oakton high, an event that was greeted with no small amount of dread from EAT and I. On Tuesday, February 18th, WOHS went off the air for major repairs and a general overhaul of the system, a tweaking that would take over three weeks to complete. That Thursday, February 20th, EAT phoned to inform me that another freshman he had been attempting to woo, Karen Cockrell, had rejected him. That evening, and again during a much longer phone conversation on Saturday, the 22nd, EAT and I sorted through what EAT knew about this Karen Cockrell, and it turned out to be much more than he realized. During our conversation on the 22nd, EAT linked Cockrell to Donna Zarin, and more ominously to Peggy coadjutor Tanya Herrell, and finally, as a result of some serious recent memory collation from EAT, to Hunk. VOT warning signals always sounded whenever a relation to a major heartbreaker could be verified. This loose nit confabulation of females that EAT and I had made jokes about was looking more and more like something that actually existed. Some actual codification of the VOT was now being done, and oh how I wish I now had more than rough jottings from the period to recall all the correlations and interconnections we were able to make. Suffice to say that there was no connection, from upperclassman dangling carrots like Cheri Allen on down to seemingly insignificant and uninvolved freshman like Diana Malone and Karen Cockrell, that couldn't be made, and made with only one or two interconnecting comm links in-between. This cast a new light (or darkness depending upon your viewpoint) on Peggy Wallace.

Understand that it was not the idea that these females had a communication network going that EAT and I found unusual or objectionable in and of itself. We were both old enough to realize that gossip was the nature of the beast we were addressing. What bothered us was the fact that rejections from within the ranks of this group were making less and less sense as time marched on, indicating the circulation of negative and false data concerning EAT and myself. Well! I didn't have long to wait for physical evidence of that false data. On the morning of Tuesday, February 25th, my first period English teacher Mrs. Leech handed me an envelope that was addressed to me. It was written on some form of rice paper, and the text was framed with various occult symbols and was sealed with a sticker that bore a picture of the eye of Horus on it. It read "Loosing a power that you can not control, like carrying a sword that you can not wield, will kill you in the end! Beware of those things that you lack the strength to control," and it was signed with a name that was written in some ancient language. My first reaction was a mixture of wonderment and trepidation, followed by a rush of amazement. After that wore off, the humor of it finally hit me. "My God!" I thought. "The rumors about me have actually attracted the attention of someone who is really dabbling in the occult". Now besides the author's rather indirect means of communication, it's possible that some genuine concern for me existed among the school's practitioners. Ultimately however, an inability to take the letter seriously arrived the moment I considered the fact that the author of the letter and Stephanie Hill had gotten their information about me from the same common pool of schoolgirl titterings. The author and Stephanie may have even known each other well enough to compare notes together.

At any rate, it was about this time that I realized the full and potential power of the "Sword" I was wielding. Oh! It was not the power referred to in that cryptic letter. It was the power of gossip, and the curious thing was that the same social hierarchy that had kept me at arms length for three and a half years had given me this power, I hadn't asked for it. Now if you cared to describe the appearance (and even, on occasion, the presence) of EAT and myself as Satanic, I wouldn't argue with you. EAT and I HAD assumed the role of Oakton's fallen angels, possessed of the same rebellious individualism and bitterness of exclusion that old scratch himself is purported to have. We trusted those we knew and liked with the ability to see through the dark façade and accept us as we were, a trust that in light of our recent rejections, was perhaps foolish and unrealistic.

The following morning, in an attempt to demonstrate how ridiculous and out of hand things had gotten, I gave Peggy the letter to read. But during lunch I discovered that Peggy had interpreted my giving of the letter to her as an accusation that she had sent the letter to me, an idea that really made me wonder what planet Peggy was on. I had to spend several minutes calming her down with assurances that I didn't think it was she that sent me the letter. I left Peggy's table with the hope that I had at least brought her closer to the realization that if her decision to not get involved with me was based on something she had heard about me, then she had bought into the same misinformation as the author of the letter, and so might as well have written it herself. With Peggy though, there was always this vagueness of being that made it difficult, at times, to know if we were truly connecting or not.

Now before I get into some of the even more bizarre occurrences that took place in March, I don't want to leave anyone with the impression that February was all doom and gloom. In fact, a number of positives helped to balance out the overall picture. For starters, while EAT and I seemed to have antibodies in our systems that fought off female companionship, our reputation (whatever it was) seemed to be attracting as many people as it had been alienating. The most notable of these was Mitchell Robinson, who actually befriended EAT and I, and was now hanging out with us regularly in the radio room. And from there on down were acquaintances like Stuart Argabright, and a number of curiosity driven peripherals like Marcia Carter. We even had our own fan of sorts in the likeness of a girl who called herself "Flash Franny."

But the biggest pleasant surprise for me that month came in the person of Carol Galane. Carol sat in front of me in my second period government class. I knew several guys who were in absolute awe of Carol, and I must confess myself to having been slightly intimidated (or hormonally disrupted, to be more accurate) by her presence in front of me everyday. But at a point only days after Peggy's rejection, Carol turned around and started talking to me, and in the process, revealed that her beauty was more than skin deep. Carol's reason for striking up a conversation with me was that she knew Peggy, and through Peggy, had some knowledge of our aborted relationship. In seeing that I was still pretty broken up over the whole affair, Carol offered some words of comfort, and an interesting bit of information. Her take on Peggy was that she still cared a great deal for me, but that she was not ready to get involved in another relationship. Apparently, according to Carol, Peggy had just suffered a severe heartbreak at the hands of a guy she had been dating named Byron. While I appreciated Carol's persistent attempts to cheer me up, her story had but the faintest ring of truth to it. It was enough of a ring, however, to leave me wondering if my appearance in Peggy's life wasn't as poorly timed as her appearance in mine.

Carol and I would speak of Peggy almost daily for weeks to come, and while her perspective on Peggy's feelings and motivations never wavered, I just couldn't make it add up. I mean, why would someone get all bent over the loss of something, and then go right ahead and push away the very thing they had just lost? My eventual post-Oakton conclusion was that not even a psychological study like Peggy would have flip-flopped like that without a goading third-party presence. Peggy may have indeed had her heart broken by this Byron character, but I felt that it was too great a stretch trying to tie this in with Peggy's late January change of heart, or imagining that Peggy couldn't just see that I was (to be blunt) not like other guys.

Along with Carol Galane, February introduced the simpler and more direct smile inducing efforts of Marcia Carter and Carrie Hindes. While displaying obvious differences in personality and approach, Carrie and Marcia had both taken to telling me to "Smile!" when passing me in the halls (and in Carrie's case, in class as well). A sweet gesture, whatever the source, and one that begs the question, how much of what I had ingested throughout the school year was now visible on my face? I honestly don't remember walking around in a cloud of despair, but the paranoia level WAS rising steadily throughout this period, thus the need to project a more stern and defensive demeanor. Around this time period, I discovered that I possessed the ability to burn a hole in someone with my eyes. During the late 70's, I came across a couple of underclassmen who claimed to have actually been frightened of me. It may have been the aura I was projecting (or the "Sword" I was wielding, if you will), or the sense that I was carrying something else around with me, as if Peggy's rejection had caused me to be shadowed by an over-protective and ill-tempered guardian angel.

February did end on a positive note. As I mentioned earlier, Karen Cockrell's rejection of EAT inspired us to begin tracking the activities and the lineage of the VOT. This inspired me to compose and record an album's worth of material on the VOT entitled "Valentine Trashcan Rain." Sometime in April I taped up a hand drawn promotional poster on the radio room wall announcing its imminent release. Though for some reason, only the first two songs had actually been recorded by this time. The other 6 songs would not be recorded (or finished) until a year later in March of 1976. Also, in late February, I wrote Holes in True to Life Fantasy. Suffice to sum up February as the post-Peggy incubation period for ideas and inspirations which would keep me busy for awhile. These ideas grew throughout the month of March, and by the nature of artistic examination, fostered the first reassessment of the whole affair. Writing about Peggy forced me to look at her in different lights. That this reassessment took place while EAT and I were drawing charts and graphs of who knew who and which gossip trial led where, accounts for the acerbic tone of some of these writings. It also precipitated an incident in early April which typifies my state of mind during the later third of my senior year. After Peggy's rejection, my presence in the cafeteria was scarce. But occasionally, I would venture into the throng to give or receive a message from Peggy (or get a brownie to munch on). I walked into the cafeteria and found, to my amazement, a veritable VOT convention going on at Peggy's table. Within the anomalous group of about 10 females, there were enough suspicious characters to inspire me to walk up from behind Peggy and lean down to whisper in her ear – "Breaking out the heavy artillery, I see." As if knowing exactly what I was referring to, Peggy immediately stood up, excused herself, and then motioned at me to join her in the hallway. From there, Peggy and I took our last walk together up the long mile to the radio station, stopping about three feet from the doorway. The ponderous slowness of our gate indicated that Peggy had abandoned her lunch with the girls in order to tie up some loose ends. Her expression was searching and sympathetic, wanting to hear my story, but giving me nothing to ignite a revelation. Even the most offhand remark from her was given with a look that said "There is something I have to say to you, but I can't say it." And I, stuck somewhere between male pride and total confusion, squandered my last chance to set the record straight with Peggy. Together, we made quite a pair. As I said, we stopped short of the door to the radio station, and finished our conversation out in the hallway, despite my repeated requests that we adjourn to the more relaxed confines of the radio room. The more we talked without really saying anything, the more I felt like jumping out of my skin. At one point, my uneasiness must have made an impression on Peggy, because with some emotional emphasis, she exclaimed, "Look at you! Robert, what's wrong?" Now Peggy would have had to spend a day as Bob Karnes to really have gotten an answer to that question, because I wasn't talking. All I wanted to do was put this lost cause to bed as quickly as possible. Understand that 10 weeks earlier, I had grown to love Peggy Wallace, and years later, I would once again grow to love her correspondingly, but at this moment in time, I did not trust Peggy any further than I could pick her up and throw her. At some point during our conversation, as Peggy had me psychically pinned to the wall with those probing eyes of hers, a very strange thing happened. Ray Denk walked by us and entered Mr. Williams' electronics classroom, which housed the radio room. Ray approached us during a particularly tense moment, and my attention was mercifully diverted from the high-beam eye contact by the sound of his footfalls. I glanced up at him for a couple of seconds, and he gave back a knowing half-grin that said, with a combination of humor and empathy –"Well Bob! I see that contact with Peggy's troubled soul has made of you, a troubled soul."

The irony of Ray's appearance at this particular point struck me even as it was happening. However! It was Peggy's curious reluctance to finish our conversation in the relative comfort of the radio room that I felt worth mentioning to EAT. EAT and I would theretofore not only think of the radio room as our sanctus sanctorum, but also as a place where members of the VOT feared to tread, and dared not enter. We were only joking, of course (to each other if not to ourselves). But as with previous attempts to keep things light, an incident followed a few days later that completely validated our assessment of the energies around us. Marcia Carter and Suzanne Zanders-Lavey visited the radio room, presumably just to say "Hi," and to check out the facility. Upon crossing the threshold, the normally cheery, confident and outgoing Marcia showed a visible change in countenance, as if she had just realized her fly was open. Now I gotta give Marcia some credit here. Whether out of courtesy or curiosity, she toughed it out for a good five minutes. But while the ever-quiet and demure along-for-the-ride Miss Zanders stood slightly behind the scene, occasionally tilting my way with a smile of recognition, Marcia looked increasingly unnerved and out-of-place as the seconds ticked away. I don't even recall her saying much while she was there (which was also way out of character for Marcia). After the two of them left, EAT said something typically irreverent like "Why did they come here?" And I know the thought must have crossed his mind that that was not the same Marcia Carter we had come to acknowledge in the halls. Though my impression of the incident had already been pre-colored by the recent memory of Peggy's aversion to the radio room, I think I was in silent agreement with EAT that the best course of action was to carry on under the pretense that we hadn't noticed a single implication in Marcia's odd behavior. The protective aura of the radio room had nonetheless been affirmed.

As my senior year was drawing nearer to its end, I began composing my senior will. If Peggy had displayed her frustration some months earlier at my failure to submit poetry that I was less than proud of for publication in the 75 Paragon, she was conspicuously silent over the publication of my senior will, parts of which I still consider to be sheer literary genius. The page it was printed on is still warm with the fuck-all attitude EAT and I had copped during those final months. And yet, It was clearly written from an insider's perspective. The idea that I might never see Peggy again was not as real as the ongoing perspective of my Oakton world, and so my pen was ablaze with the bitter tokens of unfinished business. I left to Peggy Wallace -

The heart of my Romanian vulture, to which I extracted on Friday the 13th of February 1st in the year of the swan, hardened to a crackily crunch by the embalming effects of my rat broth additive.

If the degree of innuendo over plain English kept the meaning obscured beneath the words, it was simply my way of answering a mystery with another mystery (perhaps like Peggy, out of an inability to forthrightly articulate my true feelings). I have long wondered if Peggy has ever looked back upon this time with any realization of how mysterious she was prone to be. A perfect case in point (and perhaps just as perfect an example of how well Peggy and I were suited for each other) were Peggy's written replies to my request that she sign my yearbook. It was Monday, June 2nd. The yearbook had just come out and I was busy collecting signatures. I entered the cafeteria at the beginning of B lunch to leave my yearbook for Peggy to sign. Near the end of B lunch, I returned to collect my book, but was instead given a note from Peggy, written on a napkin that to this day bears the stains of whatever Peggy was having for lunch. It read "Bob, I don't have enough time to sign it now. I need to have lots of time to think about what I'm going to say. OK? I'll see you tomorrow. Peggy." This seemed logical, but when Peggy returned my book the following day, it contained another note written on regular notebook paper. This one read-

Dear Bob,
I don't know how to say this. I can't sign your book. I can't put my feelings down on paper, and no matter how hard I try, they come out all wrong. That's why I won't write anything down. Just as long as you realize that my thoughts are with you. I'm sorry.

Love, Peggy

And there it was – Peggy's final parting testament to obliquity. Now the significance of this letter was that it was dated and delivered on June 3rd, the date of the final folly, the last hurrah. While Peggy was writing this explanation of her inability to put into words the feelings she had probably spent part of the previous evening agonizing over, the radio room was abuzz with activity. Preparations were being made, under the co-direction of Ray Denk, for a mock press assault on Peggy in the cafeteria, a folly that would expand itself under the cover of being a senior prank to much of the school proper, and even outside to the smoking arcades. This was Tonny's second visit to Oakton in as many months, and this folly was loosely planned to take advantage of his presence (and to get some use out of that movie camera of his). The contingent of folly participants was amassing in the radio room during 4th period. This group consisted of Tonny (with movie camera), EAT (with Kodak still-picture camera), Ray (with some Geiger-counter looking gizmo he was passing off as a light-intensity meter), myself (with portable cassette recorder), and at the last minute, Colonel Hash, who was probably doing his show at the time, saw us making our preparations, and wanted to get in on the action. On our way to the cafeteria, we picked up Howard as he was heading back to his 4th period class. We were 6 strong as we approached the cafeteria. Ray and I entered first, catching Peggy and her group (which from photographs of the incident included Connie Underwood, Tanya Herrell, and 2 to 3 other unidentified females) just as they were getting up to head for the trash receptacles. Colonel Hash and Howard were right behind us, brandishing pen and pad and adding to the overall effect of a media onslaught.

Peggy's friends smelled a senior prank and scattered like ants, leaving Peggy alone and at the mercy of the press. With me pushing a microphone towards her and hawking questions at her about her involvement in the "Organization," Ray taking imaginary light readings and shouting them back to the cameramen, and the Colonel and Howard providing extra physical presence, Peggy flipped out. Outnumbered and in the spotlight, Peggy went into cornered animal mode, repeatedly shouting "ROBERT!!! What are you doing?" as the four of us chased her towards the doorway and into the flashing camera of EAT and the rolling film of Tonny. Peggy's face was as red as a radish as she ran hysterical from the cafeteria, leaving Ray and I shouting, "Cut! Cut! Cut!" in the mock tone of the frustrated journalist who just failed to get the big interview.

Howard and the Colonel had to leave to return to their 4th period classes, but Tonny, EAT, Ray and I moved like a pack of wolves, fresh from the kill, down the main hallway in search of other interviews. We hit Ray King and Mr. Herndon before cutting back towards the cafeteria. Somewhere on our journey back along the main hallway, I saw Peggy approaching and signaled Ray to halt the caravan. I then called out "Peggy!" to get her attention, and it's clear from the tone of my voice on the audio-tape that I was concerned for Peggy's emotional wellbeing. The violence of Peggy's reaction to us earlier in the cafeteria was fairly shocking, even given the volatility I always sensed was present in her. I wanted to make sure some serious emotional trauma hadn't taken place. Peggy, in a more subdued but concerned tone asked, "What's going on?" I said, "It's just a joke, a senior prank, that's all," which was a white-lie placation tantamount to singing Peggy a lullaby there in the hallway. Calling it a senior prank was my way of reassuring Peggy that we meant nothing personal (which we didn't) and at the same time, linking our actions with the observance of a time honored tradition (which they weren't). Peggy, with that same tremulous look I had always seen in her eyes (and on the rest of her face a lot after January 27th), produced my yearbook and said, "I didn't sign it. There is a note in there." We then exchanged parting gestures and went our separate ways. This was the last face to face exchange Peggy and I would have, and it was unceremoniously concluded by EAT throwing back a comment at Peggy that was spiced with his special brand of impudence – "We'll send ya the negatives Miss Wallace."

Clearly more than a yearbook was exchanged here. Here we would leave our final impressions of each other. Mine, of the beautiful but secretive and sensitive woman emerging in Peggy, and Peggy's, of the last carefree flapping of wings of the child in me. I mean, look at who I was

travelling around the school with - EAT, who was yet but a sophomore, Ray Denk, who was still a child when it came to creating disruptions of this sort, and Tonny, my friend since the 7th grade, and the most direct lifeline to the spirit and reality of my youth. Could Peggy's presence have been anything other than out of place at that particular moment in my life? I was living for the moment, and it had yet to occur to me that my chances for wringing out of Peggy that which part of her always seemed on the verge of confessing were slipping away as I reveled in my merriment.

After graduation, I was still vibrating at the tension level of high school, giving my biological clock the impression I was still there. Peggy would cross my mind occasionally. I even called her one last time, in August of 1975, although she was not in the mood to talk. She claimed to be very ill, and by the hoarse craggy sound of her voice, I could tell she wasn't just saying that to sluff me off. Of course, there was the possibility that her reluctance to talk was additionally due to the fact that she did not want to talk to me, so I elected not to call her again.

It wasn't until the following March that I would REALLY start to think about Peggy Wallace. I was finally finishing the composition and the recording of Valentine Trashcan Rain, which dealt with the subjects of Peggy, Walt, and the VOT. Although there had been a part of me that had never left Oakton high, concentration on this project really put me mentally back in the thick of it. Absorption in this reverie ultimately led to an inner summons for answers from people whom I no longer had immediate access to.

I thought about calling Peggy, but decided the better course of action was to confront her at her graduation, which by this time was only weeks away, and settle things face to face. So there I was, standing on the Oakton football field in the hot June sun, watching Peggy's graduation. After the glamour and pageantry of my classes graduation at Wolf Trap, the graduation ceremony for the class of 76 seemed so pathetically makeshift. But the alphabetical seating arrangement made Peggy easy to spot, somewhere in the middle of the last row. Just as I was admiring what a beautiful woman Peggy was becoming, a young man came up from behind her. Upon becoming aware of his presence, Peggy turned around and looked upward as he leaned down to kiss her. A tender moment to be sure, but one which pierced me with its dark finality. Now if the last sentence sounds dangerously close to a paraphrasing of my description of the last time I saw Cheri Allen, then you have an inkling of the déjà vu I experienced at that moment. Needless to say, confronting her directly was now out of the question. I followed the student procession down towards the school and caught my last glimpse of Peggy as she disappeared into the cafeteria. I held out the faint hope that Peggy would see me and approach me of her own accord. But if she had seen me (which I feel certain she must have at some point), then truly, the roles of the haunted and the haunter would have been momentarily reversed. Still! As overcome with failure over this incident as I was, the feeling that there remained some unsevered link between us continued to gnaw at me.

Also! At around this same time, I discovered something that really cut me to the bone. While reading the signatures at the front of my senior yearbook and taking a short stroll down memory lane, I came across something I hadn't noticed before, something which came like a shot from the past and took the shape of a finger pointing to the future. It appeared that Peggy, for all the notes and the production she put on about not being able to sign my book, had in fact, signed my book. At a point below Carol Galane's heartfelt words was the diminutive inscription – "Always, Peggy

Anne." Now what struck me about the sudden appearance of this inscription was how much it read like the contents of a sealed letter, to be opened only when the meaning of it could be understood. What was before a vague supposition was now hard knowledge, Peggy would ALWAYS be in my heart and mind. That one word – "Always" seemed to say it all.

From late spring/early summer of 1976 through to July of 1979, I was torn between wanting to go on with the business of finding a wife, and the increasingly anxious inner voice compelling me to seek out Peggy Wallace. And none of the girls I dated during this period could silence this voice. It is amazing that I did not just pick up the phone and call Peggy, but there was something about the idea of doing that that was imposing, even frightening to me. Also, I felt that what Peggy could hide from a voice on the phone, she could not so easily keep from my eyes. Past experience with Peggy did not bear out this idea in the slightest, but I still felt that direct contact was the best way to go.

In mid June of 1976, the discovery that Peggy had a boyfriend (and so might soon marry and leave her house) demanded that action be taken before the answers that I sought became irretrievable. And so with Tonny's help, I located Peggy's house on a huge map that Tonny had (conveniently) hanging on his wall. A few days later, with heart in hand and some form of closure in mind, I took a drive out to Peggy's house. However! As I approached her neighborhood, impulse turned into hesitant reasoning. I started to think about all the other people who might be there - her boyfriend, her parents, her brothers, and all the horrible scenes that might occur if I just showed up at her house unannounced. So I simply drove by Peggy's house, an exercise I would repeat on numerous occasions over the next three years, and each time, I would receive a strange spiritual cleansing that, in time, grew to be more important than the original objective of locating Peggy.

On at least two occasions, I took friends of mine out to Peggy's street, Tom Kilbey in 1977 and Angela Sheble (who I was dating at the time) in 1979. I would park my car at the end of her street, and we would walk slowly past her house, like the mindful devout along the Wailing Wall. Tom Kilbey even commented on the Tibetan peacefulness of the experience (though the tucked-away ambiance of the neighborhood itself probably added a lot to this impression). By the summer of 1979, Peggy's house would become more of a religious shrine than anything else, but I would still half-hope/half-fear to catch Peggy on her way out to pick up the mail.

Though I never once saw a single person moving around the house or going in or out of it, on my second or third visit to the house in the summer of 76, I did see something that cleared up a little mystery. In the driveway was parked a light blue Volkswagen bug, which made little bells go off in my head. I recalled that on two occasions, as I was walking down Pickett road on my way to Tonny's apartment at Margate Manor, someone in a light blue Volkswagen bug honked at me as they drove by me, heading back in the direction of Fairfax Circle. The second time it happened, I looked up in time to see the driver wave at me, which left me wondering – "Now who do I know that drives a light blue bug?" Well! In September, I would receive further circumstantial evidence that it was, in fact, Peggy who had honked and waved at me. Tonny, who was working at the Roy Rogers at Pickett shopping center called me up after work to notify me that Peggy had stopped by the restaurant earlier that day. Tonny, God bless him, had the presence of mind to signal the girl who was working the cash register, and give her a verbal message to give to Peggy, which she did. I don't recall what the message was exactly, but the essence of it was to the effect of "Bob Karnes sends his regards," to which Tonny related that Peggy's response was one of silent, but noticeable surprise.

While I appreciated Tonny's humorous attempt to keep me in Peggy's thoughts, the greater implications of this sighting were not lost on me. Peggy's trail was getting warmer the closer I got to NOVA, which was significant because I had just started taking classes at NOVA. My September-October relationship with Diane Burley, my January - March 1977 affair with Cindy Martens, and my on-campus spring fling with Sher Weston would divert a lot of my attention during the 76-77 school year. But I still made time to engage in several unsuccessful attempts to find out if Peggy Wallace was taking classes there. And in the parking lot, my attention was drawn to anyone getting in or out of a light blue bug. Indeed! While driving anywhere between NOVA's Annandale campus and Peggy's house in Vienna, I kept a wary eye out for any light blue Volkswagen bugs, which was no small task, as cars of that make and color on the roads in Fairfax county at this time numbered in the thousands. No, the only other times I would see that needle-in-a-haystack were on subsequent visits to the Peggy shrine.

In late August of 1977, near the end of the wild summer of Tom Kilbey, Jan, Marty, and Sher, I would begin my employ at the Penguin Feather. I soon found myself attending Penguin parties (as they were called) and amassing a treasure trove of new friends and associates. Through one of those friends, I would discover a vital missing clue to solving the mystery of Peggy Wallace. At my first Penguin party on September 30th 1977, I met (and became quite week-in-the-knees over) Bob McCord's sister Patty. By the time of the Halloween party a month later, I had been largely accepted, even celebrated for who I was by the greater family of Penguins, a situation the public school system had not prepared me for. My marathon phone conversations with Laura Waddell on January 16-19 1978 drove home the point that I was as far from the environs of Oakton High as I could get. Yet, even as I was reeling from the experience of this beautiful lady bearing her soul to me (not to mention giving me a detailed description of her stuffed animal collection ala Cheri Allen), the inner voice was shouting in my other ear. Even as Patty McCord walked into the Annandale Penguin Feather on January 26th, taking my breath with her as she left, Tonny and I had already planned an expedition to George Mason University to locate Peggy Wallace. I had recently noted in the 1976 yearbook that Peggy's future plans included attending George Mason.

On January 30th, Tonny and I went to GMU and found a Margaret Wallace listed in the school directory. Unfortunately, what looked like a promising lead fell through in late February. I returned to GMU and looked for, found, and ended up excusing myself to an attractive blonde girl who was obviously the wrong Margaret Wallace. Undeterred, my next thought was that if I couldn't contact Peggy directly, I would contact one of her friends and have her either set up a meeting with Peggy and I, or at least relay a message to her. My first thought was Peggy's little jazz-dancing familiar Terry Bell. And so Tonny and I returned to GMU a few days later to have another look at their class directory. Sure enough, there was a Theresa Bell listed. The next week (now early March) I return again to GMU only to find classes have been cancelled due to snow. Curses!!! Foiled Again!!!

Ah! But a major revelation was only days away. No more than five days after my aborted attempt to contact Tinker Bell, I found myself in the Fairfax apartment of fellow Penguin Melody Ziff. Being a music lover like myself, Melody just HAD to play me one of those early Al Stewart albums she held as masterpieces. While I was sitting there trying not to nod off, a knock came at her door. Melody opened the door and ushered in another friend of hers whom she introduced to me as Chris Davia. An extremely likable fellow, we sat and chatted for 30 minutes or so while the hyperactive Melody flew off to the store to get something. At some point during our conversation (perhaps prompted by the mutual discovery that both of us had attended Oakton), Chris happened to mention the street that he lived on. This perked me up because it happened to be the exact street that Peggy lived on, and it wasn't a very long street. "Did you know Peggy Wallace?" I asked. "Oh Yeah! I knew Peggy" no sooner left his lips than I could see the light bulb of recognition cross his face. As if suddenly having realized who I really was, he asked, "Are you the guy that Peggy's parents wouldn't allow her to date because his hair was too long?" BAM!!!

There it was! For three years I had searched everything from my memory of Peggy's eyes to the wording of her letters. I had ventured down so many dead ends in search of an explanation, and here, but for the grace of God, entered Chris Davia.

Although try as I did to pump Chris for more information, all he could add was to verify that a late-January-1975 time frame sounded about right to him. As Peggy was just a casual acquaintance who shared the same bus stop with him, he was even unsure about the original source of the information. But whatever the particulars, the whole Peggy affair was no longer just a confounding mystery, it was a salt-on-the-wound tragedy. I mean! All that scenario mapping of the VOT, and the unseen third party turns out to have been Peggy's parents???? I just couldn't believe it. And yet! It made sense. When Peggy said "You're choking me," what she might have been feeling (but not saying) was "You and my parents are choking me from opposite sides."

In considering the motives of Peggy's parents, the real shit-kicker was that sometime in late January of 1975, my mother and stepfather started pressuring me to get a haircut. There were two reasons why this was easily remembered and quickly dated. 1. It stands as the largest and longest disruption of the normally harmonious relationship I had with my mother and stepfather, and 2. One of the main reasons I fought so hard against having my hair cut in the first place was that Peggy had often remarked on how much she loved my hair. On February 9th, I bowed to ultimatums issued by my stepfather and visited the dreaded barbershop, but by then, the flower of romance had already been crushed.

All indicators past and present seemed to be pushing me towards accepting the idea that it wasn't in the cards for Peggy and I. All indicators, that is, except the stubborn voice inside me, which was now saying - "Find Her! Quick!" A couple days later, and with renewed determination, I continued my vision quest to find Terry Bell at GMU. But once again, the fates were not with me. Tinker didn't show up for class, and so as I left the building, I left wondering, "Well! Was it the wrong Theresa Bell? Did she drop the class? Did she prematurely complete the assigned work?" The bottom line was that it was the last class of the quarter, and after this failed attempt, it seemed as if my only option left was to break down and call Peggy. I dreaded even confronting the idea, especially now knowing that I was the man that Peggy's parents had once seen unfit for their daughter to date. For the next 15 months, I teetered between going on with my life, and making the call. About 20 times during that period, I actually dialed the number, but I always hung up after a couple of rings, or if someone picked up the receiver. The poor Wallace's must have thought they were getting crank calls, but it was only my lack of courage.

It was actually a girlfriend of mine, Angela Sheble, who convinced me to really make the call. We were having dinner in a restaurant in Annandale, and while the benign specter of Peggy Wallace had never adversely effected our relationship, her presence in the restaurant that night prompted sweet Angela to give the gentle push of a concerned friend. Angela knew that she was just passing through my life, but that Peggy was here to stay if I didn't act. We sat there conversing idly when Angela (who was not usually given to act impulsively) suddenly pulled out a pen and started writing something on a piece of paper. She then handed the piece of paper to me. It read simply – "Peggy Wallace." And so without thinking (which is the only way that bitter pills like this are ever swallowed), I got up and walked to the payphone at the back of the restaurant and dialed the Wallace number one last time. A woman who must have been Peggy's mother answered. I introduced myself and asked to speak to Peggy. She told me that Peggy was not there, and then was kind enough to ask, "Did you know that Peggy was married?" I don't recall, but I imagine that I spent the remainder of our conversation trying to back my way out of the phone call. I then walked back to the table, picked up the piece of paper, wrote the word "Married" on it, and handed it back to Angela. The sad look in Angela's beautiful brown eyes pretty much summed up my feelings at that moment as well, but at last, it was finally over.

To lighten the mood, and to make closure of the Wallace file official, I proposed a toast to Peggy, with the hope that she would find happiness in the joys of raising a family of her own. This was a toast that I sincerely meant, and one that Angela was all too happy to raise her glass to. Though Peggy has infrequently crossed my mind in the years between this July 1979 dinner with Angela and my July 1997 decision to write this book, the thought of her has always brought with it the feeling that someday our paths would cross again. It is my sincerest hope that when and if such a meeting ever took place, I would find that troubled soul of hers to be not so troubled. And if it were at all possible to accomplish without an adverse disruption of her life, I would like to send the message to Peggy, that if I didn't love her back in 1975, I do now! ...and "Always" will.

PETER BRICHANT

One of Tonny's friends from Margate Manor during the 1972/73 period. Although some of Tonny's friends tended to be on the dry side, Brichant had loon blood coursing through his veins. I could have used a couple more like him at OHS. As it happened, Peter's brief brush with glory came in the summer of 1973, when Tonny acquired his super 8 movie camera and we started making movies. Peter assisted us in most, if not all, of these productions, his most memorable role being that of the damsel in distress in "Super Bobney." As we could not find an actual damsel to play the role, Peter came through in the clutch by donning a dress, hat and high heels that Tonny and I had procured in a raid of his mother's boudoir. It was a bright sunny day in early summer when we filmed, and although Peter looked about as ridiculous as he could possibly look, his enthusiasm made his participation in this insane act all the more heroic.

THE PETERSON SYNDROME

A set of physical and behavioral characteristics exhibited by Karen Peterson, a girl in our 72-73 Russian class that so fascinated Emmette that he felt there needed to be a syndrome codified to explain her. Although Emmette did most of his explaining of the Peterson syndrome to Elmo and myself in our little corner of Mrs. Bryan's Russian class, most of Emmette's notes and observations of Karen Peterson were made in another class that he had her in.

To better understand the Peterson syndrome, one must first take a closer look at its creator. Emmette, while being as mad and as up for the jollification of any little thing as the rest of us, was still an intellectual elitist to the core. He was also, being only a freshman at the time, still at an age where he could comfortably and conveniently distance himself from his own sexuality. We were all still young enough to convincingly overlook the physical attributes of any female and get endless laugh mileage out of the smallest quirk in her behavior. The confounding thing about many of the attractive girls we encountered in high school was that their personalities were so obviously incompatible with ours that their womanly charms were no match for our diversions into silliness. This was especially true amidst the carefree immaturity of our freshman and sophomore years. Even if Emmette did find Karen Peterson in any way pleasing to the eye (and this is a big "If" we're talking about here), nothing short of a personality transplant for Miss Peterson would have made her anything more than an object of Emmette's amusement.

Having said that, Emmette's interest in this female was undeniable. In Russian class, he would facetiously relate things he had earlier observed Karen Peterson doing or saying (as if her words and actions spoke for themselves), and then correlate these observations with the pathological profile he was constructing of the Peterson syndrome. As Karen Peterson remained studiously anonymous (a quality no doubt symptomatic of her syndrome) throughout the year in our Russian class, I could only laugh along with Emmette. That all changed when Emmette identified Gayle Alcorn as one who exhibited all the symptoms of the Peterson syndrome. Knowing Gayle as I did gave me, at last, a solid frame of reference with which to understand some of the things Emmette was looking at.

Comparing Gayle with the faint but distinct impression I had of Karen Peterson made the picture even clearer.

Now you'd had to have been a bat to be blind to the physical attributes of Gayle Alcorn, and while there was no denying Gayle an admirable degree of virtuousness and sincerity, there was a too-good-to-be-real quality about Gayle that made no further definition of the Peterson syndrome necessary. Emmette began to refer to Gayle as "Peterson 2," and then more affectionately, Emmette, Elmo and I all began to refer to her as "Petey 2." Aside from the humorous diversion that the Peterson syndrome was intended to be, my admiration of Gayle was tempered by the apparency that she was operating on some plane of existence twice removed from Elmo and I, and a good 3 to 4 times removed from Emmette. Looking at Gayle through Emmette's eyes, one couldn't help but appreciate the humor in the culture clash between this Wagner-worshipping madman and a bible toting Breck girl.

Looking at the physical similarities between Gayle Alcorn and Karen Peterson however, one cannot help but wonder what other psychological prompts Emmette may have had in singling out these two young ladies. Unfortunately, Emmette is no longer around to ask. Aside from my belief that the Coati Mundi was also a textbook case, her absence from the Oakton arena made it impossible for Emmette to make a conclusive diagnosis. Emmette occasionally noted Peterson tendencies in other females, but my memory is only good enough to recall the probable gist of his comments relating to the syndrome. I possess none of his notes or writings on the subject. I truly feel the full weight of his loss when I consider that (baring the future reminiscences of a re-united Elmo) I have just given all the information that still exists on the Peterson syndrome.

PICTURES FOR HIRE

A few weeks into the start of my senior year, I came across an enterprising young photographer who was selling 8 X 10 prints of the student (or the faculty member) of your choice for a dollar apiece. The first thought that popped into my head was a vision of the walls of my room plastered with blown up photos of CA. But as the mist cleared and I saw this fellow in front of me waiting for my answer, I placed an order for 15 photos of Cheri Allen. I made a three-album sacrifice to obtain these photographs, but it was one of the best deals I ever made, because their value to me now is priceless.

This is my personal favorite of the lot, mainly for the story written on the smirk on Cheri's face. I'm betting that this was one of, if not THE last photo of the group to be taken. Cheri appears to be hurriedly on the move, notebook in hand, to get to her next class, when suddenly that pesky photographer who has been hounding her for days in an attempt to fill this order appears again. And like a press beleaguered starlet, responding to the now familiar cry of "Excuse Me, Miss Allen!" Cheri obliges with another pose that nevertheless captures her growing impatience. Cheri would hunt me down and throttle me if she knew the laugh mileage I've since gotten from this shot.

An added bonus in this photo is that the lucky (or skilled) photographer also managed to capture Cheri's friend, the ravishing Liz Davis, who was

smoking up what appears to be the southern end of the science wing in a very simple but flattering dress. Yes! Back then, young ladies dressed to further the designs of Mother Nature, not to thwart them.

Cheri Allen – as the very essence of young womanhood. There was a flipside to the young intellectual/artisan's self-consoling view of the jock as vacuous and coarse, a female equivalent which delighted in ascribing the same deficiencies to those ladies of the Majorette/Cheerleader set. Without pondering what real-life experiences may have contributed to those stereotypes, I will hereby assert my belief that Cheri Allen had more going on upstairs than I or any of my cohorts gave her credit for having. On top of all the other attributes that this angel possessed, there was certainly no need for her to flaunt anything.

Upon delivery of the 15 Cheri photo's I had consigned, I discovered that  the photographer (perhaps owing to the fact that I was such a good customer) had actually given me 19 photos – 17 of Cheri (although one was a duplicate print), 1 of Gayle Alcorn (of all people), and 1 of Howard Koretz. When the photo of Gayle (which captured her in all her buxom glory, underscoring what a photographer after my own heart this kid was) later appeared in the 75 paragon, it became apparent that this little photos-for-hire enterprise was just a money making sideline, while he carried on the greater task of taking photos for the yearbook.

This photo of Howard, on the other hand, I was expecting. After taking all the photos of Cheri, he came to my homeroom (science class – room 120) and told me that he had one more shot left in his camera, and if there was anyone else I would like a photo of, he would take it – on the house. Caught completely off guard, I mulled it over for a second, and then turned to my left and said – "Sure! Take one of Howard here." Howard then rose to his feet and effected a pose that truly shows his penchant for addressing the world with mock solemnity, despite the faint smile that almost betrays him.

PIZZA HUT

From our discovery of it in the early 70's, the Pizza Hut became a favorite meeting place for Tonny and I. As Tonny and I's friendship in the 70's was marked by one comical misadventure after another, it's no surprise that our main hangout would oblige us with two tales of ineptitude. The first took place at a Pizza Hut in Sarasota Florida, during our second trip there in the summer of 1974. My folks had dropped us off to go have seafood and to do some shopping. Tonny and I took a seat in a corner booth and waited over two hours in an empty (and I do mean completely empty) restaurant to be served. In fairness to the Pizza Hut employees, neither of us got up and waved our hands around wildly in the air or blew any whistles, but what did they think we were there for? Was it a common practice for kids to go into Pizza Huts and just sit there goofing off for hours? As much fun as Tonny and I were having, they had to know we were there. You see, Tonny and I appreciated the humor of ineptitude in others as well as in ourselves. Ineptitude appreciation was one of the most endearing qualities that Tonny brought to the loon table.

As the minutes turned to hours, Tonny and I were in our prime watching the situation getting funnier and funnier. It may have been as long as two and a half hours before a waitress (who obviously had no idea how long we'd been sitting there) sheepishly made her way to our booth to take our order. My mother and stepfather, who warned us that they would be awhile, were amazed to discover that we had just finished eating when they arrived to pick us up. This became one of those funny stories that were destined to be told over and over again.

That should have been the end of our Pizza Hut misadventures, but during the post-Oakton 75-76 period, the Pizza Hut joke became a reality on at least two more occasions. It was at the Pizza Hut at Fairfax Circle, which was at or near the halfway point between my house and Tonny's apartment at Margate Manor. We had made the mistake of sitting in the no-man's land of the corner booth, which was apparently reserved for drug dealers who didn't want to be disturbed, for this time it took us a good hour and a half to get a visit from a waitress.

After this event, the Pizza Hut joke became a legacy. But even though at least one more event of this magnitude would sustain our joke about the timeless voids we seem to keep falling into at Pizza Huts, after 1976, the restaurant's "Don't help the customer unless he asks for it" policy seems to have been rescinded. In fact, ever since 1976, I've never received anything but prompt courteous service at a Pizza Hut restaurant, which (aside from coinciding with the period where immigrants began buying up Pizza Hut franchises in the area) leads me to believe that the aura of ineptitude that followed Tonny and I around may have had something to do with the timing of these incidents.

THE PROM

Although steadfastly resolved to maintain my self-appointed title of "Social Outcast," if you had asked me at any time during my sophomore year whether or not I would eventually be attending my senior prom, I would have bet money that it was in the bag. I took for granted my eventual success in finding a girlfriend, without being willing to play the necessary game in order to make it happen. Despite the fact that I was with about half of the student body in my view of the prom as belonging in the domain of the more popular, I still had a romantic dreamer's vision of myself attending this affair with my lady-love, and was greatly disheartened by the fact that I had not a single hopeful lined up when the event finally arrived. It never even occurred to me how out of place I might have felt at my own senior prom, because whatever separated me from the rest of the student body did not disguise the fact that this should have been a special time in my life.

Although I've to this day been unable to figure out the purpose of the Sadie Hawkins dance, I never once questioned the validity or traditional integrity of the prom, as much as its impending arrival grew to be a psychological thorn in my side. While my lack of interest in every little soc hop or sweetheart's dance that was announced during my years as an underclassman was a testimony to the distance I put between myself and the Oakton mainstream, my senior prom was a one time event, the passage of which reinforced my growing sense that things which seemed to come so naturally to others would not do so for me. At 6 years of age, I had every confidence that I would be married by my 20th birthday. At 18 years of age, with graduation fast approaching, I surely must have had the sense that in this regard, my life was moving a little bit behind schedule.

Not to cry the blues here too loudly, I must say that few (if any) of my friends or acquaintances attended the prom either, so mine was not a special case by any means. Any wish I may have expressed of attending the prom would have surely been taken as the pipe dream of a commoner attending a royal ball, and I would have no doubt been admonished to come back down to earth. And then one has to wonder if any girl that would have found me attractive (and apparently there were a few) would have even liked the idea of attending the prom. I've no doubt that there were just as many females as males thumbing their noses at the whole affair. Still, as much as my male pride suppressed the closet romantic within me, the prom's approach made me secretly long for the ability to just be someone else for one evening.

PULLER CALDWELL

Sometime during my senior year, a number of dogs were found killed and skinned in Northern Virginia. The media speculated that it might be the work of Satanists, although in the mid-70's, everything from marijuana use to long periods without rain was blamed on Satanism. An area teen, Puller Caldwell, was leading some sort of crusade to find these evil cultists and bring them to justice. Now anyone who knew a nostrils drip about Pagans and Satanists would have known that these are the last people on earth you suspect of defiling an animal in this way. But as I looked at the picture of Puller Caldwell (who was more than likely just an outraged dog lover) in the paper, it occurred to me that my appearance and behavior were things that had also been attributed to Satanism. The absurdity of it overcame me, and so I left an entry in my last will that confirmed the rumors about me with tongue so firmly planted in cheek that anyone with half an eye open would have realized - there was no truth to the rumors. I left to Puller Caldwell – "My dog-skin scarf with matching cape."

PULSE PLUS

A news/variety show that broadcast from Tampa and aired on Sarasota TV during the summer of 73. Tonny and I developed an interest in the show and its unusual cast of characters during the two weeks we spent in Sarasota that summer. Its main anchor was a plump and jolly, yet determinably earnest young man named Bruce Hutchcraft. Bruce's feeder heifer calf reports and slaughter bull price quotations belied the look and delivery of his projected serious newscaster exterior. Other amusing eccentricities of the show included the deadpan delivery overkill of their roving reporter at the state capitol - Tom Henning, their quixotic joke telling weatherman - Roy Leap, and an equally boisterous white-haired man of the sea named Salty Sal, who gave the fishing reports (dressed like a ship's captain no less).

Pulse plus was a combination of more personality in a news show than Tonny and I were used to, and the often endearing attempts of its cast to affect the pomposity of the big three network news shows we were used to. As if all this wasn't enough to solidify the position of Pulse Plus in the annals of loon history, the song they performed during one of the shows cemented it. Smack in the middle of what we thought was just a newscast came this live in the studio performance from a 4 or 5 piece jazz group, doing a bouncy bop number. As soon as Tonny noticed that the singer was one of the female anchors, I noticed Bruce Hutchcraft (on drums as I recall). Apparently the producers of the show were taking advantage of the fact that this particular news crew was musically inclined, or perhaps they were hired for their talents to fulfill the concept of a news/variety show. Whatever the reason, after 2 or 3 numbers (complete with solo's), Tonny, my stepfather and I sat in utter amazement. I was inspired to write a song about the show, and have since often wondered about the subsequent careers of its cast members. At any rate, I hope there are some gulf-coasters who look back with fond memories, as Tonny and I do, on this little slice of Florida TV history.

PUNXSUTAWNEY

A small town in the mountains of western Pennsylvania that, aside from being home to the countries most famous rodent and weather prognosticator, was where much of Tonny's non-immediate family lived. Practically all of my grandparent's family on my mother's side came from Johnstown Pennsylvania, which is just a little southeast of Punx'y. With my stepfather's hometown being Williamsport, PA, I got to see a lot of that state as I was growing up. With every successive person I would bring up the subject of family origin with, it seemed that no matter how far out the branches of their family tree would extend, part of the root system was embedded in Pennsylvania soil.

Punxsutawney has a particularly strong place in the story of my Oakton years. When I think of the town and my summer of 1974 two week stay there, many things come to mind: My rat hunt with Ganzer, the making of the film The Hand, The purchase of my first Genesis album, the Woman in My Death recording session, the general layout of the town itself, Ganzer's indoctrination ceremony, and of course - Tonny and I's hardy boys-like visit to the abandoned haunted house on Beyer Avenue. You have read about some of these things already, and when you get to Tonny's lengthy entry, you will read more about this little town than you probably ever wanted to know.

QUEEN VIPER

My on-air name for WOHS. I took the title of "Queen" to acknowledge

how much I identified with the battle between good and evil that seem to be raging on the first two Queen albums, particularly the second one, with its side white and side black. Queen II's "March of the Black Queen" became the unofficial theme song of the Queen Viper show. Just as big a reason for my title as Queen, and another study in positive and negative polarities, was the gender fencing taking place in Freddie

Mercury's mini-operas. Mercury had the theatrical sense (and the vocal ability) to play both Male and Female roles, an idea in-practice that fascinated me, as I had by this time ingested so much of CA's hyper-femininity that it seemed as if she had become a sub-entity within me.

The viper half of the name was given to leave no room for doubt that my on-air persona was meant to be a dark figure, an adversarial serpent in the garden. Viper's delivery was WGTB inspired - songs announced with the dispassionate coolness of expelled breath.

Acting on the slightly vindictive urge to put the boogens in Peggy, I signed my own yearbook as Queen Viper, effectively writing a message to myself from my darker self. It read – "No. 5 will most assuredly destroy you, for as Walt pointed out, doves must have no more than 5 wings. No. 6 will be driving a truck, like our vulture friend, have a good mourning, Bob - Queen Viper." That this dark sub-entity bore a female appellation was perhaps a reflection of an inner desire to match this mystery of the feminine mystique that had caught me unprepared and unarmed with a little mystery of my own.

QUEERBOLIC
A Tonnyism which dates to the British Insipid era of early 1971, and is meant to infer something beyond Tonny's immediate comprehension.

RADIOACTIVE FACES
An early Howard Koretz creation, and one that built up a considerable spoken (and in a few cases - written) mythology during our final two years at Oakton. Perhaps "Creation" is a poor choice of words, as it came from a dream Howard had about these glowing faces that would appear in the night sky. Howard even recorded a mini-opera on the subject, where in was given those immortal lines -

A radioactive face - I have lived
for a period of 58 years
They will pay for the life they took away
Fluctuating their radioactivity
in the minds of them and their eyes.

One truly has to hear Howard sing that verse to understand how I could have recalled it so perfectly after 25 years. Howard's fascination with this particular dream pushed radioactive faces into the loon lexicon. In fact, the radioactive faces had their own lexicon.

Navaetcoidar - Radioactive Heaven

Flucshuthon - The Radioactive face itself
Radacedes - The face particles that make up the flucshuthon
Muffalogue - The garbled static-obscured language of the radioactive faces
Zicktode - The dark domain in which the faces dwell
Rotiunzulit - The area of radioactivity

RATS

While I would leave Oakton High with a burgeoning obsession with Peggy Wallace, watching the movie ""'Willard" three times during the summer of 1971 ensured that I would enter Oakton High with an obsession of an entirely different nature - an obsession with man's greatest enemy - the rat. As a result of this obsession, the rat's place in loon lore is as solid and as entrenched as anything else in this book. I would write numerous songs about them, from 1971's "Rats in the Sewer," to 1975's "Origin Plus," though it was my 1972 instrumental ode "Sulieman in Excelsis" that struck a resonant chord in other loons, particularly Emmette. Any of these compositions held their own against Michael Jackson's syrupy sonnet to Ben Sulieman, which charted in that same summer of 1972.

While my mother refused my persistent requests for a pet rat of my own, my fascination and thirst for more information on these creatures soon transcended the fictional tale of Willard and "Ratman's Notebook," the book which the movie Willard was based on. I began using Oakton's library as a research facility, writing down every interesting story and fact I could find on the creatures in a voluminous clump of papers that Tonny would come to speak of reverently as "The Rat Notes." The most enlightening and memorable source of information I came across was Hans Zinsser's immortal work – "Rats, Lice and History" - a book that Tonny would later own in paper back form, owing to some of the incredible accounts he read in my notes. As the amount of time I put in during my freshman, sophomore and junior years preaching the greatness of rats qualifies it as some form of ministry, Zinsser's book took on an almost religious significance.

My willingness to pound the pulpit for the superiority of the rat ran a concurrent timeline with Emmette's Richard Wagner rants, and a symbiotic relationship between the two fixations nurtured our personal aspirations of greatness. No single incident exemplifies this unity of obsession better than the time our Russian teacher, Mrs. Bryan asked each member of the class to give a brief description of their plans for the coming summer. God knows what prompted Mrs. Bryan to do this, but she would soon discover that after the victorious 72-73 school year, not even a crowded classroom could deter Emmette and I from demonstrating our fealty to our obsessions, as well as to the spirit of insanity. My response to the query of my summer plans was "I plan to lead an army of rats to Rugby, North Dakota, and establish it as the capitol of the western world." Emmette's response (inspired by mine, but nonetheless - inspired) was something to the effect of "I plan a pilgrimage to Bayreuth, to proclaim it the capitol of the eastern world for the glory of Richard Wagner," to which he concluded with the added gesture of giving the triumphant insane salute.

Another incident which also dates from the spring of 1973 that demonstrates the place the rat had taken as the official figurehead mascot of the Insanist movement was Emmette's second visit to Christ United Methodist Church. For some reason, Emmette and I were rooting about the basement storage area adjacent to the youth lounge. Perhaps we had been told that a rat or two had been seen lurking around the old church. My memory is unclear on what exactly prompted this - the first of the famed rat hunts, but I have retained a vivid mental picture of Emmette and I moving stealthily about the basement storage area, with Emmette softly calling out – "Brother! Brother!" as if anticipating a screeching reply from Sulieman himself.

This was more of a spiritual exercise than anything guided by the actual belief that we would encounter a rat. I knew from what I had read about the creatures that they were primarily nocturnal, and as the mid-day sunlight was streaming through the windows, illuminating the entire area, I would say that I was listening more than I was actually looking. Emmette's choice of the word "Brother" as a call to any rat that might be sleeping beneath the clutter was as much a testimony to loon solidarity as it was an actual call to any fur-bearing entities present. While Emmette did not share my fascination with rats, he did acknowledge their importance while in my presence, in the same way that I acknowledged his theories on the Peterson syndrome - this was loon solidarity. Emmette actually expressed this during his momentous first visit to Christ United with Brian Helms. We were in the service, hymnals in hand, when Emmette noticed the words "Gloria in Excelsis" written on the top of the page we were turned to. With a broad smile of discovery and a triumphant glint in his eye, he turned to me and silently mouthed the words – "Sulieman in Excelsis."

A companion obsession to that of rats was my fascination with slum areas, old condemned buildings, warehouses and the like, because those were the places where "They" dwelled. During the summer of 1973, my grandparents (the Jarvie's) took me to Baltimore, a trip that is not remembered for its ultimate purpose as much as for the incredible sight that greeted us upon entering the city. Baltimore, in those days, did not have the shiny new face that it has today. The first thing one saw to their left upon crossing the bridge was about 8 to 10 square blocks of vacant condemned townhouses, the most ominous post-apocalyptic urban landscape imaginable, even under the glare of the noonday sun. This drew me to insist that my grandfather make an unscheduled detour to the left, that I might get a closer look at this ghost town, and being a grandparent, he indulged me. I was all eyes as we circled block after block of decay that was better seen than imagined. Pressing my luck again, I entreated my patient pop to stop the car and allow me a stroll amongst the ruins. I recall staring in wonder down an alleyway that was a good foot deep in trash. It was only after taking a few steps into the domain of the rat that my impatient grandmother insisted that we continue on to our appointed destination.

My trip to Punxsutawney in the summer of 1974 showed no abatement in my interest in rats.

Punxsutawney, despite the national attention it received every groundhog day, was an old town, whose two block long main street was lined with 19th century buildings whose backsides were undoubtedly the nightly haunts of rats the size of Ol' Yeller.

Tonny's friend Tom Henry had just donned the ceremonial underwear, been christened Ganzerareux Azziamekiassa, and was eager to prove his worthiness as a loon. As Tonny and I had just returned from investigating this intriguing L shaped alleyway that led to a mysterious set of doors, I had the perfect mission for Ganzer. With a combined sense of loyalty and adventure, Ganzer accompanied me on a return walk into town with the purpose of finding out what exactly lay behind that set of doors. Once in the alleyway, Ganzer was made clear that it was rats we were after a glimpse of, and while I don't believe I ever mentioned this to Tonny, Ganzer began calling out "Brother! Brother!" in the same delicate but imploring tone used by Emmette O some 15 months earlier, and I recall taking a second from the thrill of the hunt to note the parallel. Once at the doorway, Ganzer and I had a plan. He would throw open one of the doors, and I would step into the blackness and quickly snap a flash picture of whatever was in there. We would then run like hell in case there happened to be something else in there besides a couple of rats, say a bum with an aversion to being woken from a sound sleep by a camera flash. What the developed photograph later revealed was a room full of wood and an assortment of old junk, the very sort of place you could imagine turning into a nightclub for rats after sundown.

Not only had I read many interesting things about rats, I had been told a few remarkable first hand accounts as well by people who knew of my fascination. To this day I marvel at the story that my Uncle Bob Miller told me of an incident that happened to him when he was in Vietnam. The year before (1972), he and a buddy of his were riding in a jeep down a two-lane highway when a rat crawled out in the middle of the road. The animal was so large, his buddy had to stop the jeep and shoot the thing with his rifle. It was measured at 7 and a half feet long, and though I imagine almost half of that was tail, I was awestruck nonetheless. I was too young to have much of an interest in the Vietnam War, a war that by this time was winding down for American involvement, but this story made me wonder, for the first time, what sort of place Vietnam was that such creatures could live there.

It wasn't until the late 70's, when I started to make semi-regular trips into D.C. at night that I began to actually catch glimpses of the critters scurrying about. I remember meeting Chirpie in 1982 for a drink at a club off of Dupont Circle. Afterwards, as I was walking back to my car, I came upon a dead brown rat lying on the sidewalk. I stopped for a second and pondered my days of preaching the greatness of rats, of Harry Golden's article "The Unconquerable," which described the rat as "Everywhere dominant as well as everywhere dangerous." Perhaps I even recalled the line in David Bowie's Orwellian "Future Legend" that EAT and I loved quoting to each other – "Fleas the size of rats sucked on rats the size of cats." While the idea of a flea the size of a rat was obviously pure fantasy, here at my feet was a rat the size of a cat (a rather large cat at that). An elderly couple was conversing on the front steps of their apartment about 30 yards ahead of me. The old man saw my approach and as I came upon the rat, he narrowed his vision and shouted down to me in astonishment – "Is that a rat?" "Yes" I replied, "It sure is."

RAY DENK

One of those individuals that helped to make my high school experience so unusual and memorable. Of all the words one could have used to describe

Ray, unpredictable is the first one that comes to mind. In a recent phone conversation with Melody Rouzer, she related the amusing story of a camping trip with some Oakton friends where Ray suddenly started throwing cow chips at Jeff Wolfe. For me, this really recalled how one had to be prepared for the unexpected with Ray around.

Elmo and I learned the hard way never to get in a car with Ray at the wheel. On Ray's invitation, the two of us joined him for a 20-second round trip to the end of Sutton road and back. It appeared at first as if we were going for an innocent spin around the block with Ray, but once on Sutton road, he gunned it - hitting a speed well over 100 MPH before making a screeching 180 degree turn in the gravel lot near the corner of Sutton road and Rt. 123. I barely had time to shout "Ray! Ray!" before our rocket ride was over and we were back on school grounds. I would say the whole trip lasted no more than 20 seconds. For those who think I may be exaggerating here, I offer Ray's own account of how he was arrested for going 139 MPH on Lee Highway. Now we are talking about Lee Highway circa 1974, when traffic was thin enough on suburban Northern Virginia roads that such speeds were even possible, much less sustainable, but we are also talking about a daredevil high school male with an extremely souped-up automobile. Speaking of which, I also recall that there was an external speaker in the front grill of Ray's car. As the 3 of us were moving past the front doorway to the science department (or in this case - taxiing down the runway), a group of students (one of which was John Davies) were approaching the curb in preparation of walking across the bus lane towards somebody's car. When Ray spotted them, he slowed the car to a crawl, picked up a microphone, and with that wily smirk of his, addressed the group in state trooper fashion. As we drove passed them, I remember that the looks on a couple of their faces suggested that they had been conditioned to be startled by the sound of any voice emanating from an automobile PA. This was understandable, as this sound usually meant that the police had shown up to the party. When external speakers were later outlawed for non-police vehicles, I thought of Ray.

From the point of this attempt at breaking the land speed record (which I'd date around mid to late September 1974), Ray became an increasingly visible figure. I would see Ray at Melody Rouzer's afternoon Halloween party. It was Ray who drove me home in the middle of the party to fetch my copy of Van Der Graaf Generator's "Pawn Hearts" and bring it back to the party for Melody's edification. This was of course after I had made Ray swear that he would go no more than 10 miles over the speed limit.

It was through Howard Koretz that I got the job as a telephone solicitor for the Star, but on my first day at work, I discovered that Ray also worked there. In fact, Ray's gift of gab made him the star salesman in the office. I didn't work at the Star very long (no more than a month), but I was working there during my early January efforts to ascertain the identity of Peggy Wallace. Ray was the first person I asked about Peggy who actually knew her. Two months later, Ray saw for himself how much I had been touched by Peggy's troubled soul. Ray either had a class in Mr. William's electronics shop or assisted him there, because occasionally he would pop into the radio room on his way coming in or going out. On one such occasion, the ever-observant Ray picked up a rough draft of Holes in True to Life Fantasy. When he came across the name "yggePsiramaDirehC" (Peggy, Damaris and Cheri backwards - if you can believe how well I had absorbed Stephanie Hill's lesson on the use of backward names in Satanism), a grin of knowing recognition crossed his face. It's somehow fitting that Ray and I led the charge together into the cafeteria during the final folly, chasing a distressed and flushed Peggy Wallace from the cafeteria in tears.

I seemed to run into Ray a lot after leaving Oakton. During one memorable encounter at the Tyson's Corner mall sometime during the 1976-78 period, Ray showed me a scar on his forehead right below the hairline. He told me that he had run into a tree at 70 MPH. "Same old Ray" I thought to myself. When he told he was lucky to be alive in that nonchalant manner that implied how cheating death was a daily affair when you're Ray Denk, I told him he was lucky he was only going 70 MPH.

In contrast, the last time I saw Ray, he seemed to have mellowed considerably. He had a wife, was pushing a baby carriage, and was living on a farm west of Centerville. I recall asking him in jest if he drove his tractor through the fields at high speeds. This was in Record World at Fair Oaks mall sometime during the 1985-86 period. I can date this because Ray told me that Steve Winwood had just been out on his farm filming a video for the second single to the "Back in the High Life" album. A month or two later, I would happen to see a part of that video in passing, and catch a glimpse of the Denk farm.

The final folly was Ray's finest hour. It was the inevitable integration of our respective lunacies, and it speaks well of Melody Rouzer that she managed to independently befriend the both of us. I asked Melody recently (herself now married with children) if there were anybody from her days at Oakton that she would like to see again. The only name she could give me was Ray Denk. I must admit I'd really like to see the old boy again myself.

RAY KING

Having a last name too close to my own, arch-ruffian Ray King would bless me with his presence in homeroom for 6 straight years from 7th grade through my senior year. The quintessential freckle-faced red-haired bully, Ray taunted me daily in our 7th grade gym class, and intermittently thereafter, although as with most of Oakton's tough guys, I considered him more of an annoyance than a threat. I never really took any of Ray's taunting personally, and there never seemed to be any personal feelings of antipathy behind his jeering sufficient to spark a reaction in me.

By the start of my senior year, Ray's presence and purpose in my life was predictable and understandable. Would that I could have ascribed such consistency to the females of my conflicting fancies. No, Ray King would never send my thoughts down dark corridors of incertitude, or even, for that matter, occupy my thoughts at all when he was not in my presence. However, a few months into my bizarre senior year, I had an equally bizarre encounter with Ray. I wore my silver mylar shirt to school, which was an open invitation for Ray to start in on me about when and where the Martians were going to land and begin their invasion. For some reason, I did something I had never done before - I gave Ray an answer. I looked him square in the eye and said - "Why Yes! As a matter of fact, we ARE planning an invasion of your planet," and then I followed with a few specifics on the invasion. Ray's face could not conceal his surprise, and his body jolted backward an inch or so as if he had just been hit by a stiff wind. He had no comeback for my comeback, and he did not say as much as a word to me again in my homeroom for the rest of the year. It was as if he had been pestering me all this time just to get some sort of response. It didn't even matter if it made sense, just something to complete the cycle of communication. However! Ray had apparently been lulled into a state of unpreparedness by my years of unyielding silence. He may have been thrown into the belief that I was too unstable to risk further attempts at harassment.

Now if this incident seemed unusual, what followed it belongs in the realm of the paranormal. On a couple of separate occasions during the final months of my senior year, Ray actually acknowledged me in the halls with a respectful and affirmative nod. Compared with how willing Cheri and Peggy were to meet my gaze in the halls, Ray and I had become blood brothers. It really made me stop and think - Had the same falsehoods that would have put my name in the prayers of the revelations club, garnered the respect of those on the other end of the good and evil spectrum? I have to wonder, because Ray's diametric shift in attitude occurred around the same time as Peggy's, only going in the opposite direction.

During the final folly, as Ray Denk, EAT, Tonny and I were traversing the school in search of interviews, we came across Ray King and a group of his buddies loitering at the confluence of the two main hallways. In a flash of impulse, I pushed my tape recorder microphone in Ray's face and asked

- "Ray King! Noted ruffian and noted hood, do you have a few words to say to our Oakton audience?" With a wicked half-grin that conveyed his appreciation of a senior prank in progress, he shot back "Yeah! I think our Oakton audience sucks, Man!" My interest peaked, I'm clearly heard asking the follow-up question – "Is that all you have to say?" Unfortunately, the immediate interest of our group, Mr. Herndon, emerged from his office at that instant, diverting our attention and cutting short my interview with Ray King. But beneath the smile of the class clown who loved to perform for the amusement of the ladies, and the football field swagger of his tough-guy response, Ray may have left me a clue to the change in his behavior. If only a part of Ray actually meant what he said about "Our Oakton audience," then that would indicate that Ray, to some degree, thought of himself as an outsider. He may have taken a second look at me and realized that, in a strange way, we were now on the same side of the fence. Maybe I was right on the money when I honored all of the above possibilities for Ray's sudden change in my senior will, leaving Ray King (and Ray Denk) "The task of letting 900,000 cockroaches loose at the senior prom and a full report on Satan's desk in the morning." This was obviously a two-man job, and who better qualified to pull it off than the school's biggest terrorist (Ray Denk), and the school's biggest ruffian (Ray King). If the latter truly felt as he had expressed to me in the halls, then he would have relished even the idea of such maleficium. Perhaps that's what was really written in the smile on his face, as he passed along the affirmation to a fellow outsider, that at the bottom of it all - Our Oakton audience sucks! ....Man!

THE RECEIVING LABEL FOLLY
Sometime in early 1974, EAT and Elmo discovered a box of orange peel-and-stick receiving labels in the woods near their homes in Dunn Loring. EAT, Elmo, Kaiser and I lost no time in blanketing the school with these labels, sticking them on walls, lockers, fire extinguishers, even ceilings. I recall one instance of being the lookout for Kaiser while he took a running leap and plastered one on the ceiling of the hallway which lead to the music department. I think I also speak for the other three when I say that the appeal of this folly was in leaving a visible mark upon the school while retaining our invisibility. It was also part of the skill involved, as the four of us planted literally hundreds of those labels on various surfaces throughout the school without once being spotted or suspected. Kaiser was especially daring in his execution of this folly, though it must be remembered that it was rare for any of us to have an empty hallway in which to work our magic. We had to be extremely careful, especially in crowded hallways, but after a couple weeks of this deluge, we all started to

get a little cocky. I recall walking down the upstairs English department hallway with Earl Ragland. Upon spotting a fire extinguisher ahead of me on my right, I directed Earl's attention to the extinguisher. Now here came the tricky part - pulling a label from my pocket and peeling it while keeping it hidden from view. As we passed the extinguisher, I kept my eyes facing straight ahead, while out of the corner of my mouth passing the half-whispered suggestion to a slightly confused Earl Ragland to take a second look at that fire extinguisher. Earl glanced back and of course saw an orange receiving label plastered across its face, where-upon he let out with a hardy laugh and said "Oh! So it's you guys who are puttin' those things everywhere." It's interesting that Earl had already assessed the level of deployment and concluded that this was not the work of one man.

As Elmo kept the box of labels at home, he assumed the role of central supplier, and the one the other three of us would seek out when we had gotten rid of all our labels, like thrill junkies looking for that fix that was going to get us through the week. Elmo kept delivering the goods until he ran out of labels and the folly had to come to an end. About a week later however, EAT came to me with the news that he and Elmo had discovered another much larger cache of labels in the woods. My head immediately started inflating with mentally drawn-up plans for the blitzkrieg ahead. I went to Elmo and franticly demanded a double ration of labels, but to my dismay, Elmo refused, and inexplicably urged that we not continue the folly. Upon going to Kaiser and EAT for support, I was shocked to discover that they were in agreement with Elmo, though no reason other than we shouldn't carry on was ever given. They seemed to have either been stricken by an attack of conscience or had gotten spooked by one too many close calls. In retrospect, it was probably best that we quit while we were ahead. Elmo, perhaps feeling that my enthusiasm would get the whole group in trouble, even refused to deliver the entire bulk of the labels to me, that I might at least have the fun of continuing on my own. It was a baffling and mysterious end to a folly that was nonetheless fun while it lasted.

We had at least made a brief mark upon the school. And it was that one label that Kaiser stuck on the music hallway ceiling that remained visible for quite some time afterward. I don't recall when I noticed that it had been removed, perhaps when I returned as a guest of Rick Hockmuth in the fall of 1975, or under the auspices of Mr. Poston in 1978. I do recall checking shortly after the start of my senior year, and finding to my joy and amazement that the label was still there where Kaiser had stuck it months earlier. While discovering it gone left me with the feeling that the last bit of evidence that we loons ever attended this institution had been wiped away, I dare say the possibility exists that there is a desk or a cafeteria table in use at some facility somewhere in Fairfax county with a faded orange label still attached to its underbelly.

THE REMODS

The absolutely hilarious name of a little league baseball team that Tonny played for briefly. The team represented the Hodges Home Improvement Co., hence the name. The team's home field was Lee Graham Park, just across Lee Highway from Timberlane apartments, where Tonny was living at the time. Although Tonny never saw any action with the team, warming the bench for only 2 games, the fact that Tonny wore the uniform of the Remods conjured visions of uniforms with ladders on them, or perhaps a logo with a little slugger in paint-stained overalls swinging a paintbrush instead of a baseball bat. But in the next instance, it struck me that this name was so like something we would have cooked up in one of our skits. Fate brought Tonny and the Remods together. I'm sure of it.

RENNIE STENNETT'S HOMERUN

Near the end of my senior year, Tonny was my guest at Oakton on two separate occasions, allowing Tonny, at last, to be a part of the inner-Oakton madness. On the first of his visits, I hosted a Tonny tribute show, dubbing it "TNT Day on WOHS," with Tonny himself in the studio co-hosting. Two of Tonny's recordings with Ganzer - Boogie Woogie and Met Her in a Hog-trough were played, as well as Tonny's Wicked People of the World. In addition, the audio portion of an April 13th home run by Rennie Stennett was played over the air. Tonny was a big fan of the Pittsburgh Pirates, and well! It WAS TNT day.

THE REVELATIONS CLUB

A Christian club at OHS that I was on the verge of having an affiliation with throughout 1974. The problem I had was that unlike the self-contained youth groups at Christ United Methodist Church or the Fairfax Assembly of God, the spirit of maintaining one's station seemed to hang over the club's meetings and functions. Admittedly, it was rather unfair of me to expect that this group be divorced from the high school of which it was very much a part. This was not a group that was going to welcome me in with open arms in order to make a Christian out of me. I was either one of them or I wasn't, and when it finally sunk in that I was not going to be able to use this club to expand my circle of friends, I bailed out completely.

One rather mysterious event surrounds the club. Sometime late in my junior year, Kaiser showed me a note that had been anonymously stuffed in his locker. The note (which is still in my possession) was scrawled in pencil, in a frighteningly manic and barely legible script. It said – "If you join the revelations club next year, I'll kill you - your friend." I showed the note to Howard, EAT, Elmo, and anybody else who I thought might be able to shed some light on who its author was. Not surprisingly, everyone was as baffled about the note as I was. To know Kaiser for more than a few days was to know that science was the only religion he ascribed to, and not even for a date with one of the Alcorn sisters would he have entertained the notion of joining the revelations club. The out-of-context nature of the death threat made it impossible for any of us to take it seriously for more than a minute. Like the cryptically occult looking warning letter I would receive the following year in Mrs. Leech's English class, it was non-sequitur to the point of not even qualifying as a bad joke, and so was quickly forgotten. Still, despite the fact that the author was obviously someone who didn't know Kaiser too well, I was momentarily fascinated with the identity of this person who seemed to harbor ill feelings toward the revelations club. I also felt that the letter might have had something to do with me, because I HAD been involved with the club, which leaves us with the mystery of why the note was left in Kaiser's locker. It's a stretch, but perhaps the author had seen Kaiser and I milling around Kaiser's locker, and mistakenly thought it was my locker.

At any rate, any disparaging words I may use here to distance myself from the revelations club or its members all boil down to the fact that it simply wasn't my scene. I attended two (possibly three) meetings, one party and had a few scant encounters with the clubs two leading exponents - Kim Koan and Gayle Alcorn. Beyond these encounters (some described elsewhere in this book) I have nothing to offer in the way of an overview of the club's personality as defined by the totality of its members, or how it was going about its stated purpose of spreading the word of Christianity throughout the school.

I do have one memory I'd like to relate before closing this entry because it stands as one of the first seeds of doubt ever planted in the field of my growing agnosticism. It was during one of the club meetings, held in Mr. Everton's class (in either room 139 or room 141). During this particular meeting, a guest of some forgotten distinction came to speak to the group. He was a man in his mid to late 30's who was either an author or a minister of some sort, with what I sensed were the credentials of a minor luminary in the Christian world. Availing themselves of his experience and wisdom, the others in attendance asked his opinion on various issues pertinent to Christians. One such query was whether he thought that going to see movies like the Exorcist was potentially damaging to the spirituality of Christians. This was a very timely question in 1974, when movies like the Exorcist and lesser-budgeted movies attempting to cash in on the ensuing devil-mania were causing even non-Christians to ask the same thing.

Surprisingly, his answer was a reassuring "No!" But then he went on to suggest that a greater threat to the faith of Christians was the current wave of ancient-alien-involvement-in-human-affairs books such as Erik Von Daniken's "Chariot of the Gods."

Not having seen the Exorcist, I nonetheless found it curious that he could in such a non-alarmist tone dismiss a movie that had caused adverse reactions in its audience such as nausea, seizures, panic attacks, and fainting spells by the hundreds, and yet show such concern for non-fiction books based on actual archeological discoveries. I thought to myself – "Now, wait a minute, do those things that Von Daniken wrote about exist or do they not?" From the challenged position of this concerned Christian, one would have to assume not only that they did, but that the possible validity of Von Daniken's theories about them had become a force to be reckoned with in the Christian world. The more observations of this type I would come to make, the clearer it became that Christendom was not so concerned with a search for the truth, as it was preserving the integrity of the truth it believed to have already found. Christianity had asked me to accept an awful lot on faith, but it was the amount of hard evidence it would have had me ignore in order to preserve that faith that ultimately made me feel like a fool for having walked down that path in the first place.

RICK HOCKMUTH

Not simply the younger brother of Bob Hockmuth, but one whose place in the scheme of things followed its own distinct path. Of all the letters I mailed out during my 1997 aborted attempt at an Oakton reunion, Rick Hockmuth was the only person to respond. Sounding very much in voice and spirit like the same fellow I knew in high school, Rick heartily reminded me while recounting a Hawkwind show he had just seen that I was the one who originally turned him on to the group. I didn't remember how or when I had done this until Rick followed up with – "Don't you remember the time you brought that Hawkwind record over to our apartment?" It was then that it became apparent that when I brought that album over to play for Bob, Rick was around long enough for it to have made a lasting impression on him. I also remember all the Doors posters in Rick's room and him telling me what a big Doors fan he was (which, despite the subsequent iconization of Jim Morrison, was something I had never come across before - an actual Doors fan).

While I didn't have any classes with Rick, he seemed to appear a lot at opportune moments, the most dramatic of which was our memorable meeting at the confluence of the main hallway and the hallway that led from the front desk. Peggy was still that mysterious girl in the cafeteria who seemed to be watching me, but whose motives were as yet unknown.

 As I was talking with Rick, Peggy happened to pass by, and out of the corner of my eye I could see Peggy steel a glance at me from out of the corner of her eye. It was just one of those moments in time that will remain with me always, not only as one of the first real inklings I had that Peggy might find me attractive, but as a reminder that I would often run into and converse with Rick Hockmuth at that particular spot.

Rick also happened to be just outside one of the smoking arcades when Ray Denk, EAT, Tonny and I were doing our sweep of that area during the final folly. A very stoned sounding and at a loss for words Rick Hockmuth is heard in a brief interview on the tape.

Rick's most important role was the one he played after graduation. As EAT was no longer attending Oakton, and I did not believe that I could have counted on Emmette or Elmo's cooperation, Rick became, by default, my man on the inside. In September of 1975, Rick got me back inside Oakton on a visitor's pass, where a trip back to the radio station juxtaposed what a friend of mine Rick still very much was with what strangers Elmo and Emmette had become. Trucking around what was still a familiar place to me as the ghost of myself was quite a trip. Entering a deserted cafeteria after the lunch periods, I left a message for Peggy on the table I last saw her and her group eating at the previous June. I don't remember the exact message, only that it was fittingly cryptic and was signed – "Vindscreen Viper."

As my man on the inside, Rick could not (as EAT could have) give me reports on and pass notes back and forth to people I knew on the inside. Rick could not do this because he simply did not know these people. He did perform one last important service by procuring for me a copy of Oakton's 1976 yearbook. I couldn't thank him enough. Peggy's senior picture alone was enough to make the book one of my most prized possessions. Rick's talent for crossing my path resurfaced during the 1977-78 period, when Rick became a customer at the Annandale Penguin Feather where I was working at the time.

When we talked in 1997, Rick spoke of his brother Bob's imminent return from the Far East and the likelihood of a reunion between the Hockmuths and myself. You can be sure that once this book is finished, I will press for such an event.

RICK JUDD

Aside from Rick's revered place in loon history for his part in the Fleming-Judd election, he also bears the distinction of being the person who first introduced me to WOHS. In the first year of the radio station (that being my junior year), Rick was its manager. Rick was also instrumental in getting Kaiser the job of being his assistant at the station that year, placing him in the greater historically significant role of being indirectly responsible for the Queen Viper and Morty Sneaky shows.

As Rick was in my sociology class (the same class that had me sitting between Fausto and CA), he overheard me discussing Iggy Pop with fellow Stooges fan Sean Dorman, and was compelled to interject that he had recently received his own personal Iggy baptism, courtesy of a promotional single sent to WOHS by Columbia records. A few days later, on Rick's prompt, I brought a transistor radio into the cafeteria, and at the loon lunch table, Elmo and I bubbled with excitement as Rick played "Search and Destroy," graciously dedicating the song to me. Outside of Rick's casual mention of the station, this was my first solid memory of WOHS. EAT and I's perspective on this would be that it was a shame Rick graduated in 1974, as he had no problem playing Iggy on his show, and probably would not have made a federal case out of EAT and I playing David Bowie on ours.

In one of my letters to Tonny in the fall of 1973, I mention WOHS, Kaiser's involvement, and Rick Judd's promise to play a tape of The Bonneville Follies on the air. I don't recall whether this actually happened (or if I even supplied Rick with the tape), but owing to my assistance in getting Judd elected to the student government the previous year, my letter doesn't seem to indicate that I anticipated anything but Rick's full support.

What Rick wrote in my Junior yearbook describes him better I ever could – "Broken glass protrudes from my turgid flesh and blood pours from the gaping wounds. My arms have been severed at the neck and replaced with tungston steel. My legs no longer move to my will. Someone else controls my legs. It is a fitting farewell to Oakton – Rick Judd '74." Fitting indeed.

RICKOSHAY

Now here is an unusual and mysterious individual. His name was Rick, but I nicknamed him "Rickoshay," in part to distinguish him from the plethora of Ricks in my acquaintance. He appeared briefly my senior year as the son of the pastor of the church on Fairlee Drive. He came over to my house a few times, and on one occasion, we recorded a song that he wrote the lyrics for and sang called "Eat It Bloody in Your Minds." For someone with such a Sam Romeo/Dennis Burley air of cool about him, his lyrics were surprisingly Howard Koretzish. This song stands as the only tangible proof I have that Rick ever existed.

Rick nurtured an affinity for the macabre to rival Howard's, and though his interest in witchcraft and Satanism seems to have been partly in rebellion to his father's position as a man of God, I've no doubt as to where he inherited his good vs. evil view of the world. He seemed half-contemptuous/ half-proud of his father's vocation, despite the sense he gave me that the two of them got along fairly well otherwise. Once Rick related this story of a guy he knew who was supposedly a practicing Satanist. His story involved a description of this fellow engaged in something called "The Circle," and an instance where he turned around and looked back and smiled at Rick with glowing green eyes. No complete turn of the head, I'm afraid, but a shining example nonetheless of early 70's suburban occult lore.

At one point, Rick just disappeared. It's possible that his father had been transferred to another congregation, or his family simply moved away, but I felt compelled to remember him in my senior will. To Rickoshay, I left – "My catalogue of ancient Hebrew colloquialisms, my accumulated notes on the various methods of combating urban renewal for the preservation of existing rat hordes, and my Hockmuth originals."

THE RING EXPERIMENT

Oh! How I wish I had a copy of issue no. 1 of Tonny and I's hand drawn Insane Illustrated that featured an article on the Ring Experiment, because it was somewhat of a personal triumph for me. I was sitting next to and having a rather involved discussion with a meat and potatoes skeptic named Thomas Ring on the afternoon bus heading home. This would have been during the spring of my sophomore year. I was giving Ring a discourse on certain negative aspects of female behavior that he wasn't buying. Feeling that a demonstration was in order, I gestured backward at the female who was sitting behind us. I told Ring what I was going to say to her and exactly how she would respond. Ring continued to shake his head in disbelief, but the upper hand I had was that at this stage in my life, I knew the effect I had on females. I don't know what I said to her, but you can bet that for the sake of the experiment, it was nothing rude or offensive, though being delivered on the spot like that, it may have come off as glib or contrived. It was the kind of attempt at communication that always got a friendly response in those beach party movies I had seen as a kid. Her response however, was caustic, uncalled for, and almost verbatim what I had told Ring it would be, which brought the closest thing to a look of surprise that I would see on the face of Thomas Ring in four years of riding the bus with him.

It was actually more of a hustle than an experiment, because I knew that at 16, I was still carrying around whatever rubbed girls the wrong way all through my grade school years. The success of the Ring Experiment was that now, one of Oakton's renowned skeptics had bore witness to this phenomena. Despite the mystique built around the vagaries of the fairer sex, there were times when I found them pathetically predictable. This was one of those times.

ROBIN BURCHFIELD

My first vomit inducing taste of political correctness taken to its most self-righteous extreme. Looking back at the lack of conflict with black people that I've had in the course of my life, it makes me wish I could claim the same lack of conflict with white people on the subject of black people. In February of 1975, all I knew was that I did not like black music, but I felt that the suburbs could use a lot more black girls, and any other differences between the races were irrelevant and unimportant to me. Oakton was not plagued with the racial tensions that divided the student bodies of other area schools. In fact! The blacks at Oakton were so cool, and things were so calm there that I never even imagined that things would be otherwise in surrounding high schools.

Having said all this, my collision course with the very white Robyn Burchfield was set during B lunch, on February 12 1975. The week of February 9 - 15 was "National Negro History Week" (as it was called back then). When EAT and I entered the radio room to hang up our coats on the morning of the 10th, we were given the low down from Kaiser on how WOHS was going to be celebrating National Negro History Week. At some point during the day, a black representative from the student body was going to be bringing a stack of albums of black recording artists by the station. We were then told that during our shows for the remainder of the week, every other piece of music that we played had to be something from this stack of albums, a mandate that initially brought moans and groans from EAT and I. However! Once the stack was delivered, our previews revealed some surprisingly interesting and non-commercial music (I.E. They hadn't plopped a bunch of Motown albums in our lap). One album in particular which got the attention of EAT and myself was an album called "Astral Signs," by an artist named Gene Harris. Tied together with a theme of astrology, were jazzy melodic sections interspersed with formless Sun-Ra-like forays into the outer cosmos, occasionally throwing in a song of two to keep the listener earthbound. One of these, a song entitled "Don't Call Me Nigger, Whitey!" really caught our attention. I hadn't known it at the time, but this was actually a cover version of a Sly and the Family Stone song. At any rate, I had already resolved that the one show I was doing that week (which fell on Wednesday, the 12th – Lincoln's birthday, by chance) would heavily feature the Astral Signs album.

Flash forward one month to March 17th. I enter the radio room to sense a distinct air of anger and indignation among its 4 or 5 inhabitants. Immediately, in anticipation of a school-leveling explosion from me, Elmo and Kaiser began their premature attempts to calm me down with assurances that everything would be taken care of. I instinctively knew that I and/or the radio station had been defamed in some way, but nothing could have prepared me for what I read in the March 14th edition of the Oakton Occasional. In the letters column was a letter addressed to the editor, the administration and the student body from Robyn Burchfield (who I didn't know from Eve). It was a nauseating letter, which oozed with posturing moral rectitude. The following is the letter in its entirety.

Dear Editor, Administration, Faculty, and Students:

February 9 through February 15 was National Negro History Week. The celebration was designed to recognize the role and achievements of black people in our country's history. On Wednesday of that week, as some friends and I were eating lunch, the WOHS disc jockey made a remark that caused us to turn and stare incredulously at the PA speaker... "This is 'don't call me nigger' week."

Shamefully, a comment of this sort would have been accepted, even heralded, in the 1950's and 60's. For us to condone this ignorant attitude by ignoring it would show that we have not progressed since that time. But we HAVE advanced; we DO possess greater human understanding. Today we cannot tolerate this comment or any like it. We cannot allow the disc jockey, Bob Karnes, and his attitude to go unpunished. I call for a public apology from Karnes, as well as his immediate resignation from WOHS. I ask all of you to support me in this effort. Speak up, show you you feel (?? -an obvious typo here. I believe it should read –"show how you feel".) Put pressure on Karnes. And if he refuses to resign, Mr. Johnson, I ask you to implement his removal.

Now, ordinarily I would implore that we give a person a second chance. But what is at issue here is more than one Bob Karnes, one Oakton High School, one joking remark. This involves centuries of cruelty and black oppression by whites. We, personally, may not be to blame, but we must accept responsibility. However, we must also take the blame if we allow racial intolerance to continue. What is at stake here is the integrity of black people, of all people. As a white person, I will not allow myself to be pulled down by Bob Karnes or any fool like him. People, we can no longer afford racial bigotry. Nor can our understanding and communication be hampered by indifference. Everyone, please, demand Bob Karnes' apology and resignation.

Robyn E.
Burchfield

I don't think I have to tell you there was a fairly decent size explosion in the radio room that day. I was angered not so much that the misunderstanding had taken place, but by Robyn's knee-jerk reaction to it. Clearly here was an individual attempting to atone for previous incarnations as a brutal slave-master. Even more outrageous to me was the journalistic irresponsibility of the Occasional, who had placed the entire school square in the middle of what today would be considered lawsuit territory. Similarly incensed was Mitchell Robinson, who immediately began composing his own letter to the editor suggesting that "Someone should take the wing-wong out of that ex-douche bag's ear." Perhaps it was soothing words from Kaiser, or perhaps it was the knowledge that the language of his letter would only escalate into unprintable profanity that caused him to give up the idea.

I've got to hand it to Kaiser though, he took control of the situation. After the initial anger wore off, I began to pace with paranoia over the idea of losing the most important thing to me at Oakton high - my radio show. Kaiser and Elmo showered me with reassurances that I would not be asked, forced, or coerced into relinquishing my show. In an attempt by both the radio station and the administration to quickly defuse the situation, a March 20th meeting was set up with assistant principal Norman Bradford and myself to discuss a fitting restitution of my tarnished good name. During 5th period, I met the normally stoic Mr. Bradford in the deserted hallway which ran from the administration office to the cafeteria.

An uneasy Mr. Bradford cut to the chase and asked me what I would except as amends for this libelous letter. My conditions were simple: I wanted an apology from Robyn Burchfield over the school intercom during the morning announcements. To my surprise, Mr. Bradford gently, but flatly, refused my terms. After a few more minutes of terse persistence on my part, it was clear that Mr. Bradford was not going to give me the satisfaction I wanted. This really frosted me. I mean! If Robyn Burchfield could use her position in the press to demand before the whole school an apology from me for something I DIDN'T do, why couldn't I demand an apology from Robyn Burchfield for something she DID do. There were already erroneous rumors about me circulating around the school, I didn't need this kind of shit on top of it.

I have to believe that Mr. Bradford was thinking containment. Being desirous of maintaining the racial tranquility at Oakton, he would have been exactly what he was behaving like - a man who wanted to sweep the whole thing under the rug as quickly as possible. And so, to my knowledge, no retraction or apology from Robyn Burchfield was ever printed in the Occasional. Now aside from one ridiculous incident where some guy I didn't even know pointed me out in the hallway and jokingly shouted "There's the nigger hater," no fallout from the Burchfield letter followed my conversation with Mr. Bradford. But I've always wondered what false impressions of me Robyn's letter may have given to members of the student body who didn't know me better. Though once again, I let my senior will be the last word on the subject. To Robyn Burchfield, I left "My copy of Gene Harris's Astral Signs, containing the hit single – Don't Call Me Nigger, Whitey." Really Robyn! If you had been up on your "Negro History," you would have recognized the song when I played it.

RUFFIANS

I can't recall whether it was Emmette or I who put this word into common usage. A tone of disdain would usually accompany Emmette's use of the word, whereas I tended to employ it more as a categorical term. The height of its usage was definitely during the 1972-73 period, when Emmette was one of the inner circle, and I know that when I referred to someone as a "Ruffian," Emmette had the clearest picture of what I was referring to. So just what is the definition of the word Ruffian as it appeared in the loon vernacular of the early 70's? Well! Perhaps I should begin by explaining what a ruffian was not. A ruffian was not always … well, rough. If roughness had been the sole criteria, certain jocks and pseudo jocks would have been included, and while I do refer to Ray King as a ruffian elsewhere in this book, he really was a ruffian in the oxford dictionary sense of the word, but not in the loon sense at all. No, we are talking about Dave Olsson, Paul Dols, John Gaines, Scott Machercher and others who were rarely captured by the yearbook camera's eye, and whose senior pictures were never taken. Among the qualifying characteristics were excessive drug use, a confrontational attitude towards authority figures, a disheveled and/or unkempt appearance, and a general aura of alienation from mainstream society. The noticeable presence of any one of the aforementioned characteristics was enough to get one branded a ruffian.

Despite the psychological distance Emmette kept between himself and this rabble, one of those characteristics, the one concerning alienation, linked many ruffians spiritually with the Insanist movement. Though I was more conscious of this than Emmette, he appeared to contradict himself by showing just as much enthusiasm as I did for inviting a ruffian into the ranks of the movement in the person of Joe Gorsuch. Upon meeting Joe, Emmette seemed to have an instant and favorable assessment of his potential for insanity. Emmette seemed to also appreciate the validation Joe's arrival might afford us, and proceeded to treat Gorsuch on his visits to the loon lunch table like visiting royalty. Joe was most definitely mad. Emmette would not have opened up to anything but the real thing, and the fact that Joe crossed several social echelons to associate with us was proof of what an autonomous unit he was. Insanity bound us together for as long as it could before the differences that separated ruffians and loons caused a natural drifting apart. If I had "Partied," and had not been so keen on inventing my own forms of amusement, it's likely that I would have called a number of them my friends.

SACK O' DILL

A favorite expression of Elmo's, though I can't say for sure that he actually coined the term. Whatever vaguely unflattering connotations its usage may have carried never rose above the spirit of nonsense that accompanied its delivery. The height of its usage was late 1973, where it even shows up in a Death by Hanging lyric. However, remnants of it are to be found in the late spring of 1974, with EAT signing my Junior yearbook with the following inscription – "Nothing like a note from a Dill! Brightens up your day."

SAM ROMEO

During Tonny and I's first vacation to Sarasota Florida in the summer of 1973, we were driven to Orlando for a couple days to visit the family of an old air force buddy of my stepfather's - Merle Badders. Merle and Bonnie Badders had three children, a son named Mikey, a daughter named Danny, and another son named Bobby. Mikey was around my age, Danny was a year or two my senior, and Bobby was a year or two younger than me.

I spent a good deal of my time there running around suburban Orlando with Bobby Badders and his friends, sometimes with just his friends. Tonny emphatically opted out of these excursions (some of which went into the wee hours) in fear for his safety at the hands of these dope crazed ruffians. Oh Yes! A few of them did have long hair, and at one point, a group of about 8 of us wound up at this one guy's house where 2 or 3 in the group were imbibing in marijuana and mushrooms, but that's where the link with anything I could tie to Northern Virginia life ended. For one thing, there was something about the way that simply being there made me a part of their group that I've never experienced before or since. There was not a wit of apprehension, competitive braggadocio, or pretentiousness in the bunch. This was not the mellow south you've heard about. This was something even mellower (and further south) than that.

The eldest of the group was a young man named Sam Romeo. Sam seemed to be everyone's benevolent big brother. He had a good two years on everyone else, but unlike the obvious leader of the group that he was, he seemed just as content to lean back and let things hang until his experience and greater sense of responsibility were called for. Part of what instills that sense of responsibility is being the guy with the car, and for much of my stay in Orlando, Sam took on the responsibility of being my chauffeur and tour guide. When I showed up at any place during those two days, it was usually in Sam's car.

It really WAS like one of those songs off the first couple of Tom Petty albums, where the flavor of growing up in central Florida hadn't faded. At one point, I was even given a fake ID and employed to buy a couple of 6 packs for the group. Sam had, for some reason, been refused the sale already. Perhaps the convenience store clerk knew Sam well enough to know who he was buying the beer for. Sam reassuringly told me that I didn't have to do it if I didn't want to, but the camaraderie of this group inspired a certain amount of courage and a healthy sense of adventure. I'll never forget the hero's welcome I received when I returned to the cars with the beer in hand.

The height of the red carpet treatment I was receiving, however, was yet to come. Sam, who (along with me) did not partake of the alcoholic spoils, was nonetheless happy that his people had been taken care of. We were well into the night now, but Sam had gotten the idea that I needed to be treated to some real Southern hospitality, so off we went on a quest for something female. I was a tad dubious, but just as caught up in the thrill of the hunt. On this night, with Sam at my side, failing to score couldn't dampen the fun of trying. At one point, we ended up at this house at the end of a cul-de-sac that was a little more buried in the swampy woods than the Badders residence. Like the convenience store and the group that had followed us there, a sub-tropical small town atmosphere prevailed. Getting no response from the front door, we went around to a side door, or possibly the back door, where amidst the din of crickets and bullfrogs, one could imagine big foot watching us from the blackness of the surrounding woods. Two girls met us at the door, one was thin with teased blonde hair, and the other was a short brunette with rounded cherub-like features and frame, neither of which came within a yardarm of striking my fancy. In another display of how Sam seemed to relish his role as the youth of the community's big brother, he took the brunette, who seemed glum and downcast over something, aside for a fatherly chat. My impression, from the slowness of her movements, was that her distress had been helped along by one too many tokes and/or one too many swigs of some kind of depressant. Sam sat with her for a few minutes in an attempt to sort out whatever adolescent trauma had befallen her, but upon remembering his guest, he threw a glance my way. I could read in his look that it had just struck him that there was no one in this house that I wanted to lose my virginity with. With this, he instantly went into Southern gentleman mode and excused the both of us.

The following afternoon, when it was clear that Sam was dropping me off at the Badders house for the last time, we parted with a heartfelt handshake and well wishes for the future. I have often wondered over the years what became of Sam Romeo. On a trip down to Venice Florida to visit Bonnie and Bobby Badders in the fall of 1996, Bobby told me that he had heard that Sam had become a state trooper. When Bobby told me this, I thought to myself how much this jibed with the protect-and-serve attitude Sam seemed well on his way to developing 23 years earlier.

In my childhood and all through my adolescence, I tended to feel more at ease around people of my grandparents generation than around groups of my peers (particularly those I didn't know too well). For two days in the summer of 1973, smack dab in the middle of my tumultuous Oakton experience, this was not the case for a group of my peers headed by Sam Romeo. This puts Sam in a particular place of distinction among the entries in this book. Godspeed Sam Romeo.

SASATIOUS VON CANON (AKA HOWARD KORETZ)

A gleefully morose little Jewish man whose involvement with the Insanist movement was sheer destiny. Howard was possessed of a determinably macabre sense of humor that, like so many other facets of my Oakton experience, I've only recently come to appreciate fully. Upon acquiring the phone number of a Howard Koretz about a year ago, I called the number and got an answering machine message. It was unmistakably in Howard's commanding baritone, but it was the message itself that really reassured me that Howard was still Howard.

Contact the head honcho of this house
And you can bet at least a dime
That it's gonna be worth your time

Over the years, I have watched enough friends and lovers turn into complete strangers to find it refreshing to discover an old friend whose purity of essence has survived the ravages of time. When I finally got to speak directly with Howard on the phone, the time capsule effect was exhilarating. Not only had Howard maintained his identity and sense of the macabre, it was surprising how keen his memory of our mid 70's exploits was. Alongside the comparative amnesia of certain other Oakton alumni, Howard actually corrected and/or added to several of my "Do you remember's?"

I first met Howard in my sophomore year homeroom class. Despite the fact that Mr. Cupelli insisted on silence in his shop homeroom class - Howard, Kaiser and I managed a good deal of general goofing off from the back of the room. As this homeroom class was a launching pad of sorts for insanist activity during my sophomore year (owing mainly to Kaiser's increased interest and involvement), Howard was sort of sucked into the current. He readily confessed to insanity, and then shamed us all by not really ever fitting into our aggregate of social outcasts. One could say that Howard was an insanist in the truest sense of the word, and it was probably the knowledge of this that prevented any of us from shooing him away outright.

Howard's interjections at the loon lunch table were often so non sequitur as to completely disrupt the flow of conversation. This was particularly tedious when valuable information, reports, plans or observations were being exchanged. I found it much easier communicating with Howard one on one, because I could simply adjust by slipping into Howard's world. I believe I was alone in possessing this special ability, because in a group situation, I often found myself juggling communications between the worlds, because at best, Howard was half in his own world and half in ours.

Having said all that, Howard holds the distinction of being the only other person beside myself to be actively involved in the Insanist movement at Oakton High from its beginning to its end. Howard had a small to medium role in almost every major folly right up to the grand finale in the cafeteria in front of a hysterical red-faced Peggy Wallace.

When bodies were needed, I could always count on Howard's willingness to participate. Howard also maintained a reverence for insanity that I lost sight of during the rush of seemingly more serious events my senior year.

Howard (like Emmette) had a tendency to monomanically focus on things few others would even notice, thereby making it his own. His observations and conclusions drawn on these things were further filtered through his never sleeping sense of the macabre. Depending upon the relative interest I had in whatever he was addressing, and the impact of his conclusions, this tendency of his could appear as either an unnecessary diversion or further proof of Areteus' assertion that "Insanity is an extension of normal thought processes." Even I, who had attracted so many unusual characters by being so obviously one who accepts variant forms of behavior, had to re-adjust my set to tune Howard in. Having done so, about 6 months after first meeting him, I began to catch faint glimpses of his genius. From that point onward, I progressively viewed Howard less and less through the eyes of those I had to speak over and/or through Howard to get to, eventually reaching a point where I was able to view through my own eyes Howard's unique perspective on things. The problem with juggling communications in a group situation still existed, but I was now on Howard's wavelength enough to have a one on one relationship with him similar to the one I had with Emmette.

Sometime during the first half of 1973, Howard presented me with the first clue that my faith in him was based on something more than just wishful thinking towards the goal of expanding our group numerically. It was a recording of Howard's first composition, a recitation with piano accompaniment entitled "Death in the Essence," and it was absolutely brilliant. Part of its brilliance was that it captured Howard so perfectly, much in the same way that EAT's first solo recording – "My Baby Left Me" was 100% undistilled EAT. One particularly relevant lyric from Death in the Essence ("It was nice knowing those sunny days and bowling alleys") gives a reminder of something else Howard shared with Emmette-O (besides his singularity of vision) - a passion for bowling. Like Emmette, Howard's compulsively narrowed focus complimented the mechanics of bowling. As Tonny attested to, Emmette did not possess the tactile coordination to succeed in little league baseball, but according to Howard, Emmette did possess an above average talent for staring down a narrow lane and rolling a ball down to a specific point at the end of that lane. This was more than the sport of last resort for two individuals who were not built for football, not coordinated enough for baseball, and not tall or athletically fit enough for basketball. It had Zen-like properties that non-bowlers like myself could only watch and wonder about.

Having been encouraged by the enthusiasm I exhibited over his initial offering, Howard continued making recordings, and composing songs and poems. I ended up recording two of his compositions "Back to Old Saint Lizzies" and "The Miss Loonies of Our Minds," the latter of which (at the risk of causing Emmette to turn over in his grave) brings yet another Emmette/Howard comparison to mind. The opening stanza to The Miss Loonies of Our Minds says it all.

You meet the female of brain and mind
And insanity in the essence, you're looking to find
If she looks at you and gives you a frown
Just get the observations and write 'em down

As the second line indicates, this was written at a time when the fondest wish of each loon was to usher a female into the ranks of the Insanist movement. What it does not reveal was that all through these heady days of expansionism, Emmette had already been following the songs advice by getting the observations and writing 'em down. While unlike Howard, Emmette was dowsing his adolescent fascination with females in clinical elitism, it's interesting to note that Howard's fascination with females manifested itself with the exact same impulse to study and take notes. Though I was more proactive in actually interacting with the females that fascinated me, it only took one heartbreak for me to view with admiration the practicality of the safe distance Howard and Emmette were maintaining. As much as I romanticized the idea of examining female behavior (as if any kind of controlled environment for such a thing could have existed at OHS), in practice, my undisciplined heart would not allow me to even get close to following Howard and Emmette's example.

From the early days of my freshman year, Emmette and I's use of the word "Female" suggests that analytical distance had already been chosen over the risk of embarrassment and emotional upset. By the latter half of my senior year – "Get the observations and write 'em down" became such a catch phrase with Howard and myself that it's clear we had both realized that (at least until graduation) this was the only thing we could do - just hang back and observe. Though never amounting to more than a joke among the three of us, getting some observations, writing them down, and then actually studying them conscientiously might have benefited us. With nary a sister or a prior relationship between the three of us, I dare say our collective knowledge of how to deal with adolescent females wouldn't have filled a page. Whether taken seriously or not, this inclination to get the observations and write 'em down seems to have been addressing a real need for more information. Apart from that, it was further proof that Howard's place was with us.

Acting upon this realization, I visited Howard at his apartment at Circle Towers, shortly after hearing Death in the Essence. By the start of our junior year, my friendship with Howard was on more solid ground, and through me, Howard's involvement in follies such as Paying increased. Howard's line of Iggy Pop graffiti proved that he could originate a folly as well as go along with one. I can't recall whether or not Elmo, EAT and I's enthusiasm over the Iggy and the Stooges Raw Power LP was such that Howard was moved to purchase a copy for himself, but his fascination with Iggy was undeniable. Manifesting itself in a daily countdown of the days left until Iggy Pop's birthday written on the chalkboard in our junior year music class, this fascination was a shining example of the Emmette-like monomania I brought up earlier.

Howard drew this wonderful picture of this crazy woman that he named "Mrs. Luna Tickk." He then drew her saying "Iggy! Iggy! Rescue and cure my soul!" a paraphrasing of a line of mine that ends one of the pieces on DBH's We Were Promised a Female, - "Iggy! Iggy! Save my soul." I could have played Howard a tape of this recording, but it's more likely that he overheard Elmo or I bellowing out the phrase in an evangelistic furor, because it did become a cliché for a while. I still own Howard's early 1974 pencil drawing of Mrs. Luna Tickk. Appropriately, on the other side of the piece of paper in which Mrs. Tickk was drawn on are some notes for my oral report on insanity.

Another fond memory I have of Howard was the time I persuaded him to go up and play the piano in my junior year music theory class. Mr. Curtis hadn't shown up yet, and so certain keyboard adepts in the class were taking turns going up to the piano in the front of the room and playing various tunes that they knew. I use the word "Persuaded," because when I brought up the suggestion that Howard should be given a turn, it brought a few moans and groans from the class, making Howard a little nervous and in need of a little persuading. Well, despite Howard's unease, I knew that Howard could not resist being Howard, and so having painfully relented in giving Howard his turn, the class was treated to a very somber version of the Death March. When the class pelted Howard with demands that he play something else, I turned and gave the thoroughly Emmettian response – "That's the greatest masterpiece of all time, what's wrong with you people?" I beckoned Howard to continue, and he did.

As Tonny and I had done, Howard and I developed our own lexicon of slang, or more accurately, our own manner of communicating. This adapted mode of communication played upon (I'll say it) our mutual fascination with the macabre, and is best described by the salutation

Howard and I would begin and end many of our conversations with – "Good Mourning!" Spoken with either the deep summoning tone of a Satanic affirmation, or a somber-faced tone of solemnity which oozed with respect for the dead, "Good Mourning" became the traditional way that Howard and I would greet or say goodbye to each other.

Howard began to color (or darken I should say) his speech by prefacing key words with adjectives beginning with the same letter. A classic example of this is a note that I wrote to Howard, which I still have in my possession. It was obviously written during our senior year, when Howard and I were working as telephone solicitors for the Washington Star. As Howard's cubicle was directly opposite mine, we would occasionally slip notes back and forth to each other underneath the partition. The question I posed to Howard which demonstrates how thoroughly I had embraced his manner of speech coloration was – "How many sinister sales have you maliciously made?" This adjective inserting was at once a running joke between Howard and myself, and a gleeful affirmation of the ominous shadows that Howard cast upon all things. Indeed! The way in which Howard most resembled other insanists was his penchant for making light of the things others took most seriously, and visa versa.

While most of Howard's solo recordings, including Death in the Essence, have survived the years, I regret to say that both of the sessions Howard and I recorded together were lost by the end of the 70's. To discover one of those on an old reel to reel tape would truly be a great archaeological find. The first session was recorded during that musically fruitful spring/summer of 1973 at Howard's apartment at Circle Towers. The second and more memorable session was recorded much later at Howard's Hawthorne Village apartment on the north end of Fairfax Circle. The dark stormy nature of the music dates it to the post Peggy spring of 1975, though it's possible that it was recorded after graduation. Its infernal majesty was captured with a cassette recorder stuck in the hull of Howard's upright piano, creating an eerie reverberate effect. Sitting together at the piano, Howard played the keys on the upper register and I played the lower ones, while doing most of the singing. With very little forethought, and four hands on the piano, the flow of on the spot constructed poly rhythms that came out of Howard and I reached such levels of intensity that it felt as if we were possessed. I can recall feeling from the very first number that anything we might attempt to do musically that evening would be successful. I also recall, throughout the session, becoming aware that I was playing the piano a level or two above my native ability. It's a shame that I never got to familiarize myself with the individual pieces, and that like so many things I fully meant to hold on to, the tape quickly disappeared in the quagmire that was my room. I remember listening to a bit of the tape at Howard's to see how well it recorded, but after that - gone. I must confess here that I did not mark and catalogue my tapes as well as I should have.

Though Howard's spot at the loon lunch table was reserved by the start of my junior year, it was actually during my senior year that Howard played his most influential role. The luck of all of us having the same lunch period ran out my senior year, reducing the B lunch loon aggregate to just Howard and myself. Our locus of lunch period activity having shifted to the radio station, it's doubtful I would have visited the cafeteria at all during my senior year had Howard not been there to lunch with. This brings up one of the greatest "Ifs" of this book. If I had not befriended Howard Koretz my sophomore year, I would have probably never met Peggy Wallace my senior year. Yes! The quietude of Howard's funereal solemnity hung in the air between me and one of the most legendary "Miss Loonies of Our Minds." Howard's head is on the left side of every mental picture I have of Peggy when she was only that winsome mysterious girl who looks at me in the cafeteria.

The information Ray Denk provided, which eventually led me to track down the suddenly elusive Miss Wallace was given to me at the phone solicitor job I held in January of 1975. Again, Howard was instrumental because it was through Howard that I got this job.

Another example of Howard as being the unseen specter of dark forces was his minor but causal role in the Stephanie Hill library incident (see Stephanie Hill), which may have been a contributory factor in the early 1975 rumors about me being a Satanist. Speaking of Satanism, Howard presented me with this wonderful poem in the early spring of 1974 that I think perfectly illustrates his uncanny ability to invoke the sinister, even as he was professing goodness, as if he was born to write horror movie scripts.

Declared Change of Worship

I have a decision to declare
A change of worship, do I dare
For worshipping the devil was a horrible sin
I should not have done it at all to begin
I have now found a god to worship and trust
And he'll carry out orders which for certain he must
He'll right all the wrongs that fall on mankind
And punish wrong doers with such ways of cruel mind
They'll suffer and suffer and endure his pain long
And learn that righteousness does triumph over wrong

He'll carry out my prayers with a good sense of fame
For the Angel of Justice is mighty, and now named

Sasatious Von Canon

Before I examine this poem, I should explain something that may be confusing you. Why have I been addressing Howard throughout his entry as "Howard" and not by his assumed insanist name "Sasatious?" The answer is that while Sasatious Von Canon had become Howard's official name as a point of record, Howard had simply waited too long to christen himself for any of the people who knew him as "Howard" to adjust, and so the name Sasatious never caught on. It may have been as late as the fall of 1973 before Howard bowed to tradition and took on an insane name, whereas I cannot recall ever addressing Tonny as Tom, EAT as Doug, Emmette as Tim, or Elmo as Keith. With all of these people, an assumed name was the notary seal that authenticated the change in identity and affiliation they were undertaking, whereas with Howard it was just an afterthought.

Now as for this poem. I must first say that I don't know, nor did I ever question, Howard's reasons for giving it to me. Perhaps with all of the effort I had spent attempting to mount a conversion attempt en masse on the Christ United Methodist Church youth group, and my more recent involvement with the revelations club, Howard may have interpreted all this to mean that I had found the lord, and his Declared Change of Worship poem was his way of demonstrating his willingness to at least join me in spirit. A closer examination of the poem, however, reveals it to be Howard at his most Hitchcockian (and Howard's "Good Mourning" DID bring Hitchcock's trademark "Good Evening" to mind).

The image of God as the brutal enforcer that evolves throughout the poem, carries us to the final two lines, where Howard is either not so subtly revealing that no change in worship has actually taken place, or that like some spiritual Mafioso, Howard has just hired God to be one of his henchmen. "He'll carry out my prayers," sounds like it should read "He'll carry out my orders," and "With a good sense of fame" seems to be more of a paean to worldly ambitions than to heavenly virtues. But my favorite line is the final one, where Howard leaves us hanging with – "For the angel of justice is mighty, and now named." It helps to have known Howard to recognize that he had not within him a millimeter of piety to further realize that only someone with yards of piety could write in all seriousness such words in reference to an agent of God. Who then is the angel of justice? I believe that was left for you and me to ponder. Metaphoric clues were the stock in trade for Howard's brand of raw uncut genius. The more I look at the talents of the people I knew at Oakton, the more I feel that genius is in its purest form when it is unintentional.

SATANIC RUMORS

I remember hanging about outside the radio room while the Grand Funk song "We're an American Band" was playing inside. As I entered the room, EAT looked at me and said "We're an American band..........an American band of Satan worshippers." This typically pithy witticism of EAT's was three pronged. On the surface, he was making fun of the song by injecting substance into something he felt had none. Secondly, he was demonstrating how much of a joke we took the rumors about us being Satanists to be. Thirdly (and less obviously), he was acknowledging the fact that we hadn't the slightest intention of ever denying those rumors. In fact, our interest was peaked to the point of casually affecting the aesthetics of Satanism, if not the practice of it.

I would hazard to guess that both EAT and I had acquired our copies of Anton Szander Lavey's "The Satanic Bible" by this point. This book's paperback edition (no doubt prompted by the success of the Exorcist) hit the shelves at just about the time EAT and I's curiosities began to crave some clarity on the subject. My lurid expectations turned to shock at the book's pragmatism and logic. This was the thing that everybody was so frightened of??? This book (while of course being rather one sided on the issue) was actually my first step towards ridding myself of the myth of Satan and Satanism. Aside from the added confusion of trying to establish my own concept of good and evil while the reactionary faith-over-logicness of my Christian peers played off the sound of mind relativism of the head of the church of Satan, the only disheartening thing that either of us would carry out of these rumors was the reinforcement of the reality of what gossipy creatures females could be.

SATANISM

Sometime during the mid-seventies, while roaming the aisles of the Peoples drug store at Tysons Corner Mall, I was approached by a man in his mid to late thirties who asked me – "Excuse me! What is that on your shirt?" I was wearing a Black Sabbath T-shirt with the cover of Sabbath Bloody Sabbath (and the number 666) printed on the front of it. "This is my Black Sabbath T-shirt" I replied rather innocently. With an affirmative nod of recognition, he said "Oh! It's a band. It's a band," and excusing himself with a bowing-out gesture, he walked off, leaving me with the feeling that I'd just had a close call. His approach to me was rather confrontational, and I could tell by the way he posed his question that he was ready to lay into me if I gave him the wrong answer.

Now all I could think of at the time was what kind of Christian psycho this guy might be, because I had already been conditioned to accept the danger of an irrational reactionary response to anything I might be wearing or projecting that could be construed as being Satanic. Satanism provoked fear and hysteria (or at least worry) in Christians. This is what my experience had taught me, and I don't mind telling you, this did not endear me to Christianity, or leave me overwhelmed by the spiritual strength that Christians claimed their faith gave them. Neither was I even including the rank and file Methodist in the equation, because I could see that they did little more than attend church, and by this time, I was passed the point of placation, and was looking for answers more in the form of enlightenment than salvation.

Which brings us around to this Satanic aura I was supposed to have had in high school. Well, I won't deny having had one since so many people (including a reminiscing EAT) claim that I did. But let me state for the record that whatever back-the-fuck-up vibe I was putting out for the cowering underclassmen was an exteriorization of more earthly concerns, of the kind that drew me closer to the reality of the average adolescent male than I would have been comfortable being.

There's a passage in the bible that a number of Christians I knew were so fond of quoting that translated to the world being able to distinguish Christians by their love. I heard this scripture being bandied about a lot during the 1973-74 period, when I was still taking charismatic Christians at their word. That I was beginning to know them by their intolerance around the time of the Peoples Drug incident (which was during the 1975-76 post Oakton period) only strengthened my resolve to distance myself from them. This presumption of knowing them by their love stuck with me up until I realized that it wasn't crossing the generational lines to guarantee me the love (or even the acceptance) of my Christian peers.

I had never known any want for love or acceptance among my family and elders. Any holes in my self-esteem came from a lack of acceptance among people my own age. If I was passed the point of even considering asking a girl like Marcia Carter out, it was not for lack of women my grandmother's age telling me what a handsome young man I was. And true to form, the elders in the church showered me with the same glad-to-see-you smiles, and dealt with me as if they were nurturing a young tree so that it would grow straight and strong. I was discovering that overall, Christians were the same as non-Christians, which is something I would have discovered on my own, and wouldn't have bothered me at all if I hadn't been led to expect more from them with this business about knowing them by their love. I was discovering (whether true or false) that I could not trust people my own age whatever love they claimed differentiated them.

I mean no disrespect to those mostly over-40 Christians who tried to make me feel at home in the house of the lord, but it was Satanic literature that introduced reason into my view of this dichotomy, so I'm obliged to give credit where credit's due. This along with all those people who thought that my place was on the Satanic side of the dichotomy (if I wasn't there already) brings my empathy to rest with the true Satanist, whose lot of misunderstanding and cultural ignorance I've only received the smallest taste of.

As self-contained as EAT and I became during the 74/75 school year, the rejection and disillusionment that made this containment seem necessary hadn't stopped EAT and I from expecting the people who mattered to see us for the merry pranksters we really were. During a recent phone conversation on this very subject, EAT (with typical final-word poignancy) looked back at some of these people and said "They didn't realize that monster's need love too." Well! Hallelujah and Amen to that.

SCOTT MERRILL

Brother of Kit Merrill (the Midnight Cackeler) and a bit player in the CA drama. Scott was the greatest of the "Greats," that contingent of the Christ United Methodist Church youth group which I continually touted amongst my fellow loons as being prime for acquisition. Referring to them as the "Greats" was really my way of sugar-coating the situation in an attempt to entice my fellow loons to join me at the church for some converting of our own. Though the Cackeler legend remains a tasty chunk of loon lore, Scott was the only one of the lot (with the possible exception of youth leader Spencer Turnipseed) with any degree of greatness as we loons measured it.

Living over in Arlington, he was (like Ganzer up in Punxsutawney) a loon in absentia, and it's truly a shame that he didn't arrive on the scene until after Emmette's two visits to the church. As with Emmette and EAT, the strangeness of the circumstances surrounding their entrance into my life was often a barometer for the eventual greatness of a prospective loon. This was certainly the case with Scott. Throughout my sophomore year (1972-73), which could be viewed as my early days of discovery in the church, Scott remained a shy unassuming peripheral figure in the youth group. His sister, by virtue of her shrill insincere laugh, had long since been dubbed the Midnight Cackeler. Reverend Sheffield's daughter Coco (AKA The Coati Mundi or "The Mundi" for short) had already drawn Emmette to the church in search of more empirical data to support his theories on the Peterson Syndrome. The youth group as a whole had on numerous occasions been held up by me as a more pliant controlled group which we (the insanists) could at least practice our lunacy amongst, if not walk away with a few converts in the process.

Throughout this whole period, Scott's silent and expressionless presence graced the youth group gatherings fairly infrequently, just enough for it to register with me that he was the brother of the Cackeler. Then, sometime around late spring/early summer 1973, a dramatic change came over Scott, a change that I would love to take some credit for helping to psychically foment. Indeed! Immediately after this change occurred, Scott seemed to gravitate towards me. It was the most remarkable overnight blossoming of an individual I've ever witnessed, making it nearly impossible for me to reconcile my before and after pictures of the two Scott Merrills. His once tightly drawn face had suddenly come alive with expression. A perpetual mad glint now filled his eyes, and an accompanying smile now welcomed all into his presence. His voice, which I have no memory of hearing prior to this transformation, was now the loudest and most prevalent at the youth group gatherings (save for the piercing tone of the Cackeler). He was not simply there more often, he was there more completely, and though I would later remark on how reserved he had previously appeared, his explanation for the change in his personality boiled down to a simple change in viewpoint. My memory never retained the gist of what prompted this change in viewpoint, but whatever it was, it allowed for a healthy degree of silliness and spontaneity. This suddenly made me stand out as the only other person in the youth group vibrating anywhere near his wavelength, and so an alliance was formed. While I felt a little more secure in the group having Scott as an ally, the two of us were thrown into a rather precarious limelight.

Imagine the steady rise on the unpleasantness meter if EAT had joined me at the revelations club party at Kim Koan's house, and you have an idea of the squaring off that occurred. Like the revelations club, the bulk of the Methodist youth group were somewhat uncharismatic priggish young women. This is not to say that they wore perpetual scowls of disapproval over the improprieties of the world. They were very much the picture of the James Taylor-listening, long hair and short skirt-wearing, world peace-wishing, folk guitar-strumming adolescent female of the early 70's. But one still got the distinct impression that they viewed Scott's unrestrained merriment at times as excessive and irreverent. His sister Kit, in particular, seemed to prefer her brother the way he was before.

Aside from the change in his personality, another major sticking point was Scott's newfound willingness to proclaim the miracles of God as they were now manifesting in his life. This he did with the exuberance of a child with a new toy. Inside the Pentecostal Fairfax Assembly of God that I was even at this stage, beginning to attend sporadically, Scott would have been viewed as having been touched by the Holy Spirit. At Oakton High, I would have made the proud announcement that Scott had gone mad, and reserved a place for him at the loon lunch table. Strangely, Scott's charismatic spiritual awakening seems to have been an outgrowth of the change in his personality, and NOT the other way around. If a particular religious experience had been instrumental in effecting this change in Scott, I'm certain he would have told me. No! I think that Scott had made a decision to enjoy life rather than be stifled by it, and this was his way of reacting to the wishy-washy gray area Christianity that surrounded us there at Christ United.

This sensibilities gap came to a head one memorable Sunday afternoon when youth leader Spencer Turnipseed handed over the teaching of the youth group for the day to Scott and myself. Knowing that Scott and I were apt to present some ideas that went completely against Methodist doctrine made this a particularly bold move on Spencer's part. While Spencer liked and admired the both of us, I also felt that he was one who considered opposing viewpoints in Christendom worth discussing. The glint in his eyes indicated his pleasure at having Scott and I there to stir things up, and to make for a more interesting youth meeting by sparking such discussion. And stir things up we did. One of the ideas I had picked up from my handful of visits to the Assembly of God was that one had to be "Saved" to enter into the kingdom of heaven. Scott, who seemed to be on my wavelength 100%, had also adopted this belief. This was not an idea born out of logic or deductive reasoning as much as it was ready made ammunition for throwing into the face of our dispassionate female associates.

It was a classic sane/insane confrontation transplanted to the battlefield of the Methodist youth group. Seconds after Scott and I put the idea of being saved on the table, we were assailed with such an outcry of protest that Spencer had to intercede and insist that the group hear us out. From this point the lesson deteriorated, as discussions of these matters often do, into a stalemate argument over things no one in the group could prove or disprove. What makes it such a great memory for me is the fun Scott and I had inserting our own spirits into the group, and the vicarious enjoyment Spencer had in watching us inject a little passion into the play. If I would ultimately fail in my mission as stated in one of my late 1972 songs – "To gain the greats and take the church," it was not for Spencer's failure to provide me with a platform to reach out from.

Music, as it had been at Oakton, was to become the great separator of the sanes from the insanists in the Methodist youth group. The youth lounge was fitted with a stereo system, which had played its fair share of James Taylor records. The poor thing was pleading with me to bring my copy of Iggy's Raw Power in to blow some of the dust out of its speakers. As expected, the usual scrunched up noses and exclamations of girlish repugnance flowed from the Cackeler et al. What was somewhat unexpected was charismatic Scott's immediate fascination with Iggy. I still have this picture of Scott bouncing around the youth lounge in praise of Iggy (and I doubt that we had even gotten halfway through side one yet). In my second letter to Tonny, I mention preaching the greatness of rats and the greatness of "The Ig," as well as a "Little about my position as an outcast," in the youth lounge on Sunday September 23 1973. During the MYF meeting that morning, Scott admitted publicly that he was insane (a major event judging from my description), and good old Mary Waters signed a document stating that she did not think I was weird, despite my musical tastes and the strange effect I had on Scott Merrill.

Though it would have been foolish of me to expect a positive response from the Cackeler to Iggy and the Stooges, her reaction to Raw Power did demonstrate the dichotomy of the Merrill siblings. Scott was at his happiest when he was exploring and discovering new things, while his sister Kit, though good at heart, seemed to revel in pushing much of the world away in disdain. Scott, like the unstereotypically Christian Gary Garland, would continue to amaze me in this regard. In fact, it was from Scott Merrill that I first heard Mike Oldfield's "Tubular Bells" (the future theme music to the Exorcist). He called me up one day specifically to rave about the greatness of this album.

Scott's finest hour, however, was his involvement in the Cheri saga. Upon hearing about Cheri (and upon seeing the state I was in over her), Scott demanded that I give him her phone number so that he could at least vouch for my sincerity. My practical side thought "What the hell! I can use all the help I can get here." But the loon (or the child, if you prefer) in me started jumping up and down and thinking - Ooh Boy! Knowing Scott as I do, something is bound to occur that we'll be laughing about for months to come. What actually occurred was that Scott's call to Cheri ended up being more of a data collecting mission for my benefit, and a profitable one at that. Scott learned, as I had in my phone conversations with Cheri, that Cheri would talk to anyone, about anything, for hours on end. Though Scott was discrete enough to not ask her any leading questions such as "So, What do you think of Bob?" I do remember going over their phone conversation with him only moments after the event, and ending up feeling as if I knew Cheri a little better. Truth be told though, there was also plenty to laugh about in Scott's synopsis. A lot of the humor I derived from this was, of course, in knowing both Scott and Cheri.

The Merrill's move out of the area was so quick and without notice that I had no chance to make arrangements to keep in touch with Scott, or even say goodbye to him. Meemaw, for reasons that were not made clear to me, disapproved of my interest in the Merrills, as if she felt there was something unsavory about them. As such, my inquiries for information about them after their departure were swept under the rug. I don't know if it ever occurred to my grandmother or not, but unsavory or not, my subsequent drop in attendance to Christ United was due to the fact that without Kit and Scott Merrill (or Spencer Turnipseed, who left a month or two before Scott), the youth group had suddenly become a very dull affair. The more charismatic youth group at the Fairfax Assembly of God gobbled me up shortly afterwards. Whenever I find myself in that part of Falls Church, I recall the times Scott and I tooled about those suburban streets in that old jalopy of his. Its brakes were so worn, that he had to downshift going down hills. Times were good.

SCOTTY AND KEVIN

Two friends of mine who lived next door to my grandma Karnes' house in Falls Church. Scotty was a couple years younger than me, and Kevin was probably four years younger. I can't think of any other friends that I had more fun playing with as a child. I had no idea how far back the three of us went until my dad showed me a picture of us wherein Scotty is pushing Kevin around in a stroller. They are in this book because our friendship stretched up through my sophomore year at Oakton.

The 3 of us once had a recording session without instruments (walking around outside no less). One or two of us would make the instrument sounds with our mouths (drums, guitar solo's etc.), while the other one or two would handle the singing. Throughout the verses and choruses, the 3 of us would trade off roles in support of the other 2, and in our own primitive way, maintain a full band sound. This late summer of 1970 session marked my first attempt at the recording of original music, and at the very least put me in a frame of mind that made the first Bonneville Follies recordings an inevitable second step. The only thing I can remember from this granddaddy of long lost tapes is a refrain that young Kevin coined to a song entitled "Fuck the Fuzz." A rather harsh sentiment, given that Kevin was no more than 10 years of age at the time, but despite the fun we had making it, this tape was devoid of the silliness that would later define the Bonneville Follies.

Strangely, the three of us would have another recording session a little over a year later that even less resembled the Follies sessions that now preceded it. Perhaps it was because the three of us had grown up playing war games together, but as evidenced by our two recording sessions, Scotty and Kevin seemed to bring out in me the desire to create uncharacteristically heavy and aggressive music. Sometime before our 1971 session, I had discovered that strumming my acoustic guitar in close proximity to my cassette microphone with the levels up created a distortion effect much like that of an electric guitar cranked up to 10. The three of us assembled in my basement, with Scotty and Kevin playing various percussion and providing cued chorus support, while I strummed what the tape translated as power chords and sang. The effect was reminiscent of those wonderfully distorted late 60's Amon Duul albums. One of the songs from this session, the Willard inspired "Rats in the Sewer," was covered the following summer by the Bonneville Follies.

An entry in an old diary dated January 28, 1972 subtitled "A Day of Battle," had me leaving for my grandma Karnes' house at 9:38. When I arrived at 9:57, I met Kevin "And we immediately started battling, Scotty and the others joined us later." Now by "Battling," I meant, of course, playing war games, but two things characterized our particular brand of war gaming. Sure! We all had toy guns (I had a freakin' arsenal), but while other neighborhood kids would occasionally join us (most memorably during this period, a small black boy named "Pookie"), raising our numbers to that of a small platoon, we did not (usually) break off into teams and battle each other. We battled an imaginary enemy that each of us mocked up independently, though by virtue of my age and acutely developed imagination for this sort of thing, I seemed to be the one who would at least set the stage for the ensuing action.

The further we immersed ourselves in a particular situation, the sharper the images of the enemy became, and it's remarkable how clear some of my memories are of things that were essentially just visual mock ups. For instance, there was one particularly hard fought blood and honor session where the three of us dug in and spent the better part of an afternoon defending the hill near the back of the Scott's property (which was really nothing more than the ground sloping upward about a foot or two). With nothing but a wooden box, a couple of sacks and a pair of medium size trees for cover, we fought off, (sometimes hand to hand the occasional enemy that overran our position) an enemy that I can still see shooting at us. When at last we emerged dusty, sweaty and victorious, I recall the three of us shaking each other's hands, patting each other's backs, and reveling in the sense that we had really lived through something.

Probably my most vivid memory of the heat of battle, was utilizing this big branch that we had shoved between a Y shaped tree as a machine gun to fire at these enemy planes that were strafing us through the trees above. Both Scotty and Kevin were wounded or pinned down, and so it was a rather dramatic do or die situation for me. Each of us got his chance to be the hero and save the day, and this was one of mine. My most vivid memory of this event is the sight of a Messerschmitt swooping down towards me with both guns firing. As I was angling my gun on its 90-degree swivel, I remember that my shirtsleeves were unbuttoned and sweat was pouring down my face from the heat of the sun. Though I've always imagined that this occurred during one of the summer months, a line in the aforementioned entry leads me to believe that amazingly enough, this happened on January 28, 1972. The last line in the entry reads "The temperature was in the 70's and we were sweating." That I had noted it down in my journal suggests that I had taken note of it then, as I remember doing while I was shooting at those planes. Also, the fact that the sleeves of my shirt were open and hanging loose suggests that I wore a long sleeve shirt in expectation of cooler temperatures.

I mentioned earlier that there were two characteristics that defined our war games. The first, as I've illustrated, was the fact that except for one or two occasions, we collectively battled an imaginary mocked up enemy force. The second characteristic was the often brutal physicality of our play. It wasn't a macho thing as much as it was simply being absorbed in the intensity of the moment, and the desire to effect some form of realism. If a mortar exploded near you (whether as part of your own mock up or someone else's), you had to play along and be thrown into a wall, over a fence, or against a tree. You were obliged to obey the laws of physics and be thrown there. I remember running across the Scott's backyard (our main battleground) in an attempt to outrun an incoming shell, only to find myself flying about three feet in the air and landing hard on the ground, completely knocking the wind out of me. It's a wonder that no bones were broken after years of such adherence, though I'm sure we had our fair share of scrapes and bruises.

I remember Scotty and Kevin's parents vividly, but while I remember their dad's face and voice, I also remember him having problems with their mother, Robie, and eventually leaving the house. During the latter years of my friendship with Scotty and Kevin, I remember just the three of them, with the occasional visit from their dad. I remember Kevin (who was no more than 9 at the time) comforting his sobbing mother, and while it never really effected our play, there was at times this sense of adults having emotional problems hanging in the air. Robie Scott was a pretty lady, who despite my grandma Karnes' scandalous report to me that Robie was seen at a party smoking marijuana, seemed very motherly in a way that reminded me of my own mother. And though their house was sparsely furnished, without a bit of carpeting over the hard wood floors, it still was a place where fond memories would be stored.

April 29 1972 seems to have been another day of fun and adventure with the Scott's, though getting off to a later start than January 28th, with my arrival time logged as 11:46. Between the 10:37 time I made arrangements to come over with Scotty on the phone, and the 11:33 time I actually left my house (precise little journal keeper wasn't I?), I'm sure a good bit of pleading with my homebody mother was involved. The line "I conned mom into transporting me" should strike a chord of familiarity with anyone who remembers those pre-car years of parental dependence, especially anyone who (like me) had their friends spread out all over the county. Until my mom returned to pick me up at 4:48, Scotty, Kevin, Pookie and I battled (of course), and at one point – "We had best fall." Now after 26 years, that line is still self-explanatory. "Best fall" was a commonly held contest among boys of that era (at least I don't THINK I invented it) to see who could feign being shot and perform the most dramatic and well choreographed fall to the ground. I'm also reminded in this journal entry of the interest I took in a small shed that Scotty directed my attention to at the back of the Scott's property. The lines "It looks like a possible rats nest. It is filled with junk" recall my early 70's obsession with rats, and how that led to a similar fascination with old buildings where the creatures might be lurking.

A few odd pre-Oakton memories come to mind, like the time Scotty, Kevin and I gave a performance for some kids in their backyard. Using the Scott's raised backyard patio as a stage (which it very much resembled) the three of us utilized prop instruments and lip-synched to Banana Splits 45's, dating this at sometime in the summer of 1967. We ran through a 3 or 4 song set, to the enthusiastic applause of our audience of 4 or 5 (which included my younger half sister - Kim), but I don't recall it being worth the trouble it took setting the thing up, or talking Kevin into participating over the nagging presence of his consuming stage fright.

Another bizarre game that came out of my active imagination (which was fueled by toasted peanut butter and mayonnaise sandwiches, the sure to please specialty cuisine of my grandma Karnes) was to pretend that a section of the grass on the side of the Scott's house that faced my grandparents house was a swimming pool. We would dive into this imaginary pool and swim across the grass. This was shortly after my Golden Gate Garden's swim teacher Wally had taught me to swim, and swimming was on my mind a lot.

The last memory I have of the three of us getting together as friends was sometime in the summer of 1973, and interestingly enough, it involved me bringing over some albums for the two of them to hear. Music was becoming an increasingly important part of my life, and one that I enjoyed sharing with others. Around this time though, even young Kevin was at the age where he was beginning to amass a record collection of his own. I may have overdone it a bit by bringing over Iggy and the Stooges' Raw Power and Pink Floyd's Umma Gumma. Pink Floyd's live version of "Careful with That Axe, Eugene" actually frightened the two of them, and I was later admonished for giving Kevin nightmares.

The last time I ever saw Scotty and Kevin was in 1975. I'm guessing that it had to be at least two years later, because while Kevin was still himself, Scotty had undergone a complete personality transformation. On Scotty's prompting, the three of us walked over to this girl's house a couple of blocks away, an utterly fruitless pursuit, though the walk gave me a chance to acquaint myself with the total stranger that Scotty had become. I think Scotty had wanted to impress upon me the fact that his interests had graduated to the level of pot and girls, but throughout the ordeal, Kevin kept flashing me these "Oh! Brother" looks, and it was evident the two of us were bored out of our minds. The next time I visited my grandma and granddaddy Karnes, which may have been in my own car, I was told that the Scott's had moved. As my Oakton experience drew to an end, so too did other unrelated episodes and places of my childhood. Ah! But those were good times.

SHERRY HOGGE

Now here is someone I have not given a thought to since high school, save to recall when coming across her picture in one of the yearbooks how much I once admired her delicate beauty. So what sparked the recollection that there was something more about Sherry that would qualify her for an entry in this book? It happened as recently as three days ago. I was looking through some of Elmo's old lyric sheets when I came across a song entitled "S.H." Now if I hadn't only moments earlier been admiring Sherry Hogge's senior picture in the 76 yearbook, I might not have made the connection. But after only a minute or two of wondering "Who's SH?," it hit me. Of course! SH was Sherry Hogge.

Elmo refers to SH in his song as "A girl I once knew," and I seem to recall that their was some prior connection between the two of them, possibly going back as far as grade school. However slight this connection may have been, it was yanked into his present time consciousness by me longingly pointing her out in the cafeteria. Another line in Elmo's song, "Saw her ridin' on her bike," indicates that Sherry probably lived in the general area of Elmo's house in Dunn Loring. Whatever and whenever their acquaintance might have been, Elmo made his current standing with Miss Hogge bitingly clear with the following stanza -

Won't talk to me anymore
I won't go knock on her door
Saw her with some jock guy
I asked myself, why oh why

Now that reads like the insanist blues. The more that rose blossomed, the farther the likes of Elmo and I found ourselves towards the back of the line that was forming to pluck it from the vine. In essence, it jibes completely with the only clear memory I have of SH, outside of simply catching glimpses of her in the halls. This would have been sometime in the fall of 1973. Elmo and I were wading through the cafeteria line towards the cashier. At some point, Elmo and I became conscious of SH standing with a friend of hers about 10 feet behind us in line. I don't remember what prompted this exchange, but I recall SH hurling some sort of pretty girl nose-in-the-air kiss off at Elmo. Despite the fact that she was not addressing me, I was close enough to Elmo to get a direct feel for the vibe she was putting out, and I must tell you, what SH had in the way of looks, she lacked in ladylike temperance. I remember two things distinctly, the snarl on her face and the fact that there was nothing in the soul of the easy going Elmo that would have provoked such a snarl. Oh Yes! I recall how Elmo and I would converse lightly about SH, as would any two adolescent boys about a pretty girl, and I also recall that up until the time of this incident, I thought SH was it. Thereafter, the single fiber of my being that cared had concluded that SH was indeed IT. SH=IT – That's the name of that tune.

SPENCER TURNIPSEED
Director of the youth group for the Christ United Methodist Church during the late 1973 escapades of Scott Merrill and myself. Spencer, though stopping short of confessing to insanity himself, did appreciate and encourage the spirit of Scott and myself at a time when our behavior was razing eyebrows ever higher among other members of the youth group. Spencer had, at least, a sense of humor and a deeper understanding of manifest insanity. In recognition of this, it was discussed with Elmo and other high-ranking loons, the special honor of presenting Spencer with a ceremonial hoe (the symbol of imperial insanity). We would buy a hoe, spray paint it gold, present it to Spencer, and then encourage him to hide it. This was still being considered when Spencer was abruptly transferred to another state. Driving home the point that friendships in the transient Northern Virginia area were often short lived, the Merrills moved shortly after Spencer's transfer, bringing to an abrupt halt any interest or activity in this church.

One folly involving Spencer and Elmo does bear mentioning, as I believe it demonstrates in a small but poignant way how Elmo had become my number one brother in insanity at this point in time. It was during an evening get together in the youth lounge with Spencer present. I phoned Elmo from the lounge in a flight of whimsy and urged him to come and join us. I didn't believe he would actually come, but I had to try. He declined my impromptu invitation, but I at least wanted him to have a word with Spencer, who upon taking the receiver from me, issued his own invitation to Elmo. A few seconds of silence followed while Elmo replied, and then a rather puzzled look came over Spencer's face –"You have to pay?" he asked. This was so classic. I was doubled over in laughter. My act of whimsical bravado in calling Elmo had been matched and surpassed - game Elmo. His physical presence was no longer required. I wanted Elmo's spirit to grace the gathering, and that is exactly what I got. What is just as significant and telling was Spencer's total acceptance of my subsequent explanation of "Paying". I suppose going through life with a name like Spencer Turnipseed would tend to develop in one an accepting nature.

STEPHANIE HILL

A definite sourcepoint, though probably not the original sourcepoint, for the rumors floating about that I was a Satanist. I know Stephanie is probably somebody's mom now, and somebody else's loving wife, but at the time of this incident, I could think of her as nothing but a gossiping gadfly. It was Tuesday, January 28 1975, during my second period government class, which for some reason had adjourned to the library. We were supposed to be researching something, but of course I was ambling fancy free about the library's reference room in search of something truly interesting. Howard Koretz was looking through some kind of encyclopedia at something that caught my attention. It was some sort of thing you could imagine catching Howard's attention, like a history of witchcraft, but whatever it was, it gradually drew the attention of a few other guys, until a standing circle was formed around a seated Howard Koretz. What we were looking at must have had something to do with Satanism because Stephanie Hill (whose presence I had only seconds earlier become aware of) said "I hear that in Satanism, everyone's name is backwards" - a statement which in itself shows how naïve we were about such things back then. One of the guys gave a half interested response like "Yeah, I think so," upon which Stephanie looked directly at me and asked in all seriousness "What is your name backwards?" To which I replied – "Bob."

None of us noticed Stephanie leave. My concentration had barely been broken by her presence, but a minute or two later I became aware of the faint but distinct sound of girls whispering behind me – "Buzz buzz buzz Bob buzz buzz buzz Satanism buzz buzz buzz buzz." Upon hearing my name, I turned around and looked to see Stephanie Hill on the other side of the room, addressing a rather guarded circle of females, occasionally throwing a wary glance in my direction. My concentration had now been broken, but only long enough to contemplate how odd her behavior had been - not completely beyond the pale of what I had come to expect, you understand, but odd nonetheless. It was only some weeks later that the significance of this event grew to the point that I considered it worth mentioning to EAT. At this point, it was obvious what had not been obvious at the time of the incident - that Stephanie and her little coterie had been predisposed to the belief that I was involved in some sort of Satanic practice. If seeing Stephanie fly into gossip mode over the untimely utterance of my own name had me scratching my head for about five seconds, I soon had to ponder in depth just what Stephanie and her friends had been told about me prior to this incident.

STEVE HARLEY

No other recording artist is more emblematic of EAT and I's experience together at Oakton than Steve Harley, not even David Bowie. Oh! We were inextricably linked with Bowie by the fact that we dared to play his music on our radio shows. And then there was that bus stop cretin who taunted EAT by shouting "Doug Bowie! Doug Bowie!" While there's no denying that EAT and I loved Bowie's image and music, or that his lyrics were chock-full of quotable quotes, Harley seemed to be addressing us directly on a more personal level. Harley's lyrics were not merely quotable, they often seemed to be coming from someone who was concurrently experiencing some of the things we were experiencing, and who was expressing our joy and pain. In a few extreme examples, Harley seemed to be not only singing to us, but singing AS us, which is something I believe only a truly disturbed individual could have claimed about 1971-74 era David Bowie.

While I'm sure that EAT and I could separately list 100 different Harley lyrics that we related to in some way (individually or collectively), for brevity's sake, I'll list just a few of my personal standouts. Firstly, there was Harley's bizarre but rousing exhortation to -

Sling it! Sling it!
Let's sling it and do it again, Viper

Though the last word in the song ("Viper") does not appear on the album's lyric sheet, what was apparent on the LP in the 70's became unmistakably clear on the CD in the 90's. That line (or perhaps the entire song) was being addressed to someone named Viper. The theme of constructing a barrier of madness to cope with the condition of being on a sinking ship (or a dying planet) alone was enough to bring that song home to EAT and I. The fact that Harley used my on-air radio name of the period made it appear even more personal and timely. And if clarification of the term "Sling It" was needed, it was provided earlier on the album in the last verse of "Psychomodo" -

I've been writing a song
We all been singing along
It's like a wild schizophrenia
Wondering where we belong
Sling it all out the window
Start all over again

Cockney slang aside, the ambiguities in Harley's lyrics gave individual lines multiple applications depending on when (and under what circumstances) EAT or I happened to be in at the time we were listening to them. Enough strange coincidences had already occurred at OHS to make the Harley personality symbiosis seem quite natural. So conditioned were we to except the hidden messages of life that I would say the thing that excited us the most about Harley's lyrics was not that he seemed to be pleading our case, or giving us advice, or issuing a warning of some sort, or even setting an example (as in the wonderful "My Only Vice is the Fantastic Prices I Charge for Being Eaten Alive"), it was that Harley wrote LIKE we did. EAT and I had already adopted, to some degree, Harley's manner of allowing his open-ended imagination to fall on the page like malleable puzzle pieces to be put together by the reader. We had already surmised that the poet and the lyricist (if they be one and the same) did not just tell you something, they left you metaphoric clues. I should also point out here that EAT's lyric-writing career was, by this time, less than a school year old. Though, speaking for myself, it would take me a good 10 years more to attain Harley's command of the English language (not being English myself), Harley's greatest message to me was perhaps the affirmation that the don't-let-them-have-too-much artistic course was the one to stay on.

Having said all this, let's go back to OHS and those "Personal messages," of which Harley's first album – "The Human Menagerie" was so rife with. "Generate me limply, I can't seem to place your name,

Cherie" was a strange enough interjection of the name Cheri at a time when any mention of the name caught my attention, but a line in the album's opening track, "Hideaway," would continue to hold my attention.

It seemed we couldn't ever escape December
Every summer, summer, or maybe spring

Putting this lyric into perspective requires the construction of a Harley timeline. I was first struck by the cover of The Human Menagerie at a small record store in Georgetown in early 1974, which was possibly when I first discovered EF Sly. The store was up Wisconsin a few blocks on the left, near or possibly at the exact location that would later house "Commander Salamander." I distinctly remember making a mental note to tell EAT about Cockney Rebel and their very glitter looking album - The Human Menagerie. Bowie had trained us to suspect that any album with a glitter face on it might contain a mad genius within, so there was little surprise in learning later on the phone with EAT that he had already taken note of the album and had similarly made a decision to bring The Human Menagerie to my attention, though at this point, neither of us had heard the album.

EAT was the first one to take the plunge on Harley, buying The Human Menagerie, as well as Cockney Rebel's second (and newly released) "The Psychomodo." I taped both albums off of EAT, but found myself listening to the tape so much that I decided sometime in the summer of 74 to hunker down and buy both albums. By this time, however, the above mentioned lyric had already grabbed my attention. "It seemed we couldn't ever escape December, every summer, summer, or maybe spring" had I'm sure, a particular (though unrevealed) meaning in the mind of Steve Harley. In the summer of 1974, it seemed as if I would never escape the effects of the December 1973 rejection of Cheri Allen. As I've pointed out elsewhere in this book, a girl could reject you at any time during the school year, and the full effect of that rejection might not be felt until the overwhelming distraction of school was over with, and you had lots of free time to dwell on the matter.

This lyric gained further significance in December 1974, with Damaris Bonnell's rejection, and the introduction of Peggy Wallace. And when did I suddenly realize that I'd truly lost something I should have grabbed hold of in December of 74? Why, the summer of 1976. And when did Harley say we couldn't ever escape December? "Every summer, summer, or maybe spring." As I've also pointed out before, after graduation, your final summer vacation equates to being (or often stretches out to become) the rest of your life. "Or maybe spring" recalls the fact that spring had a significance all its own in the ballad of the lovelorn loon, as my April 1973 composition "Spring Fever" bears out. Springtime was the time of the year when young men's thoughts turned to romance (or whatever), and so in confronting each successive springtime as a begrudgingly single man, I came to wonder if I would ever escape that December cycle of spot, make contact with, invest in emotionally, and then ultimately lose.

If 1973's The Human Menagerie was the perfect epilogue to EAT and I's glitter-happy 1973-74 school year, 1974's The Psychomodo led us headlong into the emotional inferno of that 1974-75 year. As with EAT and I after the dissolution of the Insanist movement, Harley's protective coat of madness now seemed soiled with traumatic alienation and bitter reproach. The Human Menagerie's gleeful romps and baroque romanticism were replaced by The Psychomodo's graphic articulations of the pains of young manhood, from the perspective of a romantic growing up in a very unromantic world. When Harley sang in "Cavaliers" - in that pained but fuck-all tone of rebuke – "I'm getting ready to run and hide. Looking for a suitable bitch to crucify," he was keeping pace with the direction that EAT and I's heads were moving in. The two lines that proceed this, which were not totally clear to me until 1977 when I purchased an import copy (with lyric sheet) of The Psychomodo really brings the full impact of this stanza to bear.

Masturbation, getting off,
You can scoff, your ideals offer nothing new

Even the Psychomodo's most lighthearted offering "Bed in the Corner" had the object of Steve's affection telling him in the chorus -

I've got a bed here for you
I've got a bed here for me
So you can look in my eyes
And tell me what you see

During his final run through this chorus, the pained sexual frustration in Harley's voice suggests that he is on the verge of chucking his English civility and giving his lady friend a close-up view of his middle finger. EAT and I were not quite at this point yet, but we were getting there. And could we ever relate. This brings up an incident where EAT brought an article/interview of Harley into the radio station to show me, where-in Harley admits that all of the females whose names were dropped throughout the first two Cockney Rebel albums (Loretta, Lorraine, Louise, Muriel, Ruthy et al.) were not real people, but were in fact, figments of his imagination. How mad was this? Not only was Harley having his heart broken by various ladies, but Harley had himself invented these ladies, presumably for the very purpose of writing about them. Surely at the point of this revelation, Harley had become our hero, or anti-hero if you will.

Before I leave the first two albums behind and move on to 1975's "The Best Years of Our Lives," I'd like to pull one more back of the brain allusion from The Human Menagerie. Near the end of the closing track "Death Trip," Harley and a large choir lead us through a chorus of what sounds like an old English schoolyard jingle. Though, as with the "Viper" appendage on Sling It, the words are mysteriously omitted from an otherwise comprehensive lyric sheet, it sounds like they're singing -

All the boys say run like a chicken
Then you'll take some licking
My son, son, son

The actual meaning of these words in the context of the song is as obscure as it is unimportant. The one word that I do recall leaping out of the grooves of the original LP with a modicum of clarity was "Chicken." It was as if Harley just happened, at that second, to lean into the microphone a half inch or so. Please refer back to the "Femme Familiars" entry if clarification is needed on how any reference to a chicken during the period just before the release of the third album would have brought Peggy Wallace to mind. Though it's possible I had already taken note of it, it was EAT who first spoke aloud of Harley's mention of a chicken in the song Death Trip (as if anything more cryptic needed to be dragged into that song). And Yes! By February of 1975, EAT and I were still pulling things out of the first two Cockney Rebel albums, though by this time, any recent discoveries from the lyrics of The Human Menagerie more resembled ancient prophecy than up to date commentary. I can't speak for EAT, but for me, that album just wouldn't quit. I recall listening to it again in the early 80's and receiving a little jolt upon coming to the first few lines of "What Ruthy Said"

You're wearing gray today
You're from Berlin, I'd say
You're a model

I don't think more than 2 or 3 months had passed since the end of my late 1980 affair with a Nico-esque German woman named Christiane who – Yes! Was from Berlin. Yes! Had been a model in 1973. And yes! Was given to wearing gray a lot.

"European maids, hard to ignore" is the first line to the title track from Harley's 1975 release The Best Years of Our Lives. Despite the slight prophetic twist that this line would also come to have for me in the early 80's, the slightly more commercial sound of the album would take EAT and I about 2 or 3 listens to warm up to. After a week or so, it became clear to EAT, myself, and Tonny (who was now as much of a fan as we were) that Harley's genius, as well as his beloved madness, was still intact. "It Wasn't Me" and "Back to the Farm" were graphic depictions of madness, far removed from the devil-may-care whimsicality of The Human Menagerie. It was the title track that upon its timely arrival in the spring of 1975 stands as the greatest swan song to our days at Oakton High, which I think EAT might concur, were "The best years of our lives." In fact, Harley sings the song as if he were, nostalgically biding farewell to an important chapter in his life. Never mind that it's taken this long for the lump that was in Harley's throat to appear in EAT's and mine, he had hit the nail on the head again with the lines:

Fresh-faced imbeciles, laughing at me
I've been laughing myself, is that so hard to see?
Do I have to spell each letter out, honestly!
If there's no room for laughter, there's no room for me
Try looking at you, rather than me
No truth is in here, it's all fantasy

I knew even as my days at Oakton were drawing to a close, that I could have easily sung these exact words in earnest to the entire student body. And then there came what for me stands as one of Harley's most gripping passages.

Lost now for the words to tell you the truth
Please banter with me the banter of youth

What a freaking thing to say to someone. I mean, those are not just the words I should've said to Peggy Wallace back then, those are the words I should be saying to Peggy Wallace (and about a dozen other people) Now! Apparently the "Banter of Youth" is only fully appreciated as one approaches middle age.

It's interesting to observe how the emotional amplitude of Harley's artistic output and my friendship with EAT followed similar timelines, with the glorious The Human Menagerie being released around the time that I first met EAT, and Harley's determinably vapid "The Candidate" album appearing around the time that EAT and I had lost touch completely.

Harley's follow up to The Best Years exemplified the relatively uneventful mellowness of the late 1975/ early 1976 period in which it was released, and though Tonny, EAT and I would all give "Timeless Flight" a slightly tentative thumbs up, it wasn't until the CD release in the early 90's that I realized what a "Timeless" masterpiece it really was.

At the time though, the one song on the album that really stuck in my gut was "Nothing is Sacred (It's Everything Else)." Despite the conspicuous absence of madness in the album's thematic web, its lyrics were even more oblique than his previous three releases (if that's at all possible). "Nothing is Sacred" was one of Harley's image-soaked crossword puzzles that the listener could read just about anything into, but whenever I heard the song, it made me think of EAT. And whenever I sang along with the words -

Then I glanced at Lenny and saw
that my confidante was beginning to jest
Well, he came out of my subconscious
And that's where I put him away to rest
Ooh la, la, it's so fun to be depressed

- I got the strongest feeling that I was singing them to EAT, as if the words themselves had the power to capture EAT's attention across any barrier of spatial separation. It was only a few days ago, when contemplating the post-Oakton Timeless Flight era for the purpose of this entry that I recalled EAT's late 1975 composition "You got what it takes (To be my Lenny Kaye)." I then recalled the Patti Smith cloud of lust/worship we were walking around in at this time, and how her guitarist/co-composer Lenny Kaye became synonymous in our minds with sidekicks and confidantes. In this light, and during this period of my life, only EAT and Tonny could have been said to have had what it takes to be my Lenny Kaye.

It's quite possible that some sort of subconscious link in this direction had been made, but I recall getting the biggest tingle of truth out of the line – "Well, He came out of my subconscious, and that's where I put him away to rest," as if in the midst of such motionlessness and loneliness, one could suddenly wake up one day and discover that even one's closest friends didn't exist, that they (like the women on Harley's first two albums) were just figments of the imagination.

If it had become "So fun to be depressed," it was because I had Steve Harley and EAT there to make it so. Having said that, Timeless Flight was less fun than his previous three albums. Despite being less commercial than The Best Years, Timeless Flight represented the death of insanity and, as Harley pines in "All Men are Hungry," the death of youth.

Was in a frenzy from the midnight air when I saw the light
I realized only children can live upon a Timeless Flight

If this album had a message for EAT, Tonny and myself, it was that time had arrived to drag us kicking and screaming into the less interesting "Real World." In the early spring of 1976, EAT called to inform me that Steve Harley and Cockney Rebel were about to perform on TV. It was quite a thrill to see Steve Harley and band performing "Black and White" dressed in angelic white robe-like outfits. It was on an afternoon broadcast piped into one of the local independent stations of an American Bandstand-style English music show. It was also a reminder that in the mid 70's, the American television industry was still small enough that one was apt to receive their fair share of English programming.

Let's move on to the late 76/early 77 period and the release of the strange and enigmatic "Love's a Prima Donna." Aside from Harley's shape up or ship out response to Valentine Trashcan Rain's greater aspirations – "If you're looking for a valentine to love in your life, you're looking for a messiah," we were on our own with this one. Half of the album was as dry (though less inspired) as Timeless Flight, but the other half was a refreshingly hard, almost self-conscious return to the madness and frivolity of the first two albums. Near the end of what one might have otherwise deduced was Harley's most lighthearted effort to date came the 7 minute "Innocence and Guilt," a harrowingly authentic portrayal of the darker side of insanity, and a fitting theme song(?) to any of the "Psycho" sequels.

I suppose if I had to pull a message out of this album that would have been appropriate for EAT, Tonny and I as we went marching into 1977, it would be - Listen! Love is a fickle ephemeral thing (a prima donna if you will) that will blow in and out of your life with the winds of change, but you can always return to the madness of youth once a few essential truths are uncovered and the conscious decision to do so has been made. Or put another way - You can either choose your own madness, which was the madness you already chose in your youth, or you can except the madness the world gives you, which will be considerably darker because the world takes itself way too seriously.

The rest of 1977 saw the release of a best of and a double live album, two sure signs that the Cockney Rebel saga was about to come to an end. There were also sure signs during this period that EAT and I were about to go our separate ways. I had gone to work for Penguin Feather, and EAT had moved into DC with his girlfriend Samantha. It was well into 1978 when after months of not hearing from the old boy, I received a phone call at the Annandale Feather from an excited EAT. Steve Harley's first solo album – "Hobo with a Grin" had been released and EAT was driven to phone me up by the desire to have someone to share the experience with. Despite being dangerously close to being a straight pop album, it did have its moments, and a few old flames were re-ignited. 1979's "The Candidate," however, was not only Steve's cue to hang it up, it was EAT and I's cue to get on with our lives, and leave the past behind us. Of course, experiencing what we did together, moving apart only drew us closer to the day when we will re-unite. And on that day, I shall raise my glass to EAT and make the toast – "Please, banter with me the banter of youth."

STEVE LARSEN

Most of the unusual characters of Oakton High crossed my path sooner or later, and Steve Larsen was no exception. He came to my attention during my freshman year as an acquaintance of Don Frank and Fausto Bengochea. On the prowl for insanists, I had a strong feeling about Larsen just from seeing him in the halls, and after meeting him through the assistance of Don Frank, my instincts were proven correct, and then some. To begin with, Larsen's physical appearance set him apart from other students in a way that foretold the force-field effect of my senior year funereal fashions. His dress was slightly conservative and neat. His hair was shoulder length, frizzy, and at times almost Einstein-ish. Behind black horn-rimmed glasses, his large intense eyes mirrored an intelligence that seemed determined to expand itself outwardly.

I will never forget the first time Steve came to my house. He had a briefcase full of papers detailing in minutiae the various aspects of this universe he had created. He showed me (with obvious relish) page after page of things like technical diagrams of various spacecraft and their means of propulsion, illustrated maps of vast areas of outer space (even naming "The Larsen Void" after himself), and other particulars too complex for my memory to have retained. I was fascinated and admirous of Larsen for having the creativity to have cooked up all this stuff. My fascination peaked with Larsen's further description of this cosmic federation he had co-designed with a group of his pre-Oakton friends. I was anxious to verify the existence of this federation, but Larsen had just moved to Fairfax prior to his freshman year, leaving his group to languish, as the Insanist movement no doubt would have without me as a catalyst. Larsen had just been separated from his group of friends, as I had been separated from all of my Luther Jackson friends. But more importantly, Larsen had successfully worked to build a group, and a partner with group building skills was just what I needed at Oakton during my freshman year.

Though Larsen was an acquaintance of Don Frank and Fausto Bengochea, their principal bond was a shared affinity for psychedelics and psychedelic music. Beyond that, Don and Fausto's joking remarks barely concealed the fact that neither knew what to make of Larsen (an endorsement in and of itself). As I pressed the point, and was obviously interested, Fausto spoke of Larsen often, but the word for word sentence that I have the clearest picture of Fausto giving me on the subject of Steve Larsen was strangely definitive. "He's a leech for pot!" I can still hear (and see) Fausto lamenting with a half smile/half sneer. Despite the fact that Fausto, Don and Steve were all high IQ types, Fausto and Don never strayed too far from normal adolescent pursuits, whereas the condition of adolescence seemed to have left Steve Larsen untouched. While Fausto's intelligence was dispassionately removed from his rudimentary enjoyment of marijuana as a social vehicle, Larsen's genuine ties to other dimensions made any perspective-altering device his personal rite of passage. To Larsen, the Moody Blues "In Search of the Lost Chord" was not just an album to get high to. It was his favorite album, in part I believe because its statement of intent was aligned with his own deepest aspirations of transcendence. I know from sitting in my room listening to albums with Larsen that as soon as a sitar appeared in the music, his eyes would widen, as if the mere sound of the instrument itself brought him closer to "The Lost Chord."

There was something about Larsen's room that from descriptions given by Don Frank and Larsen himself furthered my opinion that his previous incarnation was spent either on a mountain in India or a planet whose sun was a dim point of light in our night sky. I remember having the idea of painting the walls of my room phosphorescent black, and then painting thousands of little white dots, to give the impression under black light that my room was floating in outer space. It's possible that this idea may have been inspired by Larsen, at least through osmosis. Larsen had definite plans for his room beyond whatever mind expanding posters he had covering his walls, though I don't recall whether he made any progress toward this end before his untimely departure.

As for any feigned detachment from Oakton society that Fausto, Don or I may have employed to maintain comfort (or coolness) levels, it paled next to the authentic detachment that was Larsen's natural state. He walked the halls of OHS completely self-contained. Despite the fact that I had only myself and a lot of big plans to entice Larsen into joining the circle of loons, Larsen calmly, almost anti-climatically, agreed to join. Unlike Fausto and Don, he had no reason not to. So he donned the ceremonial underwear, recited whatever impromptu oath I had in my head to give him, and was summarily christened "Catwalloper Larsadoodle," a wonderfully incongruous name that unfortunately did not see much usage. Shortly before or after the close of our freshman year, Larsen's family moved once again, leaving Larsen to become (like freshman year madman David Zoutes) another big "What if?" on my Oakton timeline. This was not the first, nor would it be the last time that the transient nature of government and military work, or the chess board shifting of school districts would snatch a prospective loon from our midst. Larsen's contribution would have been great, of that I've no doubt. He was missed.

STUART ARGABRIGHT

An extremely imaginative and talented artist, whose surreal landless landscapes gave our 76 yearbook the genuine look of being the fruit of young minds, while at the same time dating it in the 70's in a way that makes me long for those days. The fruit of young minds definitely had a more pleasing flavor in those days.

Stuart had a very ruddy angular face, capped by an extremely Rod Stewart looking crop of blonde hair. His robust manner and deep voice belied his shortness of stature. But it was his intelligence and artistic inclinations that fit him squarely into the Marcia Carter, Suzanne Zanders, Mitchell Robinson crowd, and this is no doubt how I came to make his acquaintance.

During the latter half of my senior year, Stuart's name came up often in my marathon phone calls with Donna Zarin, as Donna had a major crush on Stuart. Apparently this was close to being common knowledge, for during the final folly, my brief interview with Stuart consisted of the following questions. I approached Stuart upstairs near the stairway at the end of the English hallway, and hit him with this icebreaker -
"There have been some rumors around that you've been seeing known sweet potato Donna Zarin. Are these rumors true?"
To which the media savvy Stuart replied with mock seriousness -
"Yes they are! I hate to admit it, but they are true."
Pushing the rib a little further, I followed up with -
"Well! Do you have any plans on marrying Donna in the future?"
To which a game for anything Stuart shot back -
"Well, my future's kind of foggy right now, but yes! Marriage is a possibility."

Listening to this short little interview now, I'm reminded of the adaptive sense of flow that made Stuart so likable. Hit him with anything and he could (and would) play along. But in my senior will, I'm also reminded that music was the main topic of conversation between Stuart and I, as it was with Bill Dye and Earl Ragland, to whom Stuart is included with in the entry – "To Bill Dye, Stuart 'Crazy Boy' Argabright, and the Earl of Ragland - I leave the polished versions of all my musical endeavors (men of good taste don't grow old, they just learn to taste better)."

It's interesting that I would leave this triad of music lovers my own recordings. Perhaps I felt that there were lyrical references that needed to be absorbed outside of the inner circle of loons, in effect, anticipating the need for the sort of chronicle of ideas and events that this book has become. More than likely though, I was simply showing these three some mutual respect by leaving them something that was of value to me. Similarly lost behind the veil of occluded memory is the source for the nickname "Crazy Boy." It seems less imaginative and appropriate than anything I would have tagged Stuart with.

Stuart's parting inscription in my yearbook, directed at EAT and I, is as definitive as it gets. "You hard core creepers are something else," a compliment any way you cut it, coming from one who was himself "Something else." I would see Stuart only once after high school, drumming and singing for a group called the Rudiments, who were performing downstairs at a party hosted by fellow penguin Bob McCord. This would have been sometime in 1979. I was happy to discover recently that Stuart had maintained in the furtherance of music by operating his own music publishing company up in NYC. It's perhaps more pertinent at this time to point out that "Men of good taste don't grow old."

SUE SUDOR
Actually a student of Fairfax high, where Tonny was in attendance during his freshman year. Apparently, Tonny was quite enamored with Miss Suder, as evidenced by the hilarious letter that now resides in the book of artifacts. It seems that Tonny was so desperate for the attention of this female that at one point, he actually entertained the idea of sending her an anonymous letter (sound familiar?). As impulse rarely displaced rationality with Tonny, his stipulation for sending such a letter was that it was to be written by someone else. He was greatly concerned that Sue (who was in his German class) might recognize his handwriting, or perhaps show the letter to a friend who might also recognize its author. As I had been engaged in pushing the letter idea past Tonny's hesitance, I was all too happy to write the letter for him. Tonny's big mistake was insisting that I compose the letter as well. Any genuine strategic value this letter had hopes of being disintegrated the second I put pen to paper. The final product was so over the top that not even I would have dropped it in her

locker as a folly, but the effort put into its composition was well worth the amount of laughter Tonny and I got out of it.

Although the letter itself has outlived any memory Tonny might have

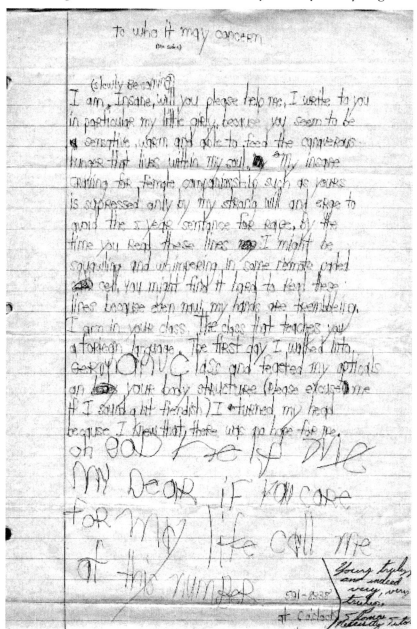

had of Sue Suder, Miss Suder would later resurface in a manner that would lead one to believe that it WAS a small world after all. Sometime during the spring of 1974 I was, for a brief period, attending a weekly discussion group at the Fairfax Assembly of God. My cousins, Linda and Betty notified me of the group, and were no doubt in attendance, as was reverend Keller's attractive and Germanic big-boned daughter. The meetings were held in the back reception area next to the kitchen, with the preponderance of female over male attendants eerily reminiscent of the revelations club meetings. On one particular occasion, one of the females in attendance was none other than Sue Suder. Two years after the fact, and long buried beneath numerous moves and two more high school changes for Tonny, Sue Suder mysteriously reappears at this conspicuously odd juncture.

No doubt having done a bit more blossoming in the interim, Tonny's points concerning Miss Suder's pulchritude were well taken. Sue was demure and soft-spoken, exuding the sort of calm well-adjusted air that I could imagine Tonny taking a fancy to. She had straight shoulder length blonde hair which, along with every other item of physical description Tonny had given me earlier, left no doubt that this girl and Tonny's freshman heartthrob were one and the same. While Sue was undeniably pretty, her almost featureless face and nondescript manner made her seem more Tonny's type than mine. I was nonetheless excited to have discovered her, and anxiously notified Tonny by phone shortly after the meeting. Tonny's surprise ruining lack of interest suggested that his heart's captivation with Sue Suder had indeed been short lived. I think that what it really indicated was that by this time, Tonny was hearing Bells, or Christmas Carols, or simply the summoning song of a girl with a certain ring to her name.

SUZANNE ZANDERS

Lovingly nicknamed "Zanders-Lavey" by EAT and I. Suzanne will be remembered for being the VOT operative who never spoke much. She was, however, spoken of often (if only in passing), because she was seen quite often in the company of other people we knew. More than this, the name of Zanders-Lavey was often invoked because her quietude belied the volume of her presence. Despite the fact that when Suzanne did speak, it was in a barely audible tone, when she was there, you knew she was there. Suzanne is the only person mentioned in this book who I saw regularly, (rode the bus with, in fact) whose voice I can not recall to save me. I can recall Tom Ring's folksy Buddy Ebsen-style husk as if I'd just gotten off the phone with him. And who doesn't have at least one vivid memory of

Ann McGrath chattling away at 100 MPH? No! All that I have to say here about Suzanne directly was derived from what I saw and what I sensed.

Beneath her teased-out hood of hair and quasi-Victorian dress, Suzanne was winsome, demure, and ladylike, allowing the sparkle in her eyes to convey a good deal of her messages. In this regard, I drew a comparison between Suzanne and myself. Like me, Suzanne appeared to have a shy streak co-existing with an intense desire to project a portion of her inner being outwardly through her appearance. As a result, though (I presume) to a lesser degree than myself, Suzanne had to contend with people who did not know her, talking and drawing conclusions about her (as I'm doing here). None of what I overheard about Suzanne was down at the level of gossip. Mostly it was in the form of an expression of wonder over that gravity-defying head of hair of hers. I confess to having been fascinated by it myself, remarking to her on the bus that her hair was "So solar." Searching for a word to describe the manner in which it shot out in all directions like atomic particles in an outwardly expanding universe, that's what I came up with.

Ultimately, the respect that EAT and I had for ol' Zanders-Lavey hinged upon our observation that beneath this otherwise unassuming schoolgirl beat the heart of a true individual. It is my sincerest hope that Suzanne's subsequent boyfriends, employers, work mates, children etc. show this jewel of individuality the respect she is due.

TANYA HERRELL

For much of my sophomore and junior year friendship with Elmo, Tanya Herrell was the spindly "Girl next door." Tanya lived next door to Elmo, and was good friends with his sister, Donna. Tanya's opinion of me as a bit 'round the bend was no doubt stoked by Donna, and fanned by the DBH sessions that were recorded at Elmo's house during this period. It wasn't until the fall of 1974 that I began to notice that the spindly girl-next-door was blossoming into an attractive young woman, and was actually well on her way to being a knee-weakening stunner a few years down the line.

Tanya had ash-blonde hair, and that same perpetually tanned complexion that made debs like Claire Schultz and Carol Galane twice as desirable. At some point during the week of January 6-10 1975, I wore my Hockmuth originals to school. These consisted of a pair of jeans and a jean jacket, fashioned by Bob Hockmuth to include sown-on patches, drawn-on stoner images, and appropriate rips and tears. I didn't shave that morning either, further contributing to the overall look of a counter-culture biker bum. I thought this Hell's Angels attire would have them cowering (or at least whispering) in the corners, but it had the opposite effect. Bonnie Tuggle complimented my outfit, and on the phone later in the day,

Donna Zarin told me that Tanya had seen me in the halls, and later commented to her that I "Looked really nice." This made me think – "Jesus H. Christ! – I buy these beautiful black textured shirts from EF Sly for 30-40 dollars (which was a fortune for a high school kid to pay for a shirt in those days), and I'm at last given compliments for wearing these rags?" Dim were my hopes for the youth of America.

I think Tanya's perception (and possibly Bonnie's as well) was that denim made me appear less threatening, or more earthy, or healthier, or some such nonsense. But honestly! This easy-rider costume was nothing the hippie-freak Hockmuths would even wear to school on a dare. I was known for dressing to shock, but in Bonnie and Tanya's reaction to these clothes, I would be the one to receive the shock. This was the one and only time I would wear denim in high school. It just wasn't me.

The next impression I would receive of Tanya Herrell (outside of my ongoing interest in her physical development) was surprise over the discovery that Tanya and Peggy had become friends. Tanya was more visible as a result, and as the possible trafficker in gossip that my paranoia led me to believe every ranking VOT member to be, her role in the overall scheme of things was suspect from this point onward. The last time I would see Tanya was as a cashier at the Merrifield Roy Rogers restaurant in the fall of 1977, and at that time, I could see that Tanya had truly become one of the beauties of Oakton.

Near the end of it all, I hazard to guess what Tanya's opinion of me was, but I did remember her in my senior will with one couched compliment, the age old male plea for her to not tread on my heart, and a tonic to take should she be stricken with Peggy's choking problem. To Tanya Herrell – I left "My recipe for fox soup, my collection of antique No Trespassing signs, and seven bottles (and I do mean seven) of my 'been-in-the-family-for-years' tonic to alleviate the CHOKING effects of heartburn." Ah! Tanya. Wherever you are tonight, I wish you well. Stay luscious.

TERRY BELL

Peggy's closest coadjutor, with the possible exception of Connie Underwood. Terry, or "Tinker" as she was appropriately called by her friends, was a gamine little sprite – possessed of the same "Now you see me, now you don't" sort of spiritual aura as Peggy had, as well as some degree of Peggy's unearthly beauty. I had no occasion to meet or speak with Terry, and aside from pegging her (no pun intended) as a possible VOT member, I had but one occasion to become more than barely aware of her presence. Peggy and I had been walking together between classes. I would date this little exchange as sometime during the week of January 20-

24 1975, after Peggy and I had become better acquainted, but before the announcement of Walt's death the following Monday would put the spooks in everybody. Peggy and I had been sort of gazing into each other's souls as we walked and talked, and I think that expectations were high at this point for both parties that something wonderful might happen soon. We had to part company at the middle stairway across from Mr. Herndon's office. As Peggy began to ascend the stairway, she turned to say a few more things, and to give the parting gesture of producing a piece of chocolate candy for me from her bag. At some point during the exchange, Peggy's eyes drifted over my head with silent recognition to a point behind me. I turned to see that Tinker Bell had suddenly appeared behind me, and was looking up at Peggy with a knowing grin. I took Terry's look to mean that the hope I had just seen in Peggy's eyes had already been expressed to her friend. The eye language between the two of them told me that Terry was not just a friend, but a confidant of Peggy's, and that I had been the subject of some of Peggy's latest confidings. This left me with a rather positive outlook.

The next time Terry Bell would come into the picture was during an unsuccessful attempt to locate Peggy at George Mason University in early 1978, and curiously, Tonny was involved. On January 30 1978, Tonny and I found a Margaret Wallace listed in the student directory. Three weeks later, hope would turn to disappointment with the discovery that this was the wrong Margaret Wallace. Undaunted, Tonny and I returned to Mason the following week and copied down the classes of a "Theresa Bell." Switching to plan "B," I return to Mason in early March with the intent of contacting Terry Bell, but was given a reminder of the weather's meddlesome ways eerily reminiscent of the storm from Hell of January 75. Yes! Classes had been cancelled due to snow. Determined, I returned the following week (it was now mid March). I waited for her, but she did not show up for the class. It was the last class of the quarter, so I deduced that she either dropped the class, or it was the wrong Theresa Bell. I may not have even gotten off campus when one of those filed-away memories surfaced to convince me that it was the former, and not the latter that robbed me of my last chance to meet Tinker Bell. I recalled making a 90% positive sighting of THE Theresa Bell driving a light colored compact car parked at a stop light at Fairfax Circle, heading in the direction of George Mason University. This was sometime in late September 1977. If only I had the yearning to contact Peggy at this time, I might have had something more to write here about pretty little Tinker.

THOMAS ASHMORE

A coadjutor of Gorsuch's during our sophomore year acquaintance. I never actually met Mr. Ashmore, but I did have the pleasure of conversing with him on the phone. It was one of those things where I was conversing with Gorsuch, and Joe decided that I should talk with his friend for a few minutes (perhaps while Joe relit the ol' tokemaster). The only reason I even recall talking to Ashmore on the phone was something that happened shortly afterward. As detailed in my journal entry of Friday February 2, 1973 - "I noted some drawings on my desk in English that could only have been made by a freak, things like 'Keep on trucking' and what have you, so in an attempt to make a communication with this person, I wrote 'Who are you?' in bold letters on the desk. In the desk was a note signed Tom Ashmore, the bloke I talked with on the phone at Gorsuch's."

It's clear that at this point, despite the fact that five other class periods equaled four other possible authors, I strongly suspected Ashmore as being the author. On Monday, February 5th, the person wrote back – "I'm the freak beside the freak in the corner, who are you?" prompting me to pop the question – "Are you insane?" In addition to receiving a reply that certainly had the tone of having been written by a friend of Gorsuch's, I also discovered an absentee pass on the floor beside the floor with Tom Ashmore's name on it.

TONNY NECESSITY TOOTER

Sit back, relax, and enjoy what will surely end up being the longest entry in the book, despite the fact that Tonny never attended Oakton (except in the spring of 1973, as a displaced member of the Woodson student body), and was living out of state during my junior and senior years.

I should first explain how mild mannered J. Thomas Hetrick became the Tonny Necessity Tooter you have been reading about in this book. I had already given myself an insane name, leaving Tonny to ponder his options. As Tommy Tooter was already a nickname I had given him earlier, the first condition he put forth (as the two of us were brainstorming on the phone) was that he wanted his initials to be T.N.T. EAT would approach the task of his own name selection in exactly the same way two years later, selecting whatever rolled nicely off the tongue as long as it met his primary stipulation that his initials spell the word E.A.T. Tommy had already mutated into Tonny, so all that remained was a middle name beginning with the letter N. After both of us had offered numerous unsuitable suggestions, Tonny, who was perhaps fending off suggestions from me that he scrap the whole T.N.T. idea exclaimed "It's a necessity that I find a word that begins with N." Only seconds later, the light bulb of discovery lit up and he blurted out – "Necessity!" And so out of necessity, Tonny Tooter became Tonny Necessity Tooter.

Tonny and I's friendship grew out of many frigid mornings spent together waiting for the school bus to take us to our 7th grade classes. As my mother had driven me to Willston Elementary throughout my years in grade school, waiting for a school bus was a new experience for me. As I recall, our Luther Jackson bus stop numbered a paltry 6 or 7 kids, which in retrospect seems odd for such a huge apartment complex as Merrifield Village. In fact, aside from Tonny (and Emmette, who would show up the following year), I can only remember one other kid from that bus stop, a small redheaded sports nut named Mike. It was only by virtue of his enthusiasm that Mike (whose name I'm only 80% sure of) left any impression on my memory.

The start of my 7th grade year at Luther Jackson was even more of a start-from-scratch than my freshman year at Oakton. True, none of the friends I'd made at Luther Jackson followed me there to Oakton, but I still knew some people, and had at least become comfortable with the idea that Fairfax was now the center of my universe. In the fall of 1969, I had

moved from Baileys Crossroads in Alexandria only months earlier. Most of my family and all of my close friends lived in Falls Church, so any aloofness I showed at my 7th grade bus stop was due to the fact that a chunk of my consciousness was still hanging out around points east.

Needless to say I had no friends going into my 7th grade at Luther Jackson (though I wasted no time in getting on the bad side of Ray King). Although I would only make one friend that year in the incredibly EAT-like John Fowler, Tonny and I did become acquaintances. While knowing John Fowler helped the shape the loon I would later become, it took knowing me to bring out the loon in Tonny. Befriending the outwardly stolid Tonny was a slow process, hampered in part by the fact that we would not share a single class together throughout our two years at LJ.

At Luther Jackson, I immediately got the sense of things to come at OHS – gym class, my own locker, a different teacher (and a different classroom) for each subject, and of course – girls with breasts. It was a whole new world, bearing little resemblance to Willston Elementary. Some of it I liked, and some of it, namely the embarrassment of gym class and the big impersonal institutional feel of the place – I hated. So there I was – in a new school, in a new neighborhood, in a new area, at a bus stop that was distinctive only for being completely unmemorable. Tonny and I had little else to do in 1970 but become friends, and though our lifelong friendship was cemented with those early 1971 Bonneville Follies recordings, it was really Tonny's first love, baseball, that brought us together.

In 1969, Tonny and his good friend Tim Kulik (the future Emmette Ophasse) went to Tysons Corner mall (which had just opened earlier in the year) and purchased their own copies of the baseball encyclopedia. Marveling at this wealth of data, the two of them poured through this phonebook-size encyclopedia, becoming master statisticians in the process. Besides affording Tonny with enough information to turn his favorite hobby into a full time passion, the purchase of this baseball encyclopedia may have made our friendship inevitable. Pushing destiny a little further, Tonny and Emmette purchased their first table-top baseball game, Kenneth Hawes Pennant Winner II, a short while later. This allowed them to pull any team from any year and pit one against the other, in time developing their own body of statistical data. Well, I can attest to the addictiveness of involvement in this sort of thing, and as Tonny recently related, the two of them would spend entire days calculating the various statistics of any given team. One has to understand that some of these averages required the employment of some mathematics that were a tad on the advanced side for a pair of 7th graders, given the pre-calculator times in which they were working in.

Kenneth Hawes Pennant Winner II game all but completed Tonny's baseball evolution from pastime to obsession, a job that would be completed two years later with Sports Illustrated's more comprehensive table top baseball game. In the late 60's, Tonny and Emmette's baseball based friendship centered around a more conventional little-league ethic of active involvement in actually playing the game. But with the acquisition of the baseball encyclopedia in 1969, and the subsequent purchase of the Pennant Winner II game, neither rain nor snow nor gloom of night could prevent Tonny's former hobby from becoming a total immersion. Neither could the dearth of neighborhood kids his age, or the absence of a usable playing field. In 1969 baseball would, for both Tonny and Emmette, make a left brain/right brain switch from being a purely physical activity pastime to being a demanding mental pursuit, full of theoretical abstractions, a multitude of variables, and page long equations that would give an onlooker the impression that atoms were being split on paper. Tonny and Emmette had now fabricated their own baseball universe, where the thrill of probability was endless. Tonny's sleeping ability with numbers had been awakened to the point where he was actually making adjustments to the Pennant Winner II game (specifically in the area of upping the walks per game ratio) to more accurately reflect real life statistics.

It was during the height of Tonny's 1970 Pennant Winner mania that I fortuitously arrived on the scene. In 1969 (or possibly earlier) I had purchased a baseball board game of my own. Being totally unconcerned with any form of statistical accuracy, and even more purposefully desirous of creating my own baseball world than Tonny, I used my extensive baseball card collection to create my own teams. This meant that the only relation my game had to real life baseball was that I was using actual major league players (whose baseball cards I owned). Unlike Tonny, I was no great fan of baseball, but I just happened to be in the thick of playing this game while Tonny was similarly absorbed with his Pennant Winner II game. Some of my earliest memories of conversing with Tonny were my periodic reports on how my rather long drawn out championship playoffs were coming along. Though the whole endeavor was just a shits and grins way to kill an afternoon for me, I had apparently seen enough of Tonny's baseball bitten soul to imagine he might have an interest in what I was doing. Though the accuracy adherent Tonny was rather bemused by some of the has-beens and never-weres who were stars in my league (I.E. Tim Cullen, Lee Elia, Dave Ricketts etc.), a chord of commonality was struck, and throughout the fall of 1970, our friendship evolved and the British Insipids were born.

So how to describe Tonny, well! Tonny was (and still is) a model of practicality, rationality, trustworthiness, and moral rectitude – a quintessentially earnest Virgo, whose logic was as rock solid as his work ethic. An early memory from our 8th grade bus stop paints a clearer picture of Tonny's moral fiber than I ever could with mere adjectives. While waiting for the bus one frosty morning, Neil Clouser came walking down Gallows Road from the direction of Dunn Loring. Presumably he had missed his own bus, and upon seeing me, he walked over to ask me some questions about our buses arrival. While he and I chatted, Neil pulled out a cigarette and lit up. He took a few drags and then decided not to wait for our bus. Gesturing to me – saying "I'll see you in school," he walked off in the direction of Luther Jackson. After Neil left, Tonny made some comment expressing his disdain for cigarette smoking, and while the code I lived by said let a ruffian be a ruffian, a jock be a jock, and a hipster like Neil Clouser be a hipster, any vices displayed for the effect of coolness did not impress Tonny in the least.

The bottom line for me was that Neil was a nice guy. That was enough to make him welcome at my lunch table, and while a wall of "Cool" may have existed between him and my inner circle of friends, it was a wall I could see and relay messages over. Tonny, on the other hand (as would Emmette for years to come), stood firmly on principal in his disapproval of cigarettes, drugs, or any ruffian activity. Despite the fact that Tonny was more steadfast in his resolve to remain on our side of the wall of cool, his disapproval of those things was to some degree shared by all of my close friends, even aspiring hipsters like Stills and Helms. I think it's safe to say that I attracted people who were devoid of common vices, yet were odd and quirky (if not outright neurotic) in other ways.

Tonny seemed to be the odd man out in his own family. His mother (who I loved and dearly miss) was a stereotypically overly emotional Italian woman, and his father was a conversely quiet man of German decent, possessed of his heritages archetypal fascination with watches and clocks. Not your garden variety generation gap, Tonny seemed to have fully accepted the moral values of his parents, while at the same time distancing himself emotionally from their shortcomings, which is to say that Tonny was not really like either of his parents. And as for siblings, Tonny did have two sisters, but they were much too young for him to have grown up relating to. The youngest one, in fact, was still in diapers when I started frequenting the Hetrick apartment.

Through the years, it became clearer that Tonny viewed himself as the emotional anchor of his immediate family, and though subsequent years may have increasingly demanded this role of him, he may have seen the writing on the wall at a much earlier age. This sort of realization shapes a person up real fast, and can make prudence, logic, and forthrightness appear at once to be tools for survival and a buttress against the stormy emotional winds of others (I.E. his mother and sisters). Though Tonny's root personality had already formed at age 13, one failsafe stability mechanism had yet to be installed – insanity. Once again, we are faced with the idea of insanity as a balancing factor. Which brings us again to the idea that as the English utilize illogic and tastelessness as comic relief against the propriety demands of English society, so too did Tonny and I employ the British Insipids. We did not invent the British Insipids as much as the British Insipids grew out of our need for comic relief. My need was primarily a need for relief from what I considered to be the dullness of my peers. Tonny, from what I observed, may have needed relief from the amorality of his peers. Whatever the situation might have been, the bottom line was that we were both young and duly bored with the status quo.

Tonny lived in Merrilee apartments, which was really only one apartment building that sat adjacent to the massive Merrifield apartment complex that I lived in. In the first five months of 1971, each of us would make numerous trips across the street to the other's apartment, and the many Bonneville Follies recordings from that time period are a testament to the silliness that went on during those visits. Meeting Tonny assured that I would carry the spirit of my youth into high school with me, despite the fact that Tonny would be with me there only in spirit. Although we were learning new things (and maturing) almost daily, the heart of a giddy grade schooler still beat within the two of us.

A comedic common ground was reached in recordings of our own commercials for products like "Zippybarbatoil," skits like "Soap Popbra," and Insipid-News-Around-the-World reports like – "Two helicopters were shot down today two miles south of the DMZ, that's Dankers and Martin's Zippers at the corner of 8th and M in downtown." Although it was Tonny's true love – baseball, that brought us together in the first place, my growing passion for music held sway, and the songs, jams, and skits of the Bonneville Follies propelled our friendship forward. The Merrilee/Merrifield phase of our friendship is best defined by the Bonneville Follies recordings that were made during that period.

Curiously, while our friendship went into a period of remission in the summer of 1971, after our respective moves from the Merrifield complex, I did run into Tonny at (of all things) a baseball game. My grandfather took me to a Washington Senator's game at RFK stadium (on August 17th – I still have the ticket stub), and at some point before the game commenced, I spotted Tonny sitting about three rows directly below me. If that wasn't peculiar enough, the last place Senators went on to beat the division leading Oakland A's, blowing Blue Moon Odom off the mound in a 10 to 0 rout, with homers from Frank Howard and Don Mincher.

Moving to Country Hill drive, Tonny attended Fairfax High his freshman year. I do have a handful of memories of Tonny's stay in that house – the fateful Wiffle Ball game with Emmette, the U235 Albump recording session, and one memorable occasion when my mother drove my bike over with me, allowing Tonny and I to ride our bikes around his new neighborhood. I remember a bit of the layout of the woods we rode into at the end of his street, and riding over a wooden bridge that crossed a small ravine that ran through the woods. I also remember a small group of neo-hippie bell bottom clad young people walking about, and I'm reminded that it was still only 1971.

Fairfax High was the birthplace of something that would become somewhat of a tradition in years to come, that of carrying a tape recorder with us to sporting events and doing our own play by play announcement of the game. While Tonny and I would later graduate to major league sporting events, our appropriately small first play by play attempt was a freshman basketball game in the gym of Fairfax High school's new state of the art building on Old Lee Highway, which sat conveniently across the street from Country Hill drive – a mere five minute stroll from Tonny's doorstep. As it turned out, we were blessed with a fairly exciting down-to-the-wire basketball game, and a surprisingly enthusiastic crowd to go along with it. Tonny was a bit more adherent to the conventions of sports broadcasting than I. My persistence in the usage of such non-basketball patter as "The shoot is up" was a typical attempt on my part at shunning convention, as well as an attempt to interject a little humor into the play by play of a game I knew only the bare basics of. If Tonny and I's friendship had become a non-stop comedy routine, then the announcing of this game showed Tonny to be the straight man, and I the clown who rarely took anything seriously. The resulting tape of the game (which I believe still exists) had many humorous, as well as authentically exciting moments, given the context of the game.

An old ticket stub from Beltsville Speedway that I still possess brings to mind a stock car race that Tonny's dad took us to, and I seem to recall an impromptu announcement of the race erupting out of our instinctual hunger for self-amusement, such as would have been the case if this race had preceded the Fairfax freshman basketball game. As there is no date on the ticket stub, and I cannot recall whether or not we recorded our announcement of this race "For Posteriorty" (as we would have called it), there is no way of conclusively honoring this event as the pre-Fairfax inspiration for doing play by play announcements (of which the Fairfax game was the first RECORDED example of).

On May 5th 1972, after a 6th period visit to the Oakton gym to view the finals of a mock political convention held by the senior class (presumably for the purpose of learning more about the political process), Tonny calls me at 4:06 in the afternoon and asks if I would accompany him to the viewing of the movie "Frogs." As the account in my to-the-minute diary entry goes, I phoned my mom up at work at 4:18 "And she approved the idea." As the film was showing up at the now defunct theatre at Pickett Shopping Center, Tonny and I met at the Pickett Giant Music record store at 7:21, where I note in my diary that Jethro Tull had a new album (which would have either been "Living in the Past" or "Thick as a Brick"). This meeting was a prelude to the hang out spot that Pickett shopping center would become for Tonny and I after the Hetricks moved into the adjacent Margate Manor apartments in the summer of 1972. My only comment on the film Frogs was "The movie was grotesque," which pretty much sums up my memory of watching leeches, snakes, spiders, lizards, and frogs exact their revenge upon a family of polluting swamplords. Frogs was another in a series of nature vs. man movies that Hitchcock's "The Birds" inspired, and the success of the previous year's Willard popularized. Tonny and I would also see the Charlton Heston classic "Soylent Green" at that old theatre, which was located in the far corner of the shopping center near the Ben Franklin's hardware store.

The beginning of my sophomore year saw not only a renaissance in the Insanist movement, but an increase in Bonneville Follies recording sessions, which brought Tonny and I's friendship back to the level of our Merrifield glory days. As I was finally amassing a group of friends at Oakton, so too was Tonny prospering socially at his new school – Woodson. Though the passage of another year without that much dreamed about first date with a girl made "Prospering" a word neither of us would have used at the time to describe our social lives, we were, in fact, much better off.

Upon first examination of Tonny's failed attempts to get a Woodson chapter of the Insanist movement going, one might conclude that Tonny's reserved nature made him one who simply did not attract loon material. Aside from the fact that Tonny had already managed to attract Emmette, John Fowler, and myself, Woodson conversion hopefuls such as Peter Brichant, Killer Keating and the Late Reverend Al Early were all odd in their own right, and though the latter two may have been a bit shy about participating in follies, it was obvious that Tonny had made some headway in weeding out the lunatic fringe from what had the reputation of being a school full of ruffians.

The summer of 1973 pretty much cemented the fact that Tonny and I's friendship would be a lifelong one. Once school let out, Margate Manor became the main hub of loon activity, with issue number 2 of Insane Illustrated giving a day by day account of a week in the life of two loons.

July 16: TONNY WALKS AROUND WITH CHICKS FROM OUT OF TOWN

On the evening of July 16, Tonny met two babes who claimed residence from Pennsylvania. A companion, whose name must be left out due to clearance problems, went along for the walk. The four got into a conversation stimulus, which stemmed from the language barrier between

Pennsylvania and Virginia. The two pulchrituders, whose names were Constance and Kathleen, forever stressed the Polish names of the residents of their area. The names included such winners as, and hold on to your seats, Casmacek, Crackavich, and Helinki. And let's not forget our old friend, Carl Gurgily. The wild one, Kathleen went "Boogying, Truckin' and Partying" all the time. Constance, although shy, maintained an air of distinction around her very well built body. Tonn, disappointed, missed a Monday Night Baseball game to be out with such flaky women."

July 17: KC REJECTS OFFER FROM PRODUCER TO STAR IN PORNO MOVIE
Kathy Cox, a renowned film star and leading woman in many motion pictures, rejected an offer from Rick Praether and Tonny to star in the nude. When asked, she replied "I would, but no, not on film, Oooohhhh!"

TNT CALLS KC A BABE
While strolling with Bobney on a search for FM (future meat), TNT noted a very certain female. It was Kathy Cox (KC). "There goes a babe," Tonny replied. "Where! Where!" Bobney screamed. "Oh, She just went behind the corner," TNT said. "$?%*#@!" cried BAB. Will BAB go sane? Is BAB through? Can he survive this terrible shock? Read next months issue for the exciting conclusion to this strange drama.

July 18: KC WITNESSES TONNY'S DOWNFALL
The score was tied 21 all in the bottom of the ninth with two out in the World Wiffle Ball Series (WWBS). The two teams consisted of Peter Brichant and Rusty Gibson, who are 15 years of age. They are opposed by the youth and experience of 29 year old Dave Wilmarth and 15 year old Tonny Necessity Tooter. The batter was Peter Brichant. Serving up the pitches was perhaps the greatest Wiffle Ball pitcher of his time, Dave Wilmarth. With that sneering look in his eye, and that gritting determination in his teeth, Pete lashed his bat back and forth as he starred menacingly at the oncoming pitch. Wilmarth wound and the pellet soared down the middle. The Ball was stroked for a long, hard one just out of the reach of the outstretched arms of TNT. Behind, the cheering section which included KC and two admirers watched in great hope. Tonny ran and ran for the ball but alas he was felled by a tree and quickly plummeted to the earth. The limbs pierced the hands and face of the all-star outfielder as the ball fell in for a home run. Scorching with pain, Tonny strode off with the look of defeat in his eyes. The reaction of KC and the two admirers was never known, but a chuckle must have passed by KC's luscious lips.

July 19: CRAZY FOAM TESTED FOR FURTHER WAR FILMS
Thursday is PlanForMovieDay and the loons planned well. The foam was tested and proved to be a success. It was used in the July 24 production "Super Bobney."

THE TWO HARASS FISH
Whence in time has such an act of stupidity been performed? Tonny and Bobney finally fulfilled their wildest dreams and got to harass the four fish who lived in Tonny's aquarium. Tonny got the idea that catching fish isn't too hard, especially when practiced in your own home. A string was cut and a weight attached to it. A hook was taped carefully on to the weight. Bobney, who couldn't help from cracking, laughed so hard the tank, which contained the four precious gilled specimens, almost fell off the sinktop. The so-called fishing line was lowered into the water with great ease and patience. Never before have two loons worked so patiently and so carefully. The fish were not attracted to the line. Instead they shyed away from this abhorrent looking creature. From the constant dipping of the line into the aquarium, water was being spilled all over the floor by Bobney. Tonny was outraged! "Get the water up off the floor. My mom'll kill me!" And so ends another exciting adventure from loonland.

July 19-20: RIPCORD!
Recording the Florida Soundtrack (later officially titled "Fading Out With Glitter") was not an easy job and it left the two loons tired and bored. "What can we do?" Tonny inquired. "Let's harass!" Bobney shouted back. But then Tonny had a brainstorm. "With my aeronautic mind and your aviated face, we could make parachutes and throw them off the balcony." So the two worked their fingers to the bone. They used cloth, string, tape, and plastic army men and women. Finally, the chutes were tested. They were complete failures as bodies hit the ground hard. Tonny suggested "Plastic would be the best solution." The hands and fingers of the two loons once again went to work. The chutes were completed and tested. Tonny miscalculated slightly and as the parachutes were flung off the porch, they didn't float safely to the ground, however, they rose and rose until the roof grasped them. Oh well, so much for the plastic chutes. But how could they give up here? They tried again and to their amazement the chutes were successful. After only two successful missions Bobney's chute perished.

July 20: UP, UP, AND AWAY, BUT WHICH WAY?

Mission One;

Weathermen throughout the world have perfected balloons capable of soaring 5000 feet and detecting weather at the time. "If weathermen can do it, so can the greatest lunatics in the world," shouted TNT. "Who needs weather? We'll just do it for the lunacy of it," BAB exclaimed. While in the house of TNT, the loons found the balloons and blew 'em up. "Now let's attach some weights to them so they'll eventually come down for re-use," TNT spewed out. "OK" Bobney agreed. After a few minutes of searching for the right weight, the balloon was tested. Tonny lofted the LoonyBalloony from his hand (this was all done off the balcony). It fell quite swiftly to the ground and upon impact, BURST! The two loons then started a'crackin'.

Mission Two;

Success was almost inevitable, but just wouldn't go the loon's way. "If no weight was on the balloons, they wouldn't go down as swiftly," said TNT. "You Betcha," Bobney replied. operation safe landing was underway. Two Balloons, one for each loon were tested. They were never seen very long. At last they were seen heading over the Halfle Tower (I think Tonny meant "Eiffel Tower"), which is a story in itself. "I wonder how the weathermen get their balloons to come down?" Tonny cried out as he pounded his head against the wall.

In addition to giving the reader some idea of how big this book might be had each of the almost 200 weeks that spanned my Oakton era proper been editorialized in this manner, these articles highlight (more than the events themselves) our ability to transform the most insignificant things into something we could get excited over. Oh, to see the world through those eyes again. A slightly abbreviated version of significant events leading up to the week this issue was written include Tonny's July 3rd filming of the first butt race, starring John Lee, Peter Brichant, and Al Early. The (according to Tonny) disappointing July 6th premier of the movie. Also on July 6th, some recording of "All Things Must Piss" was done, as well as the filming of the first film to star yours truly – "Krazy Karnes." Filming of this epic was completed the following day on July 7th. On July 12th, the "Bring Out Your Dead" album was started and finished. This was one of my solo albums, and I do remember putting in a good 8-hour day banging that baby out. Lastly, on July 13, another TNT production, "The Dives" was filmed. Tonny credits me for winning an Oscar for that one, and also credits Jay Cooper and Jeff Ashton with stellar performances. This one apparently centered around the pool that was in back of Tonny's apartment.

Aside from highlighting our brief interest in utilizing Tonny's third floor balcony for aeronautics testing, these articles bring back a period of intense creativity, where filmmaking and journalism were added to the already accelerated schedule of our respective musical endeavors. But again, while it's fun to reminisce, the ability to aggrandize the insignificant as one of lunacy's defining characteristics is what comes shining through in these accounts (as well as Tonny's unusual journalistic style).

This ability really manifested itself during Tonny and I's first trip to Sarasota Florida in August of 1973. Strange rural roadside southern businesses such as the "Kawntry Stow," and a restaurant where the waitresses literally ran about were sources of great amusement for Tonny and I, as well as perpetuating our aura as being magnets for attracting the unusual. It was during the second day of our journey, as we were pulling off the highway to get some lunch, that a big truck pulled up beside of us while we were waiting at a red light on the off ramp. On the side of the truck was the head of a smiling boy and the word "Mickey Cakes." Here was another "Little Guy." Now Tonny and I had already commented with some amusement a few hundred miles back on the rootin' tootin' lil's western fella on the "Shane's" restaurant sign, but Mickey Cakes is considered the first little guy by virtue of the fact that it was at this point that we considered little guys to be not only worthy of comment, but to be photographed and summarily immortalized as well.

Arriving in Sarasota, Tonny and I found no shortage of little guys to photograph, another testament to how new and exciting any little thing can seem when you're young and insane. Our adventures (or misadventures) in the sunshine state began with a trip to St. Armand's Square, and the purchase of an inflatable rubber raft, identical to the one that unfortunate little boy was floating on in the movie "Jaws." Tonny and I were having fun (or I should say "Beginning to have fun") taking turns floating around on the gentle waves off Lido Beach when our raft sprung a leak and promptly deflated, leaving us with the sense that our inept destiny had been fulfilled once again.

The four of us stayed in a reddish orange stuck-o covered apartment building in downtown Sarasota, about a stones throw from Sarasota bay, and about 50 yards from the famed Ranch House restaurant where Tonny and I had our legendary encounter with the waitress Laura. Also within walking distance of our apartment was a historic old hotel built by circus magnate P. T. Barnum. In the first floor of the hotel was a dimly lit restaurant where the four of us ate dinner and struck up the acquaintance of a woman who had been employed in the circus in her younger days.

Aside from the fact that we were eating in the hotel that Barnum built, Sarasota was an elephant's graveyard for old circus folk, and back in the early 70's, there were still plenty of people around with memories of the big top's heyday. This woman invited us up to her apartment, which was in an upper floor of the hotel, for tea and a few stories about the glory days of the circus. Her apartment (which like the restaurant below, was sparsely lit with small reading lamps) had an exotic gypsy-esque circus wagon motif running throughout it, and her stories (like the Ringling circus museum I would visit 25 years later) were filled with old ghosts. In fact, I recall her telling us about the actual ghosts that were presently haunting the hotel. As my 1998 visit to the Ringling museum instilled in me, at last, an interest in circus history, I'd love to go back in time and tape her reminiscences, as well as recapture the gist of the paranormal events she had brought up.

Though one could imagine ghosts walking about the old dark hotel by virtue of its ambiance alone, I recall getting the sense, if only for a fleeting moment, that it was something more. The feeling I had at the circus museum last year of almost being moved to tears by the spiritual sadness surrounding the calliopes, wagons, costumes and other relics (as if it distressed the attending spirits to see the accoutrements of their beloved profession reduced to obsolete antiques, to be gawked at by museum patrons) brought me back to this particular night, and poses the question of whether or not the strange impression I received then in 1973 was the vicarious sense of the very same longing for days gone by. Whatever it was, I stayed just long enough to take note of it, as the shorter attention spans of the adolescents that Tonny and I were made us grow fidgety, and we soon excused ourselves from the conversation of the three adults, to return to the apartment, and perhaps to resume work on the Follies album we were working on.

On a subsequent visit to the beach, Tonny and I found an old barnacle encrusted crabbing pot that had washed ashore. Tonny quickly dubbed it "The Barnacle Clavicle," and assigning it mystical powers, we insisted (against the wishes of my mother) that we bring this filthy thing back to the apartment with us. Although the Clavicle was already a qualified loon oracle by the time we reached the apartment, my mother insisted that we leave it out in the back courtyard of the apartment building. For the next couple of days, Tonny and I would make periodic visits to the yard to sit in the grass and commune with the Clavicle, but it eventually disappeared, and so another loon oracle was lost.

An unusual reminder of our Luther Jackson days greeted us on a visit to one of those wonderful waterfront restaurants that is wholly or partially suspended over the water by wooden supports. We happened to notice that Clifford Martin was sitting just a few tables away from us. He waved with a surprised outburst of recognition, and then we acknowledged each other again as he was leaving. Now Tonny recognized Mr. Martin (I suppose) as a gym teacher he had at Luther Jackson. Although I never had Mr. Martin for gym (I did have his brother Stuart as a teacher for that wonderful 7th grade gym class I shared with Ray King), I was more apt to be the one he would have recognized, as he had transferred to Oakton my freshman year.

Even eating out on this vacation was an adventure for Tonny and I, but the greatest adventure for me during this vacation would not even involve Tonny. Described earlier at length under Sam Romeo's entry, the four of us took a jaunt up to Orlando to visit the family of one of my stepfather's old service buddies – Merle Badders. Tonny may have taken a dip in the Badder's pool, but otherwise he maintained a low profile during the two days we were there. As Tonny flatly refused to accompany me on my excursions around suburban Orlando, I saw very little of the old boy during this part of our vacation. Marking him even more as the sullen outsider was the fact that I was now staying out till the wee hours and waking up just in time for lunch, while Tonny was sticking by his body clock's lifelong dictate that he rise at the crack of dawn. This separated us even further.

At any rate, Tonny was at least present for two noteworthy events that took place at the Badder's involving music, one of which was a finger pointed directly into the future, and indirectly at EAT. There was a period for a couple of hours during the first afternoon where Tonny and I were just hanging out in the Badders living room. Tonny might have been (at least part of the time) occupying himself by playing some sort of board game with Mikey, but I had become captivated in front of the Badder's stereo system with the discovery of Orlando's own progressive rock radio station. I had already discovered WHFS (then known as "Home Grown Radio" for mainly playing American artists, which meant that Frank Zappa and Miles Davis was as close to Progressive Rock as they would get), and was within a couple months of swearing off top 40 radio forever, but it would be a good 9 months before I would discover WGTB, so this was my first exposure to progressive radio - as I would later come to know it. I have Bobby Badders to thank for calling my attention to this station by tuning it in for me before leaving the house.

Whatever had been playing when the station was first tuned in, my attention was grabbed and held by the airing of Bowie's "Panic in Detroit." I had taken the plunge on Bowie early that year on the merits of his late 72/early 73 string of top 40 hits ("Changes," "Space Oddity," and "Starman"), but this was one of those Bowie songs I never dreamed of hearing on the radio. Later on, the DJ started describing a new album he had in his hands that was produced by Todd Rundgren, and proceeded to play "The Original Frankenstein" by the New York Dolls. This was my first exposure to the Dolls, and another spiritual step towards my inevitable friendship with EAT. The DJ then proceeded to play a lengthy (and particularly surreal) GTB-style set of tunes (?) which concluded with Pink Floyd's "Corporal Clegg." As I had only caught that it was a Pink Floyd piece, this initiated a search for this song that lasted until close to Christmas time, when someone recognized by my description that I was looking for a song off the "Saucerful of Secrets" album. Unfortunately, when my aunt Weezie took my Christmas list to Giant music, with Nico's "The Marble Index" and Pink Floyd's Saucerful of Secrets on it, she was told that although her nephew had great taste in music, both albums were regrettably out of print.

Late the next morning, I awoke slowly to the sounds of an already active household. To ease myself into the day, I reached around and turned on the radio that was at the head of the bed, tuning it to that amazing station. I was immediately hit with King Crimson's "Easy Money," which was followed by Black Oak Arkansas' "Uncle Elijah." This was my first exposure to Black Oak and another signpost on my way to the 73-74 triumvirate of Elmo, EAT, and myself – and the Black Oak Arkansas concert the three of us would attend 6 months later. After the better part of an hour, the station did a GTB-like hard genre shift into bluegrass music, at which time I felt it was my cue to get up and start my day.

The other noteworthy event that occurred at the Badders involving music also involved their daughter Danny. Danny was a year or two older than me, and perhaps 4 or 5 years ahead of me on the maturity meter, but Danny (God bless her) was still a girl, and with all the guy-like appreciation of this heavy progressive music going on, she felt compelled to drag me out to the family car and pop in an 8-track of some real music – Carole King's "Tapestry." I know someone was sitting with me in the backseat, and by process of elimination, I can deduce that it was Tonny, but as Tonny would not really develop his own passion for music until after high school, he was again strangely mute in the heated sexual gap argument Danny and I would proceed to have, while the organically grown sounds of Carole King's multi-platinum/uranium Tapestry album filled the car. As this was a little under a year before my total immersion in progressive rock (pending my discovery of WGTB), I was still arguing the case for Black Sabbath and Alice Cooper, so one can just imagine the led balloons that were being dropped on a disillusioned Danny, as she tried in vain to save my musical soul. When the song "Smackwater Jack" came on (which was obviously her favorite song in the world), Danny started bobbing her head back and forth up front, while I was shaking my head in the back seat. At one point, confounded, she turned to me and insisted that I – "Listen to the words, just listen to these words," as if doing so would have made this bland granola somehow more palatable. I know one thing, Hollywood's recent fascination with producing movies and TV shows that take place in the 70's will (if it ever has the guts to set a premise in the pre-disco early 70's) pass my authenticity test the second I see a teenage girl in the front seat of a car bobbing her head and singing along with Smackwater Jack.

Back in Sarasota, the four of us paid a visit to a shopping mall (which was appropriately only about a fourth the size of the four year old Tysons Corner), and visiting a record store, I made two purchases – "The World of David Bowie" and the first Hawkwind album. Now The World of David Bowie (despite the fact that it misleadingly had a Ziggy Stardust era concert photo on the cover) was an import collection of pre-Space Oddity beat era singles, but the first Hawkwind album was a significant purchase, not merely for its effect of increasing my appreciation of looser structures in rock music, but for being the album that should have silenced all criticism of the Queen Viper show (see Paula Pippert entry).

Shortly after returning from this very fun and eventful vacation in Sarasota, Tonny began preparations for his move to Punxsutawney PA, and what would become the next phase of our friendship. Tonny's first letter from Punx'y demonstrates that despite the distance that now separated us, spirits were still riding high from the many fun filled adventures of the previous year. Through a succession of letters, Tonny's role became increasingly that of caretaker for the spirit of insanity during these months of declining expansion. He not only mentions an aborted book (or story, rather) I was writing about a character named Richard (which was inspired by the character Richard Atlee in the movie "Crawlspace"), he expresses his wishes for Elmo's continued success along the path of insanity, while confirming (as Elmo would write in his song "Words" less than two weeks later) that "Crane and crack are words we know."

Crane and crack were loon words that were in such common usage at this time, that any time one of us came across either word being used outside of our group, we tended to regard it as humorous and/or at least worthy of mention, hence Tonny's need to inform me that the toilet in his new house was a "Crane" model. Telling Elmo to "Keep crackin'" was a point of courtesy that pretty much translated into – "Stay the course." Here is Tonny's first letter from Punx'y in its entirety. Dated September 1, 1973

Hello Bob,

Punxsutawney is great. We just got our stuff Wednesday and everything is set up now. I've just started school last Tuesday Aug 27. PHS may surpass Woodson as the greatest school for beauties in the world. I sure hope you're still preaching the gospel of Insanity, but I know you are so that's a pretty dumb statement. How did the pictures of the little guys turn out? And your book? Has Richard found the Kaisey Module yet? The things to do here are absolutely phenomenal. I can ride my bike all over and visit such metropolises as Cloe, Big Run, Dubois, and Indiana PA. Write to me and send me further developments in your book. I hope Elmo is still progressing and showing the skill and talent that he was blessed with. I hope you can come up to visit me this summer (1974). Well as you can see my address is at the top of this page. I am planning to make a full-length motion picture. This may prove to be impossible because it would cost exactly $104.54. Someday the loons shall take over the world. I hope you have many more loonacious moments. Tell Elmo to keep crackin.

Your Laughing Loon Attic
Tonny Necessity Tooter

ONWARDLUNATICSONWARDLUNATICSONWARDLUNATICSO
NWARDLUNATICS

Tonny's creative juices were obviously still flowing in the direction of movie making, though his ideas appeared to be exceeding his financial resources. Moving on to October 2nd, and Tonny's second letter, which begins to introduce more of the characters and places that would grow into the body of Punxsutawney lore. He name drops a number of people that were on the scene here in Virginia at the time he left. Here is Tonny's second letter from PA.

Ho Bob,

I had a rough day at work today. I make $1.60 an hour working in Stewart's drug store, in the metropolis of Punxsutawney. I thoroughly enjoyed your first two letters as they brought me back to the world I once knew and shared through insanity with you. I wish I could be back in the mighty city of Fairfax and continue to preach the gospel I know so well. In Stewart's Drug there works a 20-yr. old beaut with a ripening figure. This babe has got it all, unfortunately even a boyfriend (we loons never win). Well as I sit here and write this, I'm constantly thinking of ways to get her butt. I agree to the trade of Black Mass Lucifer for Tarkus. There is only one real loon "Prospect," and that's my cousin Bob Hetrick. His favorite expression (and one that I have come to hate) is calling me NIGGERBUNCH! How this originated I'll never know. All of the music notes will be sent soon. Around here the name Karnes is almost a household word. All my friends know about you and think you're some kind of nut, but that's what we're striving for, isn't it? My congratulations are extended to you, Brian Helms (I'll never understand that guy) Elmo Zudinski (may his hair live longer than he: no offense intended) Howard Koretz (like to meet him) Der Kaiser (never knew the old boy, but he was a good old boy) and Emmette (he's been up and down more than a super ball). Ask Emmette for me if he still thinks stormin' Norman Cash is great. I think he sucks. May Spencer Turnipseed sprout into a fine young plant. The old LC Smith & Corona is still typing away. If I sound like I'm just saying a bunch of sentences that don't pertain in the least bit to the preceding one, well I am.

GO LOONS

It's humorous to note Tonny's usage of the term "Get her butt" in this letter. If any of us were actually in pursuit of a young lady (whether in fact or simply in the wishful thinking of our dreams), we were (in loonspeak) attempting to "Get her butt." This was a commonly used term by nearly all inner-circle loons for the entirety of my stay at Oakton, and by Tonny and myself up to the end of the 70's. Tonny seems to have set his sights a little high in scoping out a 20-year-old, but at the tender age of 16, Mother Nature begins to get hard to ignore.

Tonny mentions the old "LC Smith & Corona" in a rather weird context, because he seems to be describing the typewriter I was using at the time. It was an old antique too. The damn thing was made in 1922. I suppose it's possible that he had an old Smith & Corona of his own. His letters do appear to have been typed on a rickety old bag of bolts like the one I had. Incredibly! Tonny's third letter, which seems to have been a rush letter to inform me of the loss of "The Music Sheets" (whatever those were), was dated October 4 – two days after his second letter. The letter begins with another exhortation to keep the spirit of insanity alive.

THE INSANISTS SHALL INHERIT THE EARTH   Arpochney
3:74

Bad news Bob, in moving, the typed finished copies of the music sheets were lost. Please forgive me for I repent once more to you mighty loon, king of all loons for I have done a bad deed in losing those priceless papers. However, enclosed in this envelope are the prized rat notes and the untyped music sheets.

Please continue to write your story, which I'm sure someday will be on the best seller list. Answer me this. How much % of the royalties do I receive should the book be published??? HAHAHAHAHAHAHAHA

There is one thing I have got to tell you that I completely forgot about. I am a member of the school newspaper staff. I'm the sports editor. And listen to this, the school nickname is "Chucks" for groundhog. You know the old tradition about the groundhog and his shadow? Well this is where all that garbage takes place, right here in Punxsutawney. Punxsutawney Chucks??? Give me the Woodson Cavaliers any day.

You may think my next two surprises are crazy, but I thought you'd enjoy them. This first story is from our school newspaper of 1971.

Punxsutawney?

Have you ever felt that our groundhog just hasn't made it. I know we've all felt this way when a person from out of town really slaughters our name. Pronouncing it Punxsutewney, Punfsutawney, or Punexytuna! The real winner is one sent and addressed to Pumsuramy. The letter was sent back with the notice on the envelope "No such town on state map."

As I was daydreaming in my 5th period study hall class today, I started writing a silly story. After I had finished, I handed the story over to a friend of mine. It read:

The sun was shining brightly as Paul Puney woke up feeling good inside. Paul heard a rumbling downstairs, so he went to investigate. In his haste, he tripped and fell and broke his neck as he crashed into his mother who was standing below. His mother was holding a gun that went off killing her husband. The three of them died. If you believe this story, send a stamped self-addressed envelope to "The Paul Puney Memorial Fund," Box 311, Rugby, North Dakota.

My friend could not contain himself as he started a' crackin.

And last but certainly not least, the funniest occurrence that has yet happened in this town. Rick Kerns (reader of the Paul Puney saga) and I were sitting in study hall (in the cafeteria) when we heard two ladies talking. It was a rather unusual conversation as one said to the other "That's my underwear," and the other said "No that's my rag." Well by this time Rick and I were on the floor "Chuck'ling." The lady who spoke first talked in a high pitched voice which made it all the more amusing. Apparently, nobody else in the cafeteria heard the ladies (they were, the ladies cleaning dishes) as they had probably dozed off. I think if you had been there, you would have thought this was the funniest thing that ever happened.

Well so long Bob. Continue to write to me, and send me the Richard story so I can typed it up for you. Good luck in your never-ending battle against the forces of sanity!!!!!!!!

As Tonny has recently published his second book, the Paul Puney saga (as short as it is) has been cast in the light of being an early attempt by this budding author to come to grips with the elements of good storytelling.

My next letter to Tonny was my famed account of the Cheri debacle, which I recall Tonny's sister Gina digging out for me in the early 80's (while Tonny was stationed in Japan). It was an uproariously funny trip back to the beginning of a period where anything I wrote about Cheri Allen tended to quickly assume the form of monomanic ramblings. The letter has unfortunately disappeared since then, but Tonny's reaction to it in his December 21 1973 letter was pretty much Gina and I's reaction to it 10 years later.

I would have to say your Christmas rendition of the futile encounter with Cheri Allen is the greatest example of literary genius I have ever indulged in. (Note: Please keep this letter for the hall of fame, and the others. I have kept yours). Anyway, getting back to the clash, insanity vs. female. It was of course, a victory for females, but I'm sure that will not deter the ever-producing brain of the Arch of Arpochney.

Tonny then goes on to say that he is still working at Stewart's Drug store, having amassed a fortune of $226.00 in his three month employ there, $50.00 of which had been used for camera equipment and various film production expenses. He encloses an up to date rundown of his latest movies, the length of which suggesting that Tonny was now spending as much time (or more) making movies as I was writing and recording music. He also mentions his recent purchase of a $45.95 Litronix 1100 calculator, to be used for his sports calculations. This was a significant purchase for him, because it made computing averages and statistics go fast enough that he was able to begin playing an entire season for an entire league of Sports Illustrated tabletop baseball the following summer.
Tonny goes on to express his general discontentment with Punx'y High, despite his claim that its beauxkya ratio exceeded that of Woodson's (a fact

I dispute from comparing photo's from his Punx'y yearbooks with the few times I was able to admire Woodson's finest in the flesh). He laments the loss of colorful figures such as Scotty Rigden, John Lee (not the Oakton John Lee), Lou Rainy, Chris Dukes, Rusty Gibson, and loon hopeful Al Early. Although Ganzer's continuing development would ease some of the boredom, one gets the impression that some of Punx'y's small town charm had worn off around this time. Returning to the subject of my letter, he writes:

Well, I just can't say enough for the holiday letter. I almost died of laughing, exhaustion, and whoops. My dad somehow got hold of the letter and read it. He said what you wrote was a "Bunch of junk," but you had "Great writing potential," and "Knows how to put his words together."

My response to his father's "Bunch of junk" statement in my following letter was – "He doesn't have to worry anymore. He's already married with three children," a typical insanist touché. My early 74 letters were mainly ranting laments about Cheri, countered with calls for a Bobno-Tonnian reunion and accompanying loon revival. It's interesting that I was calling for a loon revival barely a month after Cheri's rejection, as if its effect on our group as a whole were evident to me even then. The following passage from that same late January letter to Tonny puts it all in perspective.

Cheri's influence on me has caused a decrease in loon moral, in other words, she and her femininity are driving us sane. I have gone to God, Elmo has gone to Brenda, and Emmette has just gone. I'm sure that once we meet again, things will return to abnormal.

Despite my continuing involvement in two separate church youth groups, and my increasing hunger for some sort of spiritual salvation, it's clear that in the post Cheri latter half of my junior year, a part of me viewed a reunion with Tonny as an integral part of that salvation I was seeking. I go on to describe how I was given to writing "Gorsuch Lives" or "Tonny Lives" on desks, blackboards, and bulletin boards. While Gorsuch DID reappear briefly around this time (if only in body), and it was certainly true that Tonny still lived (if some 237 miles away), what I was really attempting to do in my desperation was to summon the spirit of my sophomore year, of which Tonny and Gorsuch were both symbols of. While some of my peers at the Fairfax Assembly of God may have been praying for Christ's return, I was immediately more concerned with Tonny's return, and the much-needed spiritual renewal it would bring.

Tonny's next letter to me was in cassette form, and featured the Tonny/Tom Henry collaborations "Football Frank," and "I Met Her in a Hog Trough," which was my first hard evidence that this Henry character might, in fact, be the loon that Tonny was touting him as being. I would follow with a cassette letter of my own, which featured a few of my own recordings, including "Song for Edgar Allan Poe," which particularly impressed Tonny.

We were getting into the spring of 1974 now, and with my June trip to Punxsutawney practically written in stone, much of our correspondence during this period was actually done on the phone, and was mostly in the form of getting the particulars for my impending visit ironed out. When I arrived at the Hetrick's house on Beyer Avenue, I found Tonny and family living in one of those three story 19th century monstrosities so prevalent in rural Pennsylvania. I was to bed in a sleeping bag on the floor of Tonny's room, which was a converted attic up in nosebleed territory. I remember that as Tonny's father was leading me up the winding narrow stairway to Tonny's room(?), he was relating the story that he had recently gone up there to do some work, only to find a bat flying around, a story that did not bother me in the least (that is, until I had the same story told to me by every member of the Hetrick household – at least once).

Many of the highlights of my two-week stay in Punxsutawney are chronicled elsewhere in this book, but I wish to at least list them all here again, to take this always pleasurable stroll down memory lane once more. It was late June, and for a couple days in particular, about as hot as a town in the mountains of western Pennsylvania could get. Tonny and I would take several strolls into town, passing by the graveyard as we went. Being somewhat of a history buff, I was quite impressed with the fact that some of the graves went back to the American Revolution. Once in town, we stopped by the A&P grocery store, where I bought a large bottle of prune juice. This A&P is especially memorable for the Mennonite horse and buggies I would see outside the store (there was even some kind of hitching post out front that the Amish and Mennonite shoppers could hitch their carriages to while they were doing their shopping). Being hotter than blazes, I downed the entire bottle of prune juice, an act that poor Tonny paid dearly for the following day.

The town of Punxsutawney was somewhat of a living museum. I remember going into the empty theatre and thinking as I looked over the inside that it must have dated back to the era of silent films. Tonny of course took me by Stewart's drug store, his one time place of employ. It was a dinky little place, but they did have records, and I remember browsing through them as Grand Funk's version of "The Locomotion" boomed proudly down from a wall speaker. I would make two separate trips to the department store in town. On the first trip, I caught the vinyl scent, and in a perusal of their selection, I found myself strangely drawn to an album by Genesis entitled "Selling England by the Pound." The cover and song titles were intriguing. Someone in the group played an electric sitar, and they were on the Famous Charisma label. It took until the next time Tonny and I walked by this store for me to make the decision to buy it. I remember being challenged by the music to the point of questioning my purchase, yet being fascinated enough to play the album several times in succession, until its brilliance began to reveal itself. It would not be the only album I would buy in Punxsutawney. At one point, Tonny and I walked across town to visit the house of one of his aunts (a museum in itself). While on the other side of town, Tonny and I walked into a Grants store for some reason. The very first sight my eyes caught upon entering the store was a rack of newly released albums, one of which was the latest New York Dolls album. Their first album had become a classic in the eyes of EAT and myself, and I was fairly shocked to discover that they had a second album out, much less to discover that album in Punxsutawney. It was a reminder of EAT, and the glitter appreciation the two of us shared back in Virginia.

Tonny's neighborhood in Punx'y was so small town, even coming complete with its own haunted house. It was nothing more than an abandoned house, and I'm sure that's the main reason it was deemed haunted, nonetheless, Tonny, Ganzer, and myself had to go investigate. Being fairly easy to get into (probably a matter of simply opening the door and walking in), and being nothing more than the empty abandoned house that it was, we were nonetheless mildly spooked by the experience of just being there. This brings us to the subject of Tonny's friend Tom Henry, christened Ganzerareux Azziamekiassa by me upon his donning of the ceremonial underwear and his recital of the insanist oath. Called "Ganzer" for short, he was our companion during a number of adventures we had during my stay there. The filming of The Hand, our recording session in his basement, and our wonderful rat hunt (which was just Ganzer and myself). I remember our walks from Tonny's house through the woods up to Punx'y high's football field for the filming of The Hand. It was a special time full of small town charm and youthful camaraderie.

Interestingly enough, one of my greatest memories of Ganzer was how much more empathetic he was than Tonny over the pain I was still experiencing over the Cheri rejection. In fact, Cheri seemed to be strangely creeping into my thoughts during every idle moment I spent in Punxsutawney. While a number of Punx'y's lovelies had caught Tonny's eye, Carol Bell and Mary Ann Renne in particular, Tonny had never gotten close enough to experience a major heartbreak, and perhaps wisely so, if there was any lesson to be learned from the condition I was in. Tonny was following Emmette's prudent course of maintaining his distance until a sure thing came along. Despite Tonny's claim that Ganzer was an endearing braggart, but a braggart nonetheless, whatever type of ladies man Ganzer had tried to appear as in Tonny's eyes was shunted in my presence. Perhaps having at last found a kindred spirit, Ganzer seemed to have had a similar experience, though enough time had apparently passed that he could console me with the old "Women are nothing but trouble" attitude, but with enough conviction that it was clear he had gotten close enough to get burned once or twice.

Tonny's room was in a walled off half of the attic. It was a rather spacious room, as I recall, and brighter than one might imagine, owing to a fairly large window, and the fact that the attic was that much closer to being above the tree line. It was not completely walled off from the other side of the attic, and Tonny's easy access to the dark side of the attic was occasionally called for, as there was a conveniently placed refrigerator on that side. I remember making my way over to look out the window on the other side, which overlooked the backyard and the woods beyond. There was an afternoon lightning storm raging outside, with the worst of it centered just beyond the woods. I remember just sitting there watching the storm, and then at some point getting the urge to try and photograph one of the incredible displays of lightning. I was only partially successful, as it was otherwise fairly dark where I was sitting, and fairly dark outside as well.

I remember Tonny's kitchen was infested with these weird looking roaches, and I recall Tonny being rather frustrated by their constant appearance on the counter tops. I also remember Tonny's backyard, and watching his youngest sister Beth playing with a young black cat (presumably the family pet), at one point mischievously dropping the cat into a bucket of water, which it quickly jumped out of.

One morning while Tonny and I were in need of something to do, Tonny showed me his Sports Illustrated table top baseball game, with attending charts. Though probably not overly interested at first, I soon was inspired (perhaps by the desire to impress Tonny) to proclaim that I was going to play an entire season of this game for an entire league. Being before the days of easy access to copying machines, this meant that I had to copy Tonny's charts by hand, front and back. The act of doing this must have ate up an entire day, but after about my 3rd or 4th game, I was completely hooked, playing the first 12 to 15 games of my 1971 national league season at Tonny's house in Punx'y, with Tonny rather pleasantly surprised by the sudden reawakening of my interest in baseball. Tonny would shortly join me in playing his own 71 national league season, though with somewhat different results.

Nearing the end of my stay in Punxsutawney, my mother phoned and asked if Tonny would like to join her, my stepfather and myself for another trip to Sarasota Florida. Tonny asked his folks and they said it was all right. Meemaw and Poppy drove to Punxsutawney to pick up Tonny and I, but we were not heading strait back to Virginia. Being from Johnstown originally, and as Johnstown was on our way back, Meemaw and Poppy decided it would be fun if we worked another mini vacation into the two that Tonny and I were in between. We stopped in Johnstown for a couple of days, staying at my Uncle Russell's house, and visiting with various relatives. Highlights from the trip included a ride up the incline (a trolley that ferried people up the mountain that overlooked the city of Johnstown), a trip to the small but fascinating flood museum, and a cruise around the burbs of Johnstown with my older cousin Jeff Hunt, who I believe had just finished his first year of college. I'll never forget Jeff's older and wiser words of consolation over my still aching heart. At one point during our ride, the subject turned to girls, and I took the opportunity to seek Jeff's council on the matter. Though what Jeff said exactly is lost to my memory, I do recall that it was long and profound enough to completely change my outlook on the Cheri affair from negative to positive, at least long enough for me to enjoy my second trip to Sarasota with Tonny with little or no mental intrusions from Miss Allen.

Perhaps my greatest memory of this detour to Johnstown was the fact that this was the last time I saw my Uncle Russell, who would pass away a little over a month later. He always called me "Butch," a nickname from another era to be sure, and my last clear memory of his face is a rather striking one. Pop, Russell, Tonny and I had stopped into this old church that Russell went back with possibly as far as his own baptism. No services were being held at the time, but the pastor and a few other people were there milling around the church, exchanging pleasantries and jokes with Pop and Russ. As the four of us were on our way out, Russell stopped, turned around, and moving his gaze up and around the entirety of the chapel, he said "I've got a lot of memories in this old church" in a wistful pensive tone that struck me how out of character it was coming from the always jovial man I knew as my uncle. It was as if he were viewing ALL of those memories in that moment of reflection, and though someone with youth's eternal view of life rarely picks up such clues, when I heard that he had passed on, I could only look back on the clearest image I had of my uncle, and believe that at that moment he knew he would not be making too many more visits to his beloved church.

On a brighter note, I also remember our trip to the department store that Russell worked in, and boy, was it something out of the 30's, big and busy as a Kmart at Christmas, but obviously another building that went back quite a ways with Russ.

Back in Virginia, Tonny and I had our first recording session since the previous August, yielding Tonny's classic junior year summation "Life in PA." Once in Sarasota, however, we became so engrossed in the playing of our 1971 Sports Illustrated national league seasons that outside of the Pizza Hut debacle, my stepfather accidentally running over a dog, and a local news anchor committing suicide on the air, I have few memories of this particular trip. Tonny and I had a blast nonetheless.

Back up in Punxsutawney, Tonny was bubbling with the prospect that their house would be sold. Apparently, the small-town charm had worn thin on the entire Hetrick family, and they were trying to move back to Northern Virginia. Unfortunately, in an August 1974 letter from Tonny, he bemoans the fact that the person who was looking to buy the Hetrick house on Beyer Avenue had backed out of the deal for some reason. It looked like another year of letter's to and from Tonny, all containing exhortations to look ahead to that eventual reunion.

Our senior year letters tended to be largely comments and critiques on the 12 teams and individual players of our respective 1971 national league seasons as they were unfolding (each of us was playing the full 938 game schedule). As each of these games took over an hour to play, with extra time needed to compute the various statistics, it had become a fairly consuming pastime. Essentially, Tonny and I's relationship had gone full circle from the music based friendship of the Bonneville Follies era, back to something resembling Tonny's 1969-71 baseball centered friendship with Emmette. Like the table top board game addict I'd become, I start off most of my letters to Tonny from this period begging for the monthly schedules of the games that he was supplying me with as a matter of maintaining some authenticity in replicating at least the actual sequence of games played, if not the actual outcome of the games themselves. Lines like "I should be done with May by the end of September" meant that I expected Tonny to mail me the June schedule of games by the end of the month, or as soon as possible if October was creeping up fast.

Lest my use of the word "Addict" to describe my newfound love for this Sports Illustrated baseball game cause any misunderstanding, these games actually increasingly took on the more relaxing aspects of being a nightly vacation from the pressure and tumult of my senior year. I suppose the escapist quality of these games might have qualified them for the use of drug terminology, but I prefer to think of them as a much-needed balancing factor. They did not detract from the fun I was having at school, they simply provided me with a different kind of fun, as well as a way to unwind.

A few interesting things are brought up in these senior year letters. Tonny describes the two-day move to Kentucky and triumphant return of Ganzer and family (for reasons better left unsaid here). Tonny's description of an encounter with a female named Mary Anne Renne spoke of both the pleasure and futility of longing for The 1974 Punxsutawney Area High School Queen, and so Tonny's description of this encounter thereby rates inclusion here. I should just set the stage here by saying that Tonny was at a football game between Punx'y high and Vo-Tech. He was sitting next to his friend Ed Zatsick, and found himself completely surrounded by JV cheerleaders, which Tonny describes in the Campbell soup parlance of the time as "MMMMM Good." He proceeds from there —

On the opening kickoff, we got the ball and scored, and then a funny thing happened. The 1974 Punxsutawney Area High School Football Queen — the luscious Mary Anne Renne, walked up into the stands and stood beside me. Mary Anne is an acquaintance of Ed's. WOW! As I write this, I am thinking of Poe's descriptions of various females in his stories. She was all that and more. Well, the game wore on, I being paralyzed by the fact that the "Queen" was near. We scored all night, and continued to score, and after every big play, especially touchdowns, Mary Anne would jump up and down, EXCITED, all over me. It was only after a while that she realized what she was doing, and said "I'm Sorry." I said that it was all right and kissed her (only in my dreams). But actually she WAS jumping on me, and this action proved to be quite gratifying for me.

Putting myself in Tonny's situation, (which given my popularity with Oakton cheerleaders was difficult, but not impossible) I could imagine how "Gratifying" this experience was for him. I bring up Mary Anne's name a couple times in a late 1974 letter, wherein I make the shocking confession to Tonny that — "I still call Cheri Allen 2 to 4 times a week, and she still says the kind of sweet things that force me to show her I still care." Yes! Girls were on our minds a great deal more than in the good old days of the Insanist movement, but no less an irreverent tip of the cap to those bygone days was my insistence that Tonny — "Throw Mary Anne Renne a kiss for me, and tell her that come Easter, Queen Viper shall bless her in Christ's wonderful name, and request her presence. Us Queens have to stick together." Three things are immediately recalled from this passage. Firstly, that this was using humor as a lead-in to a description of my radio show and on-air personality. Secondly, that I was planning a return visit to Punxsutawney over the Easter break, a plan that for some reason never materialized. And thirdly, that I was as close to being a full-fledged Gary

Garland style Jesus freak around this period as I would ever get, despite the fact that the great disillusionment of 1974 was only weeks away from occurring. My late 1974 letters to Tonny are distinguished by the long ranting passages that typified the undertone of desperation I was living with. That I even invoked the names of Christ and God the father in my letters to Tonny (of all people) reveals how much I was grasping for a replacement for the spiritual boost that rallying around the loon cause once gave us.

I only wrote Tonny once in 1975, in early April. The letter is a mere two pages in length, and is just another summary of what my 1971 National league was doing, with standings of both divisions, and a paragraph or two on how well my Montreal Expos were playing. Outside of my wishing Ganzer "Happy Looning," that was pretty much all I had to say. Even by the first of April I knew that Tonny's return to Northern Virginia was imminent, and would this time be permanent. As with the previous year, the knowledge of our impending reunion preceded a switch to mainly phone communications, which were more geared towards planning for that eventual reunion. I would venture to guess that the reason my much hyped visit to Punx'y on Easter of 1975 never materialized was because the knowledge that the Hetrick's would be back in Virginia by May's end made such a trip pointless. Less obviously, though letters were less important now, in light of Tonny's imminent return, I decided that I would never again include anything in a letter to Tonny that wasn't good news. Though made semi-consciously, I distinctly recall making this decision, and though the brevity of my last letter suggests sadly that my Montreal Expos were having  more luck on paper than I was at school, in addressing Tonny, I was looking to a better brighter future. As with my long gaps of not writing Tonny while he was stationed in Japan in the early 80's, my feeling was that

I did not want to revisit the negativity in my life all over again in a letter to Tonny. Basically, if I had nothing good to report, I didn't write.

Tonny's return did indeed raise spirits, and having graduated early allowed Tonny to make two visits as a guest to Oakton High before the end of my senior year. Actually, Tonny's first return visit (which was sometime in the mid to latter part of May) was done while his parents were procuring the families second apartment at Margate Manor, their second of three, I might add. Tonny may not have actually graduated Punx'y High by this point. Tonny's first visit to Oakton as my guest fell on a day that I was having my radio show. My lead-in to that particular show was to declare it "TNT Day At WOHS," even handing some of the announcing duties over to Tonny, who had enough foreknowledge of this event to have come prepared with a tape of some of his hits, and a small prewritten speech, which I will now give in its entirety.

Hello Again Everybody,

Tonny, otherwise known as TNT, is here with you today on TNT day here on B lunch in the Oakton High School. Happy to be amongst you. As most of you know, I am currently residing in Punxsutawney Pa, home of the world famous groundhog, world's greatest weather prognosticator. We have here today some great music for you. Some of you already know of my world famous exploits in Punxsutawney, recording along with Tom Henry, a one-time background guitarist for Grand Funk. Just some of the ear piercing sounds you will be hearing today will be Boogie Woogie, Met Her in a Hog Trough, yours truly doing Wicked People, and a special treat – Rennie Stennett's April 13th home run with the Pittsburgh Pirates.

As you can see, Tonny was playing along with the mock celebrity decorum that was being accorded him, most of which was an outward expression of my relief at having him back in the area again. However, aside from the fact that this radio show was as close as we would get to an official ceremony honoring his return, it must be remembered that there was not an ounce of false modesty among the lot of us. Though we wore our failures with females like purple hearts, we loons were distinguished by our healthy delusions of grandeur. No opportunity to magnify the significance of anything we said or did was wasted, and although Ganzer may have crossed the line in Tonny's observances, with his exaggerations of his successes with women, sports and music, the basic thrust of what Ganzer was doing unknowingly aligned him with the self aggrandizing spirit of the insanist inner circle. As I look back now on TNT day on WOHS, I'm left wondering what the people down in the SG office must have been thinking while this lunacy was being perpetrated.

Tonny's final visit to Oakton was really the last hurrah of my 4-year stay there, and it was only fitting that Tonny was there to be a part of it. While Ray Denk, EAT and I were reveling in the merriment of the final folly, Tonny was actually carrying on a tradition of his own that dated back to the spring of 1973, that of making his own movies. While the motion picture portion of the final folly never came out, due to insufficient lighting inside the school, it does bring to mind the fact that of all the eras and timelines that came to a close that first week of June 1975, Tonny's filmmaking career must now be included. Looking through all of his letters from Punxsutawney, his interest in making films seems to have never waned. His final letter contained a brief synopsis of what I'm assuming was his last major production, the 6 minute and 15 second long "A Game of Cards," starring Ed Zatsick. Perhaps sensing that his failure to capture the final folly on super 8 film was a sign to give it up, no other major productions were undertaken by Tonny after his return to Fairfax. In reading Tonny's letters, I'm moved to wonder what sort of movies he would have produced had he not moved to Punxsutawney, with Kaiser, Howard, Elmo, EAT, myself, and possibly even Emmette in starring roles.

At any rate, though my adventures with Tonny continue to this very day (literally), our friendship beyond the day of the final folly is for another book, suffice to state the obvious here that the size of Tonny's entry demonstrates his importance in my Oakton experience. Any future loon reunion or recording session would be incomplete without his attendance.

THE TORNADO OF 1973

Yes, on April 23 1973, a tornado came ripping through Fairfax, doing most of its damage around the Pickett shopping center area. The damage it did to Woodson High School forced the Woodson student body into a split shift school day with the Oakton student body. For the final two months of my sophomore year, our classes were shortened from 55 minutes to 45 minutes (a few minutes might have been shaved off our homeroom and lunch periods as well), ending our school day a little more than an hour earlier at about 1:10 PM, at which time the Woodson student body would be bused into their temporary makeshift home. While my heart went out to the Woodson students, having to sacrifice their afternoons and evenings as they did, I think I was with the consensus of opinion that our school day didn't seem to have gotten any shorter. In fact, my clearest memories of this period are of lodging this very complaint with my classmates, or of listening to their complaints about the continuing slow movement of time, and how in God's name did we ever survive the monotony of our classes when they were a full 55 minutes.

As for the tornado itself, I recall that it took forecasters by surprise (as they are inclined to do), being as close to a full-fledged twister as this area has seen in my lifetime. Along with the damage to Woodson high school, considerable damage was also done to Pickett shopping center, across route 236 from the school. An empty school bus was picked up and thrown through the glass front of an ABC store. I recall Tonny telling me that he had looked out his window in time to watch one of those big metal trash dumpsters being tossed around like a styrofoam cup. As Tonny was living right behind Pickett shopping center at the time, his bedroom was less than 100 yards away from the tornado's path. He told me that the sound of the wind was unearthly and deafeningly loud. The tornado continued in a northeasterly direction, taking the roofs off of some apartments on Lee Highway before dissipating in the burbs of western Falls Church. A lot of damage was done in its wake, but luckily, no serious injuries or fatalities occurred.

THE V.O.T.

An abbreviation for the "Valentines of They," a clandestine group of female operatives that EAT and I jokingly cooked up to explain the unexplainable in our increasingly bizarre and fruitless relations with the women of Oakton high. Up to a certain point, EAT and I rested our broken hearts on the cornerstone of our alliance, which was to not take anything too seriously. Beyond that point, we could no longer dismiss the reality that some sort of communication network, capable of transmitting information (or gossip) about EAT and I across the borders of class and social status with lightning speed did in fact exist. When the coadjutors of the junior and senior ladies I had pursued to a tragic end were seen breaking bread with the freshman and sophomore ladies EAT had tried to court unsuccessfully, the unlikeliness of it made every recent coincidence seem like a puzzle piece. As each successive romantic failure became increasingly difficult to explain away, the circulation of negative erroneous gossip concerning EAT and I soon became the only explanation we couldn't rule out, and so the VOT took on an increasingly ominous and adversarial role while in the 'process of taking on a life of its own.

Now I don't mean to imply that EAT and I went entirely against our nature by ceasing to crack jokes about these things, or that they disrupted our daily routine to any great degree, but they did make us mindful of what we said, unless we were in the company of all males. The radio room was generally considered a haven for free expression, but in retrospect, even Elmo could have been considered a security risk, because his sister Donna was a tie to Tanya Herrell, who was a tie to Peggy, who was a tie to Tinker Bell, who was a tie to Liz Davis, who was a tie to Cheri Allen, who was a tie to Hunk, who was a tie to Melody Rouzer. Get the picture? The efficiency (and the insidiousness) of a gossip network is that a tie to one is a tie to all, and even innocently – girls will talk, whereas you'd have been hard pressed to find one guy in that school who would have given a rat's ass whether I went out with Peggy Wallace or whether EAT and Diana Malone became an item or not.

After my mysterious/revealing library chat with Melody Rouzer on November 6 1974, a devil's triangle connecting Melody with Hunk and CA was established by EAT and I. Over the course of the following three and a half months, more connections would be made, until my February 22nd phone call with EAT concerning Karen Cockrell would prompt me to break out the ol' pen and paper, in an attempt to sort some of this out. I began to collate all of these connections and coincidences in an attempt to chart the gossip trail. The outcome of this exercise was a greater awareness of who knew who, but in general, it raised more questions than it answered. Adding to the confusion was the sheer number of people who may have been involved. Some of these people I knew, some of them EAT knew, and some were mutual acquaintances of the two of us. However, when the gossip trail ended, as it often would, with someone neither of us knew, it really ended. Had the entirety of my notes and graphs on the VOT survived the years, it's doubtful they would have gone into great detail describing things that were then common knowledge to EAT and I, rendering them partially indecipherable today. For instance, the single surviving paper in my possession, which I recognize as my first attempt to at least identify the cast of characters is merely two lists of names under two separate headings – "Possible VOT Members" and "Known VOT Members." The fact that Karen Cockrell's misspelled name appears under the "Possible VOT Members" column, with no connecting arrows to or from any of the other names means that this short list actually predates my February 22nd phone conference with EAT (where Miss Cockrell was linked to Donna Zarin, Tanya Herrell, and Hunk). Where a clearer memory and/or further explanation is needed is in the inclusion of Janice Bell's name under the Known VOT Members column. Janice Bell??? I had to pull out my 75 Paragon about a half-hour ago to confirm the existence of Janice Bell. Finding her picture among the freshman class, aside from making it interesting to note that 6 of the 13 names that comprised these two lists were freshman, did little to clarify her identity or jar any memories loose. The unfamiliarity of her face leads me to believe that whatever info I had on Janice that rated placing her among the dangerous company on the Known VOT Members list had passed through 2 or 3 hands before reaching me. It also speaks well of the reliability of my source(s) for this information, possibly EAT, possibly even our girl on the inside – Donna Zarin, that I would except this information out of hand.

I'm given to believe that Janice Bell was Tinker's younger sister, and though her yearbook picture does not bear this out conclusively, she does bear a slight resemblance to Tinker's older brother Mark Bell. An arrow was drawn from Terry to Janice Bell, pretty much cinching the familial connection between the two. Less explainable is the arrow leading to Tanya Herrell, not from Terry Bell, but from Janice Bell. At the time, this connection needed no further documentation, but it has since become lost in the memory maze of names, places, dates, and events. Sometime in late February/early March of 1975, I drew up an expanded VOT list containing over 20 names, and it's likely that, should that list suddenly reappear among my papers, it would contain one or two more names that were today unfamiliar to me. It just flat out grew to be more than I ever had the intention of keeping track of. I was not the professional note taker that Emmette was either.

The VOT was nothing that didn't exist in every other high school in the world with a modicum of the fairer sex. The damage that was done to EAT and I's high school relationships stemmed from our emotional attachment to members of the VOT existing concurrently alongside our assumed detachment from the VOT. The more unsafe it became to communicate, the more we detached, and the more our resentment was reflected in our faces and in the clothes we wore. Therein lay all the things that EAT and I never spoke aloud to those of the VOT. That no lasting relationships or friendships grew out of EAT and I's association with these ladies was the result of a stoppage in the flow of communication and information, and NOT what was otherwise apparent.

WALT ROBBINS

Although foundations were laid for future development, the Insanist movement saw little actual growth inside the halls of Oakton during my freshman year. But this did not mean attempts were not made, and I'm sure that most of my friends were aware that I was out to build something. One such a friend, Don Frank (himself a failed conversion attempt), approached me one day with the news that he had come across an individual who he felt was an open and shut prospect for "Your Group" as he called it. Don then related the incident that convinced him that Walt Robbins was someone I should meet. Don had been hanging in one of the smoking arcades with a group of people when Walt Robbins, who had been staring off into space, suddenly turned to Don and asked him in all seriousness "Did you know that doves have two wings?" Now being full of spit and hungry for converts as I was, I found this little story most intriguing, and so I set out to locate this Walt character. This was easier as an idea than it was in practice, as no one I knew had a "Walt" in any of their classes or had any knowledge of a person bearing that name, and Don's subsequent inquiries yielded only that his last name was "Robbins."

Amid the hustle and bustle of my sophomore year, I would make periodic attempts to track down Walt Robbins, but about midway through the year, his very existence began taking on mythical properties. So convinced I was at one point that Don had made the whole thing up that I consulted my freshman yearbook for proof of his existence, proof I did not find (although Walt's picture WAS in the book, it was misleadingly under the name "John Robbins").

By this point almost totally forgotten, Walt would reappear in my junior year music class. Perhaps because it was incompatible with the aura that Leslie Chessman and Howard Koretz brought to that class, but I found Walt's buffoonish behavior most distracting, and while I did chat with him briefly outside of class on a couple of occasions, I quickly concluded that he was not loon material. Would that this were the end of the Walt Robbins story. Fast forward to Monday, January 20th 1975. I am standing outside of my third period ICT class (room 129), waiting for the bell to ring, and gazing down the hallway in anticipation of Peggy's imminent passage. The 4th period bell was still probably a couple minutes away because at this point the halls were completely empty. Upon hearing the sound of footfalls from the direction of the center stairwell, I turned to see Walt Robbins shuffling towards me, red faced and wide-eyed, giving the instant impression that he was in a hyper-excited state, despite the plodding weighted forward motion of his body. With arms outstretched, and in a pleading tone he asked me "Did you know that doves have two wings?" And as he passed me, counting with the fingers of both hands, he continued at a near shouting pitch – "3! 4! 5 WINGS!!!!" And then he turned and ambled off towards the smoking arcades.

Two years earlier, a performance like that would have gotten him an instant seat at the loon lunch table with Emmette, Elmo, Boni, Kaiser, Howard and I, but as conversion efforts had become a thing of the past, I doubt that I even mentioned the incident to EAT. Oh! I stood there bewildered for a few moments, but then the hallway began to show signs of life, and then Peggy walked by – offering me the sweetest smile as she passed, and something I truly treasured snapped back into focus in the warm glow of reality. I would bask in this glow for one more week, until the morning announcements of Monday, January 27th, when the voice of a very somber Mr. Bradford announced to the student body that John "Walt" Robbins had been struck and killed on the evening of January 24th (I would later hear that Walt was hit Duane Allman style, by a bread delivery truck – how about a little toast to go along with that peach?). And then Mr. Bradford called for a minute of silence – the one glorious unified minute when the whole school could hear and feel its heart beating. It was one of the longest minutes of my life, and once within the friendly confines of WOHS, I was nervously joking with EAT and Mitch that the VOT had gone too far this time. Both EAT and Mitch angrily admonished me to show more respect for the dead, which I conceded, though privately the joke wasn't a joke. It's clearer now in retrospect that from this point onward I took the idea that external energies were whirling about with ill intent a lot more seriously, and thus the heightened desire to make light of them.

Two days later, January 29th, and my lunch with Peggy would reveal that she knew Walt. Indeed! Now that he was dead, everyone that I had occasion to speak with seemed to either know Walt or have a story to tell about him. Where were all these people, I wondered, during my freshman and sophomore years? There was a noticeable change in Peggy that went beyond the obvious remorse she felt over Walt's death. It was a change that I passed off as merely the reaction of a sensitive emotional girl to a tragedy of this sort. My final lunch with Peggy on Friday, January 31st convinced me otherwise. Wednesday's woe-be-gone uneasiness had become Friday's pea-soup tension, and believe me, the atmosphere around Peggy was that thick. And though the rest, as they say, is history, Peggy's reluctance to confide in me would forever link her with Walt in time and essence as another one of those unfinished cycles of communication that for me remains open to this very day.

Now I did not know Walt Robbins well enough to consider it proper to remember him in my last will, but in entry number 4 of the will of Howard Koretz, I did bequeath to Peggy Wallace – "Hey Tanya, How've ya been? Ya know, I had the weirdest dream last night. He was dead and doves have three wings." This was my way of leaving Peggy, through the recondite puzzlebox of a dream, not only my memory of Walt, but my last memory of Walt, which was one of a desperately confused man. I wanted Peggy to remember me in a similar way, because what she had left me with would enlighten me about as much as contemplating the idea that doves have two wings. By the way, the three wings mentioned in entry number 4 of Howard's will (with his kind permission) is, I believe, a reference to the three heartbreaks of CA, Damaris, and Peggy, though my memory on this is not 100%.

The sardonic (and at times downright stygian) tone of my last will, as compared with the sweetness and light of my December 1974 letter to Santa, demonstrate not only a loss of innocence within that period, but my willingness to use the language of obliqueness I adapted from Peggy

Wallace and Walt Robbins to express my displeasure over that loss of innocence. I can now imagine that a good deal of innocence was also lost for Walt during the three years from the time he would calmly and matter-of-factly ask Don Frank if he knew that doves had two wings, and the time he would mysteriously pose the same question to me. The look on his face told me that much, if nothing else. RIP Walt.

WANNA HEAR SOME FINAL STATS?

A Tonny quote made famous by Emmette. Tonny called Emmette out of the blue one day and announced himself with this now immortal line. Emmette thought this was amusing enough to relay to me. I would date this as sometime in 1972. It was destined through repetition to become a loon catch phrase, at least among the Emmette-Tonny sports axis, and always with the accompaniment of Tonny's inflection, which Emmette and I had absorbed into our speech somewhat anyway.

WHATABUTTAKOOKYA

Simply stated, it means "What?" or "What's Up?" depending on the content of its usage. It's interesting to note that the word contains the words "Butt" and "Kook" within its 6 syllables. The birthplace was my June 1974 vacation to Punxsutawney, growing out of the "Tonbooch?"- "Whatahooch?" call and response, which translated on its own meant simply me saying "Tonny?" and him replying "What do ya want?" Whatabuttakookya became an all-purpose response to any query. Although it hung around until the 80's, its usage was confined to Tonny and myself.

WILLARD

How much did I want to see this movie in the summer of 1971? I actually agreed to get a haircut as the condition for my father (who I was visiting in Dallas Texas at the time) to drive me to see the movie. As much as I enjoyed it on first viewing, I believe it was my second or third visit to the theatre to see it that its message for me really started sinking in. A more profound effect upon me few movies would have, certainly none during my high school years. Bruce Davidson, whose portrayal of the jittery loner Willard Stiles really hit home with me, would thereafter become my favorite actor, and Ernest Borgnine's performance as Willard's vulgar and oppressively condescending boss, Mr. Martin, made his smiling face that graced the beginning of every McHale's Navy episode a distant memory. The first (and I mean THE first) book I would ever read in its entirety was "Ratman's Notebook," the novel that the movie Willard was based on. This would have been sometime during the course of my freshman year, when the movies' influence was still quite strong. The second book I would read in its entirety was Hans Zinsser's "Rats, Lice and History," which was not a work of fiction, but chronicled the history of vermin. My interest in seeking out information about rats led me to Oakton's library, where I discovered (and checked out) Zinsser's book. Obviously, Willard was still with me.

For those of you who have not had the pleasure of seeing the movie Willard, allow me to clarify things a bit. In short, Willard Stiles was a young man who lived with his sick mother in a large old house in the suburbs. He discovers a family of rats living in his backyard, but ignores his mother's demands that he kill them. With his mother almost bedridden at this point, Willard decides to secretly keep the rats in the basement as pets, even developing a rapport with them after awhile. Willard eventually trains the rats to obey his verbal commands, giving the meek and mild Willard an unusual weapon with which to exact his revenge on a domineering boss, whom he blames for (among other things) driving his late father out of the company, and later the premature death of his mother. His deliciously ruthless boss spends the better part of his time on the screen doing things that beg for atonement (including killing Willard's prize rat Socrates), so his death at the hands of Willard's army of rats comes off as one of the greatest wimp-over-bully fantasies ever filmed.

As if this alone was not enough to make me want to see the movie several more times, the last 15 minutes absolutely floored me. After doing away with his boss, Willard returns home to have dinner with a young lady he had met at the office (but who had previously been let go by the evil Mr. Martin). With his boss gone, and a young lady in his life, Willard seemed cheerfully poised for a much happier life, when from out of the corner of his eye, he catches sight of Ben, the head rat. Knowing something was up, Willard nervously excuses himself, and walks over to the door of the basement. Opening the door, Willard discovers that the entire horde of rats has returned. Realizing how incriminating this could be for him, he fabricates some ruse about having discovered something he HAD to attend to (which was actually the truth), and practically pushes his perplexed lady friend (played by the equally mousy Sondra Locke) out the door. He then rushes into the kitchen to face Ben. He promises Ben and his cohorts food, but when Willard starts pouring poison into a big bowl, Ben is shown in one incredible scene on the counter in front of the big drum of poison, moving his upper body back and forth as if he were reading the ingredients of this stuff that Willard was doling out to feed to him and his group. As if having discovered that his suspicions were correct, Ben suddenly turns and starts shrieking in a tone that even coming from a rat sounded like an alarm. A battle erupts between Willard and what could now be considered

Ben's minions, with Willard eventually losing in the final scene of the movie, as the camera pans up to and zooms in on a seemingly gloating Ben. A more powerful visual statement of the superiority of the rat would have been hard to imagine, and this was the idea that really stuck with me throughout high school. Actually, this idea of the conqueror rat did not so much follow me around as a result of having seen this film, as much as it was being constantly reinforced by the incredible things I was discovering about this remarkably adaptable animal through what I was reading, and hearing from others with more first hand experience with the creatures than I. At some point, reality had to support the fantasy of the movie in order to maintain the interest that the movie originally sparked.

As if the movie's message needed clarification, a sequel to Willard hit the theatres in the spring of 1972. While nowhere near as successful as the original, the movie "Ben" (which Kevin Hans and I watched in an otherwise empty Fairfax circle theatre) made Ben the rat THE most highly valued animal actor in Hollywood at $10.000, more than the current Lassie, which made me the gloating thorn in quite a few dog lover's side for some time afterward. Curiously, while the movie had no shortage of scenes with people being attacked by hordes of rats, its plot line of Ben being befriended by a boy in his early teens was absolutely Disneyesque, making Michael Jackson the perfect choice for singing the theme song, and lending added significance to any Lassie comparison. For me, there was not so touching a thing as the bond between a boy and his rat.

MR. WILLIAMS

No, I'm not referring to the notorious beer swilling good ol' boy gym teacher, I'm referring to the other Mr. Williams, Mr. Hampton Williams, the one you're not likely to be familiar with unless you had an electronics class or were involved in some way with WOHS. As the faculty sponsor of the radio station, he was the teacher ultimately responsible for and in charge of its operation. He ruled, I must say, with a velvet glove, allowing Kaiser to manage the station as he saw fit, and as the keeper of the keys, dutifully letting EAT or myself into the radio room during non-broadcast hours. It must have been clear to him that he was providing not only valuable experience for the future disc-jockeys of America, but also a home-away-from-home for a couple of those displaced DJs. His only stipulation to those of us who hung out in the radio room after broadcasting hours (which was usually just me, and occasionally EAT as well) was that we not play records at a volume that would disturb the electronics class he was teaching right outside of the radio room.

In some writings of mine from the time, Mr. Williams is mentioned as the person we would be waiting for every morning to show up and unlock his electronics class (room 158), and once inside, Kaiser would have the honor of opening the radio station door. After 4th period broadcasting hours, Mr. Williams would unlock the door to the radio station proper for any wayward DJs that might wander in. Mr. Williams was a serious but quiet man, and for my money, an early example in my life of the viability of the principle that "He governs best who governs least." Would that Kaiser have followed his example a little more closely.

WOHS

Oakton's radio station, operating on 5 watts (and sounding like 10 I used to joke on the air). Actually, WOHS could be picked up fairly clearly for a mile radius around the school. The station broadcast (for the most part) during A, B, and C lunch periods, which broke down as three separate 25-minute DJ shifts. During the 1974-75 school year that I was involved with the station, the three shifts looked like this:

A lunch
Elmo Zudinski Romanoff
Ezrin Amphitron Talus (on air name – Morty Sneaky)
Jim Allewelt

B lunch
Ken Wilt (on air name – Colonel Hash)
Myself (on air name – Queen Viper)
Steve Salyer (on air name – Doctor Sal)

C lunch
Jeff Wolfe (on air name – Wolfman Jeff)
Braxton Loughran (on air name – Action Braxton)
Jeff Kaiser

WOHS was on the air for three consecutive school years – 73/74, 74/75 and 75/76. I would of course have no knowledge of any revivals that may have taken place in the 80's, but I felt a tinge of sadness upon visiting Oakton high in 1997 and discovering that the old radio room was being used for storage. Rick Judd was the program director during its first year of operation. Jeff Kaiser managed it the second year, and Elmo was in charge during its third (and to my knowledge) final year of operation.

Peter Chapman's unsolicited reproachment aside, I am defiantly proud of both mine and EAT's involvement in the station. Aside from being the one thing I would put the most effort into perfecting during my 4 years at Oakton, the stand EAT and I took at WOHS (or should I say the stand we were FORCED to take at WOHS) was perhaps our greatest blow against the forces of mediocrity. I suppose what I'm saying is that I'm not only proud of the music we played, but of the fact that we refused to stop playing it.

Lest all my venting over the pressure that EAT and I did our show's under lead you to believe otherwise, the radio station was primarily a place where good memories will forever be stored, like the time Elmo brought in Queen's "Sheer Heart Attack" for EAT and I to listen to. I also remember Elmo bringing in the Black Oak Arkansas album "Ain't Life Grand" to play for me. EAT and I had pretty much given up on Black Oak after the fairly dreadful "Street Party" album, but EAT had apparently gotten a sneak preview of this one, because I can recall him psyching me up by assuring me that this new album was "A Good One." The radio room was where I first heard a lot of albums that I play and enjoy to this very day.

The WOHS yearbook picture, taken (in the fall of 1974) for the 75 Paragon. Standing in the background are Braxton Loughran (AKA Action Braxton), Jim Allewelt, Ken Wilt (AKA Colonel Hash – sporting the famous "Hash Hat"), Steve Salyer (AKA Doctor Sal), Elmo, and Jeff Wolfe (AKA Wolfman Jeff).

Seated in the foreground are Jeff Kaiser, Doug Hart, EAT (AKA Morty Sneaky – sporting "Bipperty Bopperty Hat" with matching scarf), and yours truly (AKA Queen Viper – sporting cadaverous make-up and a homemade vampire cape, which is not really visible in the photograph).

One observation: I've mentioned Doug Hart in the context of being one with his fingers in more pies than he had fingers. A good case in point is – What was he doing in this photograph? Everyone else pictured had a radio show. I practically lived in the radio room, and the occasion of this photograph was the one and only time that I would see him there. A monetary contributor maybe?

WOLFMAN JEFF
The on air name of Jeff Wolfe, who was the voice of the morning announcements during my senior year, as well as a part of the WOHS C lunch roster.

YOU CAN'T VERY WELL DEFECT TO THE LATINS, CAN YOU?
One of Emmette's more quotable quotes. It was given in response to a fellow student's query as to why Emmette was taking Russian as a foreign language instead of a useful language like Latin. It was classic Emmette, and a damn good use of insanist logic to counter a typically sane insistence on adhering to some predetermined norm. The lesson here? – That when the point of the discussion is to direct the subject toward the status quo, the best insane response is one which precludes any further discussion.

ZIGFRIED
The nickname given to me by Don Frank, and also subsequently used by Fausto Bengochea. It's ironic that Don, who often looked with skeptical detachment upon such loon practices as the taking on of insane names, would himself be remembered as the only person in Oakton who ever gave me a nickname, and it stuck. From a point early in my freshman year, Don and Fausto exclusively and steadfastly addressed me as "Zigfried," or more informally as "Zig." While Don was my closer friend in the beginning, three years of sitting next to Fausto in the same classroom has left a clearer memory of his matter-of-fact delivery of the name.

But while never understanding Don's reasons for giving me such a nickname ("You just look like a Zigfried" is not an explanation that even my Aquarian mother would have accepted), I nonetheless bore it with cautious dignity. Having said all that, it is again the sheer irony of it that now overshadows even the memory of its usage.

BUT WHAT DOES IT MEAN?

As perplexed as you may be from having read this book once, my only advice for gleaning some understanding and (dare I say) enlightenment from it is to read it a second or perhaps even a third time. As this book is a documentary of my adolescence, those of you who are in your 20's or early 30's may still have difficulty appreciating it, for this is the period of life where one tends to consciously push away from the idea of adolescence in a mad rush to reach some personal pie in the sky. I wrote this book in my early 40's, and in the process, came to appreciate at last the "Quality" of adolescence. I am thankful for friends like Tonny and Jeff Bolton, who talked me into releasing it, because in the 4 and a half years since I first got the idea to write it, I've met so many fellow middle-agers who have been inexplicably moved to look back with fondness on their own adolescence. It's as if we were collectively awakening to a unity of generation that was deeper and more profound than the one we left behind in our youth. Old differences are cast aside as adolescence begins to more and more resemble "The Good Old Days," where any shared experience (even negative ones) grow to be treasured.

If nothing more than the quality of adolescence shines through in these pages, then my gift to you has been received. The world wastes no time in exacting its toll. While still in our adolescence, the world lets us know that it doesn't take us seriously. We have no opinions on politics, economics, religion or current events that the world would except as hard intellectual currency. No wonder we were in such a hurry to NOT be adolescents. If one is paying attention, however, the irony that will confront them in their 40's is that even adult responsibilities such as car payments, child rearing, and yard work are handled with much greater ease if one DOESN'T take them too seriously. Once this idea (which for most was abandoned along with their adolescence) is married with the wisdom and confidence that comes with decades of adult life experience, one is duly prepared to go forward and enjoy the golden years that lay ahead of them.

352

ABOUT THE AUTHOR

Robert Karnes holds no degrees from any university, has received no literary awards, refuses to pose for photographs with his chin resting on his fist, does not wear turtleneck shirts or sweaters, does not live in a cottage in New England, does not even own a cat, and yet has the unmitigated gall to expect the literary world (and you, dear reader) to take him seriously.